# The Euro Experiment

How and why did the euro crisis happen? What are the implications for the economic and political future of Europe? This book, written by a leading commentator on the economics of the European Union, provides a clear and analytical guide to the euro experiment and the subsequent crisis. Written in a balanced way that is neither pro-euro nor euro-sceptic, it explains the political forces that helped to create and maintain the single currency. Further, it argues that the recent crisis can be best understood in terms of six fundamental issues: sovereign debt, banking, private debt, macroeconomic imbalances, economic governance and the interplay of national and European politics. This accessible account will appeal to a wide readership, including general readers and students as well as academics and policymakers working in banking and public policy.

PAUL WALLACE is European Economics Editor at *The Economist*, covering the economies and public finances of the European Union. He is also a former economics editor of the *Independent*.

# The Euro Experiment

PAUL WALLACE

CAMBRIDGE
UNIVERSITY PRESS

# CAMBRIDGE
## UNIVERSITY PRESS

University Printing House, Cambridge CB2 8BS, United Kingdom

Cambridge University Press is part of the University of Cambridge.

It furthers the University's mission by disseminating knowledge in the pursuit of education, learning and research at the highest international levels of excellence.

www.cambridge.org
Information on this title: www.cambridge.org/9781107104891

First published 2016

Printed in the United Kingdom by Bell and Bain Ltd

*A catalogue record for this publication is available from the British Library*

*Library of Congress Cataloguing in Publication data*
Wallace, Paul, 1951– author.
The euro experiment / Paul Wallace.
   pages   cm
Includes bibliographical references and index.
ISBN 978-1-107-10489-1
1. Eurozone.   2. Monetary unions – Europe.   3. Financial crises – European Union countries.   4. Europe – Economic integration.   I. Title.
HG925.W346   2015
332.4′94–dc23

                                                            2015026753

ISBN 978-1-107-10489-1 Hardback

# Contents

List of figures                                    *page* vi
List of tables                                          vii
Preface                                                viii

1    A question of survival                              1

2    Defective design                                   30

3    Fragile strength                                   58

4    Greeks bearing debts                               88

5    Bad banks                                         116

6    The existential crisis                            143

7    Defender of last resort                           175

8    Sovereign remedies                                208

9    Debtors' prison                                   240

     Notes                                             271
     Index                                             315

# Figures

1 Ten-year government bond yields, 1999–2014     *page* 4
2 Euro area and American GDP, from pre-crisis peak
   in 2007–2008 to 2014     6
3 Unit labour costs, 1999–2013     74
4 Current-account balances, as per cent of GDP,
   1999–2014     75
5 Bank assets, as per cent of GDP, 1997–2013     77
6 Private debt, as per cent of GDP, 1999, 2007 and 2013     78
7 General government debt, as per cent of GDP,
   1999, 2007 and 2013     80
8 Interest rates on new loans to non-financial
   companies, 2006–2014     132
9 Euro area bank cross-border holdings of debt
   securities, 1997–2014, per cent of total holdings     154
10 Impact on GDP from an orderly Greek exit or a complete
   break-up of the euro area, per cent change in first year     157
11 Target2 balances, € billion     182
12 Euro area consumer prices, headline and core,
   per cent change on a year earlier, 2007 to January 2015     197
13 Employment protection indicator, permanent
   workers, 2003, 2008 and 2013     212
14 Product-market regulation indicator, 2003, 2008 and
   2013     213
15 Net international investment position, per cent of GDP,
   2013     249

# Tables

1 Ease of doing business, rankings in 2008, 2013 and
  2014                                                    *page* 230
2 Per cent change in GDP per person in euro area and other
  advanced countries between 1999 and 2014, unemployment in
  1999 and 2014                                                266

# Preface

There are times when history speeds up and the early 1990s was one such juncture. The decision to create a single currency in a Europe of obdurately surviving nation states was audacious and its effects continue to reverberate. The elder statesmen of France and Germany who decided to jump-start history at the Maastricht summit of 1991 were seeking to answer an old and vexed question about the role of Germany in Europe, but they posed a new and also fraught one. Could the experiment of creating a monetary union of still sovereign countries work?

Both the launch of the euro, on schedule in 1999, and the first decade of the single currency seemed to suggest that the venture was feasible in practice as well as bold in spirit. The European Central Bank (ECB) established its credentials and the overall performance of the euro area was satisfactory. Despite the diversity of the member states and the lack of any genuine economic union, it appeared that an ever-growing number of countries, rising from eleven at the start to sixteen a decade later, could indeed share a common currency while retaining fiscal and political autonomy. Even banks, which lay at the heart of the monetary union, could remain under national supervisory control. Although historical experience suggested that a single money required a single state, the euro might prove to be an exception.

But the euro crisis was another time when history speeded up, in this case revealing the early sanguine assessment of the euro area's performance as largely illusory. The creation of the single currency paid an instant dividend for the countries on the periphery, by causing their interest rates to fall dramatically. It spurred a decade of easy credit that papered over the fact that the members in southern Europe had economies that were less able to cope with the rigours of the monetary union once the good times ended.

Between 2010 and 2012, the euro area came close to disintegrating as financial markets assailed the vulnerable economies, forcing one after another to seek bail-outs even though a founding principle of the union supposedly ruled out any such assistance. In a series of hastily improvised reforms led by Germany, euro-zone governments shored up the shallow foundations of the currency union. New rescue funds were created for countries unable to access private finance in the bond markets. Fiscal rules were reinforced both at euro area level and within countries. The first steps towards a 'banking union' were taken in order to loosen the links between banks and national governments.

Most important of all, the ECB reinvented itself, sloughing off its initial conception as a narrowly circumscribed central bank and adopting a much more expansive role. Throughout the crisis, the ECB played a crucial role in supporting banks in countries such as Spain that were experiencing capital flight. But after Mario Draghi took the helm in late 2011, the central bank became more proactive, especially when he made his 'whatever it takes' vow to save the euro in July 2012, which was translated into a commitment in principle to buy unlimited amounts of sovereign bonds in countries under siege from the markets. Even though this crucial policy remained unused, at least in the first three years after Draghi delivered his historic pledge, it succeeded in dispelling break-up fears that had pushed up bond yields to punitive levels. Not only did the ECB transform itself within its existing remit, but it also won new powers following the decision by European leaders to make the central bank responsible for supervising banks within the euro area, the main advance towards a banking union.

In emerging fortified from a crisis, the ECB had much in common with other central banks in advanced economies. The Bank of England hardly covered itself in glory before and during the early stages of the financial crisis, yet it was rewarded rather than penalised by regaining its former powers as a banking supervisor. Indeed, the ECB's own short if momentous life formed part of a bigger story about independent central banks, which increasingly held sway in advanced economies. This was all the more remarkable since the gravest financial crisis since the early 1930s had happened under their watch.

The genesis of that crisis was manifold, going beyond mistakes by central banks. But to the extent that they failed to do enough to restrain risky behaviour in the preceding decade, the ECB as well as the Federal Reserve (and the Bank of England) could be blamed for a blinkered policy that concentrated on price stability while paying too little heed to financial stability. In particular, the ECB allowed dangerous credit booms and housing bubbles to take hold on the periphery of the euro area, taking false comfort from the more stable performance of the monetary union as a whole.

Indeed, the euro crisis was in many respects a second European leg of the global financial crisis of 2007–8. Greece's prominence in instigating the euro crisis in 2010 meant that it was initially characterised as a sovereign-debt crisis since fiscal improvidence resulting in high public indebtedness had brought the country to a point where it could no longer finance itself in the markets. But banking crises associated with build-ups of excessive private debt were a more common cause of difficulties on the periphery, above all in Ireland, but also in Spain and Cyprus.

Despite its similarities to other central banks (and their mistakes), the ECB remained in many ways an exceptional central bank. Uniquely, it was a supranational institution, the embodiment of a monetary union that lacked a fiscal and political union. This left it in a solitary position, which hampered a swift and appropriate response to the crisis. Although the ECB eventually adopted quantitative easing (QE) in early 2015, it was late in pursuing a policy deployed by the Fed and the Bank of England in the wake of the financial crisis. That was because QE was far more difficult in a European context since there was no euro-wide state whose bonds the ECB could purchase. As a result, the programme of sovereign bond purchases that the ECB eventually launched was one in which the national central banks bought their own governments' bonds and bore any losses that might be incurred, a significant departure from the general risk-sharing rule.

The difficulties in responding adequately to the euro crisis reflected a broader failure in European integration. In various ways and in different countries, most notably in referendums held in France and the Netherlands in 2005, voters were clearly hostile to further steps towards 'ever closer union'. Bruised by such close encounters with electorates, euro-zone leaders for their part were reluctant to adopt any steps that would require significant changes to European treaty law, requiring unanimity and referendums in some countries. As a result, they had to improvise measures that could be adopted on an intergovernmental basis or that used existing powers under the treaties. For example, some argued that the job of single supervisor should have been given to a new institution rather than to the ECB in order to ensure that monetary policy decision-making was not influenced by worries about individual banks. But the ECB was made responsible, among other reasons, because this could be done without any awkward treaty amendment.

The legal blockage reflected a wider political standstill. Opinion surveys showed that in most member states there were majorities who favoured the euro. However, that support did not translate into backing for the far-reaching steps needed to stabilise the monetary union fully and to make it work better. That required further ceding of national sovereignty, such that the currency union would be able to conduct a common fiscal policy. However, there was little genuine appetite for that either in Germany, which worried that this could become a way for countries to backslide on controlling their budgets, or in France, which feared the loss of national control.

The lack of deeper integration left the euro hostage to national politics within the various states throughout the crisis. These continued to sour even after the worst of the crisis appeared to be over and a recovery, however flimsy, got under way in 2013. Within the northern creditor countries, there was popular resentment of the taxpayer-funded bail-outs. Within the southern debtor countries, the hardship endured during the crisis spurred the sudden rise of parties that were opposed to the painful measures imposed as a condition of the rescues.

The vulnerability to the vagaries of national politics was exposed most dramatically in 2015. Just as the recovery was at last strengthening, in part because of the fillip of lower energy prices owing to the fall in world oil prices, in part because of the ECB's belated decision to undertake quantitative easing, the Greek crisis erupted again. The victory of Syriza, a radical-left party that thought it could defy German-led policies, in the Greek election of January 2015 revived the worries that had come to the fore in 2012 about the wider and damaging effects on the monetary union of a country being forced to leave the euro. As before, Greece, which had already required not just one but two bail-outs, was the most likely candidate.

Protracted and acrimonious negotiations ensued between Greece and its creditors, particularly Germany. As a crucial deadline of 30 June neared, an agreement appeared tantalisingly close. That prospect was shattered when Alexis Tsipras, the Greek prime minister and leader of Syriza, unexpectedly called a referendum on the proposed deal and vowed to campaign against it. This sudden decision was disastrous, since leaders like Angela Merkel, the German chancellor, regarded it as a breach of trust that had been painstakingly built up. Within days, Greek banks were forced to close and strict capital controls were imposed. Greece looked set to tumble out of the monetary union, with catastrophic consequences for Greeks as a new depreciated drachma replaced the euro. The immediate effects on the remaining euro area were expected to be manageable, in contrast with 2012 when it was feared that an exit could have a domino effect forcing other weak countries out. Such an event would nonetheless inflict enduring damage on the single currency by revealing it to be a harder but ultimately breakable fixed exchange-rate system rather than the capstone of European integration.

During a tense and bitter weekend summit in Brussels in July, Germany at first pressed for a temporary exit on the part of Greece from the euro area, a 'time-out' lasting at least five years. Under pressure from other big countries, notably France and Italy, Merkel retreated but it was an extraordinary occurrence in the history of the euro area and the wider European Union that Germany, which had invested so much in the cause of integration, could contemplate such an act. A grudging settlement set out steps that would pave the way to a third bail-out in which Greece would have to carry out yet more austerity and reforms in return for more loans.

Despite this reprieve, the events of mid 2015 highlighted a deep and abiding flaw in a currency union that essentially remained a club of sovereign states rather than a political federation. Joining the euro was legally an irrevocable decision. That was necessary because otherwise markets would bet on its members leaving the euro if they found it difficult to cope. Moreover, it would take only one country to leave to create a precedent for others to follow, whether willingly or under pressure from the markets. But in order for the club to function, there had to be rules and its members had to obey them. If a country like Greece refused to play by the rules, and indeed sought to exploit the wider impact of its possible exit on the rest of the euro area in order to enhance its bargaining position, then it had to be possible to show such a recalcitrant state the door.

Although the renewed Greek crisis in 2015 did surprisingly little damage to the euro-zone economy, which continued to revive, its political repercussions were disconcerting. A project supposed to draw the peoples of Europe together was instead tearing them apart. National antipathies were intensifying rather than attenuating as crude caricatures of bullying Germans and feckless Greeks were drawn. Hopes that the euro would spur deeper political integration appeared fanciful, yet without that it would remain a fragile construction.

Although the euro area remained intact – for the time being – and had indeed expanded since the start of the crisis to nineteen members, as the three Baltic states joined, mere survival was not enough. Judged by other gauges, the single currency had failed. An apparently respectable record before the financial crisis looked very different after first the sharp ensuing 'great recession' and then, after a short revival, a two-year double-dip recession followed by a weak and faltering recovery. That left growth of living standards in the first fifteen years of the euro disappointingly sluggish across the currency club as a whole. Moreover, that mediocre overall performance disguised the contrast between Germany, which fared well, and southern Europe, where outcomes were dismal. A similar story could be told by looking at unemployment, which was far higher on the periphery in 2014 than when the single currency started, in 1999, whereas in Germany it was considerably lower.

In fact, Germany had benefited from the euro not just economically but in political and strategic terms. All roads appeared to lead to Berlin and to the German government, which commanded authority owing to the strong German economy and public finances. Early fears that Germany would cast off its commitment to Europe proved false but the price that it exacted for underwriting the shaky currency union was that the rest of the euro area should become more German in spirit, especially in pursuing fiscal discipline and structural reforms. A project conceived to answer the old question about Germany's place in Europe, by taming it within the framework of a monetary union, had instead reinforced German power.

Just as early judgements on the first decade of the euro proved unduly optimistic, so verdicts reached after fifteen or so years might turn out be too pessimistic, especially if a long sustained recovery could be achieved. The danger nonetheless was that the euro area remained trapped, unable either to retreat because of the costs of dissolution or to advance because of the political obstacles to creating a European state. That could condemn its citizens to a future of lacklustre economic performance, which could be all the more problematic as population ageing took its toll, adding new fiscal pressures to strong as well as weak countries since it would be especially intense in Germany.

This account of the euro experiment is necessarily partial, because the story of the single currency can be told at many levels, ranging from the ECB itself to all the countries belonging to the euro as well as international actors such as the IMF, and spanning politics, economics and finance. It is also necessarily provisional, because the outcome of the experiment remains to be determined. That it has been possible at all is thanks to the many people who have offered me their insights and expertise while covering the euro crisis since early 2011 for *The Economist*.

I owe particular thanks to three experts for being generous in their time and their advice. Paul De Grauwe of the London School of Economics and author of a textbook on the economics of monetary union, David Marsh, who has written an authoritative history of the euro, and Niels Bünemann, a former principal press officer at the ECB and a mine of knowledge about it, were all kind enough to read an early version of the manuscript and to make very helpful suggestions. I am also extremely grateful to several journalists at *The Economist*, in particular Edward Carr, John O'Sullivan and John Peet, who read drafts and alerted me to changes that should be made. I learnt much from Zanny Minton Beddoes, editor of *The Economist* since January 2015, with whom I worked closely during the crisis. John Micklethwait, the former editor, Daniel Franklin, Andrew Palmer and Jonathan Rosenthal were sources of inspiration and bulwarks of support during the most acute phase of the crisis, in 2011 and 2012, as more recently has been Edward McBride. Roxana Willis of *The Economist*'s research department was indispensable in drawing up the tables and charts and I am also very grateful to Carol Howard, former head of the department, for fact-checking an early version of the book. My thanks also to all the people at Cambridge University Press, who have helped me, especially Phil Good, Claire Wood and Christina Sarigiannidou, and to my copy editor, Anne Valentine. Any errors or misapprehensions are my sole responsibility, and although I have sought to incorporate changes suggested by those who have read it the arguments that I have presented are mine alone, and in particular should not be interpreted as the views of *The Economist*.

Among the many debts built up in writing this book over the past year, the heaviest are to my wife, Shirley, my children, Imogen and Joseph, and my sister, Bridget; also to Sylvia, Jill, Joy, Lynn and Peter, all of whom have put up with my neglectful ways.

# I   A question of survival

In January 2009, ten years after the single currency had been founded, there seemed ample cause to celebrate in Brussels, the uncrowned capital of Europe, and Frankfurt, home of the European Central Bank (ECB). The euro was a club that other states wanted to join. Starting as a monetary union of eleven, it had expanded to sixteen, with Slovakia the latest to become a member. More important, the euro had withstood the gravest test of its first decade, the financial crisis that came to a climax in late 2008; despite its tender years, the ECB won plaudits for its prompt response when the crisis started in the summer of 2007, whereas the three-centuries-old Bank of England was rebuked for being slow off the mark. In troubled times, the single currency appeared to offer a security sorely needed by European countries that had shunned it, such as the UK whose banking system had come close to collapse. Jean-Claude Trichet, the ECB's president, described the euro as a 'shield', saying that in its first ten years it had 'proven its stability, its resistance to shocks and its resilience in the face of financial and economic turmoil'.[1]

The verdict of the European Commission when publishing a study in May 2008 that examined the decade since the first eleven members of the club had been selected was grandiloquent. Though the findings of the actual report were more nuanced, the Commission proclaimed the euro 'a resounding success'; the monetary union was 'an achievement of strategic importance' not just for the wider European Union but for the world at large in which Europe had become 'a pole of macroeconomic stability'.[2] A sense of complacency persisted among the euro-zone elite in 2009, even though bond markets signalled alarm early in the year about Greece and Italy. In December, the Commission published a study that surveyed the mostly sceptical views of American economists as the drive to create an economic and monetary union (EMU) gathered momentum in the 1990s.[3] Martin Feldstein, an economist at Harvard University and a former economic adviser to Ronald Reagan, had even speculated that the venture could spur renewed conflicts in Europe.[4] The told-you-so title of the paper was: 'The euro: it can't happen. It's a bad idea. It won't last. US economists on the EMU, 1989–2002.'

The sarcasm about American economists was mistimed. By then, the first rumblings of the euro crisis could already be felt when the recently elected Greek government revealed that its finances were far worse than previous figures had shown. The crisis, which broke out in earnest in early 2010 when Greece became unable to borrow in private markets, mutated over the following two years into an existential drama, as the markets laid siege to one country after another on the periphery of the euro area by refusing to lend at interest rates that were sustainable. Sovereign debt crises, a condition formerly confined to emerging-market economies, afflicted not just smaller euro-zone states such as Greece but large ones such as Italy. Ireland, Portugal and Cyprus followed Greece in requiring full rescues, and Spain needed a partial bail-out to secure its banks.

One crisis-fighting European summit followed another, while the ECB made increasingly bold moves to bolster the currency union's troubled banks through lavish provision of central bank funding, which indirectly propped up states as the banks bought sovereign bonds. It was to no avail – the crisis gathered in intensity. Greece became the first advanced economy in more than half a century to default on its debt. Under intense external pressure from the creditor nations in the euro area led by Germany, emergency technocratic governments took over in Italy as well as Greece in late 2011. When hedge funds and investors betting on a break-up renewed their attack on Italy and especially Spain in mid 2012, driving up bond yields again, and Greece teetered on the brink of exit, the single currency appeared close to falling apart, inflicting a crippling blow on not just the European but also the global economy.

The siege was lifted only when Mario Draghi, who had replaced Trichet less than a year before as head of the ECB, promised in impromptu remarks made in a London preparing to stage the Olympic Games to do 'whatever it takes' to save the euro. Crucially, Angela Merkel backed his stance even though Germany's top central banker vehemently opposed the ensuing 'outright monetary transactions' (OMT) policy announced by the ECB, which threw a lifeline to the sinking bond markets of beleaguered peripheral countries. In another vital step, the German chancellor decided around the same time not to expel Greece, rejecting a policy option that had been pressed by Wolfgang Schäuble, her finance minister, and agonised over for months in Berlin.

Draghi's 'whatever it takes' intervention marked a turning point. Bond yields among the peripheral countries began to fall as fears of a break-up ebbed (see Figure 1). Any remaining caution among investors was swept aside in the first half of 2014. A remarkable rally in peripheral-country debt drove down bond yields that had still been unsustainably high in countries such as Portugal just a few months earlier, in the autumn of 2013. Indeed, ten-year government debt yields in the euro area dropped to record lows, not just in the short lifetime of the euro but stretching back centuries, both in the core creditor countries, such as the Netherlands, and in the once troubled states on the periphery, such as Spain (though Greece was a notable exception). According to figures compiled by Deutsche Bank in September 2014, Spanish borrowing costs were at a two-century low, while French yields were their lowest in more than 250 years. Yields in the Netherlands, where data extended back the longest (preceding in fact the Dutch breakaway from the Habsburg empire of the Spanish king, Philip II) reached a five-century low.[5]

As financial markets capitulated, European officials declared victory. On a visit to Greece in January 2014, José Manuel Barroso, the Commission's president, could not disguise a triumphalist tone when he asserted that the euro's existential crisis was over.[6] He had made a similar claim a year earlier, which proved premature since it was followed by a tense bail-out of Cyprus in the spring of 2013.

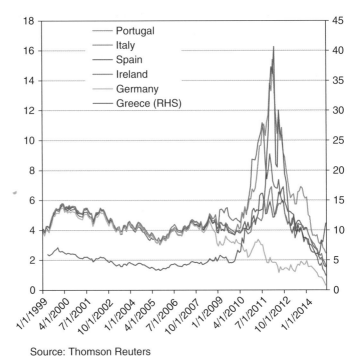

Source: Thomson Reuters

FIGURE I  Ten-year government bond yields, 1999–2014

Indeed, European leaders had repeatedly misjudged the scale of the crisis and their capacity to contain it. When Greece was rescued in May 2010, they believed that their arsenal of hastily assembled bail-out money would frighten off traders contemplating attacks on other countries. Even after the crisis had leapt one national boundary after another on the periphery, false assurances continued. In March 2012, Nicolas Sarkozy, the French president, talked about turning a page on the crisis, and crowed that for once a European summit had not been dominated by it.[7] As well as swiftly losing office two months later, he was just as swiftly proved wrong about the crisis since it resumed with even greater virulence. For most of 2014, however, Barroso was broadly correct as far as the battle in the markets was concerned, though towards the end of the year there was a temporary reverse as investors became nervous again, fretting mainly (and correctly) about the prospect of another political upset in Greece.

Any sounding of the all-clear based on the behaviour of investors and traders at a time of extraordinary monetary ease across the world failed, however, to recognise the continuing fragility of the currency union. The euro area might have survived its ordeal by fire in the markets but, as became increasingly clear during 2014, it was enduring a new ordeal by ice as its economy suffered from the chill of a recovery that barely merited the name and a collapse in inflation. The combination of weak real growth and persistently ultra-low inflation – the latter dubbed 'lowflation' by Christine Lagarde, head of the International Monetary Fund (IMF), in the spring of 2014 – meant that nominal incomes were barely rising, making it far harder to cope with the overhang of debt, private as well as public, that weighed down the weaker economies.[8] The spectre of deflation hung over the euro area, a lethal condition since when prices fall the burden of debt, which is generally fixed in nominal amounts, rises in real terms. Meanwhile, in familiar fashion, euro-zone leaders were bickering about what to do in order to make their blighted currency club work better.

By late 2014, the renewed weakness of the euro area was a matter of grave concern not just within Europe but from a global perspective. Inflation across the euro area dropped to just 0.3 per cent in September, far below the ECB's objective of close to 2 per cent, while the recovery had virtually halted in the second quarter of 2014, only a year after it had begun. In October, the IMF forecast a 40 per cent probability that the euro area would lapse into recession between mid 2014 and mid 2015.[9] If that occurred, the euro area would follow Italy in suffering a 'triple dip' downturn, following the extended double-dip recession in 2011–13, which had followed the first and most severe one in 2008–9, induced by the financial crisis.

As a result of the euro zone's second recession and feeble recovery, output in the final quarter of 2014 was 2 per cent lower than at its peak in early 2008 (see Figure 2). By contrast, American GDP was

Source: Eurostat

FIGURE 2 Euro area and American GDP, from pre-crisis
peak in 2007–2008 to 2014

nearly 9 per cent above its pre-crisis high, which it had already surpassed during 2011. Whereas unemployment in the United States had
fallen to 5.6 per cent of the labour force in December 2014 from a peak
of 10 per cent five years earlier, in the euro area the jobless rate was
11.4 per cent, still close to its high of 12.1 per cent in the spring of
2013. Moreover, even that gauge of distress for the euro area as a whole
disguised the fact that in some countries such as Greece and Spain it
was far higher, at 26 per cent and 24 per cent, respectively. Youth
unemployment rates appeared to be ruinously high at 23 per cent for
the euro zone as a whole and approaching or even above 50 per cent in
some countries, though these figures exaggerated the plight of young
people since the denominator, fifteen to twenty-four-year-olds in the
labour force, excluded large numbers who were in full-time education
and were therefore not looking for work. Even so, the scale of

joblessness as a share of the youth population as a whole was woefully high, at between 15 and 21 per cent in the worst affected countries in 2013.[10]

Manifestly, the euro-zone economy was floundering, as an unexpected slowdown in Germany in the middle of 2014 removed what had been the main source of economic resilience since the euro crisis erupted. Although some of the troubled countries on the periphery, such as Portugal and Spain, were belatedly reviving, France and Italy, whose economies were the second and third largest in the euro area, remained inert. Businesses might no longer be battening down the hatches as they had done in 2011–12 when uncertainty about the survival of the single currency was most intense, but they remained nervous about making new investments. High unemployment induced caution among households, constraining their spending. Above all, the burden of high debt when inflation was so low bore down on growth prospects. The euro area resembled a cancer patient following a punishing bout of chemotherapy; the treatment might have put the disease in the bond markets into remission, but it had left the patient enfeebled.

The renewed difficulties in the euro area in 2014 reflected the fact that the crisis was multifaceted. Indeed, a recurring pattern throughout was a failure on the part of euro-zone policymakers to grasp and to respond to the multidimensional nature of the crisis. Its origins in Greece led the crisis to be characterised at first mainly as one of sovereign debt, caused by earlier fiscal profligacy, which meant that the governments affected were unable to finance themselves in private markets. This prompted the solution of stringent fiscal austerity. But there were at least two other dimensions to the crisis. If Greece, the first country to require a rescue, succumbed because of its unsustainable public finances, Ireland, the next to need a bail-out, in late 2010, was brought low by its collapsing banks, both through the fiscal bill for saving them and the damage they inflicted on its highly leveraged economy. The rickety nature of many national banking systems was the second component of the euro crisis, as the preceding global financial crisis of 2007–8 turned out to have a longer fuse in many parts of the euro area. Compounding the misery was a third element: a macroeconomic crisis as countries on the periphery suffered sharp recessions and tried to close gaping current-account deficits that had opened up in the first decade of the single currency. Their woes reflected underlying economic weaknesses in labour and product markets that were hampering competitiveness.

The broader characterisation of the euro area's malaise as a three-fold crisis was widely accepted by 2012, following an influential paper in the spring of that year by Jay Shambaugh, an economist at Georgetown University, who emphasised the mutually reinforcing nature of the three interlocking crises.[11] Worries about the integrity of government debt undermined banks given their big holdings of sovereign bonds, while, conversely, concern about banking solvency undermined governments given the potential costs to national exchequers of rescuing toppling banks. The austerity imposed to tackle sovereign debt concerns weakened economies, which hurt banks and impaired their ability to support the economy. This in turn made it harder to fix the public finances. The German Council of Economic Experts adopted a similar approach in a study of the crisis published later that year.[12]

This was a more synoptic appraisal of the misfortunes assailing the euro area, but it still remained a partial account. For there were three other crises as well. The fourth was that troubled economies on the periphery were oppressed not only by unsustainable sovereign debt but also by excessive private debt. Measured in relation to GDP, the debt burdens of households and non-financial businesses were especially heavy in Cyprus, Ireland, Portugal and Spain. Though they were lighter in Italy, especially for its prudent households, the stricken state of its economy meant that on other gauges, such as corporate debt to equity ratios, Italian firms were in a bad way. Private debt was also worryingly high in some northern countries, particularly for households in the Netherlands, which largely accounted for the Dutch economy's bumpy ride during the crisis.

To varying degrees, other advanced countries like the US and the UK suffered from burgeoning public debt and high private indebtedness. They, too, had experienced severe economic imbalances in the run-up to the financial crisis, and their banking systems had come close to collapse. What made the difference was the fifth and most fundamental dimension to the euro crisis, a defective system of economic and fiscal governance in the currency union. The creators of the euro had brought into being a single money, but not a single government. Theirs would be a monetary union of nation states whose only concession to a broader federal principle was a weak set of budgetary rules that failed to discipline governments before the crisis. These arrangements, which included a limited conception of the ECB's role as a central bank and the national retention of banking supervision, were too flimsy to support the currency union when it came under stress.

The inadequate economic and fiscal governance left the fate of the single currency in the unsteady hands of national politicians. The uncertainty created by politics was the sixth crisis. Investors and traders posed two ever-more insistent questions. Were the creditor countries at the core of the euro area, above all Germany, willing to underpin a currency union whose shallow foundations were being so starkly exposed? Were the governments of debtor nations on the periphery prepared to play their part in dealing with the crisis by pushing through painful measures, and were their peoples prepared to accept them?

A gap opened up between the politics of the creditor countries and the politics of the debtor nations. In the former, governments needed to mobilise support both for the rescues and for more enduring reforms to strengthen the monetary union. Yet, as the crisis spread well beyond Greece, 'rescue fatigue' started to set in as many taxpayers not just in Germany but also in other northern nations like Finland increasingly resented the cost of bailing out what they regarded as wastrel economies. But if the politics in creditor countries soured, so too did the politics in the debtor states. What was initially represented as a relatively brief dose of unpleasant-tasting medicine turned into a much longer regimen, inflicting far harsher treatment on their citizens, especially through higher unemployment. The concomitant to the onset of 'rescue fatigue' in the creditor countries was that of 'austerity fatigue' in the debtor nations, especially among those in bail-out programmes overseen by the 'troika', officials representing the IMF, Commission and ECB. This caused increasing rancour, which fused especially in Greece with anti-German sentiment drawing upon the experience of the Nazi invasion and Axis occupation in the Second World War.

What made the gap particularly dangerous was that it created an environment for bluff and counter-bluff, especially in the original and most vexed rescue of all, that of Greece, as it required not just one bail-out in 2010 but a second one in 2012 followed by the third and most contentious one of all, in 2015, which was agreed upon in principle in mid July though several tricky hurdles had to be jumped for the new three-year provision of financial assistance in return for austerity and reforms to be signed and sealed. In the fraught elections of mid 2012, Alexis Tsipras, leader of the insurgent left-wing Syriza party, pledged to put an end to Greece's fiscal misery by reneging on the 'memorandum' – the Greek government's commitments under the rescue programme. This was a bluff on his part that the euro-zone creditor governments would flinch at punishing Greece by suspending the bail-out money for fear that the resulting 'Grexit' from the euro might precipitate a wider break-up of the monetary union. Countries joining the single currency were supposed to fix their exchange rates 'irrevocably'. An exit would irrevocably devalue that commitment.

Despite that danger, the German government for its part had a rather more compelling counter-bluff – making an example of Greece by forcing it out anyway, which made Tsipras's bluff all the more perilous. In the event, Syriza came second in the election to New Democracy headed by Antonis Samaras, who was able to form a coalition government that brought the country back from the edge.

But the reprieve was temporary since the game was played in earnest in 2015 after Syriza did win power and Tsipras became prime minister, bringing Greece even closer to an exit in a protracted tussle with its international creditors – the euro-zone governments led by Germany and the IMF – which culminated in an extraordinary confrontation and breakdown in trust in late June and early July.

Making matters worse, all six crises often interacted with one another to exacerbate tensions rather than to alleviate them. As well as what euro area leaders themselves dubbed, in June 2012, the 'vicious circle' between banks and governments, there was a wider susceptibility to macroeconomic imbalances. Yawning current-account deficits made economies in southern Europe and Ireland vulnerable to a 'sudden stop' in international financing and even more so if there was not just a cessation of capital inflows but also an abrupt switch to capital outflows. Unsustainable private debt held back recovery as firms and households saved more to try to pay down their obligations. As existing loans soured, many banks were in no condition to back new business ventures since the new lending would require additional capital to absorb the credit risk, which was in any case heightened by worsening economic conditions and paralysing uncertainty. Though political reassurances could counter the crisis, at various junctures worries about the resolve of governments both in the core and on the periphery to sustain the currency union led to panic-stricken sell-offs in financial markets, sapping household and corporate confidence, which in turn undermined economies as purchases were postponed and investments put on hold.

The vulnerability of the currency union laid bare during the crisis stemmed from the failure of an earlier generation of European leaders to admit the full extent of the potential sacrifices, as well as the possible gains, in merging their national currencies under the Maastricht Treaty of 1992. The benefits were accentuated while the costs were downplayed. Monetary union was above all a political project driven by Helmut Kohl and François Mitterrand following German unification in 1990. Though the deal was never expressly set out, the price exacted by the French president for unification was that Germany must give up the deutsche mark, which then held sway in Europe through a system of pegged exchange rates. The German chancellor was prepared to pay this price to win the prize of a unified Germany. Both Kohl and Mitterrand were swayed by old fears based on past conflicts, which meant that they paid insufficient heed to new dangers, in particular the risks of forging a single currency for Europe's still obstinately surviving nation states without at the same time creating stronger fiscal and political bonds.

When the time came to choose the first members of the euro area, in May 1998, politics also prevailed although the European leaders responsible for this decision no longer included Mitterrand, who had died shortly after his second presidential term ended in 1995 (when he was replaced by Jacques Chirac). If the rules set in the Maastricht Treaty had been interpreted strictly, the monetary union would have excluded countries with excessive public debt, notably Italy but also Belgium. On similar grounds, Greece would not have been admitted two years after the first eleven members, even on the conveniently flattering fiscal figures it provided when applying to join, which turned out to be false. Instead, an unwise decision was taken to start with a wider and potentially riskier currency zone. Making matters worse, rules that were supposed to enforce fiscal discipline after the currency union had started were flouted within just a few years by the two most important countries in the euro area, Germany and France, setting the worst possible example.

Creating a monetary union without a corresponding fiscal and political union amounted to political misselling. The peoples of northern Europe were invited to believe that they could gain the convenience of a single currency and a voice in a common monetary policy while retaining national control over state budgets and avoiding fiscal risk-sharing. The Germans, who were sacrificing their monetary hegemony, were assured that the ECB would be a European version of the Bundesbank, a fiercely independent central bank committed to maintaining a clear blue-water divide between the monetary and fiscal domains. That pledge could not survive the test of the euro crisis, as the ECB was drawn into sovereign bond buying.

For the countries of southern Europe, adopting the single currency became a matter of national pride, although the rush to join also owed much to a treacherous trade-off between early reward and later pain. Even the prospect of membership paid an early dividend – before the euro came into existence, interest rates fell sharply as the periphery came under the shield of German credibility. This helped public finances as national debt was refinanced at much lower costs, creating scope to reduce it to more manageable levels in relation to GDP, especially in Italy but also in Greece. However, the temptation to tuck into windfall savings by raising non-interest spending or reducing taxes proved irresistible, and weak currency union fiscal rules were no constraint. The fall in interest rates stimulated a credit boom as households and firms took advantage of cheaper borrowing costs. But the immediate gain came at the cost of longer term pain. By adopting the single currency, member states sacrificed the safety-valve of devaluation and the ability to set a monetary policy to suit their specific economic needs and differing business cycles. This meant they had to ensure that they remained competitive through other means, in particular by freeing labour and product markets, but this was an unpalatable course to pursue when everything seemed to be going effortlessly well.

Despite the failure to spell out what was really entailed in a monetary union, the euro, which came into existence at the start of 1999, got off to a good start as the upswing of the late 1990s gained momentum. The ECB had some teething troubles but established its authority. Although the euro area was somewhat slow in recovering from the global downturn of the early 2000s following the dotcom crash, it then did rather better than expected when growth picked up from the middle of 2003. Productivity performance was disappointing, but in the years between its launch and the financial crisis that started in the summer of 2007, unemployment fell and employment growth was encouragingly strong.

Paradoxically, however, the better the euro area as a whole seemed to be faring in its first decade, the worse its underlying health was becoming, as conditions on the periphery diverged from those in the core countries. Public finances in Ireland and southern Europe were flattered by credit-generated growth. Private debt burdens were rising as firms and households borrowed excessively. Bank balance sheets burgeoned even though their capital foundations were inadequate. The balance of payments deteriorated among the peripheral countries to such an extent that Spain ran the world's second-biggest current-account deficit in absolute terms (after the US) for several years, while Greece, whose economy made up only around 2.5 per cent of euro-zone GDP, chalked up the world's fifth largest in 2007 and 2008.[13]

A decade of mounting imbalances left the currency union vulnerable once financial markets ceased to hunt for returns and started to fret about risk. The removal of exchange-rate risk within the currency union had led to a big build-up of cross-border positions between investors and banks in the core countries of northern Europe and borrowers on the periphery. Even though much of the lending was misguided, the risks arising from such interconnectedness were bearable, provided that the currency union held together. But if it were to crack apart, there would be a sudden and massive adjustment in exchange rates, which would ruin firms and investors.

What lay behind the attacks in the sovereign bond and bank-funding markets was a recognition of both the fragility of the euro area and the calamity that would attend even a partial fragmentation. On the one hand, a country like Greece seemed incapable of coping inside the single currency; on the other hand, during the acute phase of the crisis between 2010 and 2012, a 'Grexit' could trigger a wider break-up, endangering not just the euro area but the global economy. The history of Greece suggested that it might be a special case, as indeed European ministers insisted it was in the summer of 2011 when preparing to flout nearly sixty years of precedent in the developed world by enforcing a restructuring of its towering public debt. Greece had after all been in default on its sovereign debt for half its existence as an independent state, an unromantic dereliction for a country whose liberators included Byron in the 1820s.[14] Yet the susceptibility to bond-market attacks of other euro-zone countries whose public finances had a less chequered history suggested a systemic weakness in the design of the monetary union.

Possession of its own currency is no obstacle to a state wrecking its public finances, but holders of its debt can still expect to get their interest and principal because the government can turn if necessary to its central bank to fulfil its obligations as they come due even if it has lost access to the markets (though whether those payments will amount to much in real terms is another matter). But investors lending to euro-zone governments could no longer look to their national central banks to act as a lender of last resort to their sovereign. That left weaker governments at the mercy of the markets because they were borrowing in what was in effect a foreign currency, a point made by Paul De Grauwe, author of a textbook on the economics of monetary union, as the crisis intensified in 2011.[15]

It was this design flaw that the ECB eventually fixed in September 2012 when it translated Draghi's 'whatever it takes' pledge into the OMT policy to buy bonds in unlimited quantities for countries in difficulty that were under the umbrella of a rescue programme. In effect, this provided a safeguard similar to the backing provided by central banks in nation states through their ability to act as lender of last resort to their sovereign.[16] This crucial commitment could be interpreted as entangling the ECB in fiscal matters, which was why Jens Weidmann, head of the Bundesbank, bitterly opposed it. But Merkel's decision to back Draghi rather than Weidmann turned the tide, and bond markets started to sue for peace. As their sovereign bond yields subsided, first Ireland and then Portugal were able to exit their three-year rescue programmes on schedule, a further cause for renewed confidence, along with a revival in the euro-zone economy that got under way in the second quarter of 2013.

By 2014, there had been progress, to varying degrees, in resolving some though not all of the euro area's multiple crises. First, to the extent that the crisis was about sovereign debt, there had been improvements in the budget balances of the worst-offending countries on the periphery. Second, euro-zone banks were looking healthier. A year-long probe into the quality of banking assets followed by a stress test in the autumn of 2014 had done something to restore confidence undermined by a succession of collapses, in some cases after previous flawed supervisory exercises. Third, the economic imbalances that had emerged in the first decade of the euro were shrinking. The cavernous current-account deficits that had opened up in Greece, Portugal and Spain turned to surpluses, an unexpectedly large adjustment. Some economies had also pushed through wide-ranging programmes of structural reforms, especially to malfunctioning labour and product markets, that should in principle have boosted underlying growth and made it easier to cope with the rigours of a single currency.

Even so, the advances in dealing with the first three components of the euro crisis fell short of what was needed. Budget balances might have improved but the legacy of the crisis was much heavier burdens of public debt. Between 2009 and 2013, government debt climbed in Ireland from 62 to 123 per cent of GDP; over the same period it rose from 84 to 130 per cent of GDP in Portugal.[17] The measures taken to deal with the grumbling banking crisis could also be viewed as a glass half-empty rather than half-full. Though some hailed the results of the European stress test in late 2014 as a watershed, others doubted whether the exercise had truly got to grips with the problems of euro-zone banks. Despite the turnaround in the current accounts of peripheral economies, a good part of the adjustment came from lower imports, reflecting the sharp contraction in domestic demand. This was particularly marked in Greece, though less so in Spain and Portugal, where exports had been surprisingly buoyant.

The record on reforms to improve underlying growth and competitiveness was also mixed. Portugal scored high for effort, but its labour market had been so extreme in the protection given to permanent workers that even after the reforms it remained rigid by international standards. Italy was more resistant, in part because it managed to avoid a bail-out. Even when Mario Monti replaced Silvio Berlusconi in late 2011, forming an emergency technocratic government, the pace of reform petered out within a few months as a shake-up of the labour market that was supposed to be historic failed to live up to its billing. Worryingly, the usual prescription of freeing labour and product markets might prove to be insufficient given the poor governance of southern European countries. The crisis highlighted deeper weaknesses in the state, especially in Greece and Italy, which were holding back their economies. In this respect, the euro crisis could be regarded as precipitating rather than causing an overdue reckoning, which required a comprehensive modernisation of public institutions, including the judicial system.

If there was mixed progress in dealing with the first three aspects of the euro crisis, the advances were even more modest in dealing with the fourth, the private debt burden, which was generally higher in 2013 than in 2007. This cast some of the apparent success stories in a darker light. Portugal might have done well in closing its current-account deficit and pushing through structural reforms, but it bore a double burden since both public and private debt were excessively high. Together with other countries that had been rescued, it was also heavily in debt to the rest of the world.

The economic and fiscal governance of the currency union – the fifth and most fundamental of the six crises – had undoubtedly been strengthened, though from a woefully deficient starting point. However hesitantly, new defences, notably a permanent rescue fund to assist states that lost market access, had been erected. Stronger fiscal controls had been imposed both at national and European levels. The euro area had also advanced towards a banking union, mainly through making the ECB the single supervisor of banks within the currency area, a role it formally assumed in November 2014 after the year-long asset-quality review and stress test. Along with this reform, a new resolution authority had been created to sort out failing banks, backed by a new common fund to be financed by bank levies. Most important of all, the ECB had moved towards the broader conception of its role that was necessary to allow the single-currency area to survive through adopting the OMT policy (though this had come under legal challenge in Germany). And it was inching forward to the further reinvention of itself that was necessary, the introduction of quantitative easing to boost the recovery and to combat lowflation.

However, euro area governance remained inadequate. Despite the intense focus on fiscal reforms during the crisis, the eventual outcome was remarkable for how little had really changed. The Maastricht system of countries that would never bail each other out had died in the spring of 2010, but the German-led response was not to bury it but rather to try to resurrect it, ensuring that the euro area would remain a monetary but not a fiscal union. The members of the currency club accepted stricter budgetary surveillance; for example, the Commission and the Eurogroup of euro-zone finance ministers saw national budgets before they were voted on by parliaments. But national fiscal autonomy remained intact, with no currency union treasury to complement the ECB. Future burden-sharing was confined to the European Stability Mechanism (ESM), the euro area's permanent rescue fund, which was strictly limited both in its scale of financing and its remit. Moreover, the ESM was established by a treaty between euro-zone states, under public international law rather than EU law, and allowing northern creditor countries like Germany to retain a national veto. An undoubted advance was that the currency club now had a single supervisor. But the ECB's ability to call the shots in this capacity was hampered by the fact that backstops for ailing banks remained overwhelmingly national, while the new resolution authority was a cumbersome outfit.

The weak governance of the euro area left the region ill-placed to deal with the renewed difficulties that beset it in the second half of 2014 and in 2015. Most troubling of all, the euro remained hostage to national politics, the sixth element of the crisis and one that was becoming more rather than less fissile. The European elections of May 2014 revealed a groundswell of protest against integration. Though this was shared in countries outside the euro, especially in Britain, such a backlash was more dangerous for members of the single-currency club, given their need for enhanced cooperation. Matteo Renzi, who had become Italy's prime minister in February, managed to hold back the Five Star Movement, which was calling for a referendum on Italy's membership of the euro.[18] But his political success was an exception to the broader trend. François Hollande, who had replaced Sarkozy in May 2012 only to become the most unpopular president on record, suffered a crushing rebuke from voters as Marine Le Pen's anti-European party won the election in France.[19] In Greece, Syriza topped the poll, while in Spain, an upstart anti-austerity party, Podemos ('We can'), came fourth. By the end of the year, the continuing rise of Podemos, which was vying for first place in opinion polls, was threatening to break the mould of Spanish politics with unpredictable consequences for the euro zone since, for example, parts of its programme sought to curb the independence of the ECB.[20]

Moreover, the tide of hostility against Europe washed for the first time over Germany. The rise of the eurosceptic party, Alternative für Deutschland (AfD), was particularly important since it broke the longstanding national consensus in favour of European integration, which had bolstered Merkel's efforts to save the euro. AfD secured 7 per cent of the vote and seven out of Germany's ninety-six seats in the European parliament. By the autumn, the party was polling still higher in two regional elections where its percentage share of the vote reached double digits.[21] Although the threat from AfD faded in 2015 as the new party split, its sudden rise had demonstrated the risk for Merkel of being outflanked by an insurgent party on the issue of European integration, giving her less room for manoeuvre in deploying German resources to shore up the monetary union.

The disputes within the currency club now involved the three heavyweight economies with Merkel at odds with Hollande and Renzi as they called for fiscal 'flexibility', which Germany regarded as back-tracking on the commitments made in the crisis.[22] Indeed, there was increasing German alarm about the condition of France, which repeatedly missed budgetary goals and was suffering from a noxious combination of a stagnant economy as well as sour politics. After heading in the wrong direction for eighteen months, Hollande had belatedly started to try to lighten the burden of the state, but he was doing so in a tentative fashion. The worry in Berlin was that continuing French economic 'morosity' would hold back the euro-zone recovery and create fertile soil for an eventual populist insurrection, calling into question France's commitment to the euro as well as the EU.

But, as before, the political upset was to occur in Greece, when Samaras called a snap election, which was won by Tsipras in late January 2015. In mid 2012, the threat of a Syriza victory had been sufficient to cause alarm about a Greek exit, inducing capital flight. Now the insurgent left-wing party had broken through, forcing banks to turn to emergency central bank funding as deposits drained out the banking system on an even bigger scale than in May and June 2012, with big cash withdrawals by Greeks as well as transfers of money abroad.[23] Yet, despite the frailty of Greece's position, the new government led by Tsipras adopted an extraordinarily confrontational stance that was bound to alienate its European creditors. Now the game of bluff and counter-bluff was being played in earnest, as the tie-less Yanis Varoufakis, the new finance minister, an economist with expertise in game theory (as opposed to practice), toured European capitals seeking to secure a better bargain for Greece and insisting that the government would not seek an extension of the bail-out that was due to expire at the end of February.

The gamesmanship yielded nothing but the slow-motion bank run, which precipitated an eventual climbdown by the Greek government in late February, when it accepted the extension of the bail-out until June. This averted a looming disaster since the country was within days of having to impose capital controls. But the confrontation continued as talks to conclude the terms on which Greece would get the release of remaining bail-out funds got nowhere because the new Greek government was still unwilling to accept that it would not after all be able to pursue its left-wing manifesto in office, but would instead have to knuckle down like its reviled predecessors to terms set by its creditors. Even so, as the new deadline of 30 June approached, Tsipras appeared to be seeing sense and both sides looked close to reaching an agreement following negotiations at the highest level with Merkel and Hollande. That was why Tsipras's extraordinary decision to call a referendum on the creditors' proposal and to campaign against it was so destructive since it breached the trust of European leaders, infuriating in particular Merkel.

With no prospect of a deal under the existing bail-out programme, the ECB could no longer permit extra emergency funding to the Greek banks which were now facing a full-scale bank run due to fears by Greeks that their country would be forced out of the monetary union, turning their hard-earned euros into worthless drachmas. The banks were forced to close and strict capital controls were imposed to prevent transfers of funds abroad. In late June and early July, the long-threatened Greek exit from the euro seemed more likely than at any time in the five-year crisis, especially when the Greeks voted decisively against the creditors' proposal on 5 July; 61 per cent backed Tsipras and voted no. Yet the apparent triumph for the prime minister was a Pyrrhic victory. The following weekend, Tsipras was involved in bruising negotiations in Brussels to try to keep Greece in the euro area. The tentative agreement announced on Monday 13 July at least achieved that goal but involved much more onerous conditions than those he had rejected at the end of June.[24]

The episode was a stark reminder of the fragility of a currency union that both required the threat of an enforced exit and yet could be fatally undermined by a departure. If a country like Greece refused to play by the rules, then the ultimate sanction for the other member states was to turf it out of the club, as Schäuble urged (to the consternation of France and Italy) at the weekend summit in July 2015 that determined the fate of Greece. That threat was necessary in order to impose discipline not just on Greece but on the other countries. If the stern line demanded by Merkel and Schäuble buckled, then this would encourage Spanish voters to flock to Podemos in the hope of gaining concessions for Spain. It was no accident that the Spanish government – though opposed to forcing Greece out of the euro – had been unsympathetic to Greece's demands for a better deal; Pablo Iglesias, the leader of Podemos, had after all joined Tsipras in a public show of solidarity at a closing rally during the Greek election campaign.[25]

Yet, even though second time round there was little of the alarm about the systemic damage inflicted by an exit on the rest of the euro area that loomed so large in 2012, the effect would still be corrosive. If Greece were to leave the euro, then the currency union would be regarded as just another transient fixed exchange-rate system. Investors would charge higher premiums on investing in countries that looked vulnerable, and Greece would then become a test-case for whether in fact a beleaguered economy might do better outside the monetary union – ironically, the better it did, the worse that would be for the long-term viability of the euro.

If the latest act of the Greek drama highlighted the continuing frailty of the euro, paradoxically there was renewed confidence about the economic prospects for the monetary union in the first half of 2015. The IMF's warning in October 2014 about a 40 per cent chance of another recession proved too gloomy as growth picked up in the final three months of that year to a more respectable 0.4 per cent increase in GDP from the previous quarter. Although outright deflation set in at the end of 2014, the further downward lurch in consumer prices was caused by lower energy prices resulting from the slump in the world oil price, which was boosting the euro-zone economy in much the same way as a tax cut. Most important of all, the ECB finally decided in early 2015 to embark upon quantitative easing, buying financial assets, predominantly government bonds, by creating money. This pushed an already weakening euro down further, and also boosted stockmarkets even before the purchases began in early March. It also contributed to the quiescence of bond markets on the periphery (outside Greece) as the latest act of the Greek drama was played out.

Five years after the euro crisis had begun in earnest with the first rescue of Greece, there was thus room for some cautious optimism as well as pessimism about the prospects for the monetary union after the jarring and persistent crisis it had endured. That drama has already spawned a number of books and will no doubt continue to do so. These include *Europe's Unfinished Currency*, by Thomas Mayer, a former chief economist at Deutsche Bank; *Europe's Deadlock*, by David Marsh, who has also written a detailed history of the euro; *The Euro Crisis and Its Aftermath*, by Jean Pisani-Ferry, a former head of Bruegel, a Brussels-based think-tank, and since May 2013 an adviser to the French government; *The Euro Trap*, by Hans-Werner Sinn, head of the influential Ifo Institute in Munich; and *Unhappy Union*, by John Peet and Anton La Guardia, both of *The Economist*.[26] These offer a variety of valuable perspectives on the causes of the crisis, an account of its stages and an assessment of the steps taken to overcome it. This book does not seek to provide a detailed narrative of events, which were in any case extensively covered at the time. Instead, it adopts a thematic approach within a broad economic and historical framework. This provides a way of comprehending a crisis of often bewildering complexity, encompassing banks, markets and governments within the different countries while involving policymakers at national, euro area, EU and global levels. The crisis was financial, economic, legal and political, but above all it was one of political economy, as European leaders and elites conducted an extraordinary experiment by creating a monetary union without a federal state.

Could it have been tackled better? In March 2014, Draghi gave a lecture at Sciences Po in Paris in which he argued that the euro area had mismanaged the sequencing of policy measures to counter the crisis, which explained why unlike the US it succumbed to a double-dip recession.[27] He said that the priority should have been to create a 'solid backstop' – his euphemism for euro-wide fiscal support underpinned above all by Germany – for both the weak banks and the weak states. Only when that had been achieved should the banks have been stress-tested with those found to be vulnerable being secured through recapitalisation. Similarly, any restructuring of public debt should have come after the creation of an effective permanent rescue fund. Instead, the reverse of this sequencing had occurred. Though this critique made eminent sense, Draghi was in effect saying that Germany should have conceded at once the reforms to euro-zone governance that it took the crisis to wrench out of it. His account of ill-timed policies rightly highlighted the deficiency of the single currency's institutions but failed to take into account the domestic constraints on Merkel, who for example was heavily criticised in Germany even at the height of the crisis in mid 2012 for conceding the banking union that Draghi argued was 'the necessary first step of a consistent strategy for a sustained recovery'.

Another relevant counterfactual is whether the national economies of the euro area would have fared any better if the single currency had been stillborn. The euro was not responsible for the dysfunctional labour and product markets and defective public institutions of southern Europe. Whatever their currency arrangements, the states belonging to the euro would have been affected by common global influences, in particular the rise of China and the plunge in long-term real interest rates, which pumped up the asset-price bubbles that burst in the financial crisis. Moreover, the member states would have been hurt by greater exchange-rate volatility after the financial crisis struck. Indeed, the Commission argued on the tenth anniversary of the euro that it had put paid to the exchange-rate realignments that 'periodically traumatised the European economies'.[28] This in turn had ensured that the single market, the other great European project, was protected within the monetary union, if not the whole of the EU, from currencies seesawing against each another, conferring competitive advantage on some countries to the detriment of others.

The question was whether one form of trauma had been swapped for another, even graver type. The euro might have prevented a repetition of the exchange-rate turbulence of the early 1990s but it contributed to the excesses leading to the financial crisis as its banks became indirectly involved in America's subprime mortgage folly and also created their own disaster within the euro zone. Both in the acute phase and afterwards, the fragility and feebleness of the euro area held back the global recovery, inhibiting growth in other advanced economies such as the US and Britain. Moreover, the fact that the UK eventually started to outshine the euro area was significant. Although the pound had depreciated, that was not the crucial factor; exporters in Spain for example did better than those in Britain. What mattered was that the retention of sterling allowed the UK to conduct its own monetary policy, including the early introduction of quantitative easing, in 2009, and an additional programme to support bank lending, starting in 2012.

In line with the thematic approach of this book, Chapter 2, 'Defective design', accordingly sets out the flaws in the original model of the euro, created in the Maastricht Treaty. They arose because the push towards a single currency was driven by politics rather than economics. As a result, the monetary union that came into being failed to comply with several tenets of optimal currency area theory, though some gaps in that theory were also revealed by the experience of the euro area during the crisis. The convergence criteria set in the Maastricht Treaty to determine whether countries were fit to join the euro were inadequate and failed to consider crucial factors such as whether labour markets were flexible enough. The stability and growth pact was supposed to ensure fiscal discipline but it buckled when flouted by France and Germany in the early years of the euro. Even though banks lay at the heart of the monetary union, they remained subject to national rather than euro-wide supervision. The euro area's defective governance made the currency union ill-placed to cope when put to the test.

Chapter 3, 'Fragile strength', shows how the euro defied the sceptics in its first decade even though it began with a broader membership than was advisable owing to the admission of countries in southern Europe whose economies were ill-suited to the project owing to characteristics such as rigid labour markets. Despite this unpromising start, the ECB established its authority in setting monetary policy for a continental economy. The record of the euro area as a whole was respectable, judged by improvement in living standards together with low and stable inflation. However, this achievement was flattered by a credit boom on the periphery that over-extended banks and built up excessive private debt. Moreover, focusing on the overall performance of the currency union left out the extreme imbalances that swiftly emerged both within and between countries as the periphery lost competitiveness and ran big current-account deficits. This distorted legacy left the euro area vulnerable once the financial crisis ended the benign environment of easy credit.

That vulnerability came to the fore when Greece suffered a sovereign debt crisis, prompting a bail-out that broke a cardinal rule of the Maastricht Treaty. Chapter 4, 'Greeks bearing debts', examines the fiscal aspect of the euro crisis not only in Greece but also across the currency union. The nature of the Greek crisis led creditor governments, especially Germany's, to depict the overall problem as one arising mainly from national fiscal profligacy, requiring austerity and, if necessary, restructuring of sovereign debt. The main concession to the systemic nature of the crisis was the creation of rescue funds, but these were inadequate. More fundamental solutions such as jointly guaranteed eurobonds were eschewed, leaving the ECB in the awkward position of having to intervene by buying government bonds in order to stem panic. As austerity was applied not just to the small, weak peripheral economies, but also in Italy and even Germany, the fiscal squeeze became too tight, contributing to a prolonged double-dip recession. And although restructuring was eventually carried out in Greece, the exercise proved destabilising and euro area governments retreated from applying elsewhere a policy that still looked necessary for other states burdened by debt.

Focusing on the sovereign debt dimension of the euro crisis was in any case too limited a perspective since weak banks as well as weak governments were involved. Chapter 5, 'Bad banks', examines the causes of the euro zone's continuing banking crisis and the eventual remedies that were adopted. The causes were both national and systemic. Within individual countries, weak supervision allowed ill-judged lending sprees while across the euro area financial integration was shallow, based on cross-border lending between banks which could be swiftly reversed, rather than deep, based on transnational ownership. Unlike the US, the euro area was slow in addressing the weak capital positions of banks and although stress tests were conducted these failed to restore confidence and if anything undermined it when banks that passed the tests subsequently had to be rescued. Eventually, however, a decision was taken to try to create a banking union, which was the right response even if the main accomplishment was the creation of a single supervisor, a role given to the ECB. But the credibility of the new arrangements was undermined by the reluctance to provide a credible joint fiscal backstop to deal with the failure of a systemically important bank. This accounted for the euro area's rush to adopt a new regime of bailing in private creditors, starting with Cyprus in 2013, despite the risks this entailed.

Chapter 6, 'The existential crisis', explains how and why the monetary union came close to disintegrating, most likely precipitated by a 'Grexit' either through Greek recalcitrance or German insistence on making an example of Greece to encourage better behaviour for the other members of the club. The history of previous currency unions suggested that they were susceptible to break-up if they lacked deep political foundations, but it also suggested that dissolution was possible without calamitous damage. However, a fragmentation of the euro area differed from previous experience because the single currency had created highly interconnected, if not deeply integrated, financial systems. A break-up would reimpose exchange-rate risk with a vengeance, inflicting heavy costs – and there was great uncertainty over who would end up footing the bill. Such fears were one crucial reason why both the rescued and the rescuing countries eventually decided to stick together in 2012 when economic stresses were most pronounced, and in 2015 when political tensions were uppermost. The other was that unlike previous currency unions the euro area had a central bank that could come to its defence.

'Defender of last resort', Chapter 7, shows how the euro crisis created a parallel identity crisis for the ECB, the very heart of the monetary union. Created in the image of the Bundesbank with a restricted conception of what a central bank should do, the ECB had to become much more like the Federal Reserve or the Bank of England even though unlike them it lacked a corresponding fiscal and economic authority. Under Trichet, the ECB was largely reactive, keeping the monetary union together by forays of bond-buying and financing capital flight but not overcoming the crisis. Under Draghi, the ECB went on to the front foot by addressing a crucial flaw of the currency union, the lack of a lender of last resort to the sovereign and the reassurance this provided for bondholders. By offering a similar backstop through the OMT policy that gave substance to Draghi's 'whatever it takes' pledge, the ECB brought the acute phase of the crisis to an end, although the policy then became subject to a legal dispute in the highest courts of Germany and the EU. But the central bank then underwent a further identity crisis as it agonised over the introduction of quantitative easing involving large-scale purchases of sovereign bonds in order to tackle low growth and ultra-low inflation. Although it eventually adopted this policy, the long delay in doing so hampered the euro area's recovery and made it more likely that it would struggle to avoid endemic Japanese-style deflation, a lethal condition for several member states given their high private and public indebtedness.

Chapter 8, 'Sovereign remedies', appraises the structural reforms that preoccupied policymakers both during and after the acute phase of the crisis as a means of making the currency union work better. Imposed on the bailed-out economies as a condition for getting official loans, they were also urged upon countries like Italy that were too big to rescue, and increasingly on France as its stagnant economy aroused concern. The reforms embraced in particular overhauls of labour and product markets to allow countries to cope better with the constraints of a single currency, but their ambition swelled into attempts to reconstruct the southern European state. Though peripheral countries needed a dose of reforming medicine this was never likely to overcome the euro crisis itself during the acute phase because any improvements would be long term rather than short term. Yet if economies on the periphery continued to do badly, this could cause a political backlash that might threaten the euro. Advances were made, but already by 2013 the reform effort was slackening and it was far from clear that enough had been done to tackle the deeply embedded deficiencies revealed during the crisis.

Chapter 9, 'Debtors' prison', shows that the euro area did make considerable progress between 2010 and 2014 in overcoming its various crises, such as the balance of payments and high government borrowing. But its prospects remained blighted by debt overhangs, both private and public, which were all the more onerous given sluggish growth and low inflation. Although there was also progress in improving the euro zone's institutions, particularly by creating a permanent rescue fund and making the ECB the single supervisor, its governance remained weak and inadequate. The euro had overcome the assault of the bond markets but remained vulnerable to political risk if it failed to deliver better economic performance for its members, particularly in southern Europe. That it had survived was remarkable, but survival was not enough, as the rekindling of the Greek crisis in 2015 demonstrated.

# 2  Defective design

The birth of the single currency in 1999 was a triumph for European integrationists whose vision had prevailed over nationalist naysayers. A monetary union that seemed fanciful a few years earlier as foreign-exchange markets cracked open its predecessor, the European exchange-rate mechanism, had become reality. On 1 January, the founder states, which included the four big economies of Germany, France, Italy and Spain, locked their exchange rates irrevocably against one another. Even though it would take three years until euro notes and coins replaced national money in circulation, at the start of 2002, the ECB based in Frankfurt now set interest rates for the whole of the euro area, affecting over 290 million people living in the eleven countries sharing a common currency.[1]

But the euro was a premature birth (as Gerhard Schröder presciently observed before he became German chancellor in 1998) because it was engendered by old national fears rather than new European hopes.[2] Politics trumped economics in the rush to curb the power of a unified Germany by creating a European currency. The compromises involved in the project meant that the design was inherently flawed. Instead of a monetary union crowning the creation of a single European state whose citizens identified themselves as European first and foremost rather than clinging to their national identities, the euro would leave the nation states in place and be run by a supranational institution, the ECB.[3] Even though the members of the currency union were to lose national monetary sovereignty, they were to preserve their power over broader economic policies while retaining their fiscal autonomy.

As well as failing to comply with the traditional alignment between money and power, the euro did not meet the minimum economic conditions needed for a common currency to work properly. In the decades before its birth, economists had devoted much thought to specifying these requirements. Judged by the criteria they had set, the design of the euro was flawed, in particular through the retention of full national fiscal sovereignty while sharing a single money. Even so, the original template might have been workable if confined to a select band of highly developed and closely integrated northern economies. But from the outset, there were doubts whether the broader and more diverse group that was admitted could share one currency since the group included southern European economies that were less suitable on several grounds.

A more optimistic view was that the creation of the euro would foster convergence so that even if countries did not belong together at the start, they would by dint of membership. The very fact of sharing a currency would induce 'endogenous' integration, turning a poor candidate at the point of entry into one worthy of admission after the event. Two American economists, Jeffrey Frankel and Andrew Rose, argued in 1996 that 'a country is more likely to satisfy the criteria for entry into a currency union *ex post* than *ex ante*'.[4] Even if this were the case. it still made the euro a risky venture.

As it turned out, the economics of currency unions, though in many respects far-sighted, failed to highlight some crucial weaknesses that were to be revealed by the euro crisis, in particular the vulnerability created for weaker countries by losing central banks that could act as lenders of last resort to their sovereign and the stresses that would emerge from shallow financial integration of banks lacking a common supervisor. This only went to underline that the euro was an experiment. Such a trial was bound to reveal flaws in the original theory that it was testing. Unlike scientists, however, the inventors of the euro could not discover its defects safely in the laboratory. Instead, they would only find out when it came close to collapse. And although that was eventually avoided in 2012, the euro area continued to perform poorly, inflicting further economic and social damage.

The branch of economics exploring the scope for common currencies was founded by Robert Mundell, a Canadian-born economist, who won a Nobel prize for his work in the same year the euro was created.[5] By then, his pioneering paper, 'A theory of optimum currency areas', was almost four decades old.[6] Published in 1961, this short article is routinely cited for its argument that mobility of labour (and capital) is essential if countries are to benefit from a common currency. But its ambition, reflected in the paper's title, stretched beyond this finding, which was in any case disregarded by the creators of the euro since labour mobility was conspicuous by its absence within the currency union.

Mundell was tilting against the received wisdom, consistent with economic history, that monetary borders should be aligned with frontiers determined by custom and power. Revealingly, Germany's own journey from a mosaic of thirty-nine states after the Napoleonic wars in 1815 to a unified country in 1871 had demonstrated the link between national power and national money.[7] As Charles Kindleberger wrote in *A Financial History of Western Europe*, the movement from eighteenth-century German particularism to nineteenth-century unity was 'one in which money and banking brought up the rear rather than serving in the van'.[8] Indeed, the newly unified Germany following the Franco-Prussian war of 1870–1 'faced a general monetary and banking chaos', according to Harold James, another economic historian.[9] In 1873, a single currency was introduced, the mark, which was backed by gold, in large part purchased from the indemnity the French had to pay after their defeat. The law establishing the Reichsbank was passed in 1875 and the central bank came into existence at the start of 1876.[10] Monetary unification followed political unification.

That link between national power and national money was reaffirmed after the Second World War. It was the creation in June 1948 of the deutsche mark, replacing the worthless reichsmark (introduced after the hyperinflation of the early 1920s), which sparked the first Berlin crisis, pitting the Allied powers – the US, the UK and

France – controlling the western parts of the city against the Soviet Union, which had occupied not just the eastern sector but the surrounding east German territory.[11] When the Allies insisted on introducing the new currency into their sectors of Berlin, the move prompted a Soviet blockade that was broken only through an airlift.[12] Currency represented much more than a means of exchange, it was the measure of national sovereignty and in this instance of international commitment on the part of the western powers.

Despite the seemingly inseparable historical link between national power and money, which included currency unions between imperial powers and their colonies, Mundell argued that traditional alignments might be subverted through developments such as the new European Economic Community, founded at the Treaty of Rome four years earlier; dubbed the common market, its six founding members were Germany, France, Italy together with the Benelux countries of Belgium, the Netherlands and Luxembourg. Indeed, he specifically asked: 'supposing that the common market countries proceed with their plans for economic union, should these countries allow each national currency to fluctuate, or would a single currency area be preferable?'. Mundell argued that the borders of a currency area should be economically defined, in particular by factor mobility, the extent to which capital and labour could move freely. 'The optimum currency area is the region', he declared provocatively. Its boundary was not necessarily national since it was delineated where capital and labour were no longer able to move freely, whether because of border controls or underlying demarcation lines such as language and cultural differences.

Mundell's paper inspired a lengthy literature on the conditions determining optimal-currency areas.[13] The researchers were seeking to create an economic cartography. More contour lines mapping economic and monetary compatibility were drawn. One was intensity of trade. The more that economies traded with one another, the more it made sense to share a currency, just as was the case in an internal national market. This held true especially for small countries whose scope for economic adjustment through exchange-rate changes was limited because both consumer and producer prices were dictated by import prices, while exporters had to set their prices according to those prevailing in their partners' markets.

A particularly important way to delineate compatibility was to assess if economies tended to move in sync with one another. In the case of the euro area, the crucial question was the extent to which an economy was in step with those of Germany and France, since by virtue of their size (making up together over half the output of the currency union at the beginning) they would tend to dominate the monetary settings of a common central bank.[14] Such cyclical convergence was linked to trade intensity, but it also reflected underlying similarities in economic structures, such as the characteristics of housing-finance markets. In particular, it mattered whether mortgage rates were generally fixed or floating, since variable-rate housing finance responded more swiftly to changes in monetary policy.

A further contour line, which together with convergence of business cycles featured explicitly among the British Treasury's five tests on whether the UK should join the euro, was the underlying flexibility of economies, especially in their labour markets.[15] This could in principle provide an alternative way of living with a single currency where labour mobility between countries was lacking, as was the case in the EU in the 1990s. If countries surrendered their own currencies, they would lose their ability to adjust their costs relative to those of the other members of the union by altering their exchange rates. If they became uncompetitive, they would at some stage have to pursue a policy of 'internal devaluation', lowering their domestic prices and wages relative to those of their trading partners in the rest of the union. Though theoretically feasible, that adjustment was typically a longer and stonier journey than simply allowing the exchange rate to fall, the course still available to countries outside a currency union. As Milton Friedman had pointed out in the early 1950s, it was much easier to change one price, the exchange rate, than a multitude of domestic prices, comparing the role of the exchange rate to the collective decision to move clocks forward in the spring.[16]

Another criterion was the extent to which the output of national economies was diversified. In principle, the wider the range of products that a country produced, the less vulnerable it would be to a shock affecting specific sectors of the economy if it no longer had the cushion of an exchange rate. However, this was a double-edged conclusion, which highlighted a tension in interpreting the tenets of optimal-currency-area theory: what might be true at the outset, might cease to be once the union was established. One of the consequences of sharing a single currency might be that countries would specialise more in the sectors where their comparative advantage was greatest as the monetary union promoted more trade. That effect would then make them more susceptible to subsequent sectoral shocks. In this instance, at any rate, endogenous integration would make matters worse rather than better.

The greater a country's cross-border labour mobility, trade intensity, labour market flexibility and economic diversity, the better suited it would be to life within a currency union, especially if its economy tended to move together with those of other potential members and shared economic characteristics, such as the way housing finance was organised. Even so, there would be times when one country in a currency club might be hit harder than others. To cope with such a contingency, some economists, such as Peter Kenen, stressed the need for some fiscal sharing to offset labour immobility so that a depressed member state would be cushioned by paying lower taxes to the centre and receiving help with unemployment benefits.[17] Research by Xavier Sala-i-Martin and Jeffrey Sachs suggested that these cushioning fiscal effects were substantial in the US. Over a third of a fall in per capita personal income in a region suffering an economic reverse would be offset by lower federal taxes and higher transfers from the centre, mainly through the reduction in taxes.[18]

Judged by the economics of optimal-currency areas, it made sense for the small and open economies of northern Europe, such as

Belgium and the Netherlands, to join a German-led monetary union. These states already traded extensively with Germany. And although changes in global energy prices affected the Dutch economy differently because of its natural gas reserves, they otherwise tended to experience similar economic shocks, which meant that they would benefit from a similar monetary response.[19] The time that it would take for such a response to work its way through to the economy would also be similar because their housing finance was organised along the same lines, with long-term fixed-rate loans being the usual form of home mortgages. For such countries, the prospective gains of forming a currency area with Germany outweighed the potential losses they might incur. As part of such a union, they would have a say in monetary-policy decisions rather than having to follow the lead of a Bundesbank setting policy with only the German economy in mind. By getting rid of their national currencies, they would eliminate exchange-rate uncertainty that hampered their financial markets and businesses. That should boost their trade with the rest of the union, and potentially boost growth too.

The economic rationale for France adopting the euro was less convincing. On the one hand, its economy did tend to move in line with Germany's, which suggested that it could live with a common interest rate.[20] Moreover, such a single monetary policy would affect it in a similar way since its housing finance was also dominated by fixed-rate mortgages. Gaining an influential voice in the setting of a single monetary policy would also be a boon. On the other hand, the French economy was large and relatively closed, based on the scale of its trade in relation to GDP.[21] Furthermore, its labour market was particularly inflexible (and about to become more so through the introduction of the statutory 35-hour working week in the early 2000s).[22] France's experience within the exchange-rate mechanism in the early 1990s was hardly encouraging; but for support from the Bundesbank forthcoming because of Kohl's willingness to back Mitterrand, it would have followed Britain in making an ignominious exit.[23]

If the economic case for France joining was mixed, there were weighty arguments for excluding the countries of southern Europe. For one thing, they were far less open to trade than those in the north. Greece, which adopted the euro in 2001, had an especially closed economy, with the lowest export share of GDP among the then fifteen member states of the EU. That was all the more remarkable given the fact that smaller economies generally trade intensively. Portugal's trade share was also low for a European economy of its size.[24] The structure of housing finance in southern Europe and Ireland created a further unhelpful divide with the rest of the euro area. In some core countries – Austria, Finland and Luxembourg – variable-rate mortgages predominated. But through their economic weight, monetary policy would be set mainly for the northern countries where long-term fixed-rate mortgages were the norm – Germany and France together with Belgium and the Netherlands – making up about 65 per cent of total housing loans in the euro area. But the changes in interest rates would actually feed through much more swiftly to the peripheral economies where mortgages were mainly floating-rate, with banks typically setting margins above Euribor, the rate at which they lent to one another, for terms between three and twelve months.[25]

More important still, countries in southern Europe would struggle to stay competitive with their main trading partners in the currency union or to claw back lost competitiveness through internal devaluation, as might prove necessary once they abandoned their own currencies. Labour markets in southern Europe were notoriously rigid, which meant that they adjusted to adverse shocks mainly through workers losing their jobs rather than through wages or hours worked falling. Italy had long relied upon allowing the lira to depreciate in order to maintain competitiveness, which was why Antonio Fazio, Italy's central bank governor, counselled against joining the single currency, likening it to 'purgatory'.[26]

Since much of Europe failed to conform to some of the criteria set out by optimal-currency area theory, why did it proceed with this revolutionary project? After all, despite the attempts of Mundell and

other economists to establish economic rather than historic bound-
aries, the link between national power and money continued to prevail. If anything, the direction was away from currency unions rather
than towards them as colonial empires were wound up and newly
independent states created their own monies. Even rock-solid links
to the US dollar, such as that adopted in Hong Kong in 1983, which
was reinforced by a currency board, remained the exception rather
than the rule.[27]

A similar story could be told for Europe. Kohl's offer in early
1990 of the deutsche mark to east Germans – overruling the
Bundesbank's objections to his generous terms – was the decisive
step in unification.[28] Whereas Germany had become reunified,
Cyprus, which did not join the EU until 2004, had been divided since
the Turkish invasion of 1974, but its experience was telling, too. The
'Green Line' through the island – a United Nations buffer zone – was
also a currency border. North of it, the Turkish lira circulated; in the
south, the Cypriot pound. A numismatic museum in Nicosia close to
the Green Line illustrated in different coinages stretching back to
ancient times that there was nothing new in this link between
power and money in an island that had fallen under one ruler after
another.

In an irony, it was precisely the historical link between money
and power that inspired the French-led drive to create a single
European currency, which was conceived above all as a means of
overcoming a new German hegemony exercised through the
Bundesbank. Despite the disavowal of history and politics that
imbued optimal-currency-area theory, it was history and politics
that propelled Europe towards a monetary union and that were responsible for its flawed design.

The political quest to create a common European money had
been longstanding as had been French support for the project. It was
after all Jacques Rueff, a prominent French economist and adviser to
governments, who had proclaimed in 1950: 'L'Europe se fera par la
monnaie ou ne se fera pas [Europe will be made by its currency or not

at all].' That declaration was to resonate as a rallying cry, although Rueff, a proponent of the gold standard, was actually advocating the need to restore monetary order to post-war Europe.[29]

In 1970, a task force headed by Pierre Werner, the prime minister of Luxembourg, had set out a plan to create a full economic and monetary union over a ten-year period. The blueprint did not envisage the precise institutional arrangements that came into shape when the ECB was created, but it spoke of the necessity of centralising monetary policy and creating a 'Community system for the central banks' that could resemble the US Federal Reserve.[30] As Gianni Toniolo observed in a history of central bank cooperation, two camps emerged in the deliberations of the Werner committee, the 'economists' and the 'monetarists', prefiguring arguments two decades later.[31] Germany and the Netherlands belonged to the 'economists', arguing that economic convergence must precede monetary union. France was the most influential voice among the 'monetarists' (not to be confused with followers of Friedman and the policy of controlling inflation by curbing monetary growth) who thought closer monetary cooperation could pave the way for an eventual currency union. Another parallel with the eventual project was the idea of making the journey in three stages.

This early push for monetary union was endorsed by the Council in March 1971, but in a watered-down version that dropped any target date for completing the project. It was in any case beached by events, in particular the collapse of the Bretton Woods fixed exchange-rate system between 1971 and 1973.[32] Yet, if anything, the switch to floating currencies heightened rather than diminished the desire to bring about monetary as well as economic integration within Europe. This reflected a deep-rooted aversion to flexible exchange rates in continental Europe that dated back to the interwar years. Nordic countries had been swift to follow Britain once it left the gold standard in September 1931. Denmark, Norway and Sweden all left the same month, and Finland followed in October. By contrast, France and the Netherlands persevered until October 1936, when both devalued. Italy, which also devalued then, had already imposed for-eign-exchange controls in May 1934.[33]

Even though France did much worse in the 1930s by staying on the gold standard, it drew very different conclusions from the overall experience of the interwar period than the UK. The British lesson, reaffirmed in 1992 when the exit from the exchange-rate mechanism allowed interest rate cuts that revived the economy, was that devalua-tion was a price worth paying if it allowed lower unemployment and faster growth. By contrast, the French lesson was that floating exchange rates gave too much power to the currency markets, allow-ing them to destabilise economies and to cause social distemper. And it was the French-inspired 'monetarist' approach to creating a cur-rency union that was to triumph.

One reason was that central bankers often found it easier to work together than politicians and finance ministers. As James observed in a history of European monetary cooperation until the early 1990s, the currency union was forged in practice by central bankers, who had developed the habit of monetary coordination in European and international forums.[34] Such collaboration flourished after the Second World War through regular private meetings held at the Bank for International Settlements (BIS) in Basel, which had been founded in 1930 to handle German reparations as part of the Young Plan.[35] And, according to James, it was a committee of central bank governors within the EEC, which had been meeting regularly in Basel since 1964, that 'decisively pushed history along' in creating the monetary union.

An advantage of taking the monetary route to integration was that it sidestepped the awkward task of spelling out to electorates what was involved in deeper economic integration, since much of what central bankers did was technical and obscure. Until the deci-sion to press ahead with a single currency at Maastricht, it also bypassed the need for new treaties. The European Monetary System (EMS) for example, which preceded the euro, was based on agreements between the central banks.[36] Created in 1979, its central feature was the exchange-rate mechanism (ERM), a grid of fixed (generally within a narrow range allowing deviations from the central parity of plus or minus 2.25 per cent) but adjustable exchange rates among its members. Adjustment was quite frequent: between 1979 and 1987 there were eleven realignments.[37]

The EMS envisaged the ecu, short for European currency unit – but also, as écu, the name of an old French coin (these things mattered) – playing a prominent part. However, it became little more than a unit of account, with interventions by central banks carried out first in dollars and then increasingly deutsche marks.[38] By the middle of the 1980s, currencies within the ERM had become anchored to the deutsche mark, stirring resentment in particular on the part of the French who bridled at the power of the Bundesbank to dictate (as they saw it) interest rates to the rest of Europe. Indeed, Jacques Attali, an adviser to Mitterrand, went as far as to claim that the deutsche mark was Germany's atomic bomb.[39] The notion was preposterous, yet it revealed how intensely the French resented German monetary hegemony.

In an effort to defuse such ill-feeling, the German government pushed at a European summit in Hanover in June 1988 for a special committee to be set up, which would study and propose 'concrete stages' leading towards an economic and monetary union. The committee was stuffed with central bankers but chaired by Jacques Delors, the Commission's president, who had already breathed new life into European integration through the initiative to complete the single European market.[40] Karl Otto Pöhl, the head of the Bundesbank, was distressed about the attempt to give new impetus to what he regarded as an unviable monetary union.[41] His misgivings turned out to be justified. Unlike previous studies that had gathered dust, the Delors Report, published in April 1989, proved to be a crucial advance by giving a technical imprimatur to the project, focusing on feasibility and implementation. Such a union, the committee said, would require a new central institution at the heart of a European system of central banks, which would be mandated to achieve price stability and endowed with independence. Though the Report did not set out a precise timetable, it advocated the three-stage process that was eventually adopted: in stage one, starting in July 1990, there would be the necessary treaty; in stage two, the institutions would come into being; while the third and final stage would feature the irrevocable locking of exchange rates and creation of a single currency that would mean full monetary union.[42]

The Delors Report might have charted a plausible course to creating a single European money, but that left open the question of why it was so urgent. One reason was that the lifting of capital controls, which accompanied the drive to complete the single market through eliminating national restrictions on trade within the European community by the end of 1992, would make maintaining separate currencies much harder. And, even though the Delors committee stressed that 'economic and monetary union implies far more than the single market programme', advocates of the single currency sought to elide the two initiatives, arguing that it was needed to make the single market work properly and hence to derive the potential economic gains from it.[43]

Consistent with this argument, advocates of monetary union pointed for example to the apparently exorbitant costs of changing national currencies within the existing European community. A tourist taking a round trip through ten (out of the twelve) member states would lose 47 per cent of the original money in conversion costs according to a European consumers' lobby in 1988. What this headline figure omitted was that over half that loss would come from just two currency conversions, from the Portuguese escudo to the Italian lira and from the Greek drachma into the deutsche mark because of fat margins charged by foreign-exchange traders to protect themselves when dealing in shaky southern European currencies.[44] If anything, what this finding showed was the risk of admitting Greece and Portugal into a monetary union.

The formal case for creating a single currency as well as completing a single market was set out in October 1990 by the

Commission in *One Market, One Money*. Though this purported to be a neutral analysis of the costs as well as the benefits of monetary union, its assessment, consistent with its provenance, was less than dispassionate, including citing the example of the supposedly extortionate cost of changing national currencies. In fact, the main way a single currency would promote economic welfare was not by getting rid of such transaction costs – the gains would be relatively small, as the report acknowledged – but through eliminating exchange-rate risk for businesses and finance and the resulting spur to trading intensity and investment. These benefits were microeconomic. The other side of the coin was macroeconomic: the corresponding loss of exchange-rate flexibility and monetary autonomy set against the potential benefits of greater price stability.[45]

What mattered was how big the benefits were and how much the costs might be. The upbeat judgements of *One Market, One Money* did not wear well. For example, it suggested that a monetary union could boost the European economy by between 5 and 10 per cent in the long run thanks to higher investment resulting from greater certainty for businesses. This proved to be wishful thinking; indeed the exceptional uncertainty generated by the shaky prospects of the single currency during the crisis weakened capital spending, which fell to half-century lows as a share of GDP.[46] Another advantage identified by the report was that 'the least favoured regions have a real opportunity for rapid catch-up'.[47] This breezy claim ran counter to the view of the Delors committee, which had worried that 'in the absence of countervailing policies, the overall impact on peripheral regions could be negative'.[48] That more sober judgement turned out to be a more accurate prediction. A long-run trend of convergence in living standards between southern and northern Europe continued in the first decade of the euro, though not for Italy and Portugal. But the divergence that opened up as a result of the euro crisis was so intense that over the lifetime of the euro until 2014, poorer countries across Southern Europe fell behind rather than gaining more ground.

But events rather than theories and arguments were to prevail. The opposition to pursuing the Delors plan remained formidable in Germany. In particular, the Bundesbank, revered by the German population as the embodiment of post-war stability and accordingly feared by politicians, made no secret of its profound hostility. What made the difference was German unification in 1990. The French could not prevent this but they could exact a price for their unwilling support. That price was to move towards a monetary union within a Europe of nation states that retained fiscal and political autonomy. This was the vital concession made by Kohl at a momentous meeting of the European Council in the Dutch city of Maastricht at the end of 1991 even though a month earlier he had told the German Bundestag that 'political union is the essential counterpart to economic and monetary union'.[49]

As the revolutionary project of a monetary union was shaped through traditional national bargaining, in particular a Franco-German deal between politicians haunted by history, the design that emerged in the Maastricht Treaty of 1992 paid little heed either to the economics of optimal-currency areas or to the traditional alignment of monetary sovereignty with fiscal and political sovereignty. The Treaty designated the goal as that of economic and monetary union (EMU) – though in reality the 'E' had little substance – and set 'convergence criteria' to determine whether countries could join. Formally, there were four criteria, three economic and one fiscal, but since the fiscal benchmark was subject to two conditions, there were in effect five. Two of the three economic tests required acceptable scores for inflation and long-term interest rates. The other one required states to demonstrate a track record of staying within the bounds of the ERM.[50] These were flimsy credentials to assure a country's fitness to join the euro, let alone its ability to stay the course within a monetary union.

Although the economic tests made some sense as gauges of nominal convergence, they still left much to be desired.[51] Compliance with the criteria was supposed to be on a sustainable basis, but working out whether good marks were the result of favourable cyclical conditions rather than long-run performance was inherently difficult. The price-stability test was assessed according to whether a state's inflation was no more than 1.5 percentage points above the average of the three best performers, for low inflation, within the EU. This might have been sensible before the currency union started, and in the event did not matter since the three best (Austria, France and Ireland) were to be among the eleven initial members. But in subsequent years, when more states applied to join the euro while the EU itself expanded, it meant that, oddly, the benchmark could be influenced by countries outside the euro area; for example, Latvia and Sweden, both outside the monetary union, were among the best three performers in 2013 when Latvia was a candidate for admission.[52]

The interest rate criterion shared this incongruity since it was assessed according to whether a country's long-term rates, gauged by government bond yields, were within an acceptable margin, in this case of two percentage points above the average for the same three countries identified as the best performers for price stability. But there was a more important reason why it was flawed. Whatever the merits of the argument that joining the euro would bring about endogenous convergence, government bond markets were susceptible to it. Provided that politicians carried through the project to create a monetary union, sovereign bond yields in weak countries would be drawn closer to those in strong economies since investors would no longer have to charge for higher expected inflation on the periphery.[53] That conviction took hold in the markets after the European Council meeting in Madrid at the end of 1995 confirmed 'unequivocally' that the single currency would start in 1999, called it uninspiringly the euro and adopted a 'changeover' plan for realising the project.[54]

The exchange-rate test, if applied stringently, was pertinent since it offered some degree of proof that economies applying to join the union could live with the rigours of a common currency. Indeed, the countries that looked most suitable according to optimal-currency-area theory also did well under this test. Austria along with Belgium and the

Netherlands had consistently managed to confine exchange-rate movements against the deutsche mark within very narrow margins for most of the 1980s and 1990s.[55] But although countries had to demonstrate compliance 'without severe tensions' that became much easier once the currency bands were widened from a maximum deviation from the central rate of 6 per cent (in either direction) before the ERM crisis to one of 15 per cent after it. In any case, the experience of the Bretton Woods system had shown that countries could often cling on to an inappropriate exchange rate for a long time before underlying economic imbalances caused a correction.

More important was what the tests left out. None of them captured the underlying suitability of a country for membership such as its trade intensity. There was no attempt to assess whether business cycles among those wanting to join had a tendency to move in line with Germany, the hub economy. And the tests paid no heed to structural shortcomings such as rigid labour markets, which would make membership much more exacting in the medium to long term, even if countries had succeeded in converging in the short term. Without wage flexibility, states that lost competitiveness would find it hard to regain it through internal devaluation. And although assessments were supposed to take account of other factors such as current-account balances, they were trumped by the convergence criteria.

Even though the British Treasury's five tests were by legend jotted down by Ed Balls, then an economic adviser to Gordon Brown, on the back of an envelope in the back of a New York cab together with the chancellor of the exchequer in 1997, at least three of them made more sense than the Maastricht criteria.[56] One asked whether economic structures as well as business cycles were compatible, so that the UK could live 'comfortably' with euro interest rates on a permanent basis. Another asked whether there was sufficient flexibility (essentially in the labour market) to deal with problems if they emerged. The concluding test was whether joining the currency union would promote higher growth, stability and a lasting increase in jobs.[57]

A particular weakness in the Maastricht model was that it lacked any form of fiscal stabilisation through a common budget, and alongside that an institutional arrangement for setting economic policy for the currency area. The aspiration to create a pure monetary union defied not just optimal-currency-area theory but past evaluations for the Commission of what was needed. The Werner Report had insisted upon 'a centre of decision for economic policy', which would exercise 'a decisive influence' at a union level.[58] In 1977, the MacDougall Report to the Commission had found that a common budget of between 5 and 7 per cent of GDP would be necessary to support a monetary union.[59] This finding was disregarded. Unlike federal countries such as the US, there would be no fiscal union with national taxpayers contributing to shared resources directed by a central finance ministry. In this respect, the euro area did not go beyond the existing design for the EU, whose budget had to be balanced and was restricted to around 1 per cent of European gross national income.[60]

Nor was the euro area to be a debt union. Each member state remained wholly responsible for its own public finances. A 'no bail-out' stipulation expressly ruled out (so it was thought) recourse to other countries; article 104b in the Maastricht Treaty said that a state would 'not be liable for or assume the commitments' of public authorities in other members of the union. In retrospect, this feature of the Treaty resembled a bluff on the part of European governments, which was duly called by the financial markets. But at the time, it was regarded as a defining characteristic of the monetary union, which was why the decision to rescue Greece in the spring of 2010 was so controversial, particularly in Germany.

Creating a monetary union without any budgetary entanglement meant that it was all the more important for member states to run sound public finances. The fiscal criterion for eligibility was that a country was not running an excessive deficit. Two stipulations were set for determining this. One was that budget deficits should not exceed 3 per cent of GDP; the other was that debt should not exceed 60 per cent of national output.[61]

The two fiscal conditions were condemned in 1992 by Willem Buiter, Giancarlo Corsetti and Nouriel Roubini in their paper, '"Excessive deficits": sense and nonsense in the Treaty of Maastricht'. The three economists argued that the stipulations were 'badly motivated and poorly designed' and threatened 'fiscal overkill' since the debt criterion in particular would be punishingly tough to reach for heavily indebted countries under the Maastricht timetable if interpreted mechanically.[62] But even on their own terms, the fiscal criteria were flawed as a means of determining eligibility to join the euro. The rule limiting budget deficits took no account of favourable economic circumstances or of special measures that might flatter performance in the period being evaluated in the tests. Since debt was a stock, it was less sensitive to the business cycle, giving more bite to the second rule. In particular, it might have been expected to keep Belgium and Italy out since their public debt in the early 1990s was not only above the 60 per cent threshold but above 100 per cent.[63] However, there was a get-out clause for states with excessive debt allowing them to be admitted if it was 'sufficiently diminishing' and approaching the 60 per cent level 'at a satisfactory pace'; what precisely that 'satisfactory' rate of decline might be was conveniently left unspecified.

In principle, the Maastricht rule about avoiding excessive deficits was supposed to apply after the currency union had been formed, with sanctions available to discipline offenders, but the German government (rightly) fretted about a loss of grip once the carrot of entry was no longer available. As a result, it pressed from late 1995 for a firmer arrangement to ensure that rules for fiscal discipline would continue to apply after the euro had come into being.[64] The eventual result was the stability-and-growth pact, which the European Council endorsed in Amsterdam in June 1997.[65] Although in a typical compromise the French had managed in earlier negotiations to add growth to the name of the pact, its substance was a Germanic insistence on stability.

The pact, which comprised two regulations and a resolution by the Council, 'put flesh on the bones of the treaty', according to Commission officials.[66] Its aim was to prevent and to deter excessive deficits through tighter fiscal surveillance and sterner corrective action. The preventive arm involved more timely monitoring on the part of the Commission, which could recommend blowing the whistle on inappropriate budget plans through an early warning. States were to set out their stability programmes, looking ahead at least three years, for meeting their fiscal objectives. In a potentially important extension of the Maastricht rules, budgets were supposed to be brought close to balance or in surplus over the 'medium term', though how long that might be was left undefined. The corrective arm was intended to enhance deterrence by speeding up the excessive-deficit procedure, setting clear deadlines, and spelling out the penalties that offenders would face if sanctions were imposed. Non-interest-bearing deposits (up to 0.5 per cent of GDP a year) for countries with excessive deficits would be turned into outright fines after two years if they were still failing to comply.[67]

The pact had three flaws. One was that in good times, it was too feeble a constraint. In principle, running budget balances that were close to balance or in surplus should have tackled high debt as well as providing room for manoeuvre for countries whose economies were struggling. But in practice the 3 per cent limit remained the constraint that mattered; and even this turned out not to be binding, since France, Germany and Italy ran deficits above the limit in three of the four years from 2001 to 2004 on figures available at the time.[68] Moreover, the 3 per cent limit was far too lenient for a country like Italy, whose perilously high debt required a sustained effort to bring it down towards the 60 per cent of GDP limit. In a glaring omission, the pact failed to specify special remedial treatment for highly indebted nations.

The second was that in hard times the pact was too blunt an instrument, leading Romano Prodi, the president of the Commission, to call the pact 'stupid' in 2002 when budget positions were deteriorating because of an economic downturn.[69] Though there were some safeguards to exempt countries whose public finances were suffering from a weak economy, they were quite restricted; in principle GDP had to fall by at least 2 per cent (though in some circumstances the fall could be between 0.75 and 2 per cent). Because of this, the pact, if implemented indiscriminately, could force a country into pro-cyclical measures to tighten fiscal policy rather than allowing the 'automatic stabilisers' – the rise in unemployment-related spending and fall in taxes that automatically help to mitigate downturns – to take full effect. This arose because the definition used for the budget balance did not take account of the business cycle.

The third and most fundamental problem was that it proved virtually impossible to enforce. The Council meeting in Amsterdam had 'solemnly' resolved to implement the pact in a 'strict and timely' manner. But when put to the test, the miscreants were led by the very government that had insisted on it in the first instance. Public finances deteriorated in Germany as its economy did badly in the early years of the euro, especially in 2002 and 2003. Already in early 2002, Hans Eichel, the German finance minister, flexed his muscles to avoid an 'early warning' about the government's planned budget deficit that year (which coincided with a federal election in the autumn).[70] The challenge to the pact came to a head in November 2003 when both Germany and France, whose economy and public finances were also in trouble, defied the Commission and got the council of finance ministers to prevent action being taken against them under the corrective arm of the pact, even though it had become clear they would not sort out their excessive deficits in 2004. Although the Commission subsequently brought and won a case challenging the council's decision at the European Court of Justice, it had lost the political battle. The row exposed an underlying weakness in the pact: the Commission might propose action but the council of finance ministers – 'sinners judging sinners' – could override its recommendations.[71]

Reforms in 2005 went some way to addressing some of the pact's defects. Stability plans were reconfigured in terms of cyclically adjusted balances (a move already under way), preferable because they captured the underlying state of the public finances.

Hard times excusing an excessive deficit were redefined to encompass any annual fall in GDP or indeed a protracted period of growth that was below trend.[72] But the overall effect of the reforms, which included longer deadlines and more extenuating circumstances, was generally to weaken the corrective arm. In an assessment by economists at the ECB in 2006, they referred to 'the proliferation of escape clauses' and argued that though the changes to the preventive arm could be seen as moving from simple to more sophisticated guidelines, those to the corrective arm were clearly associated with 'less stringent rules and procedures'.[73] The broader message of the revised pact was that the member states were not prepared to follow through the logic of the Maastricht Treaty and to enforce sanctions on misbehaving countries. As Buiter argued in late 2005, the excessive-deficit procedure was to all intents and purposes 'dead' for members of the euro zone.[74]

As well as being a flawed device for containing wayward countries, the pact also lacked ambition. Since members of the euro area could no longer tailor their own monetary policies to their individual circumstances, they were vulnerable if the common monetary settings did not suit them. In principle, fiscal policies could be used to stabilise an economy that had been hit by a shock to demand that was specific to that country rather than common to the euro area, thereby eliciting an easing in monetary policy. Such an approach was set out by the Treasury in 2003, when it envisaged the resurrection of fiscal policy, abandoned in the 1980s as a tool for managing demand, if the UK gave up its independent monetary policy by joining the euro. The British government could for example set a new rule to enforce a counter-cyclical fiscal policy, committing itself to respond with budgetary measures if the economy was running at specified margins above or below capacity.[75]

One reason why such an approach did not command support in the euro area was that monetary policy had been elevated as the primary way to steer an economy. It was more agile than fiscal policy, which required politicians to pull on tax and spending levers, more often than not too late, making it in practice pro-cyclical rather than anti-cyclical. In a speech in 2005 on the respective roles of monetary and fiscal policies in stabilising the economic cycle, Otmar Issing, the ECB's first chief economist (an informal title), accepted the role played by the automatic stabilisers since these operated in a timely fashion and symmetrically, moderating overheating during booms while supporting the economy during downturns. But he argued that discretionary fiscal policies were 'not normally suitable for demand management', noting that 'governments find it easier to decrease taxes and to increase spending in times of low growth than to do the opposite during economic upturns'.[76]

But the more important reason for the disavowal of discretionary fiscal policy was that the euro area, and in particular Germany, shunned anything that might encroach on the budgetary sovereignty of the currency zone's states. Unsurprisingly then, the stability pact was 'completely useless as a policy coordination device', argued Buiter in 2005; it was not designed to produce a euro-wide fiscal stance.[77] This defect did not matter so much in the first decade of the euro because the ECB had plenty of scope to modulate its monetary policy to offset demand shocks. But it came to the fore during the acute phase of the euro crisis, as the single-currency club as a whole tightened fiscal policy; and thereafter in the chronic phase as the ECB found it hard to foster even a feeble recovery – yet budgetary stimulus was not forthcoming.

The trade-off in Maastricht for accepting German demands for fiscal rigour was a firm date for monetary union, which was to commence no later than 1999. There was a similar compromise at the heart of the monetary union, the ECB. Germany's sacrifice was that the head of the Bundesbank, the central bank that held sway in Europe, would have just one vote in determining monetary policy on the ECB's governing council, the same as the central bank governor of Luxembourg, a mini-state the size of a local authority in bigger countries. One consolation prize was that the ECB, like the Bundesbank, would be located in Frankfurt, Germany's financial centre. But the main way that the Germans sought to soften the blow was by cloning the ECB from the Bundesbank. The ECB was to command a similar autonomy from not just one but all the governments of the euro-zone member states. That was the theory at any rate, but in practice during the crisis the positions taken by the governors on the ECB council tended to chime with the interests of their countries even though the national central banks were also to be independent under the terms of the Maastricht Treaty.[78]

The ECB was also a product of a particular phase of monetary history. It came into being as central banks around the world were focusing on achieving low inflation and winning operational independence for that purpose. But that template, of which the ECB was an extreme example, neglected the other tasks for which central banks had long been responsible. Historically they had served the interests of the state. The Bank of England for example was founded in 1694 to help provide war finance and nearly a century later, Adam Smith described it as 'a great engine of state' in the *Wealth of Nations*.[79] The German aversion to any central bank fiscal entanglement could be traced back to the part played by the Reichsbank's monetary financing of the state in the hyperinflation of the early 1920s. But the attempt to sever the ECB from any role in public finances was to prove near fatal to the monetary union in the acute phase of the crisis as the governments of countries in southern Europe found that they were borrowing in what amounted to a foreign currency without the backstop of a central bank able to create its own national money.

Another flaw in the ECB's mandate was that it lacked any supervisory grip over the banks through which it implemented its monetary policy. Again, this was to prove problematic given the historic role of central banks in promoting financial stability. The Bank of England might have been founded to help fight wars but it gradually took on the role of fighting financial crises, eventually leading Walter Bagehot in *Lombard Street*, published in 1873, to formulate its role as lender of last resort to banks suffering a liquidity shortage,. The Federal Reserve was created in 1913 to try to prevent the banking panics that had afflicted the US in the late nineteenth and early twentieth century. Such a role in fostering financial stability was difficult to achieve without supervisory control over individual banks, as the UK found out to its cost in the financial crisis after the job had been stripped away from the Bank of England in the late 1990s. But it was not until November 2014 that the ECB formally started to oversee the euro-zone banking system, following the decision to create a single supervisor in June 2012.

The flawed design of the monetary union occurred as politicians ignored the lessons not just of economic history but of economic theory. But the euro crisis was also a lesson in itself in the limits of economic theory. Some of the findings were undoubtedly prescient. The scepticism of many American economists, criticised in the paper published with such bad timing by the Commission at the end of 2009, was vindicated during the crisis. For example, in 'Europe's gamble', Maurice Obstfeld, an international macroeconomist at the University of California, Berkeley, argued that the wager could be won in the long run only if it spurred fundamental fiscal and labour market reforms and gave warning that if European leaders could not overcome domestic opposition to such measures the monetary union could prove 'unstable'.[80] Some specific risks that emerged during the crisis were also identified. For example, Peter Garber showed how potentially huge exposures could build up within the 'Target' payment system of the national central banks within the monetary union.[81] Although his analysis focused on the period between the initial locking of currencies in 1999 and the introduction of euro notes in 2002, it was to prove relevant during the euro crisis as the Bundesbank piled up claims on the ECB while the central banks of debtor nations for their part amassed corresponding liabilities.

The near-fatal defect that the euro experiment had revealed – that by giving up their own currencies governments would borrow in effect in a foreign currency – was spotted in a Treasury study that formed part of the British government's assessment, in 2003, of the case for entering the euro. The officials wrote that debt crises could be more likely in a euro area country than one with its own independent monetary policy because the former lacked the insurance against default provided by a possible bail-out by its central bank: 'it is thus in a situation like that of many developing countries, with debts denominated in a "foreign" currency'.[82] This concern did not feature in the overall assessment, which hinged upon the Treasury's judgement that the UK had not yet demonstrated the sustainable and durable convergence and the flexibility needed to make membership of the euro a sensible choice.[83]

Despite these telling insights, others proved to be far from the mark. In particular, the claim that the euro zone might endogenously become closer to an optimal-currency area, as trade intensity increased and business cycles converged did not wear well. In a survey of the euro area economy in 2009, the Organisation for Economic Cooperation and Development (OECD) found 'little evidence' that this had happened.[84] Traditional optimal-currency theory had also focused too much on the macroeconomic foundations of a well-functioning monetary union and not enough on the role of the financial system. Research on the US between the early 1960s and 1990 for example had already suggested that the resilience of a state to an adverse economic shock came more from capital and credit markets than from fiscal support.[85] Although this finding was subsequently challenged with fresh evidence showing that fiscal risk sharing predominated, especially since the financial crisis, the travails of the euro zone showed clearly just how destabilising a poorly functioning financial system could be.[86] The implication of this research was that the euro area required a banking union if it was to work properly in the long run, but the decision to start building one was taken only at the height of the crisis in the summer of 2012.

Perhaps the closest and most disturbing analogy to the European monetary union was the gold standard, which had functioned smoothly in its heyday, the four decades before the First World War, but badly when resurrected in the interwar period. A study in 2013 by

James together with Michael Bordo, another economic historian, highlighted a trio of awkward trilemmas – each a set of three choices of which any two are compatible but not all three – that had arisen under the gold standard, particularly after the First World War, and which could also apply to the euro zone.[87] The first was the 'impossible trinity'. States choosing to lock their exchange rates and allowing capital to move freely surrendered their monetary independence, a heavy sacrifice since a country slipping into recession could not cut interest rates to stimulate demand. In addition to this well-known trilemma, Bordo and James highlighted two others that were less familiar. One was that countries joining the gold standard with capital mobility jeopardised financial stability. The period before the First World War was peppered with banking crises caused by a sudden influx of foreign money, often after countries had joined the gold standard. The other was the potential incompatibility of locked exchange rates, capital mobility and democracy, illustrated by Germany's experience in the early 1930s as the country's unbearable effort to stay on the gold standard contributed to the rise of the Nazis.

The parallels between the euro and the gold standard were not exact. The European currency club had its own central bank and the euro floated against other currencies. Despite these ameliorating features, the euro area was arguably a tougher regime since leaving gold was possible, as Britain showed in 1931, even though a Labour politician famously lamented 'nobody told us we could do that'. For one thing, countries retained their currencies, making an exit much easier.[88] For another, as Bordo and James pointed out, there was a 'contingent rule' allowing suspension of the gold standard in times of emergency. By contrast, euro membership was irrevocable. Moreover, even if countries did wish to revisit the meaning of 'irrevocability', they could not because that would precipitate a system-wide banking run and 'the mother of all financial crises', as Barry Eichengreen, an economic historian, pointed out in 2007.[89] Indeed, the main reason why the crisis became existential was the fear that if an exit of just one country did nonetheless occur it could prompt a break-up of the whole system, with disastrous consequences for not just the euro area but also the global economy.

The decision to create a monetary union that was designed so badly was a chastening example of the power of politics over economics. It was politicians, driven by nationalist worries as much if not more than European aspirations, that brought the single currency into existence; in a sad irony, the euro rekindled nationalist resentments. On economic grounds, there was nothing ineluctable about such a development, still less about the fateful decision to start with a wide and riskier membership. Just as risky was the decision to cling to national budgetary sovereignty, confining any common policy to that of surveillance, which was in any case feeble. But if political will triumphed in bringing the euro into existence, the system of economic and financial governance that had been created was so inadequate that the single currency came close to a premature decease when put to the test.

# 3　Fragile strength

During its first decade, the single currency was a work in progress in more ways than one. Though the early years were difficult for Germany, France and Italy, which suffered particularly in the global slowdown from 2001 until mid 2003, the euro area as a whole made a promising start as the smaller economies in particular flourished, growing together at double the rate of the three big ones between 1999 and 2003.[1] The ECB established both its authority and the effectiveness of a single monetary policy, passing several tricky tests such as the early slowdown and commodity price shocks. The new central bank could point to a respectable record in its first decade as growth in living standards in the euro area broadly matched that of the US, while inflation remained under control. More remarkably, when the financial crisis rocked western capitalism in 2008, the single-currency club appeared to protect its member states, whereas those outside looked vulnerable. Late that year, Buiter said that there was 'a non-trivial risk of the UK becoming the next Iceland' and that the pound's status as a 'minor-league currency' was now a 'costly handicap' for London's position as a global financial centre.[2] Trichet's description of the euro as a shield in January 2009 (a term he had used before, for example in 2004) was not so obviously then the hostage to fortune that it became. In particular, although the euro itself fell against the dollar during the financial crisis it fared much better than the pound, which collapsed against both the dollar and the euro (at its nadir almost going through parity against the euro) due to fears about Britain's precarious banks.

But it was during the first decade of the single currency that the seeds of the euro crisis were sown, starting with the first and most important of them all, the admission of countries in southern Europe whose economies were ill-suited to the venture. The record for the euro area as a whole might have seemed broadly acceptable, but that overall picture disguised the emergence of economic imbalances both within and between members of the bloc. As a credit boom on the southern and western periphery gained momentum in the middle of the 2000s, these imbalances opened up on a scale matched only by the rapidity with which they emerged. Easy money caused some countries like Spain to boom and allowed others like Italy to avoid confronting structural deficiencies. The new edifice of the single currency appeared imposing, but cracks were opening up beneath the gloss of cheap and abundant credit.

The underlying weaknesses were overlooked in part because the euro and its new central bank consistently confounded the sceptics who had doubted the viability of the venture. Both the locking of exchange rates at the start of 1999 and the introduction of notes and coin three years later were accomplished with aplomb. Though there were complaints about price gouging when the new currency actually started to circulate in people's hands, public disquiet about a surge in inflation was exaggerated; despite an increase in prices in restaurants and cafés, the changeover added between 0.1 and 0.3 of a percentage point to consumer price inflation in 2002.[3] The ECB never lacked critics, but it won a grudging respect as it established a distinctive and successful regime for implementing monetary policy that enabled interest rate decisions taken in Frankfurt to be transmitted the length and breadth of what was a continental economy. Particularly after shedding some idiosyncrasies it had inherited from the Bundesbank, the ECB fitted in with the new economic policy regime among advanced countries in which independent central banks had become the principal conductors of the economy, able to stabilise the business cycle and to keep inflation low and stable with a flick of the baton of policy rates.

Moreover, the euro club was expanding. Though this flattered to deceive since the new members included three countries – Greece, Slovenia and Cyprus – which subsequently got into trouble, each new admission appeared at the time to be a fresh vote of confidence. The original eleven in 1999 were the six founders of the common market, together with five others that joined later, Ireland in 1973, Portugal and Spain in 1986 and Austria and Finland as recently as 1995. Greece brought the euro-zone membership up to twelve in 2001, two decades after its accession to the EEC. It was followed by Slovenia in 2007, Cyprus and Malta in 2008 and Slovakia in 2009, the latter four having joined the EU as recently as May 2004.[4] As had been the case on day one in 1999, the new entrants adopted the euro at the start of the year, taking advantage of the holiday to overcome the technical problems of changing their currencies.

Joining the euro at its start turned out to be less exacting when the Maastricht criteria were evaluated in the spring of 1998 than had seemed likely when the conditions were set in the Treaty of 1992. There were two main reasons beyond the easing of the exchange-rate test through the wider fluctuation bands. First, there had been more convergence than expected. By the late 1990s, European along with other advanced economies were benefiting from a secular fall in inflation, arising from sagging commodity prices and more intense international competition, notably through an influx of cheap Chinese manufactured goods, together with advances in information technology.[5] This contributed to a convergence of inflation rates, making it easier to meet the price stability test. Second and more important was the political push to start with a wider union. This partly reflected the genuine attempts made by countries in southern Europe to join the euro, but as Marsh pointed out in his history of the euro, one reason why Germany backed the admission of Italy, despite its excessive public debt, was to avoid the threat to German industry from Italian firms able to exploit a cheap lira.[6] The support for a broad membership in turn encouraged the 'convergence trades' of the late 1990s that caused bond spreads between the periphery and the core to narrow, making it easier to meet the long-term interest rate test.

The political impetus behind the euro also meant that the two fiscal criteria could be fudged even though on the face of it they looked harder to meet than the economic tests. On a strict interpretation, only three states – Finland, France and Luxembourg – of the eleven admitted at the start passed the debt test, with scores below 60 per cent of GDP in 1997. On the other hand, only two, Belgium and Italy, had inordinately high debt, above 120 per cent, double the limit. It was the get-out clause – letting nations with excessive debt off the hook provided that it was falling at an acceptable rate – that proved decisive. But though this perhaps provided grounds for admitting Belgium, whose debt had dropped by 11 percentage points of GDP in the three years since 1994, it hardly did so for Italy whose debt had fallen by little more than 3 percentage points over the same period.[7] Interpreting this as a 'satisfactory' pace of decline belonged to the linguistic school of 'when I use a word it means just what I choose it to mean'.

As for the deficit criterion – that it should not exceed 3 per cent of GDP – this was met in several countries only through manoeuvres that took advantage of flaws in the way that public finances were treated in the European national accounts. A subsequent study by the OECD unearthed 'a large incidence of one-offs and creative accounting operations', which were particularly prominent for 1997, the crucial year for assessing the candidates against the entry criteria.[8] Some were more blatant than others. Italy raised around 1.5 per cent of GDP in 1997 through temporary revenue measures. These included the notorious 'euro tax', a withholding tax on income with a commit-ment to repay it from 1999, by which time the country would be safely tucked inside the euro zone.[9] Because the repayment was a political pledge and had not been specified in law, Eurostat, the European statistical authority, allowed the temporary revenue to count against, and flatter, the budget balance.[10]

The French government used a subtler ploy, taking responsibility for the occupational pensions of a state-owned company, France Télécom, in return for a lump-sum payment from the firm. This pro-vided €5.7 billion (at the eventual conversion rate), which lowered the budget deficit by 0.5 per cent of GDP, allowing France to scrape a pass on the test. The much larger present value of the liabilities, representing pensions in payment and the accrued rights of workers, which was reckoned at €24 billion, vanished into an accounting black hole. The trick was used elsewhere, especially in Portugal, as it sought to massage deficits down both in the early years of membership and while it was struggling unsuccessfully to avoid a bail-out in the euro crisis.[11]

In practice, the fiscal tests proved as malleable as European leaders wanted them to be: they were after all marking their own papers. The political drive for monetary union dispelled caution. Even the German government contemplated a wheeze to help pass the budget-deficit test – revaluing the Bundesbank's gold reserves to allow it to pay a bigger profit to the government for the critical year of 1997 – although this was shot down by the central bank.[12] As long as potential entrants demonstrated that they wanted to join – notwithstanding its fiscal fiddles, Italy made a big effort in the late 1990s under Romano Prodi – the door was not just ajar but wide open. The only country to fail the exercise was Greece, which flunked the more objective economic tests of inflation and long-term interest rates as well as the fiscal conditions.

The decision to include the weaker brethren was one reason why the euro was ill-received in the foreign-exchange markets, whose dealers rudely dismissed it as a 'toilet currency', although the more important factor was a resurgent dollar on what turned out to be over-optimistic expectations of American growth arising from the technology-based 'new economy'.[13] Though this made for a difficult start for the ECB, it was still able to exert its authority in setting monetary policy for the euro area. The new central bank had come into existence seven months before the euro, in June 1998, just a month after European leaders had agreed upon the eleven countries that would be the first to adopt the single currency.[14] The ECB's make-up, with a central authority in Frankfurt but a continuing role for the national central banks (NCBs), reflected the compromises that had allowed this extraordinary experiment to be undertaken in the first place.

Formally, all the NCBs in the EU owned the new institution through capital shares, called 'keys', determined by their economic and demographic size, but what mattered was paid-up capital, which came almost entirely from the euro-zone central banks. Adjusted for this, the capital keys among the members of the euro area determined the risk-sharing if the ECB incurred losses and were also used to allocate the income earned on assets held against notes in circulation after the ECB's own share, which was 8 per cent.[15] Though the ECB set monetary policy, it was the NCBs that executed it. Together they formed the Eurosystem, although the ECB was commonly used to describe both since it was the ruling body at the apex of the Eurosystem.

If, in its capital structure, the ECB reflected Germany's true weight in the euro area – its capital key was 31 per cent at the outset – that was not the case in its governance.[16] Decisions relating to capital, profits and the transfer of foreign-exchange assets to the ECB were taken by the NCB governors, whose votes were weighted according to the capital keys.[17] But such procedures were the exception to the rule. In setting monetary policy and all that flowed from it, each member of the governing council, which comprised the heads of the NCBs and a six-strong executive board, had one vote. Appointments to the board were originally made by the European Council through 'common accord' (allowing national vetoes) but this was revised to qualified-majority voting among the euro-zone members under the Lisbon Treaty of 2007 (which came into force in 2009).[18] The national governors might outnumber the board members, but it was the board that drove policy and which included the crucial job of president. In an interview in 2004, almost a year after he had taken the top job at the ECB, Trichet likened the Eurosystem to a 'sports team' in which the ECB was the captain and the NCBs were the 'other players'.[19]

All members of the ECB's council were expected to act in the common interest of the euro area rather than representing their nations (or their national origins in the case of the board members). In a symbolic gesture, Hans Tietmeyer, the first Bundesbank head to join the council, insisted on removing national nameplates, saying that the governors were there in their personal capacity rather than representing their countries; where people sat was according to the alphabetical order of their names.[20] Even so, the governors from larger economies tended to carry more weight in discussions in part because they came briefed by big research teams at their central banks. And despite the good intentions, it did not rule out some old-fashioned national realpolitik on the part of European leaders over who was appointed to the board, especially who got the plum post of president.

In an inauspicious and ill-tempered deal in May 1998 between Kohl and Chirac, who wanted a French hand at the helm as soon as possible, the job went in the first instance to Wim Duisenberg, a former head of the Dutch central bank, who since July 1997 had been president of the European Monetary Institute, a proto-ECB set up in 1994, when stage two of the journey to monetary union began, on the understanding that he would not serve his full eight years of office.[21] Trichet, the governor of the French central bank, duly took over in November 2003. The unspoken pay-off for Germany accepting Trichet as the first full-term president was for their candidate to take over in 2011. At the start of that year, this had seemed to favour Axel Weber, the head of the Bundesbank, but he pulled out of the race. His unexpected decision to resign from the German central bank in early 2011 gave Draghi his chance.[22]

Unlike the Federal Reserve, which since 1977 had to pursue maximum employment as well as stable prices under a 'dual mandate' set by Congress, the ECB's primary and overriding mission was to maintain price stability.[23] And unlike for example the Bank of England, whose target was set by the chancellor of the exchequer, the ECB was given not only operational independence but also the power to specify its own goal. This was in keeping with the exceptional independence, in legal terms at any rate, which it was granted under the Maastricht Treaty. A survey by the Bank of England of inflation-targeting banks, published in 2012, found that among nine in industrialised countries, the central bank determined the target in only one, Sweden. In two, Norway as well as Britain, the government set it. In the remaining six, the target was jointly specified.[24]

The survey did not include either the Fed or the ECB because neither was an explicitly inflation-targeting central bank, although under Ben Bernanke the Fed did specify its goal for inflation (2 per cent) for the first time, in January 2012, while making clear that it continued to follow the dual mandate.[25] The ECB's approach was distinctive in a different respect. Reflecting the influence of the Bundesbank as a role-model, it started life with two 'pillars' of monetary policy, one similar to the broad macroeconomic assessment of price pressures used by an inflation-targeting bank and the other paying heed to monetary developments. Moreover, the latter was the more important, as Duisenberg said when setting out the approach that the governing council had agreed to follow. Speaking at a press conference (an early innovation was to hold one directly after the monetary-policy meeting) in October 1998, just a few weeks before the euro started, he said that money would have a 'prominent role'; the monetary pillar would be 'thicker' or 'stronger' than the other pillar.[26]

Whether 'thicker' or 'stronger', the monetary pillar proved to be the wobblier. In May 2003, the ECB formally downgraded its monetarist heritage, stating that it would rely in future more on its macroeconomic assessment, and consign monetary developments to a longer term 'crosscheck'.[27] It also used the occasion to rectify another fault in the original framework, which had defined price stability as inflation below 2 per cent a year over the medium term. This was too vague. It was wrong to suggest that this meant the ECB would tolerate deflation since the commitment specified an annual increase in the consumer price index, but the definition could be construed as tolerating very low inflation, which might in turn risk a slide into deflation. In the revamp of 2003, the ECB conceded the point, by specifying price stability more precisely as inflation that was 'below, but close to' 2 per cent, interpreted as somewhere between 1.7 and 1.9 per cent.

The rationale that the ECB gave for its reformulation was to be pored over by its governing council a decade later as inflation slid below 1 per cent in late 2013 and stayed very low in 2014, with prices falling in several euro-zone countries. The council stressed in 2003 that the more precise definition of the goal provided a 'safety margin to guard against the risks of deflation'. It highlighted the problem that deflation presented to central banks in the shape of the 'zero lower bound' for nominal interest rates. This referred to the fact that although rates could be lowered below zero, the scope to do this was limited because deposits could be switched into cash, constraining the ability of conventional monetary policy to stimulate the economy.

Although the ECB had moved a long way towards the inflation-targeting paradigm of modern central banking, it had not fully adopted it. The monetarist influence might have waned, but Trichet subsequently insisted that it had informed the ECB's decision to start raising interest rates in December 2005, despite international calls to stay its hand.[28] And although the central bank had clarified its definition of price stability, it retained its medium-term perspective, which was longer than for example the two years that the Bank of England had in mind when setting interest rates to meet its target. Even as Duisenberg beat the retreat, in May 2003, from the original over-hawkish specification of price stability, he felt compelled to say at the press conference: 'I protest against the word "target". We do not have a target ... and we won't have a target.'[29]

Once the ECB had downgraded money as a guide to policy, however, inflation expectations became increasingly important as a lodestar. If inflation either rose above the aim of just under 2 per cent, or fell well below it (as occurred from 2013), the central bank would appeal to the stability of inflation expectations over the medium term as an indicator that monetary settings were still satisfactory.[30] And when Draghi himself highlighted a fall in a particular measure of longer term inflation expectations in the summer of 2014 (which predictably became the subject of intense scrutiny), the markets interpreted this as a signal that quantitative easing was on the way, despite the aversion of Germany to central bank purchases of sovereign debt, which would be necessary for any big quantitive easing (QE) programme.

In fact, the Maastricht Treaty permitted such purchases, but the makers of the Treaty had not envisaged a policy such as QE, which would have been regarded as anathema in the first decade of the ECB. Instead, monetary policy was carried out through the orthodox method of setting short-term interest rates. The ECB's main policy rate was the refinancing rate, at which funding was provided to banks every week. There were two other rates, one above, which banks had to pay if they were short of overnight money, and one below, which the ECB paid on overnight funds that banks deposited with it. These upper and lower limits, which from the spring of 1999 until the financial crisis were one percentage point above and below the main rate, also influenced the money markets where banks lent to one another, since a bank would generally neither put money on deposit in the markets at a lower rate than that available at the ECB nor borrow at a rate higher than that of its emergency lending facility. In normal times, both in practice and through design, Eonia (the average overnight interbank rate) hugged the main lending rate because the ECB deliberately provided just enough liquidity to the banks in its weekly operations to meet their reserve requirements on average over the monthly 'maintenance period' between each policy-rate setting by the council.[31] But during the financial and euro crisis, the policy of helping banks by making available unlimited liquidity meant that money-market rates were increasingly determined by the ECB's deposit rate, which acted as a floor.

The banks borrowing from the Eurosystem always had to provide collateral. The deterioration in the quality of paper that the ECB began to accept during the euro crisis became a point of contention between the central banks of creditor nations, especially the Bundesbank, which feared having to shoulder losses on loans made to weak banks, and those of peripheral nations whose banks were desperate to get their hands on central bank funding. In fact, it was relatively easy for the ECB to adapt its ways both in the euro crisis and in the preceding financial crisis because it had been catholic about what it accepted from the outset, reflecting the wide range in practices among the individual NCBs. Indeed, for several years individual NCBs were able to accept a range of assets (such as equities until 2005) that were not permitted as a general rule.[32] This second tier of collateral that was eligible according to national rather than euro-wide criteria was eliminated in 2007 through the creation of a 'single list', but it still left the definition of acceptable collateral much wider and more lenient than the Bank of England, which would accept only a limited range of high-quality debt securities, such as gilts.[33] As it happened, this meant that the ECB was better placed than the Bank of England to respond effectively when the financial crisis erupted in the summer of 2007.

Though there were some early difficulties, such as communication mishaps by Duisenberg, the ECB was consolidating its position not just through technical prowess but, more fundamentally, for its record on inflation. Despite the grumbles about price rises at the changeover to euro notes and coins in 2002, inflation was tame in the single currency's first decade. In September 2011, shortly before Trichet stepped down, he summed up how the ECB had performed in delivering price stability in one emphatic word: 'Impeccably!'. Indeed, it had done a better job in keeping German inflation low over thirteen years, he said pointedly, than the Bundesbank had itself managed over similar periods after the Second World War.[34]

This valedictory claim was self-serving since Trichet was not comparing like with like. The Bundesbank had to grapple with the worldwide upsurge in inflation in the 1960s and 1970s, culminating in the oil-price shocks of 1973–4 and 1979–80. By contrast, the ECB took charge when the scourge of inflation had been tamed. Although there were commodity-price shocks in the 2000s, their impact was less pronounced than before. Even so, the ECB could point to a successful record, not just on inflation, which had averaged almost exactly 2 per cent a year over the first twelve years of the currency union, but also on growth, as Trichet argued in an earlier swansong in 2011.[35] Delivering a speech that June in Frankfurt entitled 'Two continents compared', he vaunted the euro area's performance. Although GDP had expanded less than in the US while the single currency had been in existence, that shortfall did not take into account slower population growth in the euro zone. Living standards, measured by GDP per person, rose at a similar pace over the whole period, pointed out Trichet.

In fact, that outcome was less satisfactory than it appeared since the euro area was less prosperous than the US, creating scope for higher catch-up growth in much the same way as between the poorer and richer states within the monetary union. Although the transatlantic gap in living standards was longstanding, the euro had done nothing to improve it.[36] More important, however, the reassuring picture that Trichet painted was premature. The currency club's relative performance worsened drastically as the euro crisis intensified. The region was pushed back into a double-dip recession, which though tamer than the downturn arising from the financial crisis lasted even longer. There were two barren years as output stagnated in the second quarter of 2011 and then fell for seven successive quarters, reviving only in the spring of 2013, whereas the earlier downturn in 2008–9 had lasted just five quarters. By contrast, the American recovery, though disappointing by post-war standards and encountering some temporary setbacks, was sustained (see Figure 2).

The sources of growth in GDP before the financial crisis differed across the Atlantic. More came in the currency union from rising employment than advances in productivity (output per worker), whereas it was the other way round in the US. Productivity growth in the euro area slowed from 1.6 per cent a year between the late 1980s and the late 1990s to 1 per cent in 2000–7. This contrasted with a pickup in American annual productivity growth from 1.5 to nearly 2 per cent a year over the same periods.[37] But some comfort could be drawn from the flipside, as employment increased rapidly, outstripping the pace in the US. The euro-zone employment rate – those working as a proportion of the working-age population – rose sharply as more women joined the workforce and pension reforms discouraged early retirement.[38]

Another encouraging sign was that despite the setbacks to the stability pact, the public finances of the euro area, considered as a single economy, were improving. On figures for the original eleven members of the euro area together with Greece, public debt fell from 71 per cent of GDP in 1999 to 66 per cent in 2007.[39] The overall budget deficit in 2007 was less than 1 per cent of GDP, lower than in 1999, and had gone above 3 per cent in only one year – 2003.[40] However, this picture could be interpreted more harshly since the improvement especially in the debt burden was disappointingly slight given the strong economic upturn in the middle of the decade.

More important, the whole looked healthier than the parts. The steady performance of the monetary union emerged as the sobriety of the economies in the core offset the exuberance on the periphery. Whereas Germany grew more slowly than the euro area, growth in Ireland, Greece and Spain was much faster. This was convergence but of the wrong kind, because for the most part it was not grounded on genuine improvements in economic performance. Moreover, the satisfactory inflation record for the euro area as a whole disguised a reversion to divergence, with higher inflation on the periphery and lower in the core, which was not so 'impeccable'. To some extent, this might be expected as the poorer countries on the rim of the euro area caught up with those in the core through the Balassa–Samuelson effect, whereby rapid wage increases in the traded sector, reflecting strong productivity growth, spread to the non-traded sector, where the scope for efficiency gains is more limited, pushing up domestic costs and prices. But that comforting interpretation did not match what was happening on the ground to the periphery, where the non-traded rather than the traded sector was driving growth.

Easy credit was stimulating housing-market bubbles and a surge in domestic demand. These sins were hardly original for the euro area: house prices were buoyant elsewhere, too, notably in the UK and the US. Indeed, Germany stood out for the absence of a credit binge, which meant that household debt (as a share of GDP) actually fell between 1999 and 2007 (see Figure 6). But the credit boom was especially intense for countries on the periphery of the euro zone because their interest rates fell so sharply as their economies came under the protective umbrella of German creditworthiness. That process had already started in the run-up to monetary union; during the five years until its start, long-term interest rates in Italy, Portugal and Spain fell by over five percentage points compared with an average of around three points for the euro zone as a whole. Once inside the union, a further stimulus got under way as the sluggish state of the German economy, making up nearly a third of the euro-zone economy, led the ECB to keep interest rates below what was needed in the peripheral countries. As a result, real short-term interest rates were negative or barely positive for long stretches in Ireland and southern Europe.[41]

Much of the effect of these inappropriate real interest rate settings occurred through housing markets, especially in countries where tax breaks favoured owner-occupiers.[42] Particularly in Ireland and Spain, this led to extraordinary house-price bubbles. Between 1995 and 2006, for example, house prices quadrupled in Ireland. Only by comparison was the Spanish experience less epic, with house prices tripling over the same period. Although Ireland and Spain stood out for their excesses – house prices rose for example in Spain by 13 per cent a year between 1999 and 2006 – the boom was widespread. Over the same period, house prices increased in Italy and the Netherlands by 7 per cent a year and in France at an annual rate of 11 per cent. By contrast, they went nowhere in Germany, which meant that they fell in real terms.[43]

This in turn spurred a broader economic boom in both Ireland and Spain as spending on construction (both in housing and non-residential buildings and infrastructure) surged to around a fifth of GDP.[44] At its peak, in 2006, residential construction as a share of Irish GDP was not only double its long-run average but also the highest in the OECD and over double the average among its then thirty member states.[45] The Irish boom was deceptive because the economy had been racing ahead for some time, causing it to be dubbed the 'Celtic Tiger'. The growth spurt that got under way in the late 1980s had been

securely grounded in favourable demographic developments produ-
cing a sharp increase in employment. Productivity growth was strong,
too, helped by an influx of foreign, especially American, multinationals, attracted by a well-educated labour force as well as kid-glove
treatment of corporate profits. But as Karl Whelan, an economist at
University College Dublin, pointed out, the nature of that economic
miracle changed at the start of the 2000s, as growth increasingly came
from the construction sector, fuelled by a credit boom, and productivity growth slowed.[46]

The Spanish economy did not career out of control to quite the
same extent as Ireland, but its imbalances mattered more because its
GDP, the fourth-biggest in the euro area, was over six times as large as
Ireland's at the outset. Spain's economic ebullience – its national
output grew at nearly double the rate of the euro area as a whole
between 1999 and 2007 – was crucial in sustaining the club's overall
performance. Indeed, Spain accounted for 40 per cent of the overall rise
in employment in the euro zone until 2007.[47] At the time, the sources
of the expansion appeared virtuous because investment grew rapidly
owing to the construction boom. But when the housing market collapsed, it turned out that much of the investment had been squan-
dered in the building of unwanted residential space, which became
ghost towns.[48]

The picture on the periphery was not a uniform one. The Greek
economy also appeared to be thriving inside the euro area; indeed, its
economy grew by 4.1 per cent a year between 1999, two years before it
joined, and 2007, almost double the 2.2 per cent growth of the euro
area (including Greece) over that period. Ireland did even better, growing at an annual pace of 5.5 per cent.[49] Slovenia and Cyprus thrived as
they joined first the EU in 2004 and then the euro in 2007 and 2008,
respectively. By contrast, growth in Italy and Portugal, at 1.5 per cent a
year between 1999 and 2007, was below that of the currency club as a
whole, even though both economies were benefiting from easy credit.
The former's lacklustre performance mattered because it was the
third-biggest economy in the euro area; the latter's was particularly

disappointing since it was the poorest of the founding members of the monetary union.

Although the reasons for the two countries' under-performance varied, they shared a common weakness in that the structure of their economies made them vulnerable to global competition.[50] Both countries had traditional strengths in products like textiles and footwear that were being undermined by low-cost producers in Asia. At the same time, the opening up of eastern Europe meant that they could no longer benefit to the same extent as before from foreign investment. For German car manufacturers for example, central European economies like Slovakia were more convenient and offered cheaper labour. Outside the euro, both economies could have regained competitiveness by devaluing. The appropriate response inside the euro was to reduce domestic costs relative to those of the other currency club members, but instead both Italy and Portugal became less competitive.

Nominal exchange rates might have been fixed between the euro member states but real exchange rates, the relative expensiveness of a country, which is often estimated using relative unit labour costs, rose generally on the periphery, making economies there less competitive. Economy-wide unit labour costs – wages and salaries together with employer social contributions per unit of output – increased markedly, whereas they remained broadly unchanged in Germany over the first decade of the euro. Remarkably, the German ability to hold their costs down occurred even though productivity growth slowed compared with its performance in the preceding decade; rather, languishing pay was the main reason.[51] By contrast, unit labour costs surged across the periphery, including Italy as well as the countries that were to require bail-outs, such as Greece, Ireland and Portugal. At its peak, in 2008, the divergence in competitiveness since 1999 between Germany and the peripheral economies in southern Europe reached between 25 and 35 per cent, while it was still higher in the case of Ireland (see Figure 3). This development troubled the ECB, and when the governing council met in Athens in October 2005,

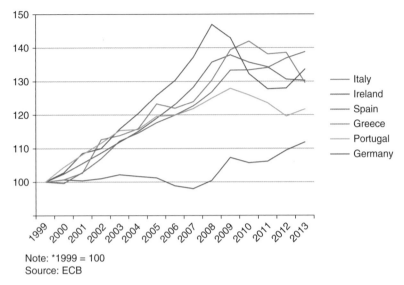

Note: *1999 = 100
Source: ECB

FIGURE 3  Unit labour costs*, 1999–2013

on one of its twice-a-year excursions out of Frankfurt (a practice that had started in 2000), Trichet used the occasion to highlight its growing concern.[52]

In another sign of trouble, the balance of payments across the periphery lurched deeply into the red (see Figure 4). Ireland's position changed from a marginal surplus in the year the euro began to a deficit of nearly 6 per cent of GDP in 2008. The deterioration in the Spanish current account to a deficit of over 9 per cent of GDP at its peak was remarkable, yet it was overshadowed by Greece's, which reached 14 per cent or more in 2007 and 2008. Even countries that were not booming suffered persistent shortfalls in their external accounts. Italy ran a string of deficits from 2002 although they were fairly small, reaching a high of 3.5 per cent of GDP in 2010. But Portugal, which had come close to balancing its accounts in the early 1990s, ran a big deficit throughout the first decade of the euro, which peaked at 12 per cent of GDP in 2008. Concomitantly, there was a swing towards big surpluses run by core countries, especially in Germany and the

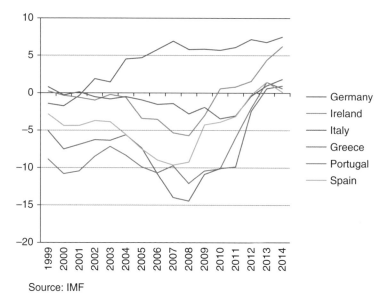

Source: IMF

FIGURE 4 Current-account balances, as per cent of GDP, 1999–2014

Netherlands. By 2007, the overall German surplus had reached 7 per cent of GDP mainly through a surplus with the rest of the euro zone of over 4 per cent of GDP.[53]

The emergence of big deficits was cause for concern, since they indicated distortions in demand and made countries vulnerable to a loss of confidence by the foreign investors financing them. As the OECD pointed out in a survey of the euro area in 2010, 'the scale and persistence of the imbalances was greater than in earlier decades', adding that 'the broad-based widening of external imbalances during the upswing was new'.[54] But in the first decade of the euro, traditional worries about the danger of running deficits were often dismissed, on the grounds that countries within a monetary union no longer faced balance-of-payments constraints. This view, which ECB officials sometimes privately expressed, could be traced back to the Werner Report in 1970, which had said that 'for such a union only the global balance of payments of the Community *vis-à-vis* the outside world is of any importance'.[55] In a hard-learnt lesson, the Commission acknowledged the riskiness of sustained national current-account deficits by including them in a scoreboard of indicators that could serve as warning signals as part of a new role in surveillance of macro-economic imbalances in the EU; deficits averaging above 4 per cent of GDP over the most recent three years were to sound an alarm in annual 'alert mechanism' reports, the first of which was issued in early 2012.[56]

The boom on the periphery was unsustainable because it was fostered by unsustainable lending. Once again, overall figures for the euro area flattered to deceive. Between 1997 and 2002, total euro-zone banking assets rose only a little, from 225 per cent of GDP to 250 per cent (see Figure 5). That was followed by a spurt that took the total size of the banking sector to 335 per cent of GDP in 2008. But banking assets rose much more sharply among the peripheral countries where lending was especially unsound. In Spain, they went from 170 per cent of GDP in 1998 to over 300 per cent a decade later. The Irish experience was even more extreme, as bank assets jumped over the same period from an already high 300 per cent of GDP to over 900 per cent. Although Ireland's figures were swollen by the presence of international banks with little connection to the domestic economy, the value of loans for house purchases and to non-financial firms tripled between 2002 and 2007. The lending surge in Spain was almost as immoderate. Cypriot and Slovenian banks also behaved with astonishing recklessness. By contrast, domestic lending barely budged in Germany and its much smaller increase in overall bank assets was reflected in the euro-zone average.[57]

The unwise lending had consequences not just for the banks and countries on the periphery but also for those in the core. The big current-account deficits on the periphery were financed in large measure by banking flows from the surplus countries. Cross-border holdings within the euro area as a share of total banking assets almost doubled in the first decade of the single currency.[58] Domestic banks in the deficit countries continued to play a crucial role as the middlemen

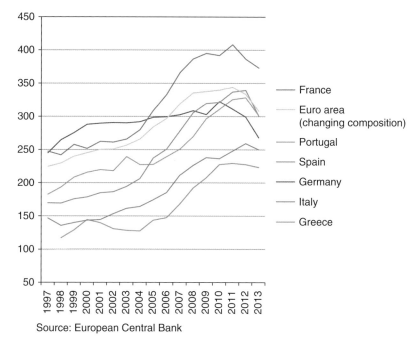

Source: European Central Bank

FIGURE 5 Bank assets, as per cent of GDP, 1997–2013

between their borrowers and the funds flowing in from banks in the surplus countries. Direct lending by foreign banks to domestic borrowers remained rare and for the most part, deeper integration through cross-border equity stakes was also lacking. In this way, European banks built up cross-border positions with one another on a scale they would have previously avoided owing to currency risk.[59]

The counterpart to the banking excesses was a big build-up in private-sector debt (see Figure 6). Spain exemplified the trend. In 1999, its non-financial corporate sector had debts worth 62 per cent of GDP while household debt amounted to 42 per cent. By 2007, both had doubled, to 125 per cent of GDP for firms and 81 per cent for households. Portuguese private debt had also risen over the same period to worryingly high levels, from 78 per cent of GDP for its companies to 110 per cent, and from 53 per cent of GDP for households to 87 per

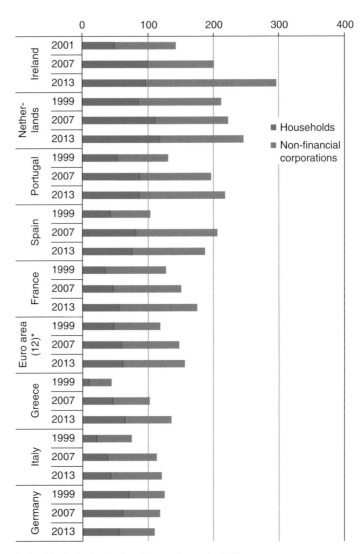

Note: *Excludes Ireland and Luxembourg in 1999,
and Luxembourg in 2007.

Source: Eurostat

FIGURE 6  Private debt, as per cent of GDP, 1999, 2007 and 2013

cent. Ireland's private-sector debt jumped from 143 per cent of GDP in 2001 to 201 per cent in 2007.

Private-sector indebtedness was another of the eleven indicators the Commission subsequently chose for its alert mechanism, choosing a level of 160 per cent of GDP as the figure above which there would be cause for concern. Although private debt for the euro zone as a share of GDP rose between 1999 and 2007, it remained below that threshold as German debt actually fell over that period. This masked some worrying developments in several countries particularly on the periphery. By 2007, debt in Ireland, Portugal and Spain had gone well above the Commission's benchmark. Dutch debt was especially high though it had not surged to the same extent since the start of the euro when it was already well above the threshold. In a study published by the BIS in 2011, Stephen Cecchetti, its economic adviser, together with two other economists at the bank, found that the thresholds when private debt became a drag on the economy were 85 per cent of GDP for households and 90 per cent for businesses.[60] On this basis, the burden was already onerous by 2007 for Dutch, Irish and Portuguese households. It was also worryingly high for Irish, Portuguese and Spanish firms on the periphery and Dutch and French companies in the core. Private debt appeared more tolerable in Italy, especially among households. However, other gauges such as debt to equity indicated increasing stresses within its corporate sector, as was also the case in Slovenia.[61]

The increase in private debt across the euro area in the first decade of the single currency contrasted with the fall in public debt over the same period, before the financial crisis and recession played havoc with public finances (see Figure 7). However, the improvement was modest and again the euro-wide figures disguised important failures and weaknesses. Government debt as a share of GDP rose markedly in Greece and Portugal between 1999 and 2007 and also edged up in France and Germany. And though it came down in Italy – debt averaged around 100 per cent of GDP in 2003–7 – it still remained far too high as the country slackened its belt-tightening effort. The primary budget surpluses

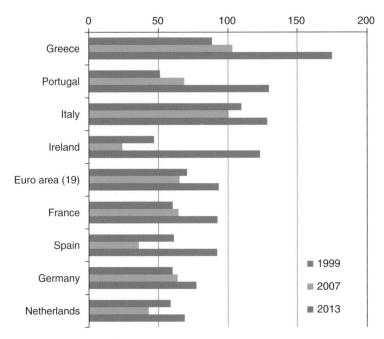

Source: European Commission

FIGURE 7 General government debt, as per cent of GDP, 1999,
2007 and 2013

(excluding interest) that had got Italy into the monetary union, peaking
at 6.2 per cent of GDP in 1997, stayed high for the first two years thanks
to the strong cyclical upturn but then declined to 1.7 per cent on average
in 2001–7.[62] This failure to exploit the opportunity afforded by euro
membership to get on top of the public debt problem rankled with
Germany when Italy got into trouble during the crisis. The country
'wasted' the fiscal dividend arising from the fall in Italian interest rates
to German levels, complained Issing in early 2014.[63] Similarly, the big
savings in interest that benefited the Greek public finances found their
way into higher spending on wages and pensions.[64]

Italy's failure contrasted sharply with Belgium's continuing
success in bringing its debt down. Belgian debt peaked in the early
1990s at 135 per cent of GDP, well above Italy's high of 117 per cent.

By the launch of the euro, in 1999, both countries' debt had fallen, though more so for Belgium, to 115 per cent of GDP, than for Italy, to 110 per cent. By 2007, Belgian debt had fallen to 87 per cent of GDP, below Italy's which was 100 per cent. The Belgian improvement was helped by a stronger economy than Italy's but it required determination to run such a long string of big primary surpluses, which averaged over 4 per cent of GDP in the two decades to 2007.[65]

Irish and Spanish public debt also fell sharply but the underlying condition of both countries' public finances was flattered by their booming economies. The strong growth in domestic demand was favourable for national exchequers because it yielded more taxes than exports (on which excise duties and VAT were not charged). There was a further bounty for countries with buoyant housing markets as transaction-based property taxes burgeoned; Ireland was a particular beneficiary through stamp duties but France, Italy and the Netherlands also gained this way.[66] When critics of austerity during the euro crisis, such as Paul Krugman, sought to challenge the explanation for the crisis favoured by the Germans – that it was essentially fiscal in origins – they seized on the fact that Ireland and Spain were running budgetary surpluses in the mid 2000s.[67] There was something in this, but it also showed how misleading headline fiscal figures could be, and that they should be adjusted for windfall effects as well as the economic cycle. In fact, both countries should have been running much bigger surpluses given the fair winds blowing their way; their small surpluses were a mark of failure rather than success.

Worse, it became clear in 2004 that Greece in particular had misrepresented the true state of its public finances both before and after joining the euro. Crucially, the deficits exceeded the Maastricht limit of 3 per cent of GDP in 1998 and 1999, the years used to assess whether Greece was eligible to join the euro. At the end of 1999, the Council had paved the way for entry by declaring that Greece had corrected the excessive deficit for which it had been in the dock since 1994. That judgement was based on figures showing that the deficit had fallen from 4 per cent of GDP in 1997 to 2.5 per cent in 1998 and an estimated 1.9 per cent in 1999.[68] These turned out to be far off the mark; the reality revealed in 2004 was a string of high deficits in 1997–9, of 6.6, 4.3 and 3.4 per cent of GDP, respectively, and the newly disclosed overruns above the Maastricht threshold continued between 2000 and 2003. The discrepancies in the late 1990s arose mainly from failing to recognise in the budget balance interest that was 'capitalised' (added to the principal rather than paid regularly) together with capital injections into public enterprises that were transfers to cover losses; thereafter, they were largely caused by under-recording of military spending.[69]

Though Greece was the most notorious for its misreporting, it was not alone in finding ways to dab some blusher on the public finances. In Portugal, for example, the extensive use of public–private partnerships kept related debt off the government's books, despite the risk of the state having to pick up the bill if projects failed.[70] The inability or unwillingness to get to grips with public finances was further illustration that to a worrying extent the apparent success of the single currency in its first decade was illusory since the whole – the euro-zone economy – was the sum of distorted parts.

But where were the private vigilantes, the bond investors, who might have been expected to spot and arrest at least some of these worrying developments? They were nowhere to be seen: until the financial crisis, government bond yields throughout the euro zone remained converged on German ones to an extraordinary extent (see Figure 1). It was as if there was no difference in creditworthiness requiring an extra premium for bond investors to compensate for holding dodgier debt. Had Greece really become barely more risky than Germany or the Netherlands? There were a number of explanations of this strangely forgiving behaviour, which was especially odd given that credit-rating agencies did draw some distinctions between the various member states and were sceptical about Greece and to a lesser extent Italy and Portugal.[71] One was that bond investors believed that the no-bail-out clause in the Maastricht Treaty was empty of content and that there was an implicit underwriting of peripheral debt by Germany and other sound creditor nations. But this was implausible since they had no way of anticipating what might happen if the matter were put to the test.

In 2005, Buiter and Anne Sibert argued that the ECB was sending a misleading signal to the markets by failing to distinguish between countries in the government debt it accepted as collateral in its refinancing activities.[72] In any such operation, the ECB would impose a 'haircut' – a discount – on the market value of the collateral according to how sound it was, as well as 'marking to market' that collateral to take account of changing valuations. The bigger the haircut the more collateral a bank would have to post in order to borrow a given amount. Despite the varying credit ratings of the twelve euro-zone governments at this juncture, four of which were not top-rated, the ECB imposed the same haircuts, which were exiguous at shorter residual maturities and still favourable on longer ones.[73]

This might have contributed to bond investors' confidence but the ECB's stamp of approval was unlikely to convince anyone harbouring real doubts about a country. The indulgence shown by the markets was more proof that they could not be relied upon to discipline governments, as the Delors committee had forewarned in 1989, pointing out that 'the constraints imposed by market forces might either be too slow and weak or too sudden and disruptive'. Presciently, it had elaborated on this by saying that 'access to a large capital market may for some time even facilitate the financing of economic imbalances'.[74] The behaviour of euro-zone bond markets was another reflection of the reckless search for yield across advanced economies in the years before the financial crisis. While all was going so well, nothing would go wrong even in potentially risky countries like Greece. It was worth collecting a marginally higher bond yield for the small risk of the good times ending.

Except that they did end abruptly, in the summer of 2007. On 9 August, the ECB provided €95 billion of liquidity to banks in a special operation to calm euro-zone money markets after BNP Paribas had shocked investors by temporarily closing three of its investment funds exposed to the American sub-prime mortgage market because it could no longer value their underlying assets. The French bank blamed this on 'the complete evaporation of liquidity' in segments of the American market in securitised products.[75]

The swift liquidity response of the ECB in the summer of 2007 was followed by a mistaken tightening in monetary policy in the summer of 2008, when it pushed its main lending rate up from 4 per cent to 4.25 per cent, even though the financial crisis was becoming graver by the day. Yet when the crisis came to a head that autumn and in the ensuing fierce recession of late 2008 and early 2009, in its own way the ECB proved quite flexible. Like other central banks, it yanked interest rates down; by May 2009, it had lowered its main lending rate to just 1 per cent. Unlike the Fed and the Bank of England, it did not go down the route of quantitative easing involving large-scale purchases of government bonds but instead pursued what it called 'non-standard' measures, in particular extending the maturity of its loans from a maximum of three months to six months and then a year, accepting worse collateral, and meeting banks' bids for funding in full. This latter policy, called 'full allotment', which was adopted in October 2008, created a surplus of central bank liquidity that in turn drove Eonia, the overnight bank rate, down below the main lending rate towards the floor set by the deposit rate, which reached 0.25 per cent in the spring of 2009.[76]

This monetary support helped to combat the recession, yet the puzzle was why the euro crisis did not begin earlier. The financial crisis had after all caused investors to reappraise everything, including their view of the euro area. Sovereign bond yield convergence gave way to divergence as investors reassessed the riskiness of places like Greece. Spreads of Italian and Portuguese ten-year bonds widened to some 1.5 percentage points above German bonds in early 2009; Irish and Greek spreads increased still further to 2.5 and 3 percentage points, respectively.[77] The euro, which had been trading around $1.60 in the summer of 2008, tumbled against the dollar after the Lehman collapse in September, falling to less than $1.30 in November.[78]

But the decline in the euro against the dollar, of 20 per cent, was greater than that of its trade-weighted value, of less than 10 per cent. The single currency rode out the crisis much better than the pound, which fell heavily against the euro as well as the dollar and whose trade-weighted value fell by around 25 per cent between mid 2007 and early 2009. Indeed, from the spring of 2009, the euro started to appreciate against the dollar, reaching around $1.50 towards the end of that year. The tensions in bond markets also eased as spreads retreated. In all, more than two years elapsed between the start of the financial crisis in August 2007 and the first tremors of the euro crisis following the Greek election in October 2009 and the ensuing revelation by George Papandreou's new government that Greek public finances were far worse than previously admitted. The easy ride given to peripheral member states of the euro zone contrasted sharply with the punishment meted out by the markets in late 2008 and 2009 to the Baltic states that were tied to the euro but not part of the monetary union.[79] Why did it take so long for the second boot to drop?

A specific reason why bond markets calmed down for a while after the jitters of early 2009 was that both the German government and the Commission hinted that the no-bail-out rule might not be enforced after all. Peer Steinbrück, the German finance minister, said in February that despite the Treaty provisions 'the other states would have to rescue those running into difficulty'.[80] Joaquín Almunia, in charge of economic and monetary affairs at the Commission, said in March that, if a crisis occurred, European help would mean that a country would not have to turn to the IMF in the first instance for assistance.[81]

That such hints could allay concern reflected a broader faith in the euro area on several grounds. First, reflecting the slowburn nature of its banking problems, the euro area compared favourably with both the US and Britain during the financial crisis. The spread between interbank lending rates and virtually risk-free overnight swap rates, a measure of the suspicion in which banks held their counterparties' creditworthiness, increased dramatically but not to the same extent as was the case for American and British banks.[82] Second, the public finances of several of the countries that were to prove most vulnerable looked much better than they really were. In 2007, Ireland's public debt was a mere 24 per cent of GDP; Spain's was just 36 per cent. Even though both countries had been treating bloated revenues from their housing booms as if these were permanent rather than temporary sources of taxation, their low debt levels appeared to afford them sufficient fiscal leeway to cope with the shock to the public finances from the economic downturn and the costs of bailing out banks. Third, the very idea of a sovereign debt crisis in an advanced country appeared inconceivable. The last time a restructuring had occurred was ironically for Germany in 1953 through the London Debt Agreement. This slashed the value both of pre-war debt upon which Germany had reneged during the 1930s together with obligations arising from the post-war assistance it had received, and set out a repayments schedule for the written-down obligations.[83] The settlement, which marked a crucial stage in Germany's economic rehabilitation, seemed to belong to another age. Indeed, as late as September 2010 the IMF published a staff position-note arguing that default in advanced economies was 'unnecessary, undesirable and unlikely'.[84]

Perhaps most important of all was the fact that the very success of the euro in its first decade had bred a complacency not only among European governments but also in the markets. Despite its shortcomings, the ECB had established its position as the second most influential central bank in the world and had responded swiftly and seemingly adequately to the financial crisis and the recession that followed. On the face of it, the performance of the euro area had been satisfactory. That overall record was marred by the fracturing and divergence that had occurred during the first decade as several of the peripheral economies experienced unsustainable booms generated by a surfeit of credit and inflated housing markets. Yet it was not until Greece revealed the true horror of its public finances that the veil of complacency was torn away.

# 4    Greeks bearing debts

The euro crisis started in earnest in early 2010 when Greece lost access to the markets and over the next two-and-a-half years it was the country that threatened the single currency the most. Trouble flared up again in 2015 as the new government, led by Tsipras, brought Greece even closer to the brink through its destructive policies and antagonistic negotiating tactics with creditors. This was part of a pattern. As the crisis in its most acute phase spread around the periphery of the euro area between 2010 and 2012, it kept on reverting in its most malign form to the nation where it had begun, shaping the actions of the European leaders trying to save it in ways that were often counter-productive. Since the Greek crisis was manifestly a sovereign debt crisis, it prompted policies not just for Greece but also for other peripheral countries that focused on tackling fiscal weaknesses, even though the sources of the euro crisis ran much deeper than budgetary misdemeanours.

For the single-currency club as a whole, the actions taken by European leaders involved the hasty erection of common defences to provide help in the form of official financing for members shut out from the markets. Although the new bail-out funds were an important addition to the euro area's institutions, they were an inadequate response. It was as if European leaders were erecting a rickety extension to the original defective building rather than carrying out the comprehensive reconstruction that was needed. What emerged from the reforms was essentially a revised version of Maastricht rather than a genuine move towards sharing debt burdens and fiscal resources through for example the introduction of jointly guaranteed eurobonds. The half-hearted measures were insufficient to overcome market fears, which meant that the ECB was forced to stave off panic through bond purchases. However, until Draghi's 'whatever it takes' pledge of July 2012, the central bank intervened in a reluctant and unconvincing way that also failed to restore confidence.

Just as important as these responses at the euro-zone level was a drive to tackle at the national level the fiscal failures that the German government in particular blamed for what had gone wrong. Merkel insisted on introducing tough new rules to enforce future budgetary discipline that would avert a future crisis. In dealing with the one that was actually happening, a prescription of tough austerity along with reforms was administered, first for Greece and then for the other countries requiring help or at risk. Eventually the euro area as a whole, including Germany even though its public finances were in no danger, donned a fiscal straitjacket.

The budgetary squeeze across the currency union was mistimed in so fragile an economic climate. By contributing to an extended double-dip recession, it exacerbated the banking and private debt crises and raised the political stakes in both the rescuing and the rescued countries by stoking public anger and discontent. Nowhere was this more apparent than in Greece itself, where a vicious circle developed in which excessive austerity weakened the economy, turning the banks, which bore relatively little responsibility for the country's initial woes, into part of the problem as their private-sector loans soured in the economic downturn, adding to the losses they faced on their holdings of government bonds.

If Greece set the pattern for austerity, it was the exception in undergoing debt restructuring. Greece broke the precedent that advanced countries do not renege on their public debt, but it did not set a new one, or so European leaders pledged, even though its eventual harsh treatment of private creditors went surprisingly smoothly. Since a write-down of debt was a standard way of dealing with sovereign debt crises, ruling it out for other countries in the euro area was arguably a mistake. But the decision eventually to treat Greece as a special case was understandable since the threat of debt restructuring contributed to the uncertainty that made the euro crisis so pernicious.

Within Greece itself, extreme uncertainty, together with the direct and indirect effects of austerity, was especially debilitating for the economy, undermining business and consumer confidence and causing a persistent deposit drain that further weakened the banks. The fog over Greece's future stemmed from a toxic mix of social discontent and political resistance to the bail-out programme that made a Greek exit appear more and more likely. But Greece was not alone in experiencing gnawing uncertainty, which damaged the euro area as a whole. This was rooted in a lack of clarity about how far Germany in particular was ready to go in saving the single currency, until Merkel endorsed Draghi's euro-saving policy in the summer of 2012 and decided around the same time against expelling Greece from the club.

The first tremors of the Greek crisis were felt in late 2009 when the new government led by Papandreou disclosed the full extent of Greece's borrowing needs. Just two weeks after a resounding victory on 4 October for Pasok (Panhellenic Socialist Movement), George Papaconstantinou, the new finance minister, had some disturbing news to impart to his European counterparts when they met in Luxembourg. A budget deficit for 2009 that the previous Greek government had estimated in the spring would be 3.7 per cent of GDP was now expected to reach 12.5 per cent. Moreover, the deficit for 2008, a figure vetted by Eurostat in April 2009, was revised up from 5.0 per cent of GDP to 7.7 per cent.[1] Even these startling revisions turned out to be short of the mark. The 2008 deficit was subsequently raised to almost 10 per cent of GDP while the 2009 deficit turned out to be over 15 per cent, respectively double and quadruple the earlier estimates.[2]

The revelations disconcerted bond markets as well as European finance ministers. By early 2010, alarm about the sustainability of Greece's public finances was raising yields on Greek bonds to rates that were becoming punitive for new issues, of which plenty were needed by the government both to finance its huge deficit and also to refinance maturing debt. Greece managed to raise €5 billion in seven-year bonds at a yield of 6 per cent, more than double Germany's borrowing cost, at the end of March, but that was the last issue it was able to make.[3] As yields jumped to quite unaffordable levels in April, the Greek state lost access to the markets.

The question facing euro-zone leaders in the spring of 2010 was whether to rescue Greece at all. That was more than a question – it was a point of principle, which posed them with a stark choice that for once could not be fudged. If they stood firm on the supposedly sacrosanct no-bail-out rule, Greece would be forced to default on its debt, because the government would no longer be able to redeem maturing bonds; there were big redemptions due in May. Losses would fall not just on Greek holders of the debt, predominantly the Greek banks, but on other European banks, especially French but also German ones.[4] One jaundiced view of the eventual decision to back a bail-out was that the German and French governments chose to save their banks indirectly by bailing out Greece. But more profound anxieties lay behind the rescue.

Any attempt by Greece to default without support from the rest of the euro area – the logic of enforcing the no-bail-out rule – while trying to stay within the currency club would be unworkable. The government would still need to finance its huge budget deficit, even if it stopped servicing its debt. Cut off from investors and the bond markets, its next move would be to turn to domestic banks. But that would be fruitless because they in turn would no longer be able to borrow from the Eurosystem since the default would contaminate their collateral in the absence of any official support from other euro-zone countries. A default would thus lead inexorably to Greece having to leave the euro in order to restore access to its central bank for both the government and the banks.

Yet such an exit would escalate the crisis by an order of magnitude, not only for Greece but also for the monetary union itself. The decisive point was that traders and investors would immediately move on to ask which state might be next in line to leave and to charge a higher risk premium on its sovereign debt. The resulting jump in bond yields of the most vulnerable countries would prompt a much wider panic with potentially devastating consequences, not least since European banks remained fragile and undercapitalised. The idea of combining a default on the privately held debt with an official bail-out, the eventual solution when Greek debt was restructured, was ahead of its time. Similar worries about rekindling the financial crisis explain why it was not seriously entertained. Such a write-down of debt was then regarded as virtually unthinkable for an advanced economy and the shock of so unexpected an event would have been viciously destabilising so soon after the global banking crisis.

Although the response to the Greek crisis lay formally in European hands, euro-zone leaders came under heavy pressure from the other side of the Atlantic to prop Greece up. President Barack Obama and Tim Geithner, the Treasury secretary, were alarmed that the attempts of the American government and of the Fed to nurse a recovery in the US would be overwhelmed if the euro area's woes destabilised banks and reignited the financial crisis. The IMF, the closest the world had to a global economic monitor, shared that concern. Headed by Dominique Strauss-Kahn, a former French politician who harboured presidential ambitions, the Washington-based institution had gained both authority and extra resources during the financial crisis, adding weight to its forebodings about the wider harm that could arise from Greece's predicament.

Such pressures explain why frightened European leaders tore up the ban on bail-outs and rescued Greece at the start of May 2010. In one step, the euro area lost its innocence as a pure monetary union free of any mutual fiscal obligations (as opposed to rules). Greece was pledged €110 billion ($145 billion at the then exchange rate) in loans, €80 billion from the other euro-zone states and €30 billion from the IMF, over a three-year period, far more than a provisional amount of up to €30 billion from the euro area with some additional help from the Fund that had been envisaged in early April.[5] This was help on an extraordinary scale, equivalent to almost half of Greek GDP, indicating the plight of the nation's public finances.[6]

Even though the IMF provided less than a third of the total, that pledge was thirty-two times Greece's 'quota', its own financial commitment to the Fund; as a rule the limit was six times.[7] This made it a record. In the IMF's unit of account – 'special drawing rights' – the pledge was exceeded only by a credit line first made available to Mexico in 2009, which had not been drawn down.[8] Moreover, the Fund admitted at the time that it was breaking one of its four cardinal criteria for sanctioning a bail-out since it could not state with a high probability that public debt was sustainable in the medium term. The IMF nonetheless went ahead with the rescue because of the 'high risk of international systemic spillover effects', officialese for financial and economic contagion.[9] In a post-mortem three years later of its role in the first Greek rescue, the IMF was frank about its purpose. Admitting that with hindsight it was 'debatable' whether two other rules – good prospects of regaining access to the markets and of the programme succeeding – were met at the time, the rescue 'served as a holding operation' that 'gave the euro area time to build a firewall to protect other vulnerable members and averted potentially severe effects on the global economy'.[10]

That time was essential for the monetary union since, wedded to the no-bail-out rule, it had never prepared for or even been able to contemplate such a contingency by setting up a rescue mechanism. As a result, the commitments of €80 billion, called the Greek Loan Facility (GLF), were provided in bilateral loans from the fifteen other member states to Greece. Each country chipped in a share based on its capital key at the ECB, making Germany the single biggest contributor, and the amounts were centrally pooled by the Commission, which coordinated the programme.[11]

Within a few months, the fifteen lenders had become fourteen. Following an election and a change of government, Slovakia, which had joined the euro in 2009, backtracked on its initial agreement to participate in the GLF on the grounds that it was poorer than Greece. Ireland and Portugal also stopped contributing once they were rescued, in late 2010 and the spring of 2011, respectively.[12] That reduced the kitty to €77 billion, of which €53 billion had been disbursed by the time Greece finally secured a second bail-out, in early 2012; the IMF had contributed €20 billion up to that point, making the total amount of the first rescue that was drawn down €73 billion.[13]

Despite the bail-out, financial markets fretted that where stricken Greece had gone, other vulnerable countries might follow. Just a week later, Europe had to go beyond rescuing Greece and to erect defences for the whole currency club. On 7 May, euro area leaders issued a statement revealing that a 'stabilisation mechanism' would be created.[14] At an emergency weekend meeting of European finance ministers, that euphemism became a pledge of a further €500 billion (with an additional €250 billion to come from the IMF) in potential rescue money to protect any other member states.[15] A debt union, albeit limited in scope, had come into being in all but name, although northern creditor nations did their utmost to deny the logic of their decision and subsequently made every effort to try to restrict the concession of mutual support.

The loss of virginity went beyond that. As the markets opened the day after this further departure from the no-bail-out world of Maastricht, there was a new buyer of sovereign bonds: the ECB. The central bank was buying government debt through what it called, also euphemistically, its 'securities markets programme' (SMP).[16] The ECB did not disclose which sovereign bonds it was buying but the purchases in 2010 were predominantly of Greek bonds together with Irish and Portuguese debt. The decision was opposed by Weber and Jürgen Stark, the German board member who had replaced Issing as chief economist in 2006, because of concern that the purchases risked making the central bank subservient to fiscal pressures.[17] Though the ECB presented a monetary rationale for the purchases, the timing of the programme (and indeed of its subsequent extensions especially in August 2011 when it pitched into the Italian and Spanish markets) showed that the underlying purpose was to quell panic among traders and investors.

The decision by European leaders to disregard the no-bail-out clause appeared illegal under the usual interpretation of the Maastricht Treaty, later incorporated in the Lisbon Treaty, although legal wriggle-room was found by distinguishing between the provision of loans and the assumption of debts. Lagarde, herself a lawyer and at this juncture French finance minister (she became head of the IMF a year later, in the summer of 2011, following Strauss-Kahn's fall from grace after charges, later dismissed, were brought against him in New York for allegedly sexually assaulting a hotel maid), candidly admitted in December 2010, after Ireland had become the second country to require a bail-out that the Greek and Irish rescues were 'major transgressions' of the European Treaty. 'We violated all the rules because we wanted to close ranks and really rescue the euro zone', she told the *Wall Street Journal*. 'The Treaty of Lisbon was very straightforward. No bailing out.'[18] Indeed, anxiety about legal challenges to their actions, especially in Germany, led European leaders to decide at the end of 2010 upon an amendment to the Treaty to create a permanent rescue fund, allowing euro-zone states to establish 'a stability mechanism to be activated if indispensable to safeguard the stability of the euro area as a whole'; the granting of any financial assistance would be subject to 'strict conditionality'.[19]

Whereas the IMF dubbed the European new fiscal defences, which it was helping to shore up, a firewall, the hope in the euro area was that the weaponry was so formidable that it would scare off any would-be attackers, with the happy implication that it would not have to be used. The IMF's analogy was misplaced since the rescue money resembled a fire engine rather than a firewall, but it was closer to the mark than the European notion that they had created a deterrent. This was as much of a bluff as the original no-bail-out clause and it was duly called within just a few months when the markets started to focus their attention that summer and autumn on Ireland and its failing banks.

One reason why the breast-beating failed to frighten markets was that the new defences, for all their supposed might, were grossly inadequate. The eventual outcome for Greece, alone, demonstrated this. At the time of its rescue, Greek GDP made up 2.6 per cent of euro area output and was a fifth of the size of the Spanish economy, which was also worrying investors owing to its housing-market bust. Yet the Greek government eventually received commitments of €246 billion in its first two bail-outs, mostly in euro-zone loans, of which €216 billion had been disbursed before the third rescue in 2015.[20] It also benefited from the biggest default in history, which eliminated €107 billion owed to private creditors, just over half of its face value.[21] Moreover, in late 2012 Greece got further help in what amounted to a covert, if smaller, additional rescue from its European creditors. As well as facilitating further debt relief through a buy-back of some of the new government bonds issued as part of the restructuring earlier that year, they agreed to defer interest payments on most of the new loans in the second bail-out for ten years and to transfer the profits made on the Eurosystem's holdings of Greek bonds, which had been spared a writedown, to Greece (after being distributed from the national central banks to their finance ministries).[22] Greece was doubtless a hard case, but the extent of its needs was an indication of just how much would be required if the crisis were to engulf a really big country like Italy, which had to borrow roughly €450 billion a year in the markets (in both treasury bills and bonds) mainly to roll over its huge public debt.[23]

The euro area's hastily assembled defences were flimsy as well as insufficient; they were complicated, too. The European contribution of €500 billion came in two forms, small and large, with confusingly similar and cumbersome names. The EU would provide €60 billion through a newly devised rescue fund called the European Financial Stabilisation Mechanism (EFSM). The EFSM was backed by the EU budget and thus all twenty-seven European member states.[24] But most of the bail-out capacity would come from another new rescue fund, the European Financial Stability Facility (EFSF), supported by only the euro-zone governments; the EFSF was to provide lending resources of €440 billion.[25] Both funds would have to raise the actual money that they lent from the markets.

Whether the establishment of the EU-backed EFSM was legitimate was questionable since it drew upon powers allowing financial assistance to a state 'seriously threatened with severe difficulties caused by natural disasters or exceptional occurrences beyond its control'. From a legal, if not an economic, perspective, this seemed dubious authority for rescuing countries whose own governments had contributed to their misfortunes.[26] Despite the small size of the EFSM, it actually contributed more than the EFSF to the next rescue, for Ireland, and disbursed almost as much to the third one, for Portugal – an unacknowledged spreading of the cost of the euro-zone bail-outs to the rest of the EU. It subsequently came in handy in the summer of 2015, after the agreement in principle to provide Greece with a third bail-out, as a source of bridging finance to redeem bonds held by the Eurosystem and to repay arrears to the IMF. As well as their indirect assistance through the EFSM, the UK, Sweden and Denmark, all three of which were outside the currency union, made contributions to the Irish rescue, of €3.8 billion, €0.6 billion and €0.4 billion, respectively.[27]

Set up as a private company in Luxembourg under its law, the EFSF, whose shareholders were the euro area's member states, stood outside the framework of the EU treaties. As Bruno De Witte, professor of EU law at Maastricht University, pointed out, its legal set-up was 'a curious mixture of public international law (the original decision) and private law', which enabled the fund to be set up posthaste.[28] It was much weaker than its notional capacity suggested because it was underpinned, not by capital, but by national guarantees in amounts set by the capital keys at the ECB which were capped to limit the respective liabilities of the countries backing it. Moreover, once it started to be used, the nations that were rescued could no longer support the fund, depleting its resources. Because of these weaknesses, the EFSF was quite inadequate in its first incarnation given the potential scale of demands upon it. In order to be rated as a top-notch borrower, a matter of pride then for the euro area, the fund's effective lending capacity was closer to €250 billion than its notional €440 billion because already only a few euro-zone states retained top credit ratings, and in the light of this, fat cash reserves had to be held to give investors more comfort.[29] This meant that to provide the originally planned €440 billion of lending resources the underlying guarantees had to be raised in 2011 to over €700 billion, which allowed it to dispense with the big cash buffers; the fund also eventually had to accept a somewhat lower credit rating.[30]

The EFSF was a stopgap solution, able to make new lending commitments only until mid 2013.[31] In late 2010, European leaders agreed to set up a permanent rescue fund, the European Stability Mechanism, which was also created on an intergovernmental basis, in this case under international law through a treaty between its member states. Together with the revision to the EU Treaty, this would put the ESM on a surer legal footing than the two funds that had been cobbled together in such a rush.[32] The ESM had stronger backing in the form of €80 billion of paid-in capital (which was eventually collected by April 2014) and could lend up to €500 billion. In one of many changes of plan by euro-zone leaders, by the time that the ESM was inaugurated, in October 2012, this was over and above the nearly €200 billion already committed through the EFSF, most of which had gone towards Greece's second bail-out, making the total effective size of the joint bail-out funds roughly €700 billion; originally, the aim had been an overall limit of €500 billion. Hopes that the EFSF would be wound up within just a few years had vanished as its loans had been extended to maturities of twenty or more years. It was supplanted for new programmes in late 2012 by the ESM, which assumed a €100 billion commitment to Spain to help shore up its shaky banks (in the event only €41 billion was used) and pledged €9 billion to Cyprus in the spring of 2013.[33]

The IMF was originally supposed to provide matching loans worth one euro for every two provided by the euro zone, but it committed proportionately much less to Greece's second rescue (€28 billion out of a total of €173 billion). Moreover, that further lending tranche was intended to keep its portion of the overall Greek bail-out at around €30 billion since from 2013 it would begin receiving repayments of its original three-year loans, whereas the euro area had by then pushed back the maturity of its first loans to Greece. In fact, because of delays in programme reviews and disbursements, the Fund's exposure to Greece fell to around €24 billion by the end of 2014.[34] In 2013, the IMF contributed only €1 billion to the €10 billion rescue of Cyprus.[35]

The inadequacy of the European response and the continued reliance on the IMF, despite its reduced financial role, in scrutinising and enforcing bail-out programmes, reflected the intense pressures on politicians in euro-zone creditor countries to contain potential claims on their taxpayers, who were infuriated at the impost. Many Germans took the view that their reward for frugality was to save the feckless, an attitude hardened by the fact that Greeks were able to claim state pensions much earlier than Germans, who had recently accepted a painful pension reform, raising the retirement age from sixty-five to sixty-seven between 2012 and 2029.[36] Similar resentments were felt in other northern countries, such as the Netherlands. In Finland, they fuelled a populist euro-sceptic protest movement in the shape of the True Finns, a party that came from virtually nowhere to win third place in the election held in April 2011.[37] The Finnish government then played hardball in the negotiations over the second Greek bail-out when it demanded collateral to cover 40 per cent of its share.[38]

As Europe's biggest economy with the soundest public finances, Germany's response was pivotal. Although Merkel contemplated a more expansive solution as the crisis deepened in 2012, her instinct was generally to do just enough to save the euro, but no more, in keeping with the grudging public mood. Despite the setback to the original Maastricht model, the German government sought to create a revised version that stayed as close as possible to the original spirit whereby each country was responsible for its own public finances. Both the EFSF and the ESM were expressions of this approach since they were organised on an intergovernmental basis, allowing

Germany to retain national fiscal control. The governing boards of both funds comprised representatives of euro-zone finance ministries (in the case of the ESM it was the finance ministers themselves) and crucial decisions on financing rescues required unanimity, which gave Germany a veto. The ESM specified that in an emergency (which would generally be the case) an 85 per cent qualified majority was required, but since the vote in this instance would be based on countries' capital shares, Germany could use its 27 per cent voting right to block any proposal that it opposed.[39] The top job at both the EFSF and the ESM went to Klaus Regling, a former senior German official who had also worked at the IMF in Washington and the Commission in Brussels and who could be relied upon to safeguard the interests of the main creditor countries standing behind the rescue funds.

The delay in introducing the ESM meant that the EFSF was the main weapon during the acute phase of the crisis. Along with its small size, a limited remit hampered the fund's effectiveness as a deterrent. The original plan confined it to providing rescue finance to countries requiring help through a bail-out programme. But that was too late if the state had been brought low by market pressures. As these mounted in 2011, and in particular spread to Italy and Spain that summer, the ECB stepped in to try to contain the rise in bond yields. This involved bond-buying on a much bigger scale because of the size of the two economies and of their sovereign debt markets, especially Italy's, but the ECB still did the minimum necessary to contain panic rather than intervening decisively to get on top of the crisis.

The reluctance of the ECB to go further reflected internal opposition within the council and the board. The German members – Weidmann, who had replaced Weber in May 2011, and Stark – argued that as well as blurring the lines between monetary and fiscal policy such purchases let governments off the hook.[40] Berlusconi seemed to prove the point when he resiled from undertakings after Italian bond yields eased following the ECB's intervention in August 2011. The foray had been preceded by a stiff letter from Trichet and Draghi (who was then the governor of the Bank of Italy) to the Italian prime minister.[41] The ECB demanded 'pressing action' on both wideranging structural reforms and swifter fiscal retrenchment in order for Italy 'to urgently underpin the standing of its sovereign signature', a florid term for national creditworthiness favoured by Trichet. Berlusconi introduced further austerity measures but then backtracked on some of them at the end of August as well as failing to make any of the deep reforms that the central bankers had stipulated.[42] The episode became a key exhibit especially in Germany for those fearing the moral hazard induced by a central bank that was over-ready to come riding to the rescue.

Trichet was desperate to disentangle the ECB from such purchases and lobbied for the EFSF to take on the bond-buying role. That required further changes to the fund's remit, in order to allow it to purchase sovereign debt. Since this would require resources well beyond €440 billion, there were calls for the EFSF to gear up its lending capacity through financial engineering that would bring in additional private funds. Though the EFSF took preparatory steps to undertake such an approach, the snag was that the fund would have had to assume more risk in its own lending in order to bring in private participation.[43] The underlying problem was that the rescue funds were being asked to do too much given the limited support that creditor countries were prepared to stump up. The notion that the EFSF or the ESM could fight the markets by purchasing bonds in secondary markets made little, if any, sense. The only institution that could credibly fight the markets was the ECB since it alone potentially had bottomless resources, by being able to create money. By contrast, traders would always know that the rescue fund had a limited pot of money, which it would in any case be unwilling fully to deplete, giving them something to bet against.

If the bail-out funds were too small even to meet the purpose for which they were originally intended, the provision of emergency financing for states that could no longer fund themselves, let alone try to take on the markets, and if the ECB was unprepared at this stage to go beyond fire-fighting, another way had to be found to save the euro from the repeated assaults of the bond markets. The logical answer was to move further towards a debt union. In the heat of the crisis, especially in 2011, eurobonds became a much touted way to take that step, even though Merkel made it clear that she would oppose such a solution.

Rather like the use of the term 'monetarist' to describe those advocating a monetary union before the creation of an economic union rather than the school of macroeconomics associated with Friedman, the term 'eurobonds' was confusing to anyone with a sense of history. Its original meaning, dating back to the birth of the eurobond market in 1963 with the Autostrade bonds was the issue of dollar-denominated debt to investors in Europe; and by extension applying to any debt severing the link between a currency and the national markets where they were placed and traded. By contrast, the defining characteristic of the eurobonds advocated as a solution to the euro crisis was that euro-zone countries should issue them together and share the responsibility for servicing and repaying them. Legally, liability would be 'joint and several', meaning that although the obligation was shared, each country was nonetheless individually responsible in principle for the full amount.[44] This was quite different from the legal underpinning for both the euro-zone rescue funds, which limited the potential liability of any one state to a share of the total; Germany's to the ESM was for example capped at €190 billion.[45] The mutualisation of debt through eurobonds offered a way out of the crisis because markets would no longer be able to pick off individual states according to their lack of creditworthiness (or sloppiness of 'sovereign signature'). The euro area could take advantage of its overall good standing (with a more moderate budget deficit and lower debt as shares of GDP than the US) in issuing such eurobonds across the single-currency zone at reasonable interest rates.[46]

The introduction of eurobonds might indeed solve the euro crisis in the short term, but the idea exposed the faultline in the currency club between the creditor and debtor nations. 'Joint and several' meant that in the last resort, readily conceivable in 2011 and

2012, the liability would cease to be joint and would become several. As weak states toppled, the full bill would end up in the reluctant hands of the stronger states left standing. It was fanciful to imagine that the Germans (or the Dutch and the Finns for that matter) would make such a sacrifice of their good credit standing without demanding a lot in return. For one thing, any introduction of eurobonds would have to be partial. For another, tight strings would have to be attached.

A far-reaching proposal for eurobonds from Bruegel, the think-tank in Brussels, in 2010 recognised that they would require both a limit and a form of discipline. Adding a dash of colour to the technical details, the French and German economists who drafted the plan – Jacques Delpla and Jakob von Weizsäcker – envisaged the eurobonds eventually making up a first 'blue' layer of sovereign debt for each country, up to the Maastricht debt threshold. Reflecting the fact that this rule was more honoured in the breach than in the observance, the portion above 60 per cent of GDP – the 'red' debt – would remain the sole responsibility of each state. Since interest rates on the blue debt would be lower, highly indebted countries like Italy would have a strong incentive to reduce their red debt, so that they could ultimately borrow solely in cheaper eurobonds.[47]

The Bruegel plan was unworkable for two reasons. First, the limit was not much of a constraint since it permitted the mutualisation of over half the outstanding euro-zone government debt, a step too far. Second, the scheme was intrinsically flawed because it introduced a credit hierarchy within any one country's sovereign debt, by creating two tranches of very different credit risk. The red debt lacking the mutual guarantee, which for a country like Italy would be as big as the blue debt, would be viewed by markets as especially risky, causing yields on it to rise and jeopardising the Italian government's ability to access the markets.[48]

Another idea, developed in the spring of 2012 by Wim Boonstra, chief economist at Rabobank, a Dutch bank, was that euro-zone countries, excluding those already in rescue programmes (at the time there were three), should be allowed to finance themselves for four years through jointly guaranteed short-term notes (with a maturity of up to two years).[49] This plan was less ambitious than the Bruegel proposal, but it was unappealing to creditor nations because once in place, like many purportedly temporary schemes, it would almost certainly have been impossible to remove. The most sensible proposal was made by the German Council of Economic Experts in late 2011. They advocated eurobonds in order to bring down excessive debt in countries where it was well above the Maastricht limit. In effect, they reversed the colour coding of the Bruegel plan: the jointly issued bonds would replace the smaller amount of debt above 60 per cent of GDP. The purpose of their plan was quite different, too, since the eurobonds in the joint fund would be temporary rather than permanent, disappearing once the excessive debt had been paid off (though this would take between twenty and twenty-five years).[50]

This redemption fund was really an ingenious attempt to solve the Italian problem that threatened to capsize the euro in late 2011, as Berlusconi's recalcitrance tested the patience not just of Merkel but also of the bond markets. Arguably, the scheme was over-ingenious. Would countries comply with the conditions set for participating in it, which included the earmarking of a portion of taxes, and what would happen if they reneged on that, say, because revenues weakened? Was it realistic to believe the scheme would eventually be wound down even if a 'legal fence' were erected to prevent its self-perpetuation, as the German economic (though not legal) experts proposed? In the event, 'the man who screwed an entire country' lost his job and was replaced by Monti, a former European Commissioner, who formed a technocratic government that pushed through harsh fiscal measures and reforms in order to satisfy Italy's creditors. Conditionality exerted under pressure from the markets was, it seemed, a lot more effective than any that might come attached to mutualisation schemes.

That critique of such well-meaning proposals went to the heart of the matter. For example, John Muellbauer, an economist at Oxford University, drafted an even more ingenious plan for eurobonds tied expressly to conditionality. Weaker countries would pay strong countries to compensate them for the extra risk they were shouldering through the joint underwriting of debt. These side-payments would be determined by their performance against a small set of indicators – unit labour costs, current-account balances and government debt – the latter two in relation to GDP. The better the vulnerable states did, the lower the payments they would have to make. Muellbauer argued that a tough 'internal vigilante', a new European body assessing performance, would replace the more familiar figure of the bond-market vigilante.[51] But this smacked of wishful thinking, given the political pressures that would be brought to bear on such a taskmaster. Conditionality had been enforceable only in the exceptional circumstances of an official rescue when creditor countries held the whip-hand. That would not apply in more normal times, not least since the very issuance of the eurobonds would restore market access. A more likely prospect was a distinctly unscary internal vigilante, feebly policing a watered-down version of conditionality.

Such fears explain why Merkel was firm in ruling out Eurobonds, both in the heat of the crisis and afterwards, making it one of her main campaign points in the 2013 election.[52] Instead, she stuck doggedly to her line that countries needed to dig their way out of fiscal holes that they themselves had created through mismanagement. Only by getting their public finances under control would they manage to get their bond yields down to sustainable levels. The clearest expression of her approach was the fiscal compact, which was signed in March 2012 by twenty-five out of the twenty-seven EU states (the Czech Republic joined Britain in standing apart), and came into force in January 2013. The by then seventeen euro states (Estonia had joined in 2011) had a strong incentive to participate since this was a condition for being able to access the ESM.[53]

Ironically, given that the policy had inspired a British veto at the summit of December 2011, the compact deviated from the classic integrationist approach since it embodied a German belief based on sorry experience that attempts to curb fiscal profligacy through European sanctions were unlikely to work. Instead, each state agreed to put into their national laws a binding balanced-budget rule. Any structural deficit (adjusted for the economic cycle and excluding one-offs) was not to exceed 0.5 per cent of GDP (unless debt was very low in which case the limit was 1 per cent).[54] This would act as a 'debt brake' since such a low deficit, even with low growth, should bring down debt as a share of GDP. Though the original goal was to incorporate such debt brakes into national constitutions (as Germany had already done in 2009) only three countries – Italy, Slovenia and Spain – did so, according to research for the German Council of Economic Experts.[55] Like the ESM, the fiscal compact was created outside the framework of EU law, through an international treaty, though in this instance more through accident – eluding the British veto – than design.[56]

But treating the euro crisis as a set of national budgetary failings made matters worse in two main ways. First, it contributed to an unwarranted tightening in fiscal policy across the monetary union. The structural budget balance tightened in the euro area by 0.7 per cent of GDP in 2011, 1.5 per cent in 2012 and 0.9 per cent in 2013. The intensification of austerity in 2012 was driven by the larger economies. In particular, Monti's 'Save Italy' programme and the budget of December 2011 on top of previous austerity measures entailed a big fiscal tightening in 2012. Italy was under pressure from the markets, whereas Germany was a haven. Yet, perversely, the austerity of 2011–12 when the crisis was most severe included Germany, which tightened its structural budget balance almost as much as the euro zone; over the three years until 2013, its cumulative tightening amounted to 2.7 percentage points of GDP compared with the euro area's 3.1 points.[57]

This was assuredly a common fiscal policy – but the opposite of what should have happened in a monetary union when some of its members were in economic trouble. In a functioning union like the US, a setback in an individual state would be partially offset by federal budgetary support. Since the euro area was not a fiscal union that was not possible, but there was still scope for the core states favoured by the markets to support overall demand, if only by not joining in a concerted squeeze.

The impact of austerity aroused bitter controversy, with some holding it largely responsible for the double-dip recession that began in mid 2011 (it certainly contributed) while others said that it was a foul-tasting medicine that had to be swallowed. The controversy escalated to a transatlantic clash in early 2013. In research first published in October 2012 and then in an expanded joint paper in January 2013, Olivier Blanchard, the IMF's chief economist, and Daniel Leigh also of the IMF, found that fiscal multipliers, measuring the impact on GDP of changes in the budgetary stance, were much higher for European economies in the wake of the financial crisis, especially in 2010 and 2011, than forecasters had previously reckoned. The conditions for such larger-than-usual multipliers arose from the fact that countries were tightening fiscal policy together at a time when the effectiveness of monetary policies was impaired by a poorly functioning financial system and there was a lot of economic slack.[58] Olli Rehn, the Commissioner responsible for economic policy, brushed aside the research findings in a leaked letter to European finance ministers in February (copied to Lagarde at the IMF), saying that the debate about fiscal multipliers had not been helpful, risked eroding 'the confidence that we have painstakingly built up over the past years in numerous late-night meetings' and had 'not brought us much new insight'.[59]

Notwithstanding his testy response (which sounded as if it was written after another late night), Rehn took a series of decisions shortly afterwards in the spring of 2013, which essentially conceded the point by easing the pressure of austerity on several European economies. The Commission sanctioned an extension of deadlines for bringing down deficits below the 3 per cent of GDP threshold. Within the euro area, France, Spain and Slovenia were given two extra years while the Netherlands and Portugal were given an additional year.[60] Quite how much this mattered at this stage was unclear. Portuguese GDP for example had already started to recover. On the other hand, the fiscal reprieve granted by the Commission appeared to make little difference to the French economy; after a strong second quarter in 2013, it hardly grew at all over the following year and a half. In the euro area as a whole, the recovery got under way in 2013 even though the budgetary stance was still tightening; it faltered in the middle of 2014 even though by then fiscal policy had become broadly neutral.[61]

Despite these doubts about the gains from the more moderate approach to fiscal policy that was belatedly adopted, the earlier lurch into concerted austerity had manifestly been damaging. Attempts by individual states to dig their way out of fiscal holes had dug a deeper economic hole for the euro area as a whole. This was not the only way in which the German determination to treat the euro crisis as a set of national failings misfired since this approach implied a willingness to allow countries to go bankrupt, which was also counter-productive given the shakiness of the monetary union. Although the very reason why Greece had been rescued was to avoid a default for fear of its destabilising effects, the German government resolved to provide for such a solution in future rescues. Merkel and Sarkozy agreed upon that plan when they met at Deauville, a French seaside resort in Normandy, in October 2010. The two leaders issued a statement with the incendiary words that the permanent rescue fund being considered should provide 'the necessary arrangements for an adequate participation of private creditors'.[62] What this meant was that the planned ESM might stipulate writing down some private debt if it was to offer help.

The resulting panic in bond markets did much to push Ireland over the edge a month later though the blame for that still rested primarily with its bust banks. Despite the Irish setback, Germany insisted on retaining the restructuring option, which was set out in a 'term sheet' specifying the main elements of the ESM in March 2011.[63] In effect, countries applying for a rescue had to pass a binary test, determining whether they were sheep or goats: could their sovereign debt be put on a sustainable path or not? If they were goats and failed the test, then some of their debt held by private creditors would have to be written down as a condition for tapping official rescue financing.

To counter the dismay in the markets following Deauville, the Eurogroup said at the time of the Irish rescue, in late November, that there would be no restructuring until 2013. Their statement implied that any such action would be phased in, applying only to new debt issued from that point (originally the middle of the year but subsequently brought forward to January) with 'collective-action clauses', which would facilitate restructuring by allowing a predetermined majority of creditors (in value) to overrule a minority of 'holdouts' that might otherwise block a writedown.[64] But the credibility of this assurance was soon undermined by what was happening in Greece. For by early 2011, less than a year after it had been rescued, it was becoming apparent not just that the programme was veering off course but also that hopes of regaining partial market access by 2012, as originally envisaged, were becoming fanciful.[65] The first country to require a bail-out would need another one.

The harsh reality was that Greek debt had been unsustainable from the beginning. Even when the rescue was mounted in May 2010, the starting point for debt, in 2009, was dangerously high, at 115 per cent of GDP. But revised figures in November showed that it had actually been 127 per cent, which in turn pushed up the projected burden for 2010 to 141 per cent of GDP (subsequently revised up again to 146 per cent). The revisions arose mainly as the debt of heavily loss-making state-controlled enterprises was brought on to the government balance sheet, even though the Eurostat rule enforcing this was hardly demanding since the threshold for including them was that their sales covered less than half their production costs.[66]

To sovereign debt specialists, the figures reported for Greece were off-the-scale. Previous defaults for emerging economies had occurred at far lower levels of public indebtedness. Some form of debt relief was surely necessary. At a conference held in April 2011 at the European University Institute in the agreeable setting of the Villa Schifanoia (whose name originally meant 'chasing away boredom') outside Florence, a plan for Greece that was anything but boring was proposed by Lee Buchheit, an American lawyer who had negotiated on behalf of embattled governments in many previous restructurings (and was later to be hired by the Greek government), and Mitu Gulati of Duke University, another specialist in this field. After demonstrating the implausibility of simply postponing the matter until 2013, they set out two self-explanatory ways in which Greek debt could be tackled by taking more immediate action: a 'light dusting' and the 'full monty'.[67]

Theirs was a broad-brush approach but it was one to which those in power were already receptive, especially in Germany.[68] The idea of a 'light dusting' – a form of 'soft' restructuring in which Greek debt would simply be rescheduled – was the first to be considered. Under such a scheme, the bonds would not be subjected to a haircut, but the repayments of principal would be delayed; there was precedent in what Uruguay had done nearly a decade earlier, in 2003. Though this 'reprofiling' would deal with the immediate problem for the official rescue, which was that so much of the financing was simply paying off private creditors as their bonds came due, it was quickly recognised that rescheduling would be quite inadequate given the scale of Greece's debts. More would have to be done.

Even so, the first formal (and confusing or maybe just confused) proposal for restructuring, made at a summit in July 2011 that also approved in principle an additional bail-out to Greece, was hardly the 'full monty' that Buchheit and Gulati had suggested as their alternative to the 'light dusting'. The plan delivered only modest debt relief as well as being unduly complicated, by providing four options for bondholders.[69] Though it purported to bring about a 21 per cent cut in the privately held debt's net present value (comparing the discounted value of the interest payments and return of principal on the bonds before and after they were exchanged in the restructuring), this seemed implausibly high at the time, as was quickly pointed out by several analysts. A subsequent study by Jeromin Zettelmeyer, Christoph Trebesch and Gulati, suggested that any creditor losses would have been no more than 11.5 per cent and could easily have been smaller.[70]

By the time the restructuring was actually carried out, in March 2012, it was the 'full monty'. As had been the case in the first official proposal, bonds bought by the Eurosystem through the SMP together with those held independently at national central banks were exempted, which removed €42.7 billion and €13.5 billion, respectively, from the restructuring. That left €205.6 billion of privately held debt, of which holders of all but €6.4 billion agreed to the terms. The 'hold-outs', whose intransigence paid off since their debt was honoured as it came due, were able to exploit the fact that their bonds were written under foreign law, which gave them greater protection. By contrast, the great majority of the debt was written under Greek law, which allowed the government to change the terms retrospectively. The crucial change was that these bonds were made subject to a restructuring provided that creditors holding two-thirds of all the debt agreed to participate – a 'retrofit collective-action clause'.[71]

In all, the face value of the Greek debt that was exchanged was written down by €107 billion, a reduction of 53.5 per cent. Those taking part got two main forms of partial recompense. One worth 15 per cent of the former debt's face value consisted of cash 'sweeteners' in the shape of one– and two-year notes issued by the EFSF. The remaining 31.5 per cent (again of the old debt's face value) took the form of twenty new government bonds maturing between 2023 and 2042 and paying annual coupons of between 2 and 4.3 per cent. In addition, they received GDP-linked warrants, which would provide extra payments if Greek growth outperformed projected medium– and long-term growth; they were reckoned, however, to be of negligible value.

The actual losses reported by banks on their holdings of Greek debt were much bigger than 53.5 per cent; typically they were around 75 per cent. This was because they reported losses in present-value terms. The new stream of payments from coupons and return of principal were discounted using the 'exit' interest rate, the one prevailing immediately after the exchange. This sum was compared with the value of the old debt, whose interest payments and principal were assumed to be repaid in full. In their 'autopsy' of the Greek restructuring, Zettelmeyer and his co-authors contested this assumption, suggesting that the value of the old bonds was anything but certain and instead applied the exit discount rates to both the old and the new debt. On this basis, they reckoned the creditor losses were 65 per cent, making the Greek restructuring the fourth harshest among comparable debt-restructuring episodes in middle-to-high income countries since 1975.[72]

And yet this biggest default in history still left Greek debt, most of which was now in official hands, at an unsustainable level, reaching 175 per cent of GDP in 2013. How could this be so after so much had been written down? There were three main reasons. The first was that the starting-point for Greek debt had been far higher than in the case of previous defaults in emerging economies; Argentina's public debt for example in 2001 was 62 per cent of GDP.[73] This reflected the fact that private lenders had treated a country apparently secure within the euro zone far more leniently than an emerging economy lacking such a status.

A second reason was that a big portion of the reduction of €107 billion was offset by additional official lending needed to meet losses incurred by Greek banks and to recapitalise them since they were the biggest losers from the haircut. Some €50 billion of the second bail-out (channelled through the EFSF) went to the Hellenic Financial Stability Fund, which had been set up in 2010 as part of the first bail-out to safeguard the banking system by providing capital if it could not be raised from the markets.[74] When this was drawn down, €15.5 billion went to cover losses in defunct banks while €25 billion was used to recapitalise the four biggest Greek banks (National Bank of Greece, Piraeus, Alpha and Eurobank).[75] Taking into account some other adjustments, €11 billion remained untapped and was returned to the EFSF in early 2015.

The third reason why the debt burden remained intolerably high was the extraordinary contraction of the economy. Greek GDP fell from its peak before the financial crisis, in the second quarter of

2007, to its trough in the final quarter of 2013 by 27.4 per cent;[76] the decline in nominal terms over the same period, which is what mattered for the debt-to-GDP ratio, was almost as big, at 23.6 per cent. The causes of Greece's great depression were many and complex. One was the wrenching fiscal consolidation, which crushed domestic demand. The original rationale for the programme was that it would restore financial confidence over the medium term and restore at least partial access to markets as early as 2012. That turned out to be far off the mark. Moreover, the impact of the fiscal retrenchment was much more punitive than in a conventional IMF rescue, since the inability to devalue meant there could be no swift offsetting recovery from net trade, which was in any case inhibited by Greece's small export sector.

But it was uncertainty arising from a political crisis that exacerbated the collapse in the Greek economy. The comparison with Portugal was telling. The conditions for its rescue were not as onerous as those for Greece, reflecting the fact that its economic and fiscal weaknesses were not as profound. But even though Portugal's economy fared much worse than the troika had expected, the decline was not comparable to Greece's. The overall contraction from the pre-crisis peak in the first quarter of 2008 to its trough five years later was 9.6 per cent.[77] Though still a grave blow, the more favourable outcome reflected the fact that Portugal had a functioning government that was committed to pushing through the bail-out programme.

By contrast, the Greek programme ran into political difficulties within less than a year, even though more than any other euro-zone country Greece needed a fundamental overhaul if it was to cope with membership of the currency union. A loss of political drive by Papandreou's government in early 2011 started to undermine confidence both on the part of the troika and the markets. That things then got so much worse in large measure reflected the severity of the political crisis especially in the two elections of mid 2012 when Greece appeared to be on the verge of leaving the euro. The downward spiral became self-reinforcing as chronic political uncertainty eroded confidence and weakened banks and the economy. Tragically, a similar process occurred in late 2014 (on worries about an election) and 2015 (after the election of 25 January) when a promising economic recovery was snuffed out, confidence was sapped and businesses suffered an intense liquidity squeeze owing to the misguided policies of the new Syriza-dominated government.

On both occasions, much of the vicious circle was generated from within Greece, but it was also exacerbated by the interactions between the Greek crisis and the broader euro crisis and attempts to resolve it. Uncertainty about whether Greece would stay the course in 2012 was matched on the broader European stage by uncertainty about how far Germany would go to support not just Greece but the other peripheral countries in trouble. The insistence on restructuring was for example a way of trying to limit German liability and enforcing prudence to avoid future crises, but in the short term it made matters worse.

As a result, although the Greek restructuring had been carried out successfully, it was to be an exception. The original plan for the ESM was toned down. Although the permanent fund still had scope to apply a restructuring, the sheep-and-goats test was no longer specified as one of the operative articles.[78] The decision to make Greece a special case was understandable at the time, but it meant that in other countries public debt would rise to levels that looked unsustainable in the long run, for example reaching 130 per cent of GDP in Portugal. The cost of avoiding a further escalation in the acute phase was that the chronic phase of the crisis would persist.

The larger failure was in conceiving of the euro crisis as essentially a set of national failures to control public finances that had pushed sovereign debt to excessive levels. Clearly, this was one aspect of the crisis that had to be addressed but the austerity that was exacted in the crisis countries was too harsh and the general lurch of the euro zone into an unwarranted fiscal tightening was unwise. As important, the conception of the crisis as a sovereign debt problem left out other crucial components, notably the fragility of euro-zone banks and the high levels of private as well as public debt, which weakened economies and undermined investor confidence. The failure to heed the self-reinforcing and damaging interaction between the banking, the private debt and the sovereign debt problems greatly intensified the overall crisis.

# 5   Bad banks

One of the many lessons of the euro crisis was that timing matters, both in the order of events and in the sequence of responses. The fact that Greece rather than Ireland was the first country to require a bail-out turned out to be highly significant. If the order had been reversed and Ireland had toppled over first, then it would have been clear from the outset that weak banks as much as weak states lay at the heart of the euro crisis. But because Greece was the first to fall, the crisis was misconstrued as predominantly a sovereign debt crisis, even though Greek fiscal improvidence was an extreme case by any reckoning. This led to a crucial delay in recognising both the problem and the solution that was necessary, the creation of a banking union (though even here only the rudiments were put in place). If some of the effort that was put into tackling the fiscal weaknesses of euro-zone governance in 2010 and 2011 had been directed instead towards swifter action in addressing the flaws in banking supervision, the euro crisis might not have intensified to such an alarming extent.

Among the other rescued countries, Portugal most closely resembled Greece. Although Portuguese banks were inadequately capitalised and over-reliant on wholesale funding, it was the dire state of the country's public finances that led to the euro area's third rescue.[1] But of the five countries eventually bailed-out during the euro crisis, fragile banks lay at the heart of the problem in at least three of them. Ireland was the first instance, but banking crises also brought down Cyprus and undermined Spain. Moreover, bust banks made Slovenia a near miss on the list of bail-outs, teetering for over a year on the brink of requiring help before finally getting to grips with them at the end of 2013.

The reluctance to recognise that the euro crisis was in large measure the second leg in Europe of the financial crisis had baleful consequences. Instead of rooting out the bad loans and cleaning up bank balance sheets, the problem was left to fester even though previous experience had shown that swift surgery was vital to prevent the gangrene spreading. The failure to tackle the troubled banks in southern Europe meant that they got weaker as investors and depositors in the core parts of the euro area shunned them, and loans soured in struggling economies. The banks responded by cutting back on lending, causing a desperate credit drought that in turn exacerbated the recession in southern Europe, hurting them further.

That was not the only vicious circle at work. The banking malaise and the sovereign debt crisis also interacted in another one, as euro-zone leaders belatedly acknowledged at their summit in late June 2012 when they vowed to break it.[2] On the one hand, deteriorating public finances and rising government bond yields weakened lenders since their wholesale funding costs were generally set by sovereign yields plus a margin. Moreover, if governments defaulted they would take the banks down with them given their holdings of public debt. On the other hand, wobbly banks weakened confidence in state finances because of the potential cost of banking bail-outs. A worrying portent for just how big such bills could be was Ireland, where the cost to the state of rescuing its wrecked banks was directly responsible for two-fifths of the increase in public debt of 100 percentage points of GDP between 2007 and 2013.[3]

Euro area leaders were if nothing else consistent in their reluctance to recognise the plight of their banks. During the global financial crisis of 2007–8, they had sought to depict it as an Anglo-Saxon affair for which they bore little or no responsibility. This version of events neglected the part played by banks in the currency union, along with British and Swiss lenders, in the financial crisis. Contrary to the self-serving narrative favoured in continental Europe, euro-zone banks were far from being innocent victims of Anglo-Saxon excesses. They too were knee-deep in the sludge of American subprime mortgage lending, which explained why losses on dodgy securities turned up in unlikely places such as German Landesbanken, publicly owned regional lenders that were a home for lost banking causes.[4]

As Charles Goodhart, an authority on financial regulation at the London School of Economics, pointed out, European banks were willing partners in transatlantic regulatory arbitrage on a grand scale, exploiting differences in the rules applying to them in their jurisdictions to their mutual advantage.[5] American banks originating the subprime lending and parcelling the loans into securities were subject to overall balance sheet limits, set through leverage ratios of capital to total assets. This meant that they needed to divest themselves of most of the mortgage-backed securities they were churning out. By contrast, European banks were prompt to adopt the latest Basel agreement on banking capital, which was specified in terms of risk-weighted assets. Without a check on their overall balance sheets, they could readily absorb the top-rated securitised products since the risk weights applied to them were low and therefore made little dent in their capital ratios. It helped that the Basel framework allowed the big banks to use their own models to gauge the risk weights; unsurprisingly, the reported riskiness of assets declined.[6]

The broader role of European banks following the creation of the euro in fostering the international credit boom took time to be spotted because it was at odds with the received wisdom about the wider macroeconomic genesis of the financial crisis. In a speech in March 2005, a year before becoming chairman of the Fed, Bernanke blamed a 'global saving glut' caused by excessive thrift in Asia, especially China, and among the big oil-exporters of the Middle East, for the low long-term interest rates that were fuelling the credit boom.[7] As these savings exceeded domestic capital formation, they were invested overseas, especially in the US, which correspondingly ran big current-account deficits, in effect acting as importer of last resort to compensate for deficient demand in the capital-exporting countries. The inflow of funds drove down long-term interest rates on US Treasuries, causing a search for higher yields in other financial assets.

Mortgage-backed securities were a beguiling alternative because they provided a higher return while offering a top-notch credit status thanks to financial engineering.

A weakness in Bernanke's saving-glut thesis was that it focused on current-account imbalances, which were financed by net capital flows. This appeared to absolve the euro area, which ran a broadly balanced current account with the rest of the world in the run-up to the financial crisis.[8] But the net capital movements could also be interpreted as the result of much bigger gross flows swelling both assets and liabilities in the sending and receiving countries. Rather than a surfeit in global saving, a 'global banking glut' might be the villain of the piece, argued Hyun Song Shin, formerly of Princeton University and since May 2014 an economic adviser to the BIS in Basel. His research highlighted the European involvement in this massive expansion of cross-border lending and borrowing and the significant part that it played in causing the global financial crisis. In an IMF lecture in 2011, he pointed out that European banks came to play a pivotal role in the US, financing their positions by borrowing from American money-market funds and the like.[9] This explained why the financial crisis prompted an acute shortage of dollar funding on the part of European as well as American banks, requiring extensive central bank swaps in which the Fed provided dollars to the ECB, which it then lent on to euro-zone banks.

Shin argued that banks generally responded to a reduction in the overall risks that they faced by expanding their balance sheets. That was why the creation of the single currency had played a substantial, if unacknowledged, part in the financial boom and ensuing crisis, by fostering the expansion of European banks, which were no longer shackled by currency risk within the monetary union. However, in its place euro-zone banks assumed a different kind of risk because stable customer deposits made up less of their funding than was the case in the US or Japan. They became increasingly dependent on wholesale sources, which were less reliable, making banks acutely vulnerable when they dried up.[10]

The impetus given to the banking sector by the creation of the single currency affected European banks outside the monetary union. London, though outside the euro area, became its financial capital while the balance sheets of British and Swiss banks also ballooned. Precisely because European banks were so heavily involved in America's own dubious lending, they emerged from the financial crisis in a bad way, requiring heavy support from their national governments. Initially, however, the banks needing help in the monetary union were in northern rather than southern Europe. State-aid figures from the Commission showed that in 2008 the main recipients of recapitalisation (relative to the size of their economies) were in Austria, Belgium, Germany, Luxembourg and the Netherlands, whose banks typically received around 4 per cent of GDP; the amounts were somewhat higher in Austria and Luxembourg. By and large, those in southern Europe did not require help, although Italian and Greek banks did receive capital injections worth, respectively, 1.3 and 2.1 per cent of GDP.[11] Support through guarantees formed a broadly similar pattern, although Ireland already had a huge implicit liability arising from the government's ill-judged decision at the end of September 2008 to underwrite deposits and debt in six banks (subsequently raised to seven).[12]

During the financial crisis, the immense problems brewing in the banking systems in southern Europe were insufficiently recognised by either the markets or national supervisors. In part, this was because the drama was being played out in the big financial capitals of New York and London, and featured assets or securities that were 'marked to market' – jargon for being regularly revalued in line with market prices, which resulted in the prompt disclosure of huge losses. By and large, southern banks had kept out of these activities, concentrating instead on lending to their national businesses and households. Potential losses on such loans did not have to be revealed unless they became 'non-performing' because borrowers were no longer keeping up with their interest and repayments (having failed to do so for ninety days); and even then there was scope for lenders to hide losses, for example by 'evergreening' loans (lending to struggling firms the money needed to make interest payments).[13]

The ECB was not alone among central banks in failing to do enough to constrain the credit boom of the early twenty-first century, but in principle it might have been expected to worry more because of the importance it attached to monetary developments, even after the reappraisal in the spring of 2003 that downgraded their influence in determining policy. However, it was following them for the wrong reason as well as thinking too much about the whole of the euro zone and not enough about the parts. In line with standard monetarist thinking, it monitored money as an indicator of long-term inflationary pressures. If instead the ECB had followed the advice later that year of Claudio Borio and William White, economists at the BIS who argued that central bankers should do more to heed and to curb excessive credit growth, it would have been more alert to the risks of future financial instability arising from the high rates of credit expansion on the periphery.[14]

As important, the ECB lacked the authority to act. Like other central banks, it started to issue financial-stability reviews, from December 2004.[15] Yet just as similar reports from the Bank of England lacked clout once its supervisory power over banks was transferred to the Financial Services Authority in the late 1990s, so also did the ECB's since it had no direct sanction over banks, a job carried out by national supervisors, generally the NCBs.[16] In common with regulators in other advanced countries, their focus in carrying out supervision was generally narrow. They also faced political pressures to stay their hand because governments and politicians regarded banks as national champions, a protectionist predisposition that was if anything strengthened by European integration since that put a premium on size to fend off foreign competitors.[17] In creating a monetary union, the political architects of the euro had neglected the crucial role the ECB would have to play in ensuring financial stability, which in turn required euro-wide supervision.

If anything, the need for the ECB to carry out such functions was even more urgent than for other big central banks because euro-wide credit provision to firms as well as households remained dominated by banks. One broad gauge of the make-up of a financial system was to compare the stock of bank credit to the private sector with the value of stockmarkets and of private-sector debt securities, such as bonds. On this basis, credit in the euro zone comprised half of total finance in the years 2005–9; by contrast, in the US it constituted only a fifth of the total.[18] Banks dominated lending to households, with much less securitisation of mortgage loans than in the US.[19] The contrast for the corporate sector was just as telling. According to figures published in 2014 by the Association for Financial Markets in Europe, banks provided only 30 per cent of the debt financing of non-financial firms in the US, whereas the figure for the EU as a whole was 70 per cent.[20] The dependence on banks was even greater in the euro area. The total debt finance raised by companies through loans as opposed to debt securities in the euro area was 85 per cent, according to analysis that year by Standard & Poor's, a credit-rating agency.[21]

The preeminence of banks rather than capital markets in the currency union in part reflected the greater importance in the euro area of small- and medium-sized enterprises (SMEs), generally defined in Europe as those with fewer than 250 employees and a turnover of €50 million or less.[22] Such firms were much more salient in the euro area than in the US, and within the currency union they were especially prominent in southern Europe. Whereas less than half of German employees in manufacturing worked in SMEs in 2011, three-quarters of Italian and Spanish industrial workers were in such firms. Among service-sector employees, two-thirds worked in SMEs in Germany compared with four-fifths in Italy.[23] Larger firms could tap the capital markets but smaller concerns relied heavily upon banks for external finance. That dependence made them the main victims of the credit drought in southern Europe during the euro crisis.

Peripheral banks were doubly vulnerable, first because of unsound loans they had made and second because they had come to rely increasingly upon funding from the markets and their counterparts in the core creditor countries of the euro area rather than from the more stable source of domestic deposits to finance loans. The average loan to deposit ratio across the euro-zone countries peaked at about 140 per cent in the autumn of 2007 and was still high, at around 130 per cent, at the end of 2011.[24] In Portugal, the ratio reached a peak of 167 per cent in June 2010.[25] Elsewhere on the periphery, the loan-to-deposit ratio was also especially high in Ireland.[26]

The snag was that this external funding was inherently fickle because financial integration within the euro area was shallow, through cross-border wholesale lending, rather than deep, through cross-border bank ownership; banking mergers and acquisitions were predominantly domestic.[27] In November 2005, Trichet extolled the advances that had been made especially in money and bond markets since the creation of the euro. In fact, that progress was shakier than he appreciated, or was prepared to admit, since one of his prime exhibits was the convergence of sovereign bond yields. But even in his upbeat presentation, which drew upon a new set of indicators assembled by the ECB for financial integration within the euro area, Trichet conceded that retail banking had lagged behind. Cross-border interbank lending had increased substantially, but there was very little direct lending from one bank in a country to a firm or household in another.[28]

As a result, the banks in the core countries could readily pull back the funds they had lent to their counterparts on the periphery when doubts emerged about the wisdom of such exposure. The contrast with the support that Baltic banks received from Swedish lenders during the financial crisis and recession of 2007–9 was telling. At the time, all three Baltic states were outside the monetary union though tied to the euro through the ERM II (its second incarnation when the single currency was born) while Sweden also retained its own currency.[29] Unlike the banks in southern Europe, those in the Baltic states were predominantly foreign-owned, ranging from almost 100 per cent in Estonia, to 85 per cent in Lithuania and 67 per cent in

Latvia in 2007. The Swedish parent banks had lent heavily to their Baltic operations, contributing to the credit boom in the three countries before the crash. But, as owners, they had a strong incentive to stay the course rather than to cut and run even when things went so badly, especially for Latvia, during the financial crisis and ensuing steep recession.[30]

Paradoxically, the revolutionary creation of the euro had bolstered the *ancien régime* of an overbanked Europe with little rationalisation across the currency area. There were some exceptions. For example, Crédit Agricole, a big French bank, made an ill-fated aquisition of Emporiki, Greece's fifth largest, in 2006. Six years later, it withdrew from the fray, selling the bank to Alpha, one of the four big domestic lenders, after incurring substantial losses while also contributing to Emporiki's recapitalisation.[31] But what stood out in the first decade of the euro was the lack of cross-border bank ownership. Ironically, that reflected the lack of a genuine single market in financial services, as countries sought to protect their domestic banks, even though one of the declared purposes of the euro was to complement and buttress the single market.

The position across the periphery was in any case diverse both between countries and within them. Ireland for example hosted a big international banking centre in Dublin but the activities there were largely divorced from the local economy.[32] The Irish banking crisis was largely though not exclusively a domestic phenomenon, in which lending by local banks fuelled a frenzied real-estate boom, although their loans were facilitated by access to international funding markets. As had occurred in other banking markets, an aggressive intruder, in this instance Anglo Irish, led the way down the path of recklessness, but other banks, unnerved by short-term market-share losses, followed, including Allied Irish, Bank of Ireland and Ulster Bank, a subsidiary of Royal Bank of Scotland, whose misjudged lending in the Irish Republic contributed to losses and continuing difficulties at Britain's giant stricken bank.[33]

Although the property boom in Spain rivalled Ireland's, there were some reasons to take a more sanguine view of its banking difficulties. For one thing, the Spanish central bank had conducted a macroprudential policy of 'dynamic provisioning' in the first decade of the euro whereby banks had to build up reserves in the good times to absorb prospective general losses (as opposed to making specific provisions for losses already incurred).[34] At the height of the financial crisis, in the autumn of 2008, Sir John Gieve, the deputy governor for financial stability at the Bank of England, was praising this policy, saying that it might well 'offer a guide for the way forward'.[35] Moreover, Spain's two big banks, Santander and BBVA, had chosen more promising territory than many northern European banks for international diversification by concentrating their overseas expansion on Latin America, a natural hunting ground given ties of language and history. Both banks benefited from that region's resilience during and after the financial crisis, which was helped by the continuing Chinese boom and resulting demand for commodities from Latin America.[36] Indeed, so strong did Santander appear, despite its still considerable exposure to the domestic Spanish market, that in 2008 it was able to take advantage of Britain's financial crisis by adding two troubled mortgage lenders to its presence in the UK, which had been established in 2004 by buying Abbey, for long the country's second-biggest building society before converting to a bank in 1989.[37]

What was missing in such an assessment of the Spanish banking system was the perilous condition of the *cajas*, regional savings banks that were central to the Spanish banking crisis when it finally erupted between 2010 and 2012. They had been off the radar of the markets because they were not publicly quoted even though collectively their share of total banking assets doubled from around 20 per cent in 1980 to 40 per cent by 2010. That testified to an aggressive expansion primarily in real-estate lending, which was financed increasingly through market funding rather than deposits.[38] The *cajas*, which were subject to unhealthy local and regional political influence, made what turned out to be disastrous construction and real-estate loans.[39]

In the second term (between 2008 and 2011) of José Luis Rodríguez Zapatero, the *cajas* were restructured and amalgamated as joint-stock companies, slashing their number from forty-five to nine by late 2012.[40] But the merged banks, especially Bankia, which was formed in 2010 from seven troubled *cajas*, the biggest of which was Madrid-based, remained weighed down by bad loans, and the bank eventually had to be rescued in May 2012, forcing Spain itself to request a bail-out in June to help recapitalise its shaky banks. The plight of Bankia, whose losses of €19 billion in 2012 were the biggest ever in Spanish corporate history, came to symbolise the shaky state of the country's banking sector, not least owing to its unfortunately chosen headquarters, one of a pair of towers leaning over the Paseo de la Castellana, a main thoroughfare in Madrid.[41]

By contrast with Ireland and Spain, banks in Greece and Italy were more sinned against than sinners themselves, though a number of Italian banks were also susceptible to unhelpful political influences. In its post-mortem on the first Greek bail-out, the IMF pointed out that 'the banking system was perceived to be relatively sound when the programme began' (in the spring of 2010). 'Financial-sector distress was a result of the protracted recession and sovereign debt problems', noted the Fund, 'in contrast to Ireland and Spain where causality ran the other way'.[42] In Italy, there were some exceptions such as the Tuscan lender, Banca Monte dei Paschi di Siena, the oldest bank still in existence (just), which showed that corporate age was no obstacle to rash mistakes. More typically, Italian banks had a conservative business model and avoided the worst excesses of the credit boom on the periphery. As the Commission noted in a report on Italy in 2014, its banks 'weathered the first phase of the global financial crisis in 2008–9 relatively well'.[43]

But the misfortunes of Italian banks were to multiply. First, from the middle of 2011 they got caught up in the sovereign debt crisis, as foreign investors pulled out of Italian bonds, whose yields duly surged, and northern banks withdrew funding. That pushed up wholesale borrowing costs and forced the banks into the arms of the ECB in order to cover the funding hole. Second, the banks' loans started to turn sour in ever-greater amounts as Italy slipped into another recession, which undermined firms' ability to pay back their borrowing. The ratio of non-performing loans to total lending rose from 5 per cent at the end of 2008 to 16 per cent in late 2013.[44]

Portuguese banks looked riskier, in part because they were so dependent on funding from the rest of Europe, in part because their capital positions were weak and in part because the private sector was so heavily indebted. Yet Portugal had at least escaped a housing bubble in the run-up to the financial crisis. When the bail-out terms were set in May 2011, €12 billion of the total €78 billion was allocated to replenish banking capital. In the event, only about half of this amount was used in the three years of the rescue.[45] But then shortly after Portugal exited the programme in the spring of 2014, the reserve of €6.4 billion came in handy as the country's second largest private bank, Banco Espírito Santo, collapsed, not because of its exposures to the Portuguese economy but rather owing to losses incurred by the parent family-controlled group of companies. The government had to pump in €4.4 billion to buttress Novo Banco, the imaginatively named 'good bank' that was excised from the wreckage of the old one.[46]

With a population of just two million, Slovenia was too small to attract close scrutiny from the markets, which helped obscure the fact that its banks went on a reckless lending spree around the time that the picture-postcard country in central Europe joined the euro. A long boom had been under way from as early as 1993, two years after it had broken away from Yugoslavia. This catch-up growth got a second wind after Slovenia joined the EU in 2004 and still more so on adopting the euro in 2007 when its GDP expanded by almost 7 per cent, the fastest rate among the thirteen countries belonging to the single-currency area after its accession.[47] In that year alone, credit to the private sector surged by 34 per cent, following growth of 27 per cent in 2006.[48] The wild boom stoked up problems for Slovenia's thinly capitalised banks, arising particularly from loans to construction and financial-holding firms that soured as real-estate and financial bubbles burst. Through much of 2012 and 2013 Slovenia struggled to contain a banking crisis, which was so serious that by 2013 its three main banks (all state-controlled) were bust, able to carry on only because of an impending public bail-out whose exact size was not determined until a review of bank balance sheets and stress tests was published in December.[49] The cost of propping up the banks between 2008 and 2013 amounted to 14 per cent of GDP.[50]

In contrast with Slovenia's stealth crisis, the Cypriot banking system blew up in spectacular fashion. Its experience again illustrated the diversity of banking problems in the euro zone. Much of the damage had been done in an expansion of the banking sector before and after joining the EU, in 2004, rather than after adopting the euro, in 2008. Its banking system had reached Icelandic proportions by 2009, with banking assets worth eight times Cypriot GDP.[51] Unlike other banks in southern Europe, the Cypriot banks were not short of deposits and benefited as late as 2009 and 2010 from outflows from Greece. The failure of the two biggest banks was rooted in poor lending decisions as they sought to exploit the abundance of funds deposited in Cyprus and built up a fatal exposure to the Greek economy and state. Supervisory grip was lacking and effective corporate governance within the banks was 'close to non-existent in practice' according to an independent inquiry.[52]

Despite the diversity of the national banking crises on the periphery, they shared two crucial systemic characteristics. One was that much of the extra lending had been financed through cross-border loans from banks in the core of the euro zone. This was a fickle form of funding and as doubts arose about the creditworthiness of the banks on the periphery it headed for the exit. As Jaime Caruana, general manager of the BIS, which monitored global banking activities, showed in a paper with Adrian Van Rixtel, such international lending from one euro-zone bank to another surged dramatically between 2003 and 2008, only to collapse back to the starting point by the end of 2011 as funding within the euro area reverted to being segmented on national lines.[53]

Banks on the periphery that were haemorrhaging funds as creditors in the core pulled out their money were able to borrow copiously from the Eurosystem. Though that alleviated the crisis, it did nothing to address the reasons why northern creditors were running scared, which was the underlying weaknesses of the peripheral banks and their economies. Moreover, any bank that came to rely heavily on central bank funding was manifestly weaker than one that could do without it. Just as the provision of abundant liquidity was insufficient to overcome the global financial crisis of 2007–8, whose turning point came when banks were recapitalised after the collapse of Lehman Brothers, so the provision of abundant and cheap funding from the ECB could not fill the capital holes in southern banks.

The other systemic characteristic of the banking crisis arose from the vicious circle between governments and banks. In general, this worked through the erosion of banks' strength in the economies whose sovereign debt was shunned by raising their funding costs; bonds issued by Greek, Irish and Portuguese big banks were penalised for example during 2010.[54] But the decision to impose restructuring on Greece meant that sovereign weakness destroyed banks during the acute phase of the crisis. Not only were the Greek banks brought low, but the two big Cypriot banks (Bank of Cyprus and Laiki) were also mortally wounded through the losses they incurred on their holdings of Greek sovereign bonds, in part because they had taken recklessly big bets on them, with holdings of €5.7 billion (equivalent to about 30 per cent of Cypriot GDP), on which they incurred losses of €4.5 billion.[55] Since Greece remained the exception, however, banks were by and large not undone through their exposures to sovereign debt.

Paradoxically, however, the link between governments and banks strengthened during the crisis in terms of banks' direct exposure to public debt. Across the euro area as a whole, domestic sovereign bond holdings made up a higher share of total banking assets in early 2014 than in 2009 – though at close to 6 per cent it was still lower than at the end of 1998, on the eve of the euro, when it stood at 7.5 per cent. There had been particularly sharp rises in Italy and Spain, whose banks' exposure doubled, from around 5 per cent of their total assets in 2009 to about 10 per cent five years later.[56] Spanish and Italian banks in particular feasted on the extensive three-year funding offered by the ECB in the winter of 2011–12. As well as using this to refinance their own debt, they also used some to buy their national sovereign bonds. Between November 2011 and March 2012, Italian banks' holdings of government debt rose from €247 billion to €324 billion, an increase of almost a third. Spanish banks were greedier still. Their pile of sovereign bonds rose from €178 billion to €265 billion over the same period, an increase of just under a half.[57]

Shortly after the ECB's initiative to provide three-year funding was announced in early December, Sarkozy indiscreetly noted at the European summit, 'this means that each state can turn to its banks, which will have liquidity at their disposal'.[58] In effect, the ECB action could thus be interpreted as backdoor QE as banks pursued what was quickly dubbed the 'Sarko trade', a bespoke version of a standard carry trade.[59] The banks were paying rock-bottom interest rates for their borrowing from the ECB (the rate was the average over that period, starting at 1 per cent and falling by September 2014 to a mere 0.05 per cent). They could use that finance to buy high-yielding Spanish and Italian bonds (whose ten-year yields were 5.4 per cent and 6.9 per cent, respectively, at the start of 2012). This raised their sovereign exposure but if the government went down the banks would, too, so the carry trade still made sense, certainly far more so than using the funding to lend to small businesses, which had a high risk weighting under the Basel rules and were particularly risky in hard times. If market conditions improved, as they did, then the venture would pay off. In 2014, the Commission noted that the carry trade pursued by Italian banks had 'significantly supported the profitability of several institutions'.[60]

If the threat to banks from their holdings of sovereign bonds was for the most part averted, the problem of excessive private debt nonetheless persisted, weighing down not just their balance sheets but their economies by prolonging the credit drought that had started when external funding dried up. The debt overhang was particularly grave among companies. Figures for 2011 published by the IMF showed that 30 per cent of corporate debt in Italy was owed by firms whose pre-tax earnings were insufficient to cover their interest payments. The position was even worse in Spain and Portugal where the share of similarly frail firms was 40 and nearly 50 per cent, respectively. This compared with close to 15 per cent of French and German debt that was owed by such weak companies.[61]

Unsustainable levels of private debt spelt trouble everywhere for the banks that had lent so much of it. The surprise was that the necessary deleveraging, on the part of both the banks and the borrowers took so long to get under way in earnest. Indeed, total banking assets in the euro area continued to expand well into the crisis, reaching a peak of almost €35 trillion as late as May 2012.[62] Over the following two years, they fell by €4 trillion but that still left a collective balance sheet that was three times GDP, far higher than was the case for American banks, whose total assets were worth roughly the same as national output.[63] The form of the shrinkage over the two years reflected the fragmented nature of the currency club. In the vulnerable countries on the periphery, a third came about through a contraction in loans to the non-financial private sector – households and businesses. By contrast, these stagnated elsewhere, and a fall in derivatives accounted for half of the overall decline in the core countries.[64]

The switch from credit glut to dearth on the periphery, especially for businesses, contributed to the economic difficulties of the crisis countries in two ways. First, it became much harder for viable firms, especially small ones, to get any loans at all. Between the end of 2008 and the end of 2011, loans to private non-financial firms in the vulnerable countries contracted by around 5 per cent. That fall gathered pace, and by early 2014 the overall decline exceeded 20 per cent. By contrast, business lending slightly rose over the whole period in the rest of the euro area.[65]

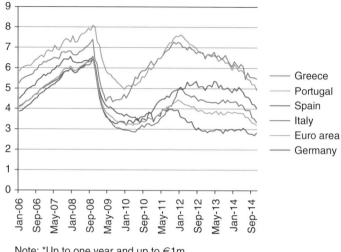

Note: *Up to one year and up to €1m.
Source: ECB

FIGURE 8 Interest rates on new loans to non-financial companies*,
2006–2014

Second, the cost of corporate borrowing was now much greater
on the periphery than in the core, putting firms in the afflicted countries at a competitive disadvantage (see Figure 8). The interest rates
paid by Portuguese and Greek firms were higher before the crisis, but
the gap widened markedly. Spanish and Italian companies had previously been able to borrow at rates around the euro-zone average, but
a differential opened up that was even larger compared with Germany
whose firms were favoured by extremely low interest rates. An arche-
typal case of the penalty being paid by businesses according to where
they were located was the disparity between the borrowing costs of
companies on either side of the border between Austria and Italy. In
the summer of 2012, Italian businesses there complained that they
were paying twice as much in interest on their loans as neighbouring
firms in Austria.[66] A big gap persisted between the core and the
periphery in 2013, even as the overall crisis subsided and sovereign
borrowing costs fell. Not until 2014 did it narrow appreciably.

But disentangling cause and effect was tricky. Regular surveys of bank lending by the ECB showed that demand for loans was in any case low, which was hardly surprising given the depressed condition of economies in southern Europe.[67] And banks in peripheral economies had good reason to be tougher on prospective borrowers because they were in turn made vulnerable by the weakness of their economies. Even so, in May 2014 Draghi said in a speech in Portugal that the 'credit gap' between the actual provision of loans and what would normally have been available was contributing up to a third of the economic slack in the stressed countries.[68]

To the extent that much of the problem lay with fragile banks as well as frail customers, this reflected the mistaken way in which the euro area dealt with its banks. When the financial crisis began, economists contrasted the ways in which Sweden and Japan had dealt with their banking crises in the 1990s. Sweden had been swift to isolate the bad assets in state-backed asset management companies whereas Japan had resisted such a decisive action, which had allowed the underlying problems to get worse.[69] Clearly, Sweden was the model to follow, yet in the event the euro area's response more closely resembled Japan, with countries reluctant to own up to the full extent of the problems. As a result, the banking crisis persisted and the bill got higher as economies with impaired banks continued to deteriorate. According to a study published by the ECB in April 2015, the total public cost of financial-sector bail-outs between 2008 and 2013 was 5 per cent of euro-zone GDP (in 2013) – around €500 billion.[70]

The failure to get on top of the problem meant that many investors harboured suspicions about what lay hidden in bank balance sheets. They had learned through bitter experience that banks could one day show ostensibly respectable capital ratios and go bust the next. In particular, stress tests had been not just ineffective but counterproductive. Instead of raising investor confidence in both banks and supervisors, as was the case in the US, they further undermined it. The sorry story of European stress tests encapsulated the mistaken way in which the festering banking crisis was handled owing to the deficient governance of the euro area.

Stress-testing banks had been pioneered in the US. Just as engineers had long used stress tests to work out how robust physical structures like airplane wings were to extreme events, so banking supervisors would use them to assess whether banks had enough capital to withstand a combination of financial and economic shocks.[71] The tests simulated what would happen to banks' balance sheets under both a 'baseline' scenario, in which the economy and financial conditions evolved in line with central forecasts, and an 'adverse' scenario. The first test, conducted in the spring of 2009 on nineteen big banks holding two-thirds of the assets in the American banking system, was designed to allay continuing worries about hidden weaknesses on the balance sheets of American banks, even though they had already been forcibly stuffed with public capital under the 'Tarp' (troubled asset relief programme), starting in October 2008.[72] The exercise worked. A subsequent study by researchers at the IMF concluded that the release of the results 'effectively halted and then reversed the two-year slide in investor confidence towards the country's banks'.[73]

By contrast, the stress test coordinated in the EU later that year for twenty-two big cross-border banks by the Committee of European Banking Supervisors (CEBS) failed to reassure investors when it reported on the 'resilience of the banking system'.[74] This was in part because it did not disclose the specific information that the markets were seeking. The results were published at an aggregate level, whereas the American authorities had provided findings for each bank. The lack of transparency vitiated the purpose of the exercise, which was to rebuild confidence through disclosure. Moreover, CEBS, 'an independent body for reflection, debate and advice' (to the Commission), was a paper tiger that could not insist on measures being taken to rebuild capital.[75]

That was bad enough, but subsequent rounds of tests eroded confidence. The exercise in 2010 covered many more banks – ninety-one in all, covering two-thirds of total banking assets in the EU – and was an improvement on the first round in that it disclosed information about individual banks as well as the overall picture. When the findings were published in July, seven banks failed but CEBS said that the aggregate results indicated a 'rather strong resilience for the EU banking system as a whole'. But their credibility was swiftly undermined since two Irish banks passed the test just months before Ireland's domestic banking system fell to pieces.[76]

The round in 2011 further sapped the credibility of European supervisors even though it was carried out by the European Banking Authority (EBA), which had replaced CEBS as part of a set of reforms in response to the financial crisis and had a specific if still limited remit to strengthen cross-border supervision and to harmonise banking regulations across the EU in a 'single rule book'.[77] When the results were announced, in July 2011, Dexia, a Franco-Belgian bank that had required a bail-out in 2008, passed with flying colours, ranked twelfth safest out of the ninety banks participating in the exercise. Three months later, in October, it required a further rescue from the French and Belgian governments. A serial offender, it needed yet another bail-out, its third, a year later.[78]

Although there were particular failings in the tests such as the unsatisfactory treatment of the risks of sovereign debt held by banks, the fundamental reason why they exacerbated rather than alleviated worries was that the euro area was not a fiscal union. The American one helped to restore confidence and to stabilise the banking system because it was backstopped by federal money. The availability of this backstop was flagged in advance, reinforcing the credibility of the exercise since any capital gaps revealed by the test could be filled if necessary.[79] By contrast, the European tests lacked any such pledge, leading the markets to suspect that the results were doctored to put the best face on things, a doubt hardened by the subsequent collapse of banks that were supposedly viable.

That suspicion would remain as long as euro-zone banks remained under their complaisant national regulators. This was why the decision to create a single supervisor, taken by European leaders at the heat of the crisis in June 2012, was so important. The job was handed to the ECB, despite some initial misgivings arising from the conflict of interest for any central bank of carrying out banking supervision as well as monetary policy. Typically, it took much longer than expected to give the ECB its new powers, owing to attempts by the European parliament to flex its muscle over the accountability and transparency of the new single supervisor.[80] Not until October 2013 was the final regulation passed under which it would take formal overall control a year later, in early November 2014, after conducting a thorough review of the main banks for which it would henceforth be directly responsible.[81] The aim of the probe was both to restore credibility in euro-zone banks and to protect the ECB from future mishaps that might sully its reputation.

In carrying out this 'comprehensive assessment', the ECB sought to learn lessons not just from the contrasting American and European experience in stress-testing but from supervisory reviews that had also been carried out at national level within the euro area. Ireland had led the way in 2011, followed by Spain in 2012 with two rounds of tests and Slovenia in 2013. These exercises were by no means the only factor at work nor even the most important in stabilising these banking systems. Confidence in Irish banks continued to fall for several months after the publication of the results in the spring of 2011 and even after it had troughed in September that year stayed at a low ebb. Spanish banks remained shunned after the first set of tests were published in June 2012, and the turning-point was Draghi's 'whatever-it-takes' pledge in late July. Yet the second set of tests in Spain and the ones in Ireland and Slovenia differed from the wider European stress tests in one crucial way: they were based on asset-quality reviews, a granular inspection of banks' books that sought to shine light on the murkier corners of their balance sheets.[82]

That was why a similar root-and-branch probe lay at the heart of the ECB's 'comprehensive assessment' in 2014 of 130 banks in the monetary union, which made up 82 per cent of the euro area's banking assets.[83] As well as conducting this painstaking asset-quality review, the assessment featured a stress test (which was coordinated across the EU by the EBA). The new test was more exacting than that of 2011. The adverse macroeconomic scenario and attendant financial shocks, including a sharp rise in bond yields, envisaged a cumulative drop in euro-zone output of 2.1 per cent over three years, whereas in the 2011 test output fell by only 0.7 per cent over two years. Relative to baselines, which in both instances envisaged growth, the cumulative shortfall in output over the period – 6.6 per cent over three years compared with 4 per cent over two years – was also greater.[84] An important change in the stress test was the treatment of sovereign bonds in the adverse scenario. Unlike the exercise in 2011, which had confined any shock to the bonds held in banks' trading books, the one in 2014 also affected those held as 'available for sale' in banking books, about half of the total government debt held by European banks, although the effect of losses on capital was dampened, with only 20 per cent of any losses feeding through in 2014, rising to 40 per cent in 2015 and 60 per cent in 2016.[85]

Despite these more exacting requirements, the eventual results revealed in late October 2014 for the euro zone were not the cathartic moment once expected. Although twenty-five – nine of which were Italian – out of the 130 banks failed, the total capital shortfall, of €25 billion, was surprisingly low; moreover, in around half of them it had already been filled by capital-raising in the first nine months of 2014.[86] These comforting findings were challenged by financial economists, Viral Acharya and Sascha Steffen, who examined a smaller group of thirty-nine publicly listed large banks, and found that they remained worryingly undercapitalised. Their estimate of potential capital short-falls under a market-based stress test came to €450 billion, including sizeable ones for three big French banks that had fared satisfactorily in the official exercise. In explaining the discrepancy, they pointed to the use of risk-weighted rather than actual assets in the official test together with supervisory leniency in measuring capital.[87] The currency union was becoming more and more the domain of zombie banks, contended Buiter (who had become chief economist at Citigroup in 2010) shortly afterwards.[88]

To the extent that the findings of the year-long review retained at least some credibility, one reason why the outcome turned out to be a damp squib was that it had come so late in the day following successive rounds of capital strengthening. Altogether, euro-zone banks had raised around €270 billion through new equity issuance between 2007 and the spring of 2014.[89] But probably the most important reason why the exercise failed to carry conviction was that it had not been supported by a clear European backstop. In September 2012, finance ministers from three creditor countries, Germany, Finland and the Netherlands, meeting outside Helsinki, had dashed hopes in Ireland and southern Europe that the agreement reached at the June summit on breaking the vicious circle between banks and states meant that common funding would be available to plug capital holes arising from existing – 'legacy' – assets. The northern creditor nations made clear that they would not have such bad debts dumped upon the ESM, the common rescue fund, whose use in recapitalising banks directly could be undertaken only for problems arising once the new single supervisor was in place.[90] Existing capital shortfalls would have to be met from national safety nets if private sources were unavailable. Despite intense lobbying by the ECB, Germany stuck to its guns.

Moreover, other steps to create a banking union had been half-hearted. Such a project ideally would have had three pillars: in addition to the common supervisor, there would be a single body to resolve failing banks, and a joint deposit-guarantee scheme. This would be broadly similar to the American approach where the Federal Deposit Insurance Corporation dealt with failing banks as part of its wider remit in insuring deposits.[91] Rather than this sturdy tripod, the euro-zone banking union was lopsided: the original three pillars became one-and-a-half, not the sturdiest of designs. The third pillar – creating joint deposit guarantees – was abandoned as politically unfeasible. Northern creditor nations feared that their depositors (and behind them their states) would do the guaranteeing, while southern depositors would do the claiming. As for the body to deal with failing banks, the Single Resolution Mechanism (SRM), this became in effect half a pillar.

After fractious meetings in Brussels in December 2013 and subsequent negotiations with the European parliament, euro-zone countries agreed upon a convoluted plan for the SRM. Under legislation due to come fully into force in 2016, the SRM would indeed be created. But it would take eight years for a common fund to be built up, starting in 2016, through levies on the euro-zone national banking systems (though 60 per cent would be mutualised after two years), which could be drawn upon in dealing with failing banks.[92] The amount that would ultimately be available, €55 billion, was less than Ireland alone had needed to bail out its banks. The decision-making process of the SRM was less cumbersome than in initial drafts, but it remained highly complicated for a body that would have to act typically over a weekend when the markets were closed. In the strained criticism of an IMF Report in July 2014, there were 'questions about the ability of the framework to deliver least-cost, effective and timely resolution in a systemic banking crisis'.[93]

Despite the weaknesses of the banking union, European leaders were still determined to break the pernicious link between banks and states, by ending taxpayer-financed bank bail-outs. The new approach was heralded in the Cypriot rescue in the spring of 2013, which broke with the customary official bail-out of bust banks. Though lending from the ESM was used to prop up the island's cooperative banks, there was an abrupt change in strategy towards its two largest ones, Bank of Cyprus and Laiki, which together had balance sheets worth four times Cypriot GDP.[94] Bank creditors who had generally been spared in previous rescues would be 'bailed in' to sort out the two Cypriot banks.

An eye-rubbingly bad first proposal to get all depositors, including those whose deposits were supposedly covered by an insurance guarantee of up to €100,000, to contribute to such a bail-in was hastily dropped after protests in Nicosia and condemnation across Europe. The initial endorsement of this plan by European finance ministers, led by inexperienced Jeroen Dijsselbloem of the Netherlands (who had replaced the wily Jean-Claude Juncker as head of the Eurogroup at the beginning of 2013), together with senior representatives of the IMF, cast a harsh light on the poor decision-making capacity of the euro area and its partner in Washington. A week later, they came up with a more sensible, if still flawed, plan. The Bank of Cyprus, a virtually bust bank into which the domestic assets and liabilities of Laiki, a completely bust bank, were shunted, was eventually recapitalised from the uninsured deposits, a raid made easier by the fact that many of those were held by Russians (and Ukrainians), either directly or indirectly.[95]

That shift from bail-out to bail-in was planned across the EU through the Bank Recovery and Resolution Directive (BRRD), which got the go-ahead in December 2013. Under new provisions generally taking effect in 2016, two years earlier than originally envisaged, bail-ins would involve not just shareholders and holders of subordinated debt (a weaker form of banking capital), as had already occurred in countries like Ireland, but also creditors who had previously been protected for fear of exacerbating the crisis, in particular senior bond-holders (to the vexation of the Irish who wondered why they should shoulder the burden on behalf of the wider euro area) and also large-firm uninsured depositors.[96] In extreme cases, large deposits of smaller-sized firms and individuals might also be at risk.

The desire to get banks off the backs of governments was understandable, leading Germany for example to apply the bail-in provision even earlier, from 2015. The suspension of the normal rules of capitalism for banks during the crisis had undermined public faith in business. But the switch from bail-out to bail-in held particular risks for the interconnected euro zone where cross-border wholesale funding had already proved to be flighty. Even if a systemically risky bank (owing to the size of its balance sheet) avoided trouble, the effects of bailing in just a small bank could rattle confidence more widely, if depositors found themselves out of pocket, as could occur under the rules. Even though small depositors (those with less than €100,000) would continue to be protected, that would make big depositors all the more likely to remove their funds at the mere whisper that something was up.

Moreover, the example of Cyprus was hardly reassuring, not least since the imposition of the bail-in was accompanied by deposit freezes and capital controls. The economy, which had already shrunk by 2.4 per cent in 2012, contracted by 5.4 per cent in 2013, and fell by a further 2.3 per cent in 2014.[97] The Bank of Cyprus, the country's main lender, was bolstered by a big capital injection from investors, including a group led by Wilbur Ross, an American private-equity specialist, in the summer of 2014, which plugged the gaping hole revealed by the stress test later that year.[98] But it was weighed down by its non-performing loans, which reached an astonishing 53 per cent of its gross loans at the end of 2013, up from 36 per cent just six months earlier. Indeed, it was able to carry on only thanks to continued emergency funding from the Cypriot central bank (permitted by the ECB).[99]

To the extent that the Cypriot bail-in was characterised as a success (though it took two years for capital controls to be fully lifted), that reflected a mixture of wishful thinking, size and distance.[100] Especially in Germany, the tempers that had flared over the misdemeanours of the Cypriot banks in accepting Russian slush money had died down. Cyprus was too small and its banks too isolated to matter once the immediate crisis was over. It had been forgotten, along with the main lesson to be learnt from its unhappy experience: that bail-in of systemically important banks (in this case for the Cypriot economy) was far from trouble-free and was unlikely to work if applied to much larger and more interconnected banks in a big euro-zone economy.

Of course, the euro area was not alone in embracing bail-in as the way to deal with future banking problems. Outside the monetary union, Denmark had pioneered this approach with senior bondholders, when Amagerbanken (nicknamed 'Armageddonbank') collapsed in

2011, though it subsequently had to beat a retreat when investors penalised other Danish banks.[101] Along with Germany (and Austria), in the euro area, the UK also introduced the regime a year earlier, in 2015.[102] And in late 2014, the Financial Stability Board, a global forum for banking regulation, set out a plan for dealing with the most tricky problem of all: how to deal with the collapse of a large international bank, or to use the preferred regulatory jargon, G-SIB (global systemically important bank).[103] All countries had a compelling interest in trying to avoid further recourse to taxpayer bail-outs in a future financial crisis. But the interest in the euro area went beyond that since what concerned northern countries, especially Germany, was shielding their taxpayers from bank collapses in other states. The reluctance to provide a credible fiscal backstop to the euro-zone banks – the ESM set a limit of €60 billion once the single supervisor was in place – together with the lack of mutual deposit insurance meant that the vaunted banking union was a fragile construct.[104]

Euro area banks were not alone in getting into trouble. That honour had been amply shared by their counterparts in Britain and the US. But the euro area was much slower than the US and the UK in tackling their weaknesses. National supervisors within the single-currency club tended to support their banks as local champions and were reluctant to own up to their fragility. The prolonged failure to clean up the currency union's banks helped to explain the intensity of the crisis in the markets, especially in 2011, when investors took fright at the entire banking sector, pushing their equity prices down and causing a funding famine that was relieved only by the extraordinary steps taken by the ECB in the winter of 2011–12. The failure continued to hurt the monetary union even after the acute phase of the crisis was over as banks were still seeking to reduce their overall balance sheets, which made them reluctant to extend new loans, causing a constricting decline in credit on the periphery. All along, the euro area's troubled banks had been a crucial reason why the euro crisis was so severe.

# 6   The existential crisis

The idea of European monetary union was a distant dream when the Eagles released their album, 'Hotel California', in 1976. But the west-coast band's spaced-out lyrics turned out to be prescient for the euro thirty-five years later as the currency union stumbled into a crisis that threatened to tear it apart. Was the euro area, like the hotel, a place where you could check in but never leave? If that was the nightmare for a country like Greece as its citizens weighed the immediate pain of a 'Grexit' against an uncertain future gain as an economy unshackled from the euro, the existential nightmare for the euro area was that a country might indeed leave, and in the process destroy the single currency itself.

That prospect looked most threatening in 2012. Yet three years later, Greece went even further to the edge. The potential economic harm to the rest of the euro area in 2015 appeared to be much more contained than in 2012, although no one could be entirely sure about this in practice. By contrast, the political damage of the clash among euro-zone leaders at their weekend summit in July as Greece desperately sought to remain a member while Germany openly pressed for an enforced exit was profound. The disharmony caused soul-searching about a project that was dividing the peoples of Europe rather than bringing them together.

The history of currency unions cast a sobering shadow. If the European version were to survive, it would be the exception to the rule. Shortly before the financial crisis erupted, Andrew Rose, an economist at the University of California, Berkeley, estimated that sixty-nine countries (or other territorial entities) had left currency unions since the Second World War. In fact, this was an underestimate because Rose's figures did not include the break-ups following the collapse of the Soviet Union and of Yugoslavia. The exits generally occurred as the former imperial powers shed their colonies and newly independent countries adopted a new currency. The departures peaked in the 1960s and 1970s; by the end of the latter decade, sixty-two out of the sixty-nine noted by Rose had taken place. The end of currency unions did not necessarily coincide with the date of independence. Typically, there was a delay of seven years after the formal handover of power to a new state though in some cases countries left a currency union before becoming independent.[1]

Delving deeper into history there were earlier precedents in Europe for the problems that could beset currency unions, bringing about their eventual demise. The Latin Monetary Union, formed in 1865, lasted formally until it was disbanded in 1926, but it had withered away long before that. Founded by France, Belgium, Italy and Switzerland, the LMU has been called the first international monetary union, but its scope was more limited than that since it was a coinage convention that did not cover bank notes.[2] Specifically, it was a bimetallic system, with a fixed relationship between gold and silver, in which common standards were agreed for the issuance of high-value coins, in both metals, which were to be mutually accepted by national treasuries.[3]

The union might have been called 'Latin' but that was window-dressing. The driving force behind the union was France, which saw it as an opportunity to contest the rising power of Prussia by asserting economic leadership in Europe, showing if nothing else the consistency of French policy over more than a century.[4] Félix Esquirou de Parieu, the French chief negotiator at the convention establishing the LMU, aimed even higher at an international conference held in Paris shortly afterwards, in 1867, when he sought to marshall agreement for a 'universal money'.[5] The lofty aspirations came to nothing and hopes of further progress were dashed when Prussia defeated France in the war of 1870–1, after which a unified Germany switched to gold, paving the way for the high noon of the gold standard and the increasing irrelevance of the bimetallic alternative enshrined in the LMU, whose members first restricted and then ceased new minting of silver money in the 1870s (though the existing stocks were not withdrawn).[6]

The LMU's own history showed how vulnerable monetary unions were to abusive behaviour by member states manipulating a common currency to fund budget deficits, argued Thomas Mayer in *Europe's Unfinished Currency*. Greece, which had joined the LMU in 1868, soon after it had been created, was eventually kicked out after it debased its gold coins.[7] The admission of so unsuitable a member was an uncomfortable portent for Greece's adoption of the euro, in 2001, again shortly after the venture had started. But for the use of the word 'league' to describe the union, it would be hard to discern that an early history of the LMU was describing Greece's membership of it rather than of the euro, and had been published in 1901 rather than 2001: 'In no sense was she a desirable member of the league. Economically unsound, convulsed by political struggles and financially rotten, her condition was pitiable.'[8]

The LMU's shadowy existence long after it had lost its initial rationale following the adoption of the gold standard and the growing importance of bank notes highlighted another lesson that was to be pertinent at the height of the euro crisis: its members were loth to wind it up because that would have exposed severe losses for some member states. In the case of the LMU, these arose from the fall in the market value of silver against gold. Specifically, they would have materialised if France had insisted on other countries like Belgium and Italy redeeming in gold at the union's fixed parity the large stocks of their silver coins that it held.[9] As Luca Einaudi, a modern historian of the LMU, wrote, it 'survived its own decline because member states did not want to pay the cost of its termination'. Another reason for its survival was that France, the pivotal monetary power within the union, was reluctant to lose the political influence it still derived from it. The union eventually ended after the exigencies of war finance caused the liquidation of the silver stocks during and immediately after the First World War.[10]

The Scandinavian Currency Union, formed initially between Denmark and Sweden in 1873 with Norway joining in 1875, worked better because it was based on the gold standard and, unlike the LMU, had a common unit of account, the krona. The SCU was further underpinned by the fact that Sweden and Norway were joined in a political union in which they shared a monarch and conducted a common foreign policy while exercising domestic home rule. From the late 1880s, a clearing agreement between the three central banks allowed them to draw funds readily from one another and the monetary union was extended to notes between 1894 and 1901, the high point of the union.[11]

Although the SCU was more successful than its Latin cousin, its history revealed that monetary union was not necessarily the integrative force, both economically and politically, that the architects of the euro had in mind. Despite their close geographical and political ties, the three member states failed to forge a customs union and the share of trade between them declined from 22 per cent of total exports in 1872 to 10 per cent in 1910.[12] Far from binding countries closer together, the opposite happened when in 1905 Norway decided to sever the political union with Sweden, a move prompting restrictions on the clearing agreement. As a result, the SCU was vulnerable to the further retreat into nationalism during the First World War, even though the three Scandinavian countries stayed out of the conflict. By 1917, it had in effect broken up, although it was not formally dissolved until 1924.[13]

If the First World War put paid to currency unions between states, it also demonstrated the tight interlocking of sovereignty and money. The disintegration of the Austro-Hungarian empire, which had commenced shortly before the war ended in November 1918, was swiftly followed by the break-up of the monetary union among the successor states. Yugoslavia, initially called the Kingdom of Serbs, Croats and Slovenes (joining parts of the former empire with previously independent Serbia) was first out of the gate in January 1919, 'overstamping' Austro-Hungarian notes in its territory in order to turn them into national legal tender. Monetary financing of the war had already unleashed inflation, but the creation of new national monies and central banks was messy and accompanied by hyperinflation in Austria and Hungary, although Czechoslovakia experienced deflation and a jump in unemployment.[14]

Just how ominous this record of break-ups was for the euro could be questioned on grounds of relevance. The Latin and Scandinavian monetary unions came closest in spirit in that they were formed between otherwise sovereign states. But they were far more limited in scope than the euro area, which created a common money however it was held, including bank deposits as well as notes and coin. There was no overarching central bank with ultimate authority similar to the ECB. Moreover, central banks had limited responsibilities when money was backed by gold or silver since their main task was to ensure that national currency was adequately buttressed by bullion, although the Bank of England was forging a new role in ensuring financial stability, notably through its intervention to orchestrate a rescue of Baring Brothers in the 'crisis that never became a drama' of 1890.[15] By contrast, the ECB's role as guardian of price stability made it ultimately responsible for the euro-zone economy given the link between economic activity and inflation.

If anything, the historical examples of currency fragmentation associated with the end of empires were even less pertinent. For one thing, the context was quite different. Whereas the euro formed part of a broader project of European integration, the earlier break-ups occurred as the consequence of political disintegration. The inflation accompanying the collapse of the Austro-Hungarian empire formed part of a broader monetary disorder, of which the German hyperinflation of the early 1920s was the most egregious example.[16] The end of so many currency unions after the Second World War also accompanied a broader dismantling of colonial empires. Financial systems in these earlier unions were in any case far removed from the scale, sophistication and integration of that of the euro area.

Most of the break-ups after the Second World War had occurred in the 1960s and 1970s, but there were two more recent instances. One was the short life of the rouble area, which began in 1992 with the fifteen former Soviet republics as members but counted just two at the start of 1994, Russia and Tajikistan; the status of Belarus was unclear since it was seeking to rejoin, but that came to nothing and it retained its new currency, making it the sole legal tender later that year.[17] The rouble zone had turned into rubble in just two years. The currency union established between the Czech Republic and Slovakia after the two countries parted political company at the start of 1993 had an even briefer existence, falling apart within less than six weeks.[18]

Once again, however, these break-ups occurred in the context of political ruptures, in both the Soviet Union and Czechoslovakia, whereas the euro was rooted in the wider European project of ever closer union. Indeed, in an odd coincidence, the end of the Soviet Union, in December 1991, coincided with Europe's leap forward at Maastricht.[19] The three Baltic states, which had been annexed by the Soviet Union in 1940, were determined to reintroduce national currencies to affirm their independence. Tellingly, Estonia was both the first country to make a clean break from the rouble area, resurrecting the kroon in June 1992, and the first Baltic state to abandon its currency, adopting the euro in January 2011.[20]

In addition to their opposing directions of political travel, another crucial distinction between the rouble zone and the euro area lay in their respective budgetary starting points. For all the weaknesses in the Maastricht criteria, they did at least seek some fiscal sanity among prospective members, with good reason as the rouble area's short-lived existence proved. The collapse of the Soviet command economy undermined the public finances of the new states. Though the Baltic states managed to keep theirs under control, several of the new republics ran prodigious budget deficits in the first year of the currency union. Predictably, they were covered by printing money. Although the Russian central bank was the only one that could issue roubles, the other central banks, formed from the former republican offices of Gosbank, the Soviet state bank, were able to issue their own supplementary currencies, which circulated locally. Equally predictably, the result was ruinous inflation, and even hyperinflation in Ukraine.[21] Again, the relevance of this episode, which echoed the disastrous consequences of the collapse of the Austro-Hungarian empire, appeared remote for the euro area where the ECB was the supreme authority over the national central banks. Indeed, fifteen years after the euro started. the opposite fear, that of Japanese-style deflation, had come to the fore.

Despite the differences between these more recent break-ups and the experience of the euro area, they nonetheless provided some worrying lessons. One was the ability of national central banks in the rouble area to circumvent restrictions from the centre, through issuing parallel currencies. In principle, the primacy of the ECB ruled out such rogue behaviour, but the structure of the Eurosystem with the continuing presence of the NCBs rather than their conversion into ECB branches allowed room for national manoeuvre.

As the euro crisis intensified, exceptions to the rule of a single monetary policy became more widespread. Central banks in Ireland, Greece and Cyprus provided emergency liquidity assistance (ELA) to their endangered banks, which added to Eurosystem base money. There were precedents: the Bundesbank for example had resorted to ELA during the financial crisis in 2008.[22] There were safeguards, too. The national central bank in question bore the credit risk on the lending to the banks in question. However, this assurance was flimsy since the collateral was of poorer quality and the NCB's assumption of that risk relied essentially on the ability to call upon its national treasury in a country that was in deep economic and fiscal trouble. More important, the ECB's governing council in Frankfurt could block a national central bank from such action if it was deemed to 'interfere with the objectives and tasks of the Eurosystem', provided that two-thirds of the council decided that was the case.[23]

This was a powerful threat though something of a nuclear weapon in that the consequence might be to force a country out of the euro. However, the ECB used it to force both Ireland and Cyprus into accepting official bail-outs (and bail-ins for Cypriot banks) when it lost patience with persistent and extensive use of ELA and the risks that posed to the rest of the Eurosystem.[24]

In 2015, ELA played a crucial part in the Greek crisis, both in allowing it to drag on for several months and then in finally resolving it.[25] In February, the ECB stopped accepting Greek sovereign debt (and more important, bank bonds guaranteed by the Greek government) as collateral on its usual lending to banks. That had been possible despite its junk status because the Greek state was underpinned by the support of euro-zone creditors and the IMF while carrying out policies under the terms of the bail-out, but this could no longer be assured through a successful review of the programme. The decision shunted over €40 billion of lending to banks into the ELA category, which then became the main way in which the Bank of Greece supported Greek banks. It also offered a means on the part of the ECB's governing council to intervene provided that a two-thirds majority could be mustered. The council's decision on Sunday 28 June to freeze the amount of ELA available to Greek banks at €89 billion even as a full-scale run was under way following Tsipras's calling of a referendum swiftly brought home why this was such a disastrous move on his part. Since banks could no longer borrow further funds from the Bank of Greece to make up for the drain of deposits, capital controls were immediately imposed and the banks did not open on Monday, with cash withdrawals from ATMs limited to just €60 per day.

In a previous less disruptive instance of the fraying of the monetary union, national central banks were permitted from early 2012 to lend against riskier forms of collateral (additional credit claims) than were generally accepted by the Eurosystem. Seven (five of them in troubled countries on the periphery) grasped the opportunity to accept such bank loans, which lacked market valuations, at their own risk.[26] Unlike the provision of ELA, such lending would not be subject to limits set by the governing council. Although the euro area had started with diverse collateral practices, it subsequently sought to mould them into a unified pattern; now it was reversing direction even though the concession was supposed to be temporary. In a note issued shortly after the council approved the specific approaches proposed by the seven NCBs in February 2012, Buiter asked: 'Is the euro zone at risk of turning into the rouble zone?' He worried that 'a sequence of bad decisions' could lead to a fracturing of the monetary union in what he called 'roublezoneification', a process that threatened to be as ugly as his neologism.[27]

The Czech–Slovak monetary divorce in 1993 also offered disconcerting lessons for the euro. One was that capital flight – in this instance from Slovakia into the perceived haven of the Czech Republic during late 1992 and in early 1993 – could swiftly undermine a currency union. The money moved because people feared its dissolution followed by a Slovak devaluation. A second was that it took over six months to introduce new banknotes in both countries (from early February until the end of August). The Czechs and Slovaks were able to provide temporary cash through the Austro-Hungarian device of overstamping existing banknotes, but the long delay in issuing new notes was one reason why an exit from the euro area would be chaotic since such a policy could not be adopted for euros that were still valid elsewhere.

No matter what the exact relevance of these earlier break-ups might be, they did at least demonstrate that they were feasible, but were they nonetheless costly? Strikingly, given the worries about the break-up of the euro area, Rose found that the countries leaving currency unions since the Second World War generally did not suffer much macroeconomic turbulence or jolts to their living standards though inflation tended to rise.[28] On the other hand, in earlier research with Reuven Glick, an economist at the San Francisco Fed, he found large declines in trade between countries after unions ended, with bilateral trade eventually falling by half.[29] Since the greater intensity of trade and the associated increase in competition was one of the main ways in which a monetary union was supposed to promote prosperity, this suggested that the break-up of the euro would be very damaging.

However, this finding was not that relevant to the euro area since it was based mainly on the experience of post-colonial states, a diverse bunch of small and poor economies. An alternative explanation for the sharp declines in trade was that they formed part of a broader deterioration in economic performance arising from poor policies pursued by post-colonial governments. If that was the case, the link between currency unions and trade was more apparent than real. The end of the sterling link between the Irish Republic and the UK in 1979 appeared to have had no significant impact on their bilateral trade.[30]

A paper in 2006 by Richard Baldwin, of the Graduate Institute of International Studies in Geneva, argued that estimates pointing to a strong link between currency unions and trade were unreliable. He found that the boost to trade within the euro area from the creation of the single currency was modest: between 5 and 15 per cent with a best estimate of 9 per cent. He also showed that the gain had essentially been a one-off adjustment, achieved by bringing down the fixed cost for exporters of introducing new goods into euro-zone markets, which had benefited the three countries that had stayed out of the monetary union – Britain, Denmark and Sweden – almost as much as the twelve that had by then adopted the single currency.[31]

If so many break-ups had previously occurred without lasting damage and the euro area itself did not have much to lose in trade since the gain had been minor, this might seem to imply that the single currency could also be dissolved or fragment without too much damage. Indeed, a study of the Czech–Slovak monetary divorce published in the year that the euro began, argued that though it took its toll on GDP, especially in Slovakia in 1993, the costs were relatively low. This led the authors to conclude that dissolution of the European monetary union or secession by some of its members could be 'swift and without prohibitively high costs'.[32]

Such a view appeared to inform the German government's initial response to the Greek crisis in early 2010 when it seemed ready to countenance a Greek exit (though this differed from the assurances Steinbrück had made a year earlier). In March 2010, Schäuble said that if a country could not sort out its public finances or restore its competitiveness, as a last resort it should exit the monetary union (while staying in the EU), a view he first expressed in the *Financial Times* and then, more trenchantly, in an interview with *Bild*, Germany's top-selling paper.[33] Merkel echoed this sentiment shortly afterwards when addressing the Bundestag, but soon changed her tune.[34] By May, the chancellor was defending the unpopular Greek bail-out by arguing that the survival not just of the euro but of the wider project of European integration was at stake; 'if the euro fails, then Europe fails', she told the Bundestag.[35]

This claim was questionable, but the economic alarm was justified because the single currency had become inextricably embedded within the European economy. More than a decade of monetary union, removing internal currency risk among its members, had denationalised assets and liabilities across one of the richest and biggest economic regions in the world. The continued existence of the single currency had also informed decisions taken outside the euro area by investors and businesses.

That denationalisation of assets was especially notable in the ownership of government debt. By 2010, just over half of euro area government debt (52 per cent) was held outside the country of origin, both within the currency club and outside it. Such holdings were particularly high for smaller countries, reaching over 70 per cent for Austria and Finland in the core and 63 per cent for Portugal on the periphery. But they were also extensive in the big peripheral economies of southern Europe, at 45 per cent for Italy and 42 per cent for Spain.[36] The increases that had occurred since the euro was created were dramatic. A case in point was Italy, where foreign ownership of Italian government securities had been just 27 per cent in 1998.[37]

Banks had become intertwined within the currency union through the interbank market. Their exposure went beyond that to encompass cross-border holdings of both sovereign and private debt within the euro area, which burgeoned during the years before the

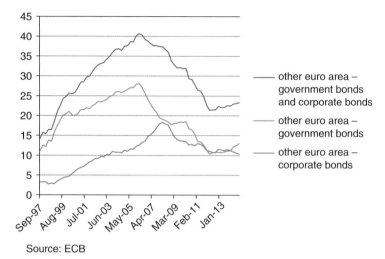

Source: ECB

FIGURE 9 Euro area bank cross-border holdings of debt securities, 1997–2014, per cent of total holdings

financial crisis (see Figure 9). The interlinkages went beyond the boundary of the monetary union. British banks held little sovereign debt issued by peripheral countries but were vulnerable to them, directly through private-sector loans especially in Ireland but also in Spain and Italy, and indirectly through their exposures to German and particularly French banks, which were themselves heavily exposed to the vulnerable countries on the periphery.[38]

Indeed, concern about the fate of the euro was of overarching importance not just to the European but also to the global economy, which was why the American government pitched in to try to sort out the mess. The euro had after all become a reserve currency second only to the dollar. Its share of official foreign-exchange reserves increased from 18 per cent at the start of the monetary union in early 1999 to 28 per cent a decade later at the end of 2009 (over the same period the dollar's share fell from 71 per cent to a still dominant 62 per cent).[39] Already by December 2006, the value of euro banknotes surpassed that of dollars in circulation (helped by the appreciation of the euro against the dollar at that time). At the end of 2007, there were some 12 billion banknotes in circulation with a value of €677 billion.[40] No previous currency union had brought about the sheer interconnectedness of the euro area. Accordingly, the price of a break-up was feared to be dauntingly high.

Working out just how high those costs might be was hard because there were so many imponderables, not least whether a break-up might be contained to just one country or might trigger a broader fragmentation. Another question was whether an exit, most likely of Greece, would occur in chaos and acrimony or in a planned and relatively conciliatory manner. A German exit was politically inconceivable for a country whose post-war redemption owed so much to its embrace of European integration, but this did not prevent the idea being mooted, causing further nervousness in the markets. For example, Hans-Olaf Henkel, a supporter of monetary union in the late 1990s when he headed the Federation of German Industries, had become an influential opponent of the euro and advocated splitting it into a northern hard-currency area and a southern soft-currency zone. In the summer of 2011, he made the case for Germany leaving with a select group of small, solvent economies – Austria, Finland and the Netherlands.[41]

With so many uncertainties and a reluctance on the part of official organisations even to contemplate the idea of a break-up, few estimates of the potential bill were published. One from economists at UBS, a Swiss bank, found that if a strong country like Germany were to leave, it could incur costs worth 20 to 25 per cent of GDP in the first year; if a weak country like Greece were to quit, the first-year cost would be 40–50 per cent of GDP.[42] These estimates were implausibly pessimistic, in part because they assumed that countries exiting the euro would also be forced out of the EU altogether, thus incurring trade obstacles as well as currency disruption. Yet more sober attempts to estimate the economic impact still portrayed a trainwreck in the making.

According to the IMF, which broke the official omertà on the subject in March 2012 in what was in effect a warning shot to Greece, an exit would cause the Greek economy to shrink by around 13 per cent in 2012 rather than the 5 per cent they then expected it to contract anyway. The decline in domestic demand would be significantly larger because an exit would require an immediate correction of Greece's swollen current-account deficit through lower imports. The Fund's economists provided no figures for the wider impact on the rest of the euro area, but they highlighted 'negative spillover effects' – jargon for the wider damage that an exit would inflict, most of all by shattering the notion that euro membership was forever. In January 2013, when the immediate risk of a Grexit had receded, the IMF estimated how big those effects might be, ranging from a loss of euro-zone output in the first year of 1.5 per cent to as much as 6 per cent if a Greek departure 'turned out to be a catastrophic event like the collapse of Lehman Brothers'. The impact was 'fundamentally uncertain' and it was 'not possible to establish that contagion risk from euro exit would be limited and manageable'.[43]

Simulations by Mark Cliffe, an economist at ING, a Dutch bank, provided figures for two scenarios: an orderly Greek exit and a complete break-up of the monetary union, in each case working out what would happen to GDP compared with a baseline projection in which the euro area remained intact (see Figure 10). His estimate for the impact of an orderly Grexit was similar to the IMF's; the Greek economy, already contracting sharply, would slump by an extra 7.5 per cent in the first year. Across the euro area, it would be responsible for a decline of 1.6 per cent in the first year, reaching 2.2 per cent over two years. A full disintegration of the currency union would devastate the euro zone (as was), causing an output loss of almost 9 per cent in the first year and of 12 per cent over two years. That would far exceed the precipitous slide induced by the financial crisis, when GDP fell between the first quarter of 2008 and the second quarter of 2009 by 5.8 per cent (see Figure 2).

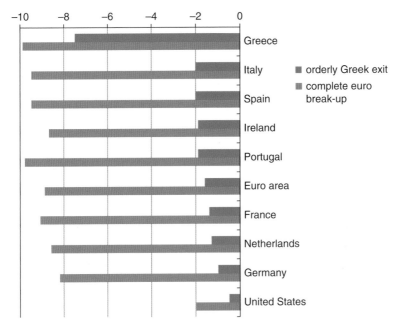

Source: ING, December 2011

FIGURE 10 Impact on GDP from an orderly Greek exit or a complete break-up of the euro area, per cent change in first year

Why would the break-up costs be so heavy? The main reason was that the dissolution of the monetary union would recreate the very currency risk that the euro was supposed to have eliminated. Whereas cross-border investors and borrowers could for example factor in such risk for countries that retained their own currencies, countless transactions across the gamut of financial instruments and commercial contracts had been made on the assumption that exchange rates had been fixed for good within the euro zone. The currency risk from a break-up would be far greater than the usual fluctuations in exchange rates, with potentially huge changes in the values of the restored national currencies. Across the former euro area, there would be a wave of bankruptcies as businesses found themselves either owed money in a depreciating currency or owing money in an appreciating currency.

The reappearance of such risk scared not just investors and businesses within the single-currency club but those outside it, as they contemplated a range of alarming outcomes that might occur even if a full dissolution of the union could be averted. Suppose for example that a break-up following a Greek exit could be contained to the southern debtor countries, which might either go their own ways or stay together in a single bloc, while the northern creditor states retained the euro. This form of break-up would see the euro, which would remain the currency of the majority of the euro-zone members, soar while the new currencies of the peripheral debtor countries (or their new currency if they stayed together) would plunge. The extreme exchange-rate movements would make it impossible for both private and public debtors on the periphery to honour their obligations to lenders in the remaining euro area because their own new currencies, in which income was generated and taxes were paid, would be worth much less in relation to the euro. As they were forced to default on the debt, the losses would be spread back to the creditors in the remaining euro zone and beyond.

That risk of such a blowback was one reason why the core countries in the euro area were so worried about a possible break-up arising from an exit by debtor nations. But there was no easy way out for the creditor countries. Suppose alternatively that Germany might after all lose patience with the whole enterprise and resurrect the deutsche mark. At the outset of the euro crisis, this would have bankrupted the German banking system, observed Daniel Gros, director of the Centre for European Policy Studies, in May 2010. Bank deposits would have to be redenominated from euros into new deutsche marks one-for-one since no government would dare to make depositors poorer overnight as the euro sank against a resurgent deutsche mark. That would inflict big losses on the banks since their extensive foreign claims in euros would now be worth much less in deutsche marks. The government would be forced to save them with a 'massive infusion of capital'. Leaving the euro was thus 'a rather expensive proposition for a creditor country like Germany', said Gros laconically.[44]

This specific threat became less of a worry as German banks reduced their exposure to the debtor countries in the euro area; according to a study by economists at the BIS, such claims on five peripheral countries (Greece, Ireland, Italy, Portugal and Spain) halved from just under €600 billion in the first quarter of 2008 to €300 billion in the second quarter of 2012.[45] However, this pushed the risk on to the German public sector since the only way that the banks could be repaid was through the Bundesbank raising its exposure within the Eurosystem to the debtor central banks. Bringing back the deutsche mark would be no panacea. One way or another the German taxpayer would pick up a heavy bill and the economic damage would go well beyond this since the restoration of a hard currency would inflict a crippling blow, at least in the short term, on Germany's vital exporting industries.

The precise form that fragmentation might take, ranging from the contained and planned exit of one country to a chaotic departure, from the exit of several nations to a complete collapse of the currency union, was just one uncertainty among others. A particular anxiety was legal uncertainty, a fog as dense as the one enshrouding the Victorian law courts in *Bleak House*. If there was a contract, say between a creditor in Germany and a debtor in southern Europe, what was its legal status in the case of a break-up?

Suddenly, a knowledge of *lex monetae*, literally the law of the money, meaning the law of the state that issues the currency, became pertinent. This stated that the country in whose currency a debt was denominated determined what that currency was. If a German borrower took out a loan in dollars governed by English courts, only American law could determine what a dollar was under the agreement.[46] Cobwebbed precedents were dusted down, such as the ruling of the highest German court after unification under Bismarck on whether holders of Austrian railway debt, repayable either in

Austrian silver guilders or the thalers that had previously circulated in Germany and were converted into marks based on gold, could insist on being repaid in the latter, which had become more valuable since gold had appreciated against silver. Even though the bonds were governed by Austrian law and there was no agreed place of payment in Germany, the court ruled in favour of the bondholders, endorsing the principle that a sovereign state must be able to determine its own currency.[47]

A difficulty in applying this doctrine to the exit of one country from the euro area or a partial break-up was that the euro would continue for the remaining members. The prospect of fragmentation rather than dissolution contrasted with previous instances, such as Austria-Hungary, when currency unions had completely disintegrated. The crucial question was whether euro-denominated obligations would still be payable in euros or in the new currency issued by the departing country or group of countries. Posing the question was easier than answering it, since that might depend upon whether the contract described the euro as the currency of the euro area or that of the state which was leaving, whether the place of payment was in the departing country or not, and what the governing law of the contract was. If payments were specified to be made outside the exiting state, this would suggest the contract should continue to be honoured in euros, even if they were to be made outside the euro zone (typically in London). Where contracts were written under, say, English law, disputes could be judged in English courts, which were likely to decide that the obligation should continue to be paid in euros. Summarising these complex issues in relation to a possible Greek exit, Charles Proctor, a London-based lawyer, said that 'contracts with a significant international dimension would remain outstanding in euro'.[48]

Yet, despite a plethora of briefings from City-based international law firms, their guidance failed to provide businessmen with the certainty they craved. What for example would be the status of euros held in London with an American bank by a Spanish company if the euro area broke up? No one could provide straight answers, confided a prominent Spanish businessman after the acute phase of the crisis had ended.[49] Moreover, even if the law favoured foreign creditors of companies in an exiting country, enforcing their rights would be counter-productive if it pushed the businesses into bankruptcy, as was quite likely since the debts would become far more onerous as the euro appreciated. For once a firm became insolvent the obligations would be converted into the domestic currency. The court proceedings that would ensue were likely to be drawn-out, leaving the creditors with big losses owing to currency depreciation no matter how much of their lending was formally recovered.[50]

It was as if the statesmen who had conjured up a single currency were in fact sorcerers' apprentices. The tale of the magic broom that brought a flood of water was familiar to Germans in particular as *Der Zauberlehrling*, written in 1797 by Goethe, their national poet, and the (misquoted) line *Die Geister die ich rief* (the spirits that I called) was a common saying. That spell could be broken by the sorcerer on his return. But one senior German official reportedly feared that 'we have invented a machine from hell that we cannot turn off'.[51]

Making matters worse, the spell applied even in the apparently limited case of just one country leaving or being forced out of the currency club. A country like Greece might be on its knees but its bargaining power was enhanced by the threat of an exit since, however disastrous this might be for the Greek economy, it might wreak havoc on the rest of the currency club. Resenting the potential for blackmail and worried about its broader implications for other countries in trouble, creditor countries led by Germany could not give cast-iron assurances that an exit would not happen. With familiar unhelpful feedback, the uncertainty generated by fraught bargaining unnerved markets, exacerbating the crisis in 2011 and 2012.

Whether through accident or design, the construction of the monetary union, certainly as long as the ECB stuck to a restricted view of its role, resembled in physical respects the fragile strength of a brittle material, which would snap if overstressed. In strict legal terms, it was a union that did not even contemplate the possibility of exit. The lack of any such provision was deliberate. The architects of the euro needed to convince financial markets that there could be no retreat from monetary union (though no one anticipated the full extent of the dangers from an exit that loomed so large during the crisis). Accordingly, currencies adopting the euro fixed the exchange rates of their former national currencies for good; the conversion rates were 'irrevocable'.[52]

The lack of any emergency escape-hatch created a legal disjuncture. As part of the vexed reformulation of the European Union to deal with its expansion from fifteen to twenty-five members in 2004, the Lisbon Treaty formally acknowledged for the first time the right of a member state to leave the EU, while omitting to acknowledge that a state might want or need to leave the euro. This legal incoherence was all the more striking since, with the exception of Britain and Denmark, which had negotiated specific opt-outs, all EU member states were supposed ultimately to join the currency union.

If states could leave the EU, but not the euro, could a country leave the euro and stay in the EU? No, said Phoebus Athanassiou, a legal counsel at the ECB, in a paper published by the central bank in December 2009. His judgement, uncharacteristically succinct for a lawyer, was that 'withdrawal from EMU without a parallel withdrawal from the EU would be legally impossible'.[53] If that was the case, an exiting state would lose access to the single market (and financial help from the EU through regional funds directed to poorer countries) as well as having to recreate its own national currency. Whether or not such a strict legal interpretation would hold in the event of an actual exit was not so clear-cut. A possible solution would be for a country to withdraw from the EU and then to be readmitted as quickly as possible, suggested Proctor in his own paper on the issues raised by a fragmenting euro area. A snag with this legal legerdemain was that such readmission would be subject to all the EU member states ratifying it.[54] Politics in any case seemed likely to trump legalities, not least since the Commission would want to preserve the single market. After all, when Schäuble, himself a lawyer, aired the idea of an exit from the monetary union in March 2010, he explicitly said that a country leaving the euro would be able to remain a member of the EU.

If, as seemed plausible, politics were to prevail at a European level, they would surely be paramount on the national stage. A remarkable feature of the acute phase of the crisis, between 2010 and 2012, was that the peripheral countries put up with the austerity and reforms imposed in the rescues rather than seeking to leave the euro. Although there were popular protests, such as the *indignados* movement in Spain, the only country where an insurgent party came close to winning power was Greece, in the early summer of 2012. The mobilisation of popular discontent came with a lag, notably in the European elections of May 2014, although the nihilist Five Star Movement led by Beppe Grillo had previously come close to a breakthrough in the Italian general election of early 2013.

One reason for the quiescence of the periphery was a reluctant recognition that harsh measures were necessary. This was apparent in Ireland, following the madness of its housing-market bubble and of the bank lending that had financed it. The election in February 2011, just three months after the rescue, delivered a new coalition government dominated by Fine Gael, which had previously been in opposition. Despite electoral rhetoric about revisiting some of the terms of the bail-out, Enda Kenny, the new Irish prime minister, knuckled down to the task of complying with the terms of the bail-out programme.[55] Irish voters had on previous occasions used referendums on European issues as a form of protest, but in May 2012 they backed one required to ratify the fiscal compact; concentrating electors' minds, a rejection would have rendered Ireland ineligible to get future help from the ESM.[56] A readiness to push through reforms was also notable in Portugal, where Pedro Passos Coelho, who became prime minister after winning an election in June 2011, held shortly after the previous government had been forced to accept a rescue, was personally convinced of the need for tough measures to enhance competitiveness and reduce the weight of the state on the economy.[57]

Moreover, at the time of the rescues the full extent of the economic downturns that would ensue was not appreciated. That was most glaringly the case in Greece, but it also affected other countries that were bailed out. When preparing their first assessment of the Portuguese economy under its three-year programme, the troika forecast declines in GDP of 2.2 per cent in 2011 and 1.8 per cent in 2012, with output picking up by 1.2 per cent in 2013. In fact, GDP fell for three consecutive years, by 1.8, 4.0 and 1.6 per cent in 2011–13. Instead of the unemployment rate peaking at 13.4 per cent in 2012, as envisaged by the troika in May 2011, it reached 16.4 per cent in 2013, going above 17 per cent in the winter of 2012–13.[58] Yet even though the reality was so much worse than expected, there was still a case for carrying on rather than switching horses in mid-stream.

Small states took the view that the long-term advantages of clubbing together with larger ones outweighed the short-term disadvantages of staying the course. Big states had more options because they were better placed to go it alone, making the threat of their exit more plausible. Of these, Italy arguably came closest to the door, under Berlusconi. In December 2012, just over a year after he had had to resign as prime minister, he declared that Italy would be forced to leave the euro in order to be competitive if Germany did not accept that 'the ECB must be a real central bank'.[59] More important, it later transpired that he had been raising the issue of a possible exit in discussions with other leaders while he was still in charge in late 2011.[60]

Berlusconi's brinkmanship contributed to his downfall in November 2011. This was an Italian affair, engineered by Giorgio Napolitano, the elderly president, but under strong pressure from Germany and France.[61] In Brussels the previous month and then again in Cannes where a G20 summit was held in early November, Merkel and Sarkozy upbraided Berlusconi for failing to put Italy's house in order and demanded action.[62] As in other southern countries, a greater distaste for national politicians than for European demands seems to have swung the balance as far as the public was concerned. Italy had been ruled by technocrats before, most recently when

Lamberto Dini was in charge between January 1995 and May 1996. In the tense closing weeks of 2011, Italians accepted the need for a similar administration of ministers recruited from outside parliament under Monti which would carry out his 'Save Italy' programme; eight, including Monti himself, were university professors.[63]

A démarche by European leaders also precipitated a change in Greek leadership in November. First, Papandreou was denied the referendum he wanted to call on the new bail-out programme, which euro-zone leaders had outlined in late October, along with the deep restructuring of privately held Greek government debt that was eventually carried out in 2012.[64] Merkel and Sarkozy were aghast at such an idea, which the Greek prime minister had dreamt up without consulting other European leaders or indeed Evangelos Venizelos, his finance minister; whatever its democratic legitimacy, it would have further destabilised an already shaky currency union. Papandreou was summoned to Cannes, where the G20 summit had been hijacked by the euro crisis, and was told bluntly that if he was to hold any referendum at all, it would have to be on whether Greece wanted to stay in the euro or leave it. This was an extraordinary response since it brought into the open the possibility of an exit, which was supposed to be unthinkable. But Barroso used the occasion to forestall any referendum at all by encouraging Venizelos to shoot the idea down, which he duly did on his return to Athens.[65] Within a few days, Lucas Papademos, a former vice-president of the ECB, had replaced Papandreou as the technocratic head of a national-unity government.

Such interventions together with the unremitting pressure from the troika were one reason why throughout the crisis the country that seemed most likely to leave was Greece. But despite the hardship they were suffering, Greeks were wary of breaking with the euro. Opinion polls showed that even as the economy slumped the Greeks still backed the single currency. Campaigning in the elections of May and June 2012, Tsipras, leader of the insurgent Syriza left-wing group, reassured voters that Greece could stay in the euro while calling for an end to the 'barbarous' bail-out programme.[66] In effect, he was declaring that he would call Merkel's bluff, betting on the fact that the German government would back down on Greek austerity rather than put the euro to the test of a Grexit.

Tsipras adopted a less intransigent stance ahead of the election of January 2015, helping him to win, but he then became locked into a battle with the country's creditors that involved precisely the game of bluff and counter-bluff that had been feared in 2012, gambling on the notion that Germany would blink for fear of the wider consequences of an exit in destabilising the monetary union. Both in prospect in 2012 and in reality in 2015, the danger was that the Germans would stand their ground since if they conceded to Syriza this would foster similar populist parties in other debtor countries. The decision by Tsipras to pursue the strategy in 2015 was all the more perverse since the Greek position was weaker than in 2012. Financial linkages between Greece and the rest of the euro area had become attenuated while bond markets in the periphery were subdued by the ECB's adoption of quantitative easing in 2015 involving the purchase of sovereign bonds (though not those of Greece).

In both 2012 and 2015, there were two main paths to an exit. One was short, through a sudden ejection. This would happen if the ECB were no longer able to permit the lending to Greek banks through ELA to make up for their loss of deposits. In 2012, for example, if the Syriza leader had won then and unilaterally called the debt moratorium he was threatening, this would have put the ECB in an impossible position since Greece would then lack the support of the euro-zone creditor nations. In 2015, a failure on the part of Greece to redeem debt of €3.5 billion held by the Eurosystem that was due to be paid on 20 July, just a week after the fraught weekend negotiations that resulted in the first steps towards Greece's third formal bail-out, would also have been a moment of peril, undermining the credibility of the ECB if it did not make a stern response. A decision by the ECB to cut the ELA lifeline would have caused the banks to fold, enforcing an exit since this would be the only way that the Greeks would be able to restore a banking system. To reinforce such a move, the ECB could cut the

Greek banks off from the Target2 payments system. However, the ECB would take such action only if euro area leaders had taken a decision to expel Greece.[67] The threat of such an expulsion was most potent in 2015 when the Germans came to the July summit armed with a proposal to impose a 'time out' of at least five years from the euro area if Greece did not accept much harsher terms than its voters had rejected only a week earlier.

Alternatively, the exit could have been a more gradual though still ineluctable process, as the Greek government simply ran out of money to pay its own pensioners and workers, not to mention commercial creditors with which it was running up big arrears by suspending payments. In these dire straits, it could start to finance itself by issuing its own IOUs direct to its domestic creditors. The notes ('scrip') would rapidly fall in value, creating in effect a new depreciated parallel currency. Such a scenario was set out at the height of the crisis in the summer of 2012 by Mayer, then an adviser to Deutsche Bank, and came close to being realised in the middle of 2015 as the Greek government ran out of money. A precedent was what had happened in Argentina as it struggled to hang on to its link with the dollar before it was severed in early 2002. Desperate regional governments began to pay their employees in scrip, such as the *patacones* issued by Buenos Aires Province. But such a manoeuvre was likely only to postpone an exit and would itself cause monetary disorder and inflation.[68]

Whichever way an exit could occur, whether in 2012 or 2015, its effects on Greece would be catastrophic, at least in the following year or so. The horror story of a Grexit began with chaos as, overnight, the euro became a foreign currency. Greece would lack its own notes and coin since it would take several months to print and mint them. And whereas the Czechs and Slovaks had been able to overstamp notes, this would probably not be possible for Greece since the euro would still be in existence for the other members of the currency union and would continue to circulate as tourists visited the country.

If the new currency would take time to be issued as notes and minted as coins, it would immediately come into being for all other domestic assets and liabilities. These would be redenominated into drachma, most likely at parity through a one-for-one conversion. But, reborn in such unpropitious circumstances and awakening earlier painful memories of depreciation, the new drachma would immediately plummet in value, scything through the value of savings and deposits. In its estimates of early 2012, the IMF anticipated a fall in the exchange rate of 50 per cent. As had happened in Argentina in 2002 when it severed its decade-long fixed exchange-rate link with the dollar, this could create unstoppable pressure on the government to mitigate the impact on depositors. Yet, as had also occurred in Argentina, the banks would be ruined by any such 'asymmetrical' redenomination of their balance sheets.

Though the Greek government would have a free hand at home in converting euros into drachmas, it lacked the same authority over foreign debts, whether private or public. But that offered scant comfort to foreign holders of Greek debt. Whatever its legal status, the burden of such debt would rise dramatically in drachma terms, as the euro appreciated against the new currency. This would force outright default upon both the government and private companies on their euro-denominated debt to external creditors.

The nightmare for the Greek public was that an exit would ignite inflation. This would come about in the first place through the depreciation of the reborn drachma, which would push up import prices. The initial shock would be met by a central bank lacking the credibility of the ECB and under pressure to create money to cover the government's borrowing requirement. This would lead to a surge in inflation; the IMF estimated in early 2012 that prices would rise by 35 per cent in the first year.

Some of these worries might have been overdone. The immediate changeover in currencies would undoubtedly have been messy given the delay in creating the new notes and coin. But in increasingly cashless economies, the temporary lack of national notes might prove less problematic than feared. The Greeks could have got by for a few months by making more payments electronically and using existing euro notes and coin in circulation for small transactions (in effect accepting dual pricing), according to Roger Bootle of Capital Economics, in a paper proposing how countries might leave the euro, which won a competition set by Lord Wolfson, a British businessman, in 2012.[69]

Whether a Grexit would have inflicted more lasting domestic damage after the initial shock was questionable, especially if it were allowed to remain within the EU and thus to continue benefiting from the single market. In particular, the economy would have gained from the sharp correction in competitiveness that it still urgently needed, assuming that it was not frittered away in runaway inflation. Argentina's experience a decade earlier offered a more optimistic prognosis for Greece. The peso had been tied, one for one, with the dollar in April 1991, in order to break supposedly once and for all Argentina's addiction to inflation. The link was reinforced by a currency board, an institutional arrangement designed to stop the central bank from creating more domestic currency and bank reserves than its holdings of dollars and foreign currency. A similar board in Hong Kong since 1983 had withstood a series of shocks.

In Argentina, the constraint of the currency board was less binding than was the case in Hong Kong since up to a third of the central bank's assets could consist of dollar-denominated Argentine government debt, but the system had nonetheless survived a decade before the crisis.[70] The system had been sufficiently credible for much of the economy to have become dollarised. By the end of the 1990s, about 60 per cent of bank deposits and loans were denominated in dollars.[71] The extensive dollarisation of the Argentine economy meant that breaking the link, which occurred in early 2002 in the wake of its debt default (on what was then a record of $82 billion) at the end of 2001, was expected to be traumatic, inflicting long-lasting damage.[72]

The immediate effects were unquestionably dire but the worst fears turned out to be exaggerated. Inflation did surge initially to over 40 per cent by the end of 2002, but it then subsided to 4 per cent a year later. The restoration of competitiveness helped the economy to recover quite swiftly. After declining by 11 per cent in 2002, GDP grew the following year by 9 per cent.[73] Indeed, Argentina thrived during much of the ensuing decade, growing at around that hectic pace. The economy was helped by a commodity-price boom, with food prices doubling between 2003 and 2008, from which Argentina benefited as a big agricultural exporter especially of soya beans and associated products (just as it had been hurt by low agricultural prices in the late 1990s).[74] On the other hand, it was shut out of international capital markets because of continuing disputes over its default, despite settling with most bondholders in restructurings in 2005 and 2010 that exchanged 91 per cent of the defaulted debt for new performing bonds. Though growth was checked in 2009 by the global recession, it bounced back to 9 per cent a year in 2010 and 2011.[75]

The economic revival faded in 2012 and by the start of 2014 Argentina was once again in the grip of a currency crisis as the peso plunged in value, declining by more than at any time since the devaluation of 2002.[76] In the summer of 2014, it defaulted again on its debt owing to a clash with a group of investors holding bonds that had not been exchanged in the restructurings. These dogged 'holdouts' ('vulture' funds was the preferred term used by Argentine ministers) were pressing for full repayment following an American court ruling in their favour, which prevented the government from making payments due to the bondholders who had settled.[77] Argentina's renewed economic difficulties and its continuing battle with the holdouts appeared to vindicate those who had argued against Greece following a similar course in severing the currency link as well as restructuring its debt. But at the height of the Greek crisis in 2011 and 2012, Argentina's experience suggested that an exit from the euro might have been possible without the lethal effects that so many dreaded.

Greece was centre-stage in this existential drama, but the final decision on whether it stayed in the euro or left it was made by politicians in Berlin rather than Athens. Even after Samaras narrowly won the second Greek election in June 2012 and was able to form a coalition government (helped by an automatic boost of 50 out of the total 300 seats in the Greek parliament that went to the party getting the most votes), there was plenty of scope for things to go wrong because his new administration sought a softening in the terms of the second bail-out.[78] That was dangerous since the German government was initially suspicious about Samaras, who had failed to support Papandreou in the first bail-out, and remained frustrated by what it regarded as endless footdragging. As a result, it continued to consider enforcing an exit, even though the Greek public had voted against such an outcome.

The case in Berlin for pushing Greece out of the euro, which was pressed by Schäuble, rested on several points. First, confidence in the Greek government had been drained dry: if the state were indeed not just a special case but a lost cause, it would be better to face up to this even at this late hour. Moreover, the destabilising effects of a Greek exit that had loomed so large two years earlier were less salient because far less debt was owed to private creditors following the purchases of the ECB, the repayments of maturing bonds made possible by official loans and the restructuring in March 2012. On top of that, there was another possible advantage. By making an example of Greece, the remaining countries in the euro area would be forced to be on their best behaviour, in order to avoid such a fate. And if Greece was the weak link in the chain, removing it would make the rest of the union stronger.

An enforced Grexit remained on the table until the late summer of 2012 when Merkel returned to Berlin from a walking holiday in the Tyrol region of the Alps and decided against forcing Greece out for much the same reasons that European leaders had always shied away from any form of break-up. The crux of the matter was that her advisers were unable to provide her the assurance she wanted that the risks of a Grexit could be contained and would not trigger an even deeper crisis.[79] Arguably, this was her characteristically cautious way of rejecting the policy since any such assurance would have to be qualified. The departure of Greece would immediately put back in the frame other bailed-out economies such as Ireland, which were making encouraging progress and had complied with European conditions. Markets would also call into question the viability of Spain and Italy as members of the monetary union. If a Grexit created a further panic, the cost of containing it for Germany might paradoxically be an even bigger concession, such as a move towards eurobonds or explicit guarantees for the sovereign debt of stressed states.

In 2015, Merkel's stance was again cautious even in the face of provocative tactics on the part of the Syriza-led government, especially on the part of Varoufakis who appeared to go out of his way to alienate his fellow finance ministers on the Eurogroup, not least and inadvisably Schäuble. The German chancellor did her best to sort out a deal in meetings in late June, which would have provided temporary help to the Greek government until later that year, using funds still available from the second bail-out, including €11 billion returned to the EFSF because it had not been needed to recapitalise the banks after they managed to tap private sources in 2013 and 2014. However, Tsipras's decision to call a referendum on the creditors' proposal and to campaign against the plan was a provocation too far, destroying trust on the part of not just Germany but also the rest of the euro area. Moreover, the damage done to the Greek economy by capital controls and the bank closures meant that the amount of bail-out money that would subsequently be required, for a three-year period, was much larger, up to €86 billion, than had been envisaged earlier in the year when for example Luis de Guindos, the Spanish economy minister, talked of assistance between €30 billion and €50 billion.[80]

As a consequence, Merkel took a very different stance in the summit of 12 July which ran on into the following morning. Gone was the broadly conciliatory stance that she had adopted in late June. Instead, she initially backed the hardline position of

Schäuble, who came to the negotiations in mid July armed with a plan for Greece to take a five-year 'time out', if it failed to agree to much stiffer terms. The notion of a temporary exit was one that Schäuble had entertained in March 2010, shortly before the first Greek bail-out. It made little sense either then or in 2015, for it was inconceivable that Greece could entertain rejoining a currency union from which it had parted in such political bitterness and with such attendant economic agony, which a mooted humanitarian package would scarcely salve.

As much as anything, it was the heavy divorce bill for both a parting country and the remaining states that convinced politicians on either side to plough on rather than to start again, both in 2012 and 2015. From one perspective, this could be seen as a strength of the euro: the costs of any form of demerger were such that it made better sense to cling together. Yet this was an unsatisfactory defence, rather like an unhappy marriage whose partners reluctantly stay together for fear of the disruption and financial losses that separation would bring. That unhappiness was much in evidence in the days after the summit as Tsipras said that he did not believe in the agreement he had made at the summit, while Schäuble continued to press the case for Greece leaving the euro.

Despite these deep political rifts there was a crucial reason why the euro area defied the sceptics and stayed intact. The pressures on the monetary union were after all extreme especially once they started to affect the big economies in southern Europe in 2011 and 2012. According to the IMF, capital outflows from Italy in the year to June 2012 amounted to €235 billion, 15 per cent of its GDP in 2011. The outflows from Spain over the same period were even higher in both absolute terms and as a share of GDP, totalling €296 billion, 27 per cent of its national output in 2011.[81] A capital exodus on this scale would have overwhelmed any fixed exchange-rate system. What made the difference was the ECB, whose interventions were ultimately to prove decisive in the battle between bond markets and governments that raged in 2011 and 2012.

The existential crisis of the euro during its acute phase was at root one of credibility: did irrevocable really mean irrevocable? Plenty of earlier currency unions had after all come unstuck and their demise seemed to emphasise the preeminent link between national sovereignty and currency. But such examples differed from the euro in that for all the weaknesses of its original design, it did form part of a wider project of 'ever closer union' and was underpinned by Germany, the hub economy and hegemonic state. The euro area also differed from previous ventures because the costs of break-up were potentially so much higher given the financial interconnectedness of the member states after more than a decade of sharing a currency. As well as this reason for sticking with the union, the euro area had a potent weapon to deal with the bond markets, a powerful modern central bank – provided that it was willing to rise to the occasion.

# 7   Defender of last resort

Throughout the crisis there was a Faustian battle for the soul of the ECB. That struggle was most earnest in Germany, coming close to parody when Weidmann invoked Goethe's drama as a warning against succumbing to the temptation of unbridled money creation.[1] Should the ECB stay faithful to its first incarnation, the circumscribed conception of a doughtily independent central bank that was essentially the Bundesbank writ large on the European stage? Or did it have to shed that skin and assume a more ambitious and expansive role akin to that of the Fed or the Bank of England, even though unlike such traditional institutions embedded in their sovereign states it was uniquely a supranational monetary authority? As the euro crisis itself metamorphosed from a trial in the markets to a broader economic failure of stalling growth and protracted low inflation, the ECB was called upon to reinvent itself again, by adopting a programme of quantitative easing that would involve large-scale purchases of sovereign bonds, a policy shift as fraught for a central bank lacking a single state as the decisions it took in the heat of the crisis between 2010 and 2012.

A change of leadership in late 2011 was almost certainly pivotal in determining the outcome of the ECB's identity crisis. Under Trichet, who had taken charge in November 2003, the central bank repeatedly crossed lines it had drawn in the sands, but its French leader sought to build and to represent a consensus on the council. Since that was generally lacking during the euro crisis it was hard to widen the ECB's remit beyond the bare minimum needed to sustain the currency union. The central bank's approach in combating the euro crisis in 2010 and most of 2011 was accordingly reactive and hesitant rather than proactive and decisive.

When he was campaigning for the top job, Draghi paid homage to Germany as an economic role model for pushing through structural reforms to improve its competitiveness; and he went out of his way to praise the Bundesbank at his first press conference, in November 2011, expressing 'great admiration' for the institution and its tradition.[2] His wooing of the German public earlier that year paid off when *Bild* backed him. The influential tabloid had initially campaigned against Draghi, saying that inflation belonged to the Italian way of life as tomato sauce to pasta, but within a few weeks it changed its mind and endorsed his candidacy, crowning him with a *Pickelhaube*, the spiked helmet of the nineteenth-century Prussian army.[3] But Draghi was not the honorary German that the newspaper fondly imagined and he was prepared to go where Trichet had feared to tread, to the increasing discomfort of the Bundesbank as the ECB ceased to follow its made-in-Germany manual.

Ironically, it was the ECB's lurch into unorthodox territory under Trichet, in particular its decision to purchase the sovereign bonds of peripheral countries under siege, that gave Draghi his chance. Until the euro crisis erupted, Weber, head of the Bundesbank, appeared to be the front-runner in the race to replace Trichet as president when his term expired at the end of October 2011.[4] For one thing, he had a solid grounding as an academic macroeconomist. For another, and more important, the job of running the ECB, for which Germany had sacrificed the Bundesbank's former hegemony, had gone first to a Dutch and then to a French candidate; now surely it was time for a German to take charge. That orderly flightpath was disrupted when Weber, unhappy about the direction the ECB had already taken, aborted take-off in February 2011 by announcing that he was going to resign from the Bundesbank for personal reasons at the end of April, a year before his term was due to expire.

This opened the door for Draghi, governor of the Bank of Italy since the end of 2005, who could himself boast strong macroeconomic credentials as a former academic as well as long experience in the public sector, having held high office in the Italian Treasury as well as the central bank. He had also spent time in the private sector, working at Goldman Sachs between 2002 and 2005, which provided invaluable insights into the way private markets work in practice as opposed to theory (although his stint as an investment banker also led to criticism from some quarters).[5] Despite his laudatory remarks about the Bundesbank, his conception of what the ECB should do differed radically from what Weber, faithful to the German central bank's tradition, believed.

Before long Draghi was to be helped by another reshuffle as Stark, who vehemently opposed bond purchases, decided to leave the board early. He was replaced at the start of 2012 by Jörg Asmussen, a more emollient and less dogmatic figure, who was to prove an important ally for Draghi in the battle for German public opinion as the Italian steered the central bank in a direction that put it on collision course with the Bundesbank.[6] The new president was also able to capitalise on Stark's departure by prising away the influential job of chief economist from the German member of the board for the first time since the ECB was created. In a surprise move, responsibility for the economics department was handed not to Asmussen, for whom the German finance ministry had lobbied, but to Peter Praet, a former director of the Belgian central bank where he had been firefighting the banking crisis before joining the ECB board a few months before Draghi.[7]

Trichet's defensive stance during the euro crisis, which contrasted with the bold steps he had taken to fight the financial crisis and ensuing recession, reflected not only his consensual style of leadership, but also the fact that mustering agreement became far harder to achieve as the euro crisis segmented the monetary union between the core creditor countries and the peripheral debtor nations. This created corresponding splits in the governing council, both among the sixteen governors of the NCBs (rising to seventeen in 2011 when Estonia adopted the euro), and in the six-strong executive board. Such national differences of opinion were not supposed to happen, especially on the board, but the sharply opposed views and styles of Stark and Lorenzo Bini Smaghi, an Italian board member in charge of international relations, conformed uncannily to national stereotypes as well as the economic traditions of post-war Germany and Italy. And if nationality were so irrelevant, Bini Smaghi would not have had to leave the ECB early in order to make room for a French member on the board, once Trichet had departed, resolving a diplomatic row between France and Italy.[8]

The precise points of contention varied in salience during the crisis but the question remained the same: how much should the ECB do to save the euro, and therefore necessarily assisting the struggling states on the periphery, without forfeiting its monetary independence in all but name? The first and continuing flashpoint was over buying government bonds, initially through the securities markets programme (SMP). The purchases under the SMP were made in secondary markets, which meant that formally at least they did not flout the ECB's mandate. The Maastricht Treaty forbade 'monetary financing', which ruled out central bank purchases in the primary market, when governments were raising money through new issues. But it permitted buying in secondary markets, where bonds already issued were traded, as part of its monetary operations, and there were no restrictions on including sovereign debt in such activities.[9]

Such purchases of public debt had long been part of the repertoire of central banks as a means of providing more liquidity to steer short-term interest rates down, which could be reversed through sales that withdrew liquidity, steering rates up. Since the financial crisis and ensuing deep recession, the Fed and the Bank of England had gone a step beyond such standard open-market operations by making large-scale purchases of government bonds (the Fed also bought mortgage securities that were in effect state-backed). The purpose of these quantitative-easing programmes was both to inject money directly into the economy, bypassing the impaired banking sector by selling to institutional investors, and to drive down the term premium between long- and short-term interest rates. This gave fresh impetus to monetary policy even when short-term rates had fallen to their floor, set by the 'zero bound'. The central banks targeted sovereign bonds both because they were the safest asset and also because government-debt markets were easily the largest and most liquid, allowing scope for bulk purchases.

But the ECB's purpose for the SMP was not to inject more money into the euro-zone economy, since it claimed to be sterilising the liquidity created through its purchases by withdrawing the same amount of money through offsetting operations (specifically, by tying it up in weekly fixed-term deposits that it induced banks to hold).[10] Nor was the SMP intended to lower overall long-term interest rates in the euro area. Yet for both legal and presentational reasons, the ECB had to argue that the bond-buying was for monetary purposes. The rationale it presented for the SMP – that the purchases were necessary to counter 'malfunctioning' securities markets that were 'hampering the monetary-policy transmission mechanism' – was tortuous.[11] The timing of the programme suggested that the real reason was to quell panicky markets and to buy time for governments to reach more durable solutions to the euro crisis, involving both changes in the overall governance of the currency union and reforms at national level. As Buiter subsequently noted, 'the true purpose of the programme was first and foremost to prevent disorderly default of an EA [euro area] sovereign' as well as forestalling a 'full market meltdown' of the undercapitalised European banking system.[12]

The two German members on the council – Stark and Weber – were distressed by what they regarded as a covert form of fiscal support. The purity of the Bundesbank's opposition was besmirched by the fact that it had itself purchased German government bonds in the mid 1970s in order to lower long-term interest rates. In 1974 and 1975, it built up a portfolio of government paper worth DM7.5 billion. It abandoned the policy in October 1975 on the grounds that it was ineffective, but the central bank's outright holdings of government debt were not fully eliminated until 1996.[13] Though this previous foray into bond-buying was useful ammunition for its critics, the Bundesbank had grounds to worry about acquiring risky peripheral as opposed to safe German debt since it would bear the single biggest share of any losses under the Eurosystem's risk-sharing arrangements.

Despite German opposition, the ECB authorised bond purchases between May 2010 and February 2012 whose value (based on what it had paid for the bonds) peaked at almost €220 billion, by which time the holdings included not just Greek, Irish and Portuguese bonds but much larger amounts of Italian and Spanish debt. Most of the bonds were on the books of the national central banks; the ECB itself acquired 8 per cent. The shifting pattern of purchases reflected the ebb and flow of the euro crisis, with two main phases of buying, the first in the middle of 2010 and then to a lesser extent towards the end of that year and at the start of 2011, as markets fretted about Greece, Ireland and Portugal; and then in the second half of 2011 as Italy and Spain caused alarm. The ECB did not disclose the breakdown until February 2013, a year after it had halted purchases and a few months after it formally ended the programme (in September 2012). It revealed that at the end of 2012, the value of the holdings stood at €209 billion, lower than at the peak owing to subsequent redemptions. Of this total, almost half (€99 billion) were Italian bonds; Spain accounted for €43.7 billion, Greece for €30.8 billion, Portugal for €21.6 billion and Ireland for €13.6 billion.[14]

But the SMP was not the only way in which the ECB was propping up the rickety currency union. Behind the scenes it was conducting a much bigger rescue than any financed through the hastily assembled bail-out funds. As the crisis showed no sign of subsiding, not only did private funding of balance-of-payments deficits on the periphery dry up but also capital took wings. Moreover, that capital flight was not just from the small economies in difficulty but also from the big countries in southern Europe. What happened next demonstrated how the euro area with its shared central bank was more robust than a fixed exchange-rate system.

A cessation of capital inflows and even more so the onset of capital flight typically sounded the death-knell of pegged currencies as the central bank in the afflicted country ran out of foreign-exchange reserves to defend the exchange rate. Such a 'sudden stop' caused currencies such as those of Thailand, Indonesia and South Korea to buckle in the Asian financial crisis of 1997–8.[15] But the euro area had a lifeline that could make up for the missing capital inflows and indeed cope with capital flight, as long as the Eurosystem was prepared to extend it. And that is what happened. As private funds were pulled out of the periphery and into the core, this was made possible by the peripheral central banks borrowing from the Bundesbank and other northern NCBs.[16]

The resulting positions within the Eurosystem were hidden in the entrails of the Target2 payments system (this had replaced the first-generation system in 2007–8).[17] Before the financial crisis, when private investors in the surplus countries were financing current-account deficits in peripheral Europe, the individual NCBs ran Target accounts that were broadly in balance (see Figure 11). However, during the euro crisis they ballooned. As the flight to safety in the core havens mounted, the Bundesbank in particular amassed a huge claim against the ECB, which peaked in August 2012 at €750 billion (worth over a quarter of German GDP) while the central banks of countries like Spain and Italy piled up big liabilities. Though the Bundesbank's position was easily the biggest, the Dutch and the Finnish central banks also accumulated big claims; the latter's at its peak was even higher as a share of GDP than the German central bank's.[18]

The emergence of these enormous claims and liabilities within the Eurosystem sparked a heated controversy after Hans-Werner Sinn, head of the Ifo Institute in Munich, drew attention to them in 2011. Sinn originally argued that they had built up since the financial crisis through financing current-account deficits on the periphery, whereas other economists interpreted them as the financing of abrupt capital flight.[19] In fact, depending upon the country and the time period, there was something in both explanations, as a subsequent analysis by economists at the BIS showed.[20] However, the actual pattern of the Target2 liabilities among the stressed economies on the periphery,

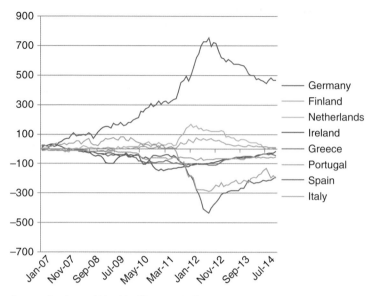

Source: Institute of Empirical Economic Research,
Osnabrück University

FIGURE 11  Target2 balances, € billion

which did not increase smoothly but rather jumped as fears mounted
about their viability, suggested that capital outflows were the dominant factor.[21] Ireland was an early case in point. Its pre-crisis current-
account deficit, which peaked at nearly 6 per cent of GDP in 2008, had
swung into a small surplus by 2010 and 2011 (see Figure 4). Yet
between the autumn of 2010 and the autumn of 2011, the Irish central
bank was the biggest Target2 debtor as Irish banks haemorrhaged
foreign deposits owing to capital flight. Where Ireland led, Italy followed with a spectacular jump in its Target2 debt from the summer of
2011 even though it continued to run a relatively small current-
account deficit. Since capital also began to flee Spain on an even bigger
scale, the Target2 balances within the Eurosystem soared.

From one perspective, the controversy was an unwarranted fuss
about internal bookkeeping arrangements within the Eurosystem. On

a consolidated basis – the position of the ECB itself – the sum of the claims held predominantly by the Bundesbank cancelled out the sum of the liabilities owed by the southern and Irish central banks. The weakness in this interpretation was that the ECB was not just a head office with regional branches. The NCBs had distinctive balance sheets reflecting their different histories (the Bundesbank's was stuffed with gold) and their governing boards had their own specific national responsibilities for which they (and not the ECB) could be held accountable.[22] It was this autonomy for example that allowed them to provide emergency liquidity assistance. As the ECB itself pointed out in 2002, there was 'a dense network of relations between NCBs and the political institutions of their respective countries', which included annual reports and parliamentary hearings.[23] And although all the NCBs were independent that did not stop national finance ministries worrying about having to meet capital shortfalls in their central banks. Though some economists argued that central banks could never go broke, this was a hard sell and central bankers worried about the cost to their credibility if institutions that were supposed to embody financial rectitude themselves went into the red.[24] Moreover, national governments were keen on pocketing their central banks' shares of the Eurosystem's monetary income.

Reflecting the NCBs' continuing national role, the external positions on their balance sheets were included under balance-of-payments and national-accounting rules in scoring the net international investment position (NIIP), the net balance for any one country of assets held abroad and national liabilities to foreigners. The borrowing done by the Central Bank of Ireland through the Target2 system, which peaked at €145 billion, nearly 90 per cent of GDP, at the end of 2010, and stayed high in the following year, counted against Ireland's external indebtedness, contributing to a negative NIIP position of over 100 per cent of GDP in 2011.[25] Correspondingly, the Target2 credits extended by the Bundesbank were scored as part of Germany's external assets, contributing to its positive NIIP position of 35 per cent of GDP in 2012.[26] The story told by the national accounts was a very different one from the one dismissing Target2 balances as internal entries in the Eurosystem's books. What they revealed was that in the core countries of the euro area, the official sector was conducting a discreet yet enormous bail-out of private creditors through their central banks.

The two perspectives could be reconciled. As long as the euro area remained a going concern, the national central banks' claims on and liabilities to the ECB were notional and did not represent a separate source of risk. The build-up of the Target balances was a symptom of the tensions within the euro area rather than a problem in themselves. What mattered for the Eurosystem as a whole was the credit risk that had been taken in the debtor countries in lending to their banks and any losses arising from that.

That credit risk had increased a lot as the ECB kept on easing the conditions for collateral against which it lent. Among a myriad of changes, the most important was the decision taken in October 2008 to lower the minimum credit quality threshold required for most assets to be eligible from A– to BBB– (the lowest investment-grade rating), from at least one of the four credit-rating agencies that the ECB recognised. Though this was supposed to last only until the end of 2009, it stuck. Moreover, starting with Greece in May 2010, even the minimum threshold was suspended for bonds issued or guaranteed by governments in countries complying with the terms of a rescue programme. Rules on the eligibility of asset-backed securities (ABSs) were relaxed in December 2011 and again in June 2012. A sign of both the increasing riskiness of the collateral being accepted, and the efforts being made to mitigate that risk was that the average haircut applied to collateral rose from 3 per cent at the start of 2008 to 14 per cent in early 2013.[27]

But if the currency club were to break up then worries about the increased credit risk of accepting more dubious collateral would appear quaint compared with the potential losses that might arise on the Target2 positions. What had been internal Eurosystem accounting entries would become anything but notional since debtor NCBs in the exiting and devaluing countries would be unable to honour their pledges to the ECB. In principle, any losses would be shared among the remaining NCBs according to their capital keys. If that were the case, the fact that the Bundesbank's Target2 position was swelling so ominously would not matter since its key was 27 per cent.[28] Such orderly burden-sharing might work in the event of a limited fragmentation of the euro zone. If it were to disintegrate, however, the rules could be difficult to enforce, leaving the Bundesbank – and indirectly German taxpayers – facing enormous potential losses on its exposure.

Unnervingly, the only way to avoid such an outcome was to keep raising the stakes against those betting on the euro's downfall. Under Draghi, the ECB did just that. In December 2011, just one month after he had taken over from Trichet, the central bank moved decisively to avert an impending funding crisis for both banks and governments. In the first quarter of 2012, banks were due to repay €230 billion in bonds they had issued while sovereign financing requirements were around €300 billion.[29] That posed a mortal danger to banks and governments in the stressed economies since unnerved northern private creditors were no longer prepared to meet these needs.

The ECB's response was to offer banks unprecedentedly long funding. Whereas normal lending to banks was on a weekly basis, with funding also regularly provided at maturities of three months in 'longer term refinancing operations' (LTROs), the longest term on ECB lending had previously been one year, made available on three occasions, from the middle until the end of 2009, mostly in June.[30] In Trichet's final month at the helm, the ECB announced another round of one-year operations, the first of which was to take place that October and the second in December.[31] But in December 2011, the ECB pledged instead to provide three-year loans. The cost to banks was negligible since they were charged the average of the ECB's main lending rate over that period, during which it fell from 1 per cent to 0.05 per cent.[32] In two such dollops of funding, one later that month (which replaced the second of the planned one-year liquidity operations) and one at the end of February 2012, the ECB lent banks €489 billion and €530 billion. Together that took its total three-year provision of funding to an extraordinary €1 trillion (amounting to 3 per cent of the euro-zone banking balance sheet and equivalent to 10 per cent of euro-zone GDP). Since a big chunk of this was used to replace other shorter term funding, the net increase in liquidity was not so large, but the ECB's balance sheet still rose by an impressive €500 billion between mid December 2011, before the two three-year LTROs, and March, after them.[33]

The LTROs were a lifeline for the embattled banks and sovereigns of southern Europe. Italian and Spanish banks each acounted for around €300 billion of the total €1 trillion of long-term funding.[34] By the spring of 2012, the infusion of long-term liquidity into the banking system appeared to have restored calm to the euro area. Another reason to be more optimistic was that there were new governments in both Italy and Spain, the two peripheral economies that were of most concern to European policymakers due to their size. But the apparent tranquillity was deceptive. By the summer of 2012, the crisis was raging even more fiercely than in late 2011 when Italy, still under Berlusconi, teetered on the brink. But this time it was Spain that was in the sights of the bond vigilantes, so much so that it seemed to be heading inexorably to a full bail-out similar to those already necessary for Greece, Ireland and Portugal.

Spain was in trouble for a number of reasons. Despite the commanding majority that Mariano Rajoy had won in the election in November 2011, the new Spanish prime minister was maladroit in his first few months of office. His prevarications compared unfavourably with the prompt measures taken by Monti's government in late 2011. In particular, although Rajoy pushed through an important labour market reform, he failed to exploit the comparative calm in financial markets at the start of 2012 by owning up swiftly to the problems facing Spanish banks, concentrated among the *cajas*. By the time their losses came to the fore, in the spring, it was too late. Moreover, Spain's public finances remained stricken as the budget deficit stayed stubbornly high, actually rising from 9.4 per cent of GDP in 2011 (the same as in 2010) to 10.3 per cent in 2012.[35] Indeed, a comparison of the IMF's forecasts in April and October 2012 for that year revealed that among thirty advanced economies, Spain's budget balance had deteriorated the most.[36]

High external indebtedness also made Spain vulnerable. Its liabilities to foreign creditors exceeded its foreign assets by 90 per cent of GDP in 2012, up from around 30 per cent in 1999. Italy's position was much more favourable, owing a net 29 per cent of GDP, having deteriorated only a little from owing a net 5 per cent when joining the euro. This was a clear demarcation line between the two big economies of southern Europe. Disconcertingly for Spain, it was in the same camp as the smaller peripheral countries before they had to be bailed out. In 2009, the external balance sheets of Greece, Ireland and Portugal had shown negative positions of 86, 89 and 108 per cent of GDP, respectively.[37]

By the summer of 2012, the euro crisis was more virulent than ever and looked set to claim Spain as its next and most important victim. Even though Spain secured €100 billion of euro-zone rescue money in June to deal with its troubled banks, its ten-year government bond yields touched 7.75 per cent in late July. Even worse, two-year yields briefly went above 7 per cent, constraining the Spanish government's ability to borrow in anything other than short-term Treasury bills (letras). The Spanish sickness was infectious: Italian ten-year bonds went above 6.5 per cent.[38]

It was at this point that Draghi delivered arguably the most successful verbal intervention ever made by a central banker. In unscripted remarks at an investment conference in London, the ECB's president said that the political capital being invested in the single currency was underestimated, declared that the euro was 'irreversible', and then uttered his historic pledge: 'Within our mandate, the ECB is ready to do whatever it takes to preserve the euro. And believe me, it will be enough.'[39] A few days later when presenting the first sketchy details of what that shoot-from-the-hip commitment might mean in practice, Draghi spelt out his message about irreversibility: there would be 'no going back to the lira or the drachma or to any other currency. It is pointless to bet against the euro.' It was pointless 'because the euro will stay and it is irreversible'.[40]

What this would require was an undertaking to unleash, if necessary, the ECB's money-creating power to buy bonds without limit on the markets. Draghi's experience when working at Goldman Sachs meant that he understood the mentality of traders. A credible commitment to purchase unlimited amounts of bonds could in itself bring to heel investors betting on a break-up of the euro without it necessarily ever having to be carried through. For such a policy to command credibility, Draghi, who had led from the front in London before getting support from the bank's governing council, had to build a convincing consensus to back his proposal. Since Weidmann was bound to oppose such an initiative (though not necessarily by invoking Goethe's *Faust*) what this entailed was a diplomatic offensive to peel away the governors of northern creditor countries who normally sided with the Bundesbank, such as Finland's Erkki Liikanen. Draghi was able to achieve this for two main reasons. First, the gravity of the situation and an instinct for self-preservation concentrated minds. If the ECB did not act, the crisis might become uncontrollable and consign the central bank and the euro to history as another failed currency union. And second, Draghi could offer a convincing rationale, which drew in particular on De Grauwe's influential analysis.

This research had pinpointed the reason why euro-zone governments in the embattled peripheral economies had become so vulnerable in the bond markets. Clearly, there were specific reasons why Spain was under attack, whereas Germany was a haven. The housing and construction bust had wounded Spanish banks, and their plight threatened the state itself owing to the costs of cleaning them up. By contrast, Germany had escaped the housing bubble altogether, and its economy recovered strongly from the spring of 2009 (although it then faltered during the euro-zone double-dip recession). Even so, the markets' polarised treatment of the two economies was hard to reconcile with the fact that the pre-crisis starting point for Spanish public debt in 2007, of 36 per cent of GDP, was considerably lower than Germany's 64 per cent.[41] Nor was it self-evident why Spain should be treated so much more harshly than the UK, outside the euro, which became a haven during the euro crisis even though it had also experienced a burst housing bubble and its entire banking system came close to collapse in the financial crisis.

The explanation was that by joining the euro states lost more than the ability to change their exchange rate and to set interest rates according to the needs of their domestic economies. They also started to issue debt in what was in effect a foreign currency. In the first decade of the euro, this worked to the advantage of formerly distrusted economies in southern Europe by lowering their borrowing costs, but it left them cruelly exposed once bondholders took fright. By forfeiting monetary independence, their central banks could no longer act as a lender of last resort, not just to their banks but also to their sovereigns, stripping away from private bondholders the assurance that, come what may, they would be repaid. 'The absence of such a guarantee makes the sovereign bond markets in a monetary union prone to liquidity crises and contagion', argued De Grauwe, comparing this vulnerability to banking systems before central banks became lenders of last resort to banks.[42] The vulnerability was exacerbated as markets started to fear the worst, a break-up of the monetary union.

When Draghi's 'whatever it takes' pledge was formalised as OMT in September 2012, the new bond-purchase undertaking replaced that lost safeguard for countries in trouble. The bland designation, 'outright monetary transactions', belied its clout, which Draghi was keen to highlight. The central bank chief presented it as a counter to break-up worries – 'unfounded fears of reversibility'. Large parts of the euro area, he said, were in a 'bad equilibrium', namely one where there could be 'self-fulfilling expectations that feed upon themselves and generate very adverse scenarios'. That made a case for intervening to 'break' these expectations, which concerned not just specific countries but the euro area as a whole.[43]

At the heart of OMT was a simple commitment: 'no *ex ante* quantitative limits' would be set on the size of the purchases. This was the godfather moment for the bond markets, the horse's head in the bed to terrify them into submission. It made OMT quite different from the SMP, which had not included any such threat and whose intermittent interventions had in practice been quite limited. Moreover, the policy was not a temporary programme like the SMP. On the face of it, OMT appeared more restricted than the SMP with respect to the maturity of the bonds eligible for purchase, which would be confined to debt with a residual maturity of between one and three years. But that commitment applied to all bonds, whatever their original term, which were within that range of redemption. The new policy thus provided something similar to the implicit protection for bondholders that had been removed when states joined the euro and in so doing created what Draghi called a 'backstop' to counter fears that the single-currency zone might disintegrate.

The effectiveness of the backstop was enhanced by another feature of OMT that distinguished it from the SMP. The ECB's insistence on preferred-creditor status in the restructuring of Greek debt contributed to the worsening in the euro crisis in the middle of 2012 since it set a precedent for what might happen in other countries where the Eurosystem had also bought bonds. In effect, these purchases had pushed the remaining private bondholders down the credit hierarchy and that increased risk was reflected in higher yields. If bonds were bought on similar terms through OMT, it might be self-defeating. Investors still holding the debt would fear that the new purchases would make them more vulnerable in the event of a default because it would be imposed upon the diminishing share of the debt in private hands. To avoid this danger, the ECB said that bonds acquired through OMT would rank the same – *pari passu* – as those of private creditors.

The final difference with the SMP was that OMT would be expressly linked to 'conditionality': states would not be eligible unless they were complying with one of two forms of euro-zone assistance programmes that set conditions in return for the help and were closely monitored. One was the type requiring deep economic and fiscal adjustments and reforms as the *quid pro quo* for the bail-outs. The other was more limited, a precautionary form of support that euro area leaders had decided to add to the armoury of the rescue funds in July 2011, making available lines of credit subject to less onerous conditions but still requiring strict surveillance.[44] Both had to include the possibility of rescue-fund purchases of a state's debt in primary markets. Being in such a programme would not, however, lead automatically to OMT since the ECB retained full discretion over the policy.

When Draghi unveiled the policy to the press on 6 September, the first question was whether the governing council had unanimously backed it. No, was the answer: there was 'one dissenting view'. There were no prizes for guessing who that might be. But the fact that Weidmann was alone in opposing OMT mattered. Draghi was fortunate that Stark had been replaced by Asmussen, who was ready to do whatever it took to back Draghi's 'whatever it takes' pledge. Even so, Weidmann represented more than just one vote. As he himself said in remarks pointedly posted on the Bundesbank website over the summer: 'We are the largest and most important central bank in the Eurosystem and we have a greater say than many other central banks in the Eurosystem.'[45] What proved fatal for Weidmann's campaign was that the policy secured the support of Merkel whose decision to back Draghi against the wishes of the Bundesbank was crucial in lending authority to OMT.

The weapon had been primed, but for it to be fired a country had to apply for support from a euro-zone rescue fund. As Spain continued to struggle in the autumn of 2012, Draghi appeared impatient for Rajoy to make the necessary application (the support for Spain's financial sector did not make it eligible for OMT), so that the ECB could turn words into action. When the governing council decamped in October to Brdo castle near Ljubljana, the Slovenian capital, on the second of its twice-a-year outings from Frankfurt, the ECB's president declared in martial tones: 'We are ready with our OMTs. We have a fully effective backstop mechanism in place, once all the prerequisites are in place as well.'[46]

For the ECB, the 'prerequisites' meant that a state was willing to carry out the terms of a rescue programme – the necessary though not sufficient condition for it to launch OMT. But for governments applying for such help, the 'prerequisites' meant political pain and national humiliation. Politicians in the creditor nations could also expect a hard time in their national parliaments when making further requests to send more money south. Both Rajoy, a procrastinator by nature, and Merkel, who also tended to defer decisions, opted to wait and see.[47] Their caution paid off as bond yields started to subside. Before long the ECB, too, began to see the merits of OMT being a deterrent rather than being deployed since as long as it remained unused its actual power could not be measured, which if anything made it all the more potent. Extraordinarily, the policy that had saved the euro in the acute phase of the crisis and was subsequently to feature in legal battles at the highest level in Germany and Europe lacked any formal documentation beyond a short press release (fewer than five hundred words) detailing its technical features when Draghi announced it in September 2012.

Nonetheless, OMT remained bitterly controversial in Germany. Weidmann might have been overruled, but his role as president of the Bundesbank, a still revered institution for many Germans, gave him a pulpit to express his continuing disapproval. Indeed, it was shortly after Draghi unveiled the policy that Weidmann invoked Goethe's *Faust* to illustrate the perils of central bank power. The Bundesbank's opposition was visceral since it contested the central rationale for the policy. Asked in September 2012 whether it was for the ECB to decide that the single currency was irreversible, Draghi declared that this fell 'squarely within our mandate'. But the Bundesbank argued that it was not the role of the central bank to keep the monetary union together; that was the prerogative of the still sovereign states that belonged to it and their citizens.[48]

Such a clash between the presidents of the ECB and of the Bundesbank, which Draghi had so extolled when taking up office, was unprecedented. And although the Bundesbank had been over-ruled, not just by the governing council of the ECB but also by Merkel, what mattered now was that another great power in the land was taking an interest, the German constitutional court based in Karlsruhe, whose scarlet-robed judges struck fear into the hearts of the country's rulers, including the chancellor herself. German citizens opposed to OMT turned to the court, bringing a case against the policy on the grounds that it flouted the German constitution ('Basic Law'). Quite what business it was of the German court to consider the case at all given that the ECB was a European institution and therefore sub-ject to the European Court of Justice (ECJ) in Luxembourg was open to question. But the court had reserved the right to check whether a European institution was overreaching the terms on which Germany had transferred powers to it.[49] Public hearings in June 2013 featured a gladiatorial spectacle as the two German members on the ECB's council put their respective cases, Asmussen defending the policy and Weidmann arguing against it.[50]

The court had developed a habit of baring its teeth rather than biting in previous cases challenging the government's actions fight-ing the euro crisis. The judges had for example sanctioned controver-sial measures such as the original Greek loans and the creation of the rescue funds in May 2010 despite the no-bail-out clause in the European treaties because Germany's contributions to the assistance were subject to parliamentary control.[51] That led the markets to expect another 'yes, but' verdict, but they were wrongfooted. When the court finally delivered its provisional judgment, in February 2014, which was backed by six out of the eight judges (the other two declar-ing that the case should have been rejected as inadmissible), it ruled that the ECB had exceeded its powers when adopting OMT and that the doctrine violated the ban on monetary financing of government budgets.[52]

At the hearings in June 2013, Asmussen had argued that OMT complied with the ECB's mandate, the use of monetary policy to secure price stability, because it was designed to restore the effectiveness of interest rate decisions made by the central bank. In parts of the euro area, 'the steering of monetary policy was not functioning fully, or was in part not functioning at all', he said, adding that 'the key interest rate had lost its key function'. The OMT policy was the 'necessary and appropriate step to eliminate the disruption in the transmission of monetary policy caused by concerns that there would be an unwanted break-up of the euro'.[53] The German court was unimpressed by this defence, arguing that OMT was an economic rather than monetary policy, which breached the ECB's mandate since under European law it could not pursue its own independent economic policy. The judges reached this view because the purchases would favour only some states, whereas the ECB's monetary policy was not supposed to differentiate between the various members of the currency union. In this context, the policy appeared functionally equivalent to bail-outs 'without their parliamentary legitimation and monitoring'. And the court found that the policy in effect gave the ECB the power to remedy any deterioration in countries' credit ratings, which 'would largely suspend the prohibition of monetary financing of the budget'.

Despite the harsh verdict, financial markets took it in their stride, focusing on the fact that, in an unprecedented step for a court jealous of its powers, the German judges had referred the case to the ECJ. Since the Luxembourg court was reliably integrationist, it was expected to back the ECB. A preliminary opinion in January 2015 from Pedro Cruz Villalón, an advocate general at the ECJ, duly found in the ECB's favour, ruling that OMT was compatible, in principle, with European Treaty law. Villalón backed the ECB's view that OMT lay within its mandate, finding that it was 'an unconventional monetary-policy measure'. As important, he said that the OMT policy could be carried out without infringing the ban on monetary financing.[54] Though Villalón's opinion was not binding on the ECJ, the ruling of an advocate general normally pointed in the direction of its eventual judgment. But even if this transpired, this would not necessarily end the legal dispute since the German court's decision to refer the case to the ECJ did not mean deferring to it. According to De Witte, the German judges had not thrown in the towel; rather they would take the ECJ's views into account when reaching their final rather than provisional judgment.[55]

A clash between the courts looked likely because Villalón dug his heels in on two of the three conditions that the German court had in effect set out as a possible compromise. His ruling was arguably consistent with one of them, which stated rather vaguely that 'interferences with price formation on the market are to be avoided where possible'. The advocate general said that the policy must be carried out and in particular timed in such a way that the ECB's interventions in secondary markets did not become blurred with the primary markets, where governments raise fresh funds. He also ruled that if OMT were implemented, which could occur only for countries in a rescue programme, the ECB would at that point have to detach itself from all direct involvement in monitoring the programme, since otherwise that could call into doubt OMT's credentials as a distinct monetary-policy measure. But Villalón rejected the second condition set by the German court, that the ECB should enjoy superior status to other creditors rather than be on an equal footing with them. And he gave short shrift to the third stipulation, that purchases should not be unlimited. Both proposals, he declared, entailed the risk of 'seriously calling into question the effectiveness of the OMT programme'.[56]

The legal dispute over OMT thus remained unresolved in early 2015, with both courts still due to pass their final verdicts. There might still be scope for compromise. Although the issue of the creditor status of the ECB would be tricky to finesse, it might be possible to fudge the issue of limits, owing to the fact that while the buying might be unlimited *ex ante* it would necessarily be limited *ex post*. Indeed,

Asmussen had said at the hearing in June 2013 that 'the design of OMTs makes it clear to everyone that the programme is effectively limited, for one by the restrictions to the shorter part of the yield curve and the resulting limited pool of bonds which may actually be purchased'. The opinion submitted to the court by Frank Schorkopf of Göttingen University on behalf of the ECB gave a figure of €524 billion in December 2012 for that pool of debt in the one–three year range for Italy (accounting for almost two-thirds of it), Spain, Portugal and Ireland, not all of which would be bought by any means.[57]

Assuming that the ECJ's actual judgment followed the advocate general's opinion, as occurred in June 2015, the German court might nonetheless stood its ground when passing its own final judgment, based as before on whether OMT flouted Germany's constitution. If the Karlsruhe judges did dig in their heels, they could try to stop the Bundesbank from participating in the policy if it were ever implemented. Though the ECB could insist that OMT was still intact since the purchases could be made by other central banks, such a legal conflict would corrode the credibility of both the policy and the monetary union.

Yet, arguably, the judicial jousting was beside the point, not least since in time-honoured legal fashion it took so long (which some cynics thought was the point). Whatever its legality, the unused policy of OMT had already served its purpose by turning the tide in the markets, although other factors had contributed to the rally, not least the further flood of liquidity into global markets following the Fed's decision to start a third programme of quantitative easing just days after the ECB's announcement of OMT in early September 2012.[58] Moreover, even if the full purport of the German court's ruling had initially been misinterpreted, the markets still had grounds for brushing it aside by the time it was eventually handed down, for by early 2014 OMT had become largely irrelevant to investors. Another market play was in hand: an increasing expectation that the ECB would itself eventually have to introduce quantitative easing to tackle low inflation. If that were the case, peripheral debt markets would get

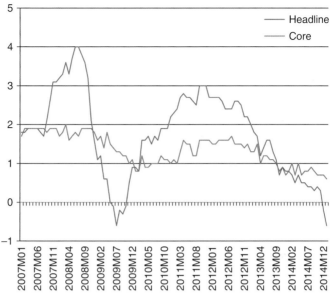

Notes: *Changing composition
      **Excludes energy, food, alcohol and tobacco.
Source: Eurostat

FIGURE 12  Euro area* consumer prices, headline and core**, per cent
change on a year earlier, 2007 to January 2015

another boost regardless of the fate of OMT. And markets being for-
ward-looking, the smart strategy was to anticipate the effect of QE and
to buy ahead of the ECB.

The fall in inflation that gave a second wind to the bond-
market rally on the periphery took the ECB by surprise. In the
middle of 2013, the Eurosystem's staff were forecasting inflation
of 1.3 per cent in 2014; the outcome was a mere 0.4 per cent.[59] The
unexpected tumble in inflation occurred in the autumn of 2013 as
the headline rate fell from 1.6 per cent in July to just 0.7 per cent
by October (see Figure 12). As it weakened further in 2014, it
became clear that Lagarde's diagnosis in April 2014 had been accurate: the euro area was indeed suffering from lowflation. Although
the collapse in the world oil price in the second half of 2014 was

responsible for the onset of outright deflation at the end of the year, core prices, which excluded energy along with food, alcohol and tobacco, revealed a more troubling underlying weakness. Core inflation dropped from around 1.5 per cent in 2012 to euro-era lows of 0.7 per cent at the end of 2013 and for much of 2014; in January 2015 it fell to 0.6 per cent.

The collapse in inflation was a triple blow to the euro area. For one thing, it made the task of regaining competitiveness on the periphery harder. Just as Germany had regained its competitive edge in the pre-crisis era by keeping its path of inflation below that of the periphery, so the easiest way for the periphery to win back the ground it had lost would be by containing price pressures while German inflation now ran higher than usual. But since German inflation itself fell below 1 per cent in 2014, the crisis countries did not have the same room for manoeuvre. In August 2014, for example, when inflation was 0.4 per cent across the euro area, and 0.8 per cent in Germany, prices were falling in six members of the currency club. These included Italy and Spain, the third– and fourth largest euro-zone economies, where prices were falling at an annual rate of 0.2 per cent and 0.5 per cent, respectively.[60]

The second way in which subsiding inflation and the threat, or reality, of deflation were a menace was because of the high level of indebtedness in the euro zone's troubled economies. With the exception of some inflation-linked government bonds, private and public debt were obligations set in nominal terms. This meant that if prices were now falling in some countries, the real value of debt was actually rising. Ultralow inflation also hurt borrowers because the incomes and revenues servicing their debts were rising less than they had expected when they took out the loans.[61] The fall in inflation and associated decline in inflation expectations had a third harmful effect. Since there was now little scope to lower nominal rates, which were already close to the zero bound, real interest rates would rise, thus inadvertently tightening monetary policy, as Draghi stressed at the ECB's press conference in December 2014.[62]

As inflation lurched down in late 2013, the ECB had three main possible remedies. One was to cut interest rates again, if necessary moving them into negative territory since they were already so low. The second was to pump more liquidity into the banking system, if possible directing it to the real economy rather than supporting government bonds, as had happened before. The third was to conduct full-blooded QE, which would entail buying sovereign bonds since they were the only asset class large enough to allow bulk purchases. It was clear that QE would be the remedy of last resort. In December 2013, Yves Mersch, a member of the executive board, highlighted the lack of a central government for the euro area whose debt the ECB could buy and said that although it could purchase a basket of the individual governments' bonds 'this would pose immense economic, legal and political challenges'.[63] The story of the year that followed was how the ECB was forced ever closer to overcoming those 'immense' challenges as the first two policies looked increasingly inadequate, concluding in the historic decision at the start of 2015 to embark upon QE in March that year.

Already, in November 2013, the ECB had cut its main lending rate, from 0.5 to just 0.25 per cent. This eased conditions for banks on the periphery that continued to rely upon central bank funding. But it barely affected those in the core that could fund themselves in the money markets for which the crucial rate was the ECB's deposit rate, which formed a floor and had stood at zero since July 2012. The question was whether the ECB would dare to move into negative territory, in effect charging banks for depositing money with it. This would be an unprecedented move for a big central bank, although the Danish central bank had already adopted the policy – the first time one of its interest rates had gone negative in its nearly 200-year history – on the same day that the ECB lowered its deposit rate to zero in July 2012. Danmarks Nationalbank had responded later that afternoon by taking this historic step in order to fend off unwelcome upward pressure on the krone, which was pegged to the euro, at a time when confidence in the single currency was at a low because of break-up fears.[64]

Unlike Denmark's central bank, the ECB was not seeking to defend a fixed exchange rate, and the exchange rate was not a policy target, as Draghi on occasions had to point out.[65] However, it was desirable to bring the euro down because its appreciation after OMT had restored confidence in the single currency's viability contributed to the fall in inflation. A further argument in favour of going negative was that the move might regalvanise the interbank market, since banks in countries like Germany that were flush with funds would now lose money if they simply parked the spare cash at the ECB, giving them a sharper incentive to lend again to banks on the periphery. Set against these possible gains, the effect of the policy in squeezing bank profits could make it counter-productive.[66]

Despite this potential disadvantage, the ECB did finally pluck up its courage and introduce negative interest rates in June as well as cutting the main lending rate again. After further reductions in September 2014, the deposit rate stood at minus 0.2 per cent while the lending rate was just 0.05 per cent. The main effect was to bring down the euro. In the spring of 2014, the single currency was trading at close to $1.40 – around 6 per cent up on its value a year earlier and some 15 per cent above the low that it had reached shortly before Draghi's 'whatever it takes' pledge. By the start of November, it had fallen below $1.25, a decline of 10 per cent since early May, and its lowest for over two years. Though the depreciation was in part a reflection of a resurgent dollar, the euro had fallen by 4 per cent on a trade-weighted basis over the same period. Moreover, Draghi had gone out of his way to emphasise that monetary policy in the euro zone was 'on a diverging path' to that of the Fed, the one still easing, the other heading towards tightening once its programme of asset purchases was fully phased out, which duly occurred at the end of October.[67]

As well as lowering interest rates into negative territory for the first time, the ECB had also adopted the second of its remedies, a new long-term lending programme to banks. This resembled the Bank of England's 'funding for lending' scheme, introduced in July 2012 in order to foster lending to firms and households by relieving the rising costs of British bank funding stressed by the worsening euro crisis.[68] Unlike the three-year funding provided by the ECB in the winter of 2011–12, which banks had used to buy sovereign bonds, the new initiative aimed to stimulate lending to the private sector – non-financial firms and households, excluding mortgages; hence the scheme was called targeted longer term refinancing operations (TLTROs).[69]

Starting in the autumn, the ECB offered long-term funding, stretching until September 2018, in two stages. In the first two operations, in September and December 2014, banks would be able to borrow up to 7 per cent of their stock of eligible loans (those in the 'targeted' category). Then in six further operations, each quarter in 2015 and the first half of 2016, extra funding would be linked to the flow of bank net lending. The terms were very generous. Initially, the rate was fixed at the main lending rate plus ten basis points, meaning that banks could borrow at just 0.15 per cent a year. Then the ECB decided in January 2015 to remove even that wafer-thin margin for the remaining six operations, meaning that banks could borrow at a nugatory 0.05 per cent. The only condition was that the banks receiving the loans should improve their lending record to the private sector, a benchmark calculated in such a way that some could qualify even if their loans fell at a more moderate rate than before.[70] If banks failed to comply with their benchmarks, the penalty was no more than a slap on the wrist in that they would have to repay the funding to the ECB early, in September 2016.

The further relaxation in the terms in January 2015 reflected the fact that the new scheme had got off to a poor start. The first two operations allowed banks to borrow up to €400 billion. However, the take-up in September and December 2014 was little more than half that, amounting to just €212 billion.[71] What this suggested was that the constraint on credit lay less in the supply of loans from banks (and, indirectly, in their funding costs) and more in the demand from borrowers.

This did not prevent the ECB from taking further steps to try to spur bank lending to the private sector. In September, it announced that it would buy both covered bonds, issued by banks and backed by mortgages and loans to the public sector, and asset-backed securities. The decision to purchase covered bonds was uncontroversial since the ECB had gone down this route before, having bought €60 billion between mid 2009 and mid 2010. It had also launched another programme of purchases worth €40 billion at the end of 2011, although in the event it bought less than half of that as the initiative was in effect superseded by the big three-year loans of December 2011 and February 2012.[72]

A snag in trying to help banks by buying covered bonds was that the help was misdirected, going mainly to countries whose banks did not require assistance. Spain was the only peripheral economy with a big covered bond market. Within the euro area, the use of covered bonds was most prominent in Germany and accordingly it was German banks that would benefit the most from the ECB's purchases.[73] This was one reason why the ECB decided also to buy ABSs as well. More generally, together with the Bank of England, it was striving to revitalise the impaired European securitisation market in order to widen the range of funding sources for banks and to provide alternatives to bank lending for businesses.[74]

The ABS-buying initiative which started in late November, a month after the new covered bond purchase programme, aroused concern, especially in Germany. Critics of the ECB, such as Sinn, accused it of a further lurch towards becoming a bail-out agency.[75] The commotion was unwarranted since default rates on securitisations had been much lower in Europe than in the US.[76] In fact, the real criticism was that the stunted size of the market meant that the ECB could not buy that much anyway. Although the covered bond market was considerably bigger, it was not large enough to allow the central bank to make the scale of purchases needed to ramp up its balance sheet and ease monetary conditions further in the euro area. The crux of the matter was that the central bank was trying to fight lowflation from a position of unilateral disarmament by treating full-blooded quantitative easing, which would involve buying sovereign bonds, as the weapon of last resort.

Although controversial at the time, the big QE programmes launched by the Fed in late 2008 and the Bank of England in early 2009 had not stoked up inflation as some had feared. An upsurge in British inflation in 2011, when it briefly went above 5 per cent, was largely caused by temporary factors such as a rebound in commodity prices and the rise in VAT in January of that year.[77] Five years after their QE programmes had begun, inflation in both the US and the UK was unusually subdued, with consumer prices rising by 1.4 and 1.7 per cent, respectively, in the year to the first quarter of 2014.[78] Yet subsequent analysis of their impact did suggest that they had helped to bolster the American and British economies at a time when their central banks had run out of room to lower policy interest rates any further.[79]

Given the international experience of conducting QE and the reality of euro-zone lowflation, the economic case for adopting the policy was a 'no-brainer', according to one top international economic official. The obstacle was a familiar one, arising from the exceptional status of the ECB as a central bank without a state. When the Bank of England embarked upon QE, it confined its purchases almost entirely to gilts, the bonds issued by the British government. Similarly, the Fed bought US Treasuries, or mortgage-backed securities that were in effect guaranteed by the federal government. Both American and British sovereign bonds were highly rated, even if they had been downgraded in the aftermath of the financial crisis.

By contrast, the euro area was marked by extreme variation in the quality of its sovereign debt. In January 2015, just two countries – Germany and Luxembourg – retained AAA status from the three main agencies (Fitch, Moody's and S&P). At the other end of the spectrum, three states were rated as junk, notably Cyprus and Greece, but also Portugal, though it was only just below investment grade (DBRS, a fourth agency, rated it above junk, which meant under the ECB's rules that Portuguese debt remained eligible as collateral). Italy was rated

BBB-, the lowest investment-grade rating, by S&P following a down-grade in December 2014.[80] This variation in credit quality meant that a broad programme of QE under the ECB's usual risk-sharing arrange-ment would be much riskier for the central banks of sound countries than those of the less creditworthy ones. Indeed, such a venture could be interpreted as the backdoor creation of implicit eurobonds by the ECB.

After months of acrimonious debate within the council, the ECB eventually found a way forward at a momentous meeting in January 2015. The programme of buying private assets launched in late 2014 was extended to encompass sovereign bonds and debt issued by European institutions, increasing its scale by an order of magni-tude, from purchases averaging about €12 billion a month of private assets (mostly covered bonds) to €60 billion a month. In all, the ECB pledged to buy €1.14 trillion of financial assets by creating money in the nineteen months between March 2015 and September 2016. Of this, around €200 billion would come from the existing covered bond and ABS programmes. Of the additional €900 billion through the new public-sector asset purchase programme, 12 per cent would be debt securities issued by European institutions such as the venerable European Investment Bank, the rescue funds established during the crisis and other international organisations located in the euro area. The lion's share, of around €800 billion, would consist of sovereign bonds issued by the euro-zone states.[81]

The ECB's decision to embark upon QE might have been delayed but it was on a bigger scale and over a longer period than many had expected. Moreover, the ECB indicated that its undertaking might be open-ended. Draghi said that the purchases were intended to be carried out until the end of September 2016 and would 'in any case be con-ducted until we see a sustained adjustment in the path of inflation' consistent with achieving the aim of nearly 2 per cent. As the policy became ever-more likely in late 2014 and then was finally unveiled in January 2015, it paid early dividends in a lower euro, which fell to $1.14 on the day of the announcement and then even further, reaching lows of around $1.05 in mid March after the buying began. That represented a fall of almost 25 per cent from its level twelve months earlier; the trade-weighted exchange rate was down by 14 per cent over the same period. Whatever Draghi's disavowals of an explicit exchange-rate policy, the ECB appeared to be very keen on a lower euro, which was one of the main ways QE was expected to stimulate the euro-zone economy.

The combination of a cheaper currency and the stimulus from falling energy prices seemed to be working in early 2015, as confidence revived and the Euro zone economy grew by 0.4 per cent in the first quarter.[82] Even so, there were grounds for caution about the policy's longer term success. The size of euro-zone QE was still considerably smaller, at 11 per cent of GDP, than asset-purchase programmes conducted elsewhere; the Bank of England's eventual purchases of £375 billion were twice as large as a share of GDP. And QE was inherently less potent in an economy still dominated by banks than in one like the US where capital markets were so much more prominent.

Moreover, the ECB's council was able to overcome German objections to QE only by undermining a central risk-sharing principle in its monetary-policy regime. Some restrictions were necessary, notably to deal with Greece, due to hold the election just three days later that brought Syriza to power. The ECB set rules that in effect ensured there would be no purchases of Greek bonds in the immediate future.[83] Countries in bail-out programmes whose compliance was being reviewed, as was the case for Greece, would not be eligible. Moreover, a limit of 33 per cent on the amount of a country's bonds that could be purchased also excluded Greece given the Eurosystem's existing holdings of Greek sovereign debt.

However, the governing council went well beyond these specific rules to a more fundamental retreat from the usual risk-sharing arrangements. These would continue to apply to the acquisition of European and international debt. But the far bigger purchases of euro-zone sovereign debt would be handled quite differently. The capital keys would continue to determine how much debt was bought, meaning that German bunds would make up a quarter. But rather than each of the NCBs buying euro-zone sovereign debt across the board and parcelling out the risk according to the capital keys, they would instead confine their purchases to their own governments' debt with each bearing the risk of any losses on it. A mutualisation of risk on the €800 billion or so of euro-zone sovereign bonds to be bought through QE would be confined to buying carried out by the ECB itself, amounting to 8 per cent of the total public-sector purchase programme. The purchases by NCBs of securities issued by international institutions, amounting to 12 per cent of the programme, would also be subject to the usual regime of risk-sharing.

Quantitative easing had finally arrived in the euro zone, but on German terms, preventing the creation of implicit eurobonds on the balance sheet of the Eurosystem. The scale of the programme was bigger than expected, but the German price was a breach in the ECB's usual risk-sharing arrangements, which created within the very heart of the monetary union the fragmentation it had been seeking to fight. That was a worrying aspect to a programme on which so many economic hopes rested. Moreover, even with this concession the adoption of QE remained unpopular in Germany and, unlike OMT, was not endorsed by the German government. Although Merkel refrained from openly criticising the ECB when the council took its decision in January, she fretted about the effect of ultra-loose monetary policy in softening the pressures for reform in the debtor countries.[84]

The ECB had managed to reinvent itself to a considerable extent during the crisis. But it had done so in a faltering fashion and after long delays. This reflected both its origin as a central bank with a narrow remit and constricted conception of its role and the difficulty in behaving like the Fed or the Bank of England, given the lack of a fiscal counterpart. The fact that it had travelled far from that starting point owed much to the severity of the crisis. But the frequent hold-ups on the journey contributed to the crisis. Draghi's 'whatever it takes' pledge might have saved the euro but the fact that it came so late in the day left the currency club in a debilitated condition. The long delay in resorting to QE made it more likely that the chronic phase of the crisis might persist as the euro zone followed where Japan had led and found it equally hard to banish deflation.

# 8    Sovereign remedies

As one country after another was admitted into the intensive-care ward of a bail-out, the regimen was the same: a combination of austerity and structural reforms. Countries like Italy and Spain seeking to avoid the humiliation of a full rescue (Spain's national pride was salved by confining its bail-out to its banks) self-administered some of the same medicine. The balance and timing of the treatment was ill-gauged: there was too much austerity at the start and insufficient reforms. But the need for the latter appeared indisputable. Indeed, one interpretation of the euro crisis was that the single currency had exposed underlying flaws, in particular defective labour and product markets, in the crisis countries that would eventually have had to be tackled in or out of the monetary union.

One purpose of the reforms was to make southern economies more flexible and thus better able to regain competitiveness through lowering domestic costs. Another was to foster stronger growth, which would allow economies to deal with excessive debt, both public and private. As one senior German official put it, the new fiscal rules were needed to deal with the numerator – the government debt itself – while the structural measures were required to boost the denominator – GDP. Pension reforms were part of the remedy. Though generally slow working, they had the advantage of operating on both the numerator by making budgetary savings and the denominator by keeping older people in work, thus increasing the labour supply and potential output.

An alternative interpretation of the euro crisis was that the faith placed in reforms was overstated and that the difficulties afflicting the periphery had arisen by joining a monetary union that put them into a straitjacket. The case for overhauling the supply-side of European economies was after all long-standing, informing the 'Lisbon agenda', set out at a summit in Portugal in March 2000, which aimed to turn the EU over the ensuing decade into 'the most competitive and dynamic knowledge-based economy in the world', a vision that was not realised.[1] The OECD had been urging its thirty or so mainly rich member states to embrace reform even before the euro started. In 1994, for example, the Paris-based intergovernmental think-tank published its *Jobs Study*, which identified labour market reforms to tackle the scourge of persistently high unemployment; and, in the 1990s, it developed indicators of job protection and business regulation to highlight impediments to labour and product markets. Since 2005, it had chivvied along its member states, a majority of which were not in the euro area, by publishing *Going for Growth*, which specified policy priorities for countries based on their performance against international benchmarks.[2]

Structural reforms could be narrowly and widely defined. When *Going for Growth* got going in 2005, its recommendations focused on labour and product markets, and to a lesser extent on education; but it subsequently widened its remit to include other areas such as innovation policies.[3] As the problems in some countries in southern Europe appeared increasingly intractable during the crisis, the ambition of the externally driven reform also widened, seeking to shake up not just labour and product markets but the governance of southern European states, including their judicial systems.

The German government was especially insistent on structural reforms, starting with the 'pact for competitiveness' in February 2011, which was intended to spur bracing overhauls such as more flexible wage-setting arrangements for countries to cope better with the rigours of the currency union. With some amendments, it was adopted a month later but renamed the 'euro-plus pact', with other countries outside the currency union joining it, though little came of it.[4] Germany continued to press for reforms once the acute phase of the crisis was over, though with less success, confirming the fears of those who suspected they would occur only under market pressure. In particular, Merkel was rebuffed in her attempt to get countries to agree upon 'contracts' for reform (in return for financial help) – or, as the revealingly obfuscated language of the communiqué put it, 'mutually agreed contractual arrangements and associated solidarity mechanisms' – at the European summit in December 2013.[5] Though this did little to dent the chancellor's commitment to the cause of reforms, senior German policymakers started to worry that Italy and France in particular would not do enough to ginger up their struggling economies.

In insisting on reforms, Germans invoked their own experience within the single-currency club. That had got off to a rocky start. When the euro came into being, the German economy was labelled the 'sick man of Europe'.[6] Eventually, the government led by Schröder, chancellor between 1998 and 2005, grasped the need to prescribe unpalatable medicine, especially for the labour market through the 'Hartz reforms', which came into force between 2003 and 2005, toughening up welfare rules for the unemployed and increasing pressure on them to look for work while helping them to find it by deregulating temporary jobs and reorganising the employment service.[7] Since such reforms had apparently restored German economic health, similar treatment (though without the toleration of deficits Germany had then demanded) should be administered to the sick countries in peripheral Europe.[8]

This homily was questionable as an account of what had really cured the ailing German economy in the early 2000s, let alone what was necessary to tackle the euro crisis. Though Germany undoubtedly did regain competitiveness by keeping down wages, the Hartz labour reforms were less instrumental in this than generally portrayed. Research by German economists published in the *Journal of Economic Perspectives* in 2014 argued that the pay restraint emerged from an inherent adaptability within Germany's traditional collective bargaining arrangements, which became much more decentralised between 1995 and 2005 as firms increasingly used 'opening clauses' in industry-wide agreements that allowed them to strike their own deals with their workers. The willingness of trade unions to curb wage demands was itself a response to the enhanced power of employers once it became possible to move production to low-cost central and eastern European economies after the collapse of communism.[9]

The conviction with which the German government pressed for structural reforms in the crisis countries was all the more remarkable given its increasing reluctance to implement them at home. Merkel was taught a lesson she never forgot in 2005 when she came close to losing the chancellorship, which had seemed hers for the taking, after campaigning on a reforming ticket. Although she pushed through a pension reform in her first term, which set in motion a gradual increase in the retirement age from sixty-five to sixty-seven, she was reluctant to make other changes, such as opening up German services to more competition. The footdragging continued in her second term, from 2009 until 2013. None of this seemed to harm the German economy which snapped back from the severe recession in 2008–9 induced by the financial crisis, surpassing its pre-crisis peak in early 2011, six months before the United States (though it subsequently fared worse than the US as the euro crisis took its toll).[10]

Merkel's authority in urging reforms on the periphery was eroded when, in her third term starting in late 2013, the footdragging at home turned to backpedalling. Her new coalition government, formed with the left-of-centre Social Democrats (she had shared power in her second term with the more economically liberal Free Democrats), weakened the earlier pension reform by opening up an early retirement window in the state pension system that allowed employees who had started to work when they were young to retire at sixty-three on a full pension.[11] In a further lapse from virtue, a national minimum wage was introduced, starting in 2015. Whatever the social case for such a move, it introduced a new rigidity into the German labour market.

Depicting the euro crisis as a biblical tale of sin among peripheral economies that required the penitence of structural reforms played well to national audiences in the northern core of the euro

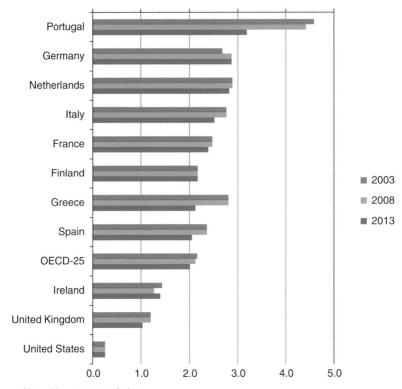

Note: *6 = most restrictive.
Source: OECD

FIGURE 13 Employment protection indicator*, permanent workers, 2003, 2008 and 2013

zone who resented having to bail out their southern neighbours. But the story failed to explain why Ireland had succumbed despite an economy that conformed more closely to the ideal version that structural reforms were supposed to achieve than Germany's itself. Ireland needed few lessons from the troika – or Germany – about the case for flexible labour markets because it already had them (see Figure 13). That had not prevented a steep rise in unit labour costs during the first decade of the euro. Its record on product markets was less exemplary, but it scored better than Germany on this aspect of economic

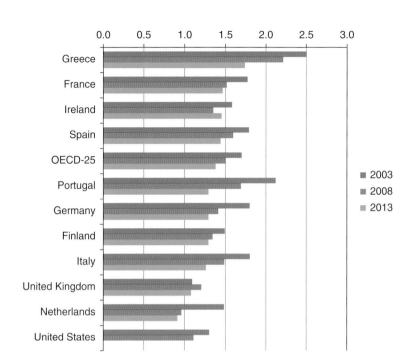

Note: *6 = most restrictive.
Source: OECD

FIGURE 14 Product-market regulation indicator*, 2003, 2008 and 2013

performance in the early years of the monetary union, though it eventually lost that advantage (see Figure 14).

However, the prescription of structural reforms did make sense for floundering southern European economies, which were failing not only to cope with the discipline of the currency union but also in realising their underlying potential for growth. When the euro was launched, levels of GDP per person in Portugal and Greece were around half those in Germany; in Spain they were three-fifths and in Italy they were about four-fifths.[12] Such relative backwardness was an opportunity for catch-up growth through the adoption of new technologies and best managerial practices together with higher investment. Convergence within Europe had indeed occurred for much of the post-war period, but already by the 1980s that process was weakening and becoming more uneven. Greece fared badly in that decade and by the 1990s Italy was already under-performing. Elsewhere on the periphery, however, Ireland was flourishing as a 'Celtic Tiger' economy.[13]

In the first decade of the euro, the underlying problems of southern Europe were obscured in Greece and Spain, as their economies prospered thanks to easy credit, but they were already evident in the disappointing growth records of Italy and Portugal. The mix of causes for the poor performance varied from one country to another, but it was plausible to find a common factor in labour and product markets that were failing to work properly and were hindering adjustments to competitive pressures. Such deficiencies would be unwelcome in any country, but they were especially grave for members of a monetary union, which could no longer depreciate their own currencies in order to regain competitiveness. Instead, they had to achieve 'internal devaluations' by lowering their domestic costs relative to those in the euro area as a whole. As Friedman had pointed out long ago, this was a harder and slower road to follow than a fall in the exchange rate, which would swiftly realign relative costs as long as workers and producers did not resist by pushing up wages and prices in response.

Far more than countries retaining their own currencies those in the euro zone needed flexible labour markets. But hopes before the launch of the euro that it might promote reforms had come to nothing.[14] If anything, the pace of reform then slackened, in part because joining the monetary union meant that countries could no longer so readily provide a stimulus to demand to offset the short-term pain of reforms, making them politically less feasible, as Charles Bean of the London School of Economics (who subsequently became chief economist at the Bank of England) had warned in 1998.[15] Labour markets were particularly inflexible and uncompetitive in southern Europe. In particular, regulation and judicial practices favoured permanent employees who already had jobs. Although some safeguards were necessary to prevent arbitrary dismissal and unfair discrimination, they could be a double-edged sword. The harder it was to fire workers, the more reluctant employers were to hire them: insiders gained, but outsiders lost.

An indicator of job protection showed that permanent employees throughout southern Europe were well defended in the first decade of the euro, although there were also tough rules in northern countries such as the Netherlands. Higher scores up to a maximum of 6 indicated stricter employment protection legislation (EPL), which encompassed a range of restrictions such as dismissal procedures and severance pay stipulations (see Figure 13).[16] In 2008, Portugal had easily the highest score in the OECD, of 4.4 for permanent employees against individual dismissal. By way of comparison, the UK's labour market where it was much easier to fire people, scored 1.2.

As the high scores of countries like Germany, whose labour market was on the mend by 2008 suggested, these gauges did not tell the full story. In the case of Italy for example, as the OECD itself pointed out, the EPL gauge understated the real cost of making workers redundant, much of which arose from judicial delays and the fact that reinstatement of employees was the main sanction for unjustified dismissal.[17] The indicator also failed to fully capture the difficulty of dismissal in Spain. That led Spanish employers typically to acknowledge that dismissal of workers was unfair, shelling out the maximum amount of severance pay (forty-five days per year worked) that was due, in order to avoid entanglement in judicial proceedings.[18] The prevalence of temporary workers in Portugal and Spain where a fifth and a third, respectively, of employees were on such contracts before the financial crisis, bore clearer witness to employers' attempts to free themselves from the onerous terms of permanent contracts.[19]

Over-zealous job protection for permanent staff meant that the pain of labour market adjustment fell overwhelmingly on those temporary and generally younger workers. Not only was this socially and generationally divisive but also it made no economic sense since employers had to undertake dismissals according to the legal status of their employees rather than their individual merits. The insider–outsider gap hindered the integration of young people into the workforce and stunted the growth of human capital since businesses lacked incentives to train and develop temporary employees to the same extent as for permanent staff. Meanwhile long-standing staff became reluctant to move jobs even if a new offer better suited their talents for fear of losing the protection they had built up with their existing employer.[20]

Labour markets in southern Europe were also fouled up by outdated collective bargaining arrangements that worked badly. Permitting firms to strike deals with their workers – the American and British way – fostered flexibility since it allowed companies to vary working hours and pay as demand fluctuated. But if wages were to be determined through sector-wide arrangements, then it was better for these to be coordinated nationally since both sides of industry then had to take account of the impact of excessive pay settlements on employment. This was the most common pattern in northern countries like the Netherlands and was also followed in Italy where negotiations remained highly centralised at sectoral level, despite attempts to give more freedom to firms as long ago as 1993. As pursued in Italy, the system did not work well; a review of the Italian economy by the Commission in 2014 complained that collective bargaining was 'largely unresponsive to firm-level productivity and local labour market conditions'.[21] The worst model, followed by Spain, was for bargains to be struck predominantly at an intermediate level, such as by industry and within regions, which prevented the discipline of market pressures on individual companies and their employees and allowed only feeble coordination at national level.[22]

The inflexibility of the Spanish labour market was notorious. Collective bargaining, which covered most workers despite low union membership, was predominantly at sectoral level, within each of the fifty provinces (seven of which corresponded to regions). These agreements were then automatically extended to all the firms in the sector and province regardless of the degree of unionisation. Only a tenth of workers negotiated their pay at firm level.[23] The labour market was made still more rigid through multi-year agreements, including price indexation clauses. Two-thirds of workers were covered by such arrangements before the euro crisis compared with a third in the euro area as a whole.[24] The overall result of these arrangements was a labour market in which pay responded glacially to cyclical fluctuations in demand, and was only weakly related to productivity in firms and industries. A case in point was that real wages rose by 4.1 per cent in 2009, even as national output fell by 3.6 per cent.[25]

The toll of labour market inflexibility was heavy, as employers pulled hard on the one lever that they could use and sacked temporary workers in droves. In both Spain and Portugal, falls in employment exceeded the declines in GDP, in each case measured from their respective peaks in 2008 before the financial crisis reached its climax and troughs reached in the euro crisis. The disjuncture was most extreme in Spain: GDP fell by 8 per cent over that period, employment by 18 per cent. By contrast, employment fell by 0.5 per cent in Germany as firms adjusted their working hours even though output contracted by 7 per cent in its much shorter recession between the start of 2008 and of 2009.[26]

Rigid labour markets in southern Europe went hand in hand with strict regulations that impeded competition in product markets, in part because the more that employers dominated their sector, the harder they found it to resist union demands for greater job protection.[27] This joint pattern of rigidities differed from the northern economies, where the effect of strict rules for labour markets tended to be offset by looser ones for product markets. Another gauge produced by the OECD sought to measure the extent and intensity of such product-market regulation (PMR); the higher the score, the more restrictive the rules were. The coverage was extensive, including for example retail distribution, but there was a particular focus on network industries in energy, telecommunications and postal services, and transport, together with professional services, which could burden the trading sector of the economy, imposing high costs on it if regulations allowed them to be run as local monopolies.[28]

Although product-market regulation (unlike job protection) was becoming less onerous in the first decade of the euro, southern Europe still stood out for the scale of such anti-competitive rules (see Figure 14). In 2008, for example, the average PMR score across twenty-five broadly comparable members of the OECD was 1.5.[29] The UK and US were lower, at 1.2 and 1.1, respectively. Northern members of the euro area, were also below average, especially the Netherlands (just under 1.0) – in marked contrast with its high degree of employment protection. By contrast, every state in southern Europe was at or above the OECD average, led by Greece (2.2), Portugal (1.7), Spain (1.6) and Italy (1.5).

This was fertile ground for professional cartels to flourish, charging excessive prices for their services. Even though such restrictions were particularly prominent in southern Europe, they were not confined to it. Professional services in particular were heavily protected in Germany, where for example its regulation of prices for architects and building engineers was a restrictive practice unique within the EU in 2014.[30] But the strength of the manufacturing sector in Germany enabled it to shrug off the effects of such restrictions in a way that was not possible in southern Europe. Their grip was particularly tight in Greece, which was a particular problem since services provided by hundreds of tightly regulated professions accounted for a third of private employment.[31]

Such monopolistic practices often went beyond professionals to include other groups of workers that had managed to divvy up a slice of the economy to benefit their members. In Greece, there was a long-standing restriction on the number of permits for firms specialising in trucking, an impediment to competition that forced firms to carry out their own deliveries, raising costs through empty lorries on the way back. Even as Cyprus suffered a steep economic downturn in 2013 and 2014, the cost of taking a taxi from Larnaca airport by the coast in the south of the island to Nicosia, the capital, in the centre – a ride taking only about thirty-five to forty minutes – was €50, while the tariff for short trips within Nicosia was exorbitant.[32]

As well as protected professions and trades, there were the sheltered sectors at the heart of the non-traded sectors of southern European economies, particularly monopolies in essential utilities, which hurt the trading sectors of the economy by imposing excessive charges. This contributed for example to high electricity prices in Italy, which were 50 per cent above the European average, according to a report from the IMF in 2012. Industrial users were particularly hard-hit, making it harder for them to compete.[33] The monopolies responsible for imposing such burdens in southern Europe were tough nuts for politicians to crack because their privileges were defended not just by the bosses but by the workers.

Malfunctioning labour and product markets attested to a more general weakness in the southern European state. One gauge was the Worldwide Governance Indicators project, supported by the World Bank, and based on surveys of households and businesses together with the views of experts among non-governmental organisations and the private and public sectors. Four of the six indicators produced for countries around the world were relevant, relating to government effectiveness, regulatory quality, the rule of law and control of corruption. The scores in 2013 for the crisis countries told a remarkably consistent story. Ireland ranked along with Germany above the average for the OECD. Portugal and Spain stood somewhat below. Slovenia scored relatively poorly on regulatory quality. But the two countries that stood out as poor performers on all four indicators were Greece and Italy. Dispiritingly, their rankings deteriorated between 2003 and 2013.[34]

Southern European states were at best inefficient, through heavy handed regulation and a creaking judicial system, at worst corrupt to varying degrees (though they were hardly alone in that). These defects in governance tended to reinforce a feature of the southern European economy that was becoming a disadvantage: the predominance of smaller family-based firms. Small firms were bound to feature since many activities such as hairdressing and restaurants were often best undertaken by independent entrepreneurs while start-ups especially high-tech ones were welcome since they increased competition and a few might grow into large companies. But there were bad as well as good reasons for the preponderance of smaller firms in southern Europe. In Italy, once firms employed more than fifteen workers they became subject to stringent labour market regulations, making it costly to get rid of poorly performing employees.[35] By staying small, firms could also reduce their exposure to risk from clients failing to pay their bills. Since chronic delays made it hard to enforce contracts in the courts, firms had an incentive to confine their trading relationships to a smaller circle of businesses that they could trust.

The shortcomings of the state hurt the Greek economy in particular by shackling its goods exports, making it over-reliant on tourism and shipping. A study published by the Commission in 2014 estimated that, despite Greece's strengths in those two sectors, exports of goods and services were a third lower than an economy of its size and nature should have delivered, with particular weakness in manufacturing products such as electrical equipment and machinery. The researchers blamed the shortfall largely on a variety of institutional failings such as those identified by the Worldwide Governance Indicators and other international surveys.[36]

Widespread corruption in the Greek tax system weakened economic performance by creating incentives to operate on a small scale in order to escape official attention. The failure to crack down on widespread tax evasion by professionals meant that the way to get on was to join the racket of those providing services in sectors penned off from competition by cosy state regulations. It was no accident that Greece had the highest rate of self-employment; at almost 30 per cent of working-age employment in 2010 it was double the euro area's 14.5 per cent. But Greece was not alone in creating such incentives to stay under the radar of the state. Indeed, a ranking of the self-employment rate within the euro area tallied tellingly with the countries that got into trouble. Next highest after Greece came Italy with a rate of 23 per cent, followed by Portugal at 17.5 per cent. Self-employment was also above average in Spain, at 16 per cent, and in Cyprus and Ireland, at 15 per cent.[37]

Making matters worse, the family-based firm was losing its economic allure. Italian businesses had once combined the advantages of remaining small – lean management and low overheads – with economies of scale and marketing by forming a 'cluster' in which several firms specialised in specific components, including the machinery and equipment used in production, allowing them to cooperate through intense trading relationships with one another. The Italian clusters in sectors such as textiles and clothing (including for example footwear, handbags and travel goods), household products, and personal products like spectacles were extolled in 1990 by Michael Porter in his *Competitive Advantage of Nations*.[38] But despite Italian flair in fashion and design, such sectors were vulnerable to competition from cheaper operations in Asia, causing the clusters to hollow out, while the advantages of size had become more apparent as markets became ever-more global. One way in which Italy had failed to adapt to globalisation was that it had too few big international companies like Luxottica, an eyewear producer, argued Bill Emmott, a former editor of *The Economist*, in *Good Italy, Bad Italy*.[39]

The gravity of the crisis of the southern state might seem cause for despair but it also gave grounds for hope. The difficulty in pushing through tough reforms was manifest since vested interests were deeply entrenched in maintaining the ancien regime. Correspondingly, however, the prize might be greater than usual. The IMF spelt this out when estimating the size of these potential gains for Italy in 2012. Its economists worked out that a package aimed at halving the gap between the country's defective product and labour markets and those where they operated well elsewhere could in itself raise GDP by 5.7 per cent over five years. Furthermore, the total boost to GDP in the long term (including that over the first five years) could be as high as 10.5 per cent.[40] Similar simulations published in 2014 for the eurozone periphery as a whole (Greece, Ireland, Italy, Portugal and Spain) estimated an increase in GDP of 3.7 per cent over five years from a package of structural reforms; the long-term rise (again, relative to the baseline) would be as high as 12.7 per cent.[41]

Such estimates were encouraging though inherently speculative but the real difficulty was in making the reforms. The troubled countries of peripheral Europe did undoubtedly make headway especially during the acute phase of the euro crisis and particularly among the bailed-out economies as they complied with conditions set by their rescuers. Judging by an OECD indicator for reform effort, the countries under pressure in southern Europe surpassed their previous records between 2010 and 2013 as well as exceeding the performance of OECD countries as a whole.[42] Contrary to the commonly held view that Greece was the slacker in the class, it actually did the most in 2011 and 2012 when the crisis was most acute; and even more so when taking into account the fact that its reforms were in areas such as labour markets that were typically difficult to tackle. On a similarly adjusted basis, Spain and Portugal also stood out. By contrast, Italy lagged behind in reform effort in part because little was done until Monti replaced Berlusconi in late 2011. Germany, so eager for the peripheral countries and in particular Greece to change their ways, scored especially low for its own effort.[43]

Gauging the efficacy of the reforms on the periphery was tricky, not least since there were so many of them, with some mattering much more than others for their impact on the economy as well as differing in the social and political sensitivities involved. In Portugal for example, the government led by Pedro Passos Coelho adopted 400 measures as part of its adjustment programme and a special minister, Carlos Moedas, was appointed to coordinate them across ministries.[44] Though the troika and international monitors like the OECD could document legislative acts, implementation was harder to assess. Moreover, even if they were carried out in full it would still take time for the changes to affect the economy.

A centrepiece of reforms was an overhaul of labour markets. Spain's worked so badly that significant changes were eventually made. In the final years of Zapatero's government, some efforts were made to reduce the privileges of permanent staff. In particular, firms were given more leeway to justify dismissals on grounds of economic difficulties, allowing them to make a lower redundancy payment. However, this merely chipped away at the wall between permanent and temporary workers. The reforms also did little to address the other crucial flaw in the Spanish labour market, the imposition on firms of collective agreements. Though companies seeking opt-outs no longer required the consent of the two sides of industry that had negotiated the deals, they still had to get the agreement of their staff.[45]

Armed with a decisive election victory in late 2011, Rajoy went further than Zapatero had dared go. A labour reform in February 2012 gave individual businesses a much freer hand to strike their own bargains with their staff by opting out from collective pay-setting tariffs. The power of employers still negotiating together was enhanced by setting a one-year limit on the automatic extension of existing agreements if new deals could not be mutually agreed. The economic grounds for justifiable dismissal of permanent employees were clarified to include nine months of falling revenues, and firms no longer had to prove that this was essential for their future profitability. The maximum amount of severance pay for unjustified dismissal was reduced to thirty-three days per year worked (with a lower overall maximum of twenty-four rather than forty-two months), both for new contracts and for future years of service on existing ones, and companies no longer had to pay 'interim wages' while judicial proceedings were pending.[46]

The overall verdict on the reform was mixed. On the one hand, the overhaul of collective bargaining represented a breakthrough though mainly for larger firms since the process of opting out of the collective arrangements could be cumbersome.[47] On the other hand, the attempts to reduce the segmentation of the labour market did not go far enough. In a cautiously positive evaluation of the reform, the OECD said that it appeared 'to have brought more dynamism into the

Spanish labour market', but noted that severance pay for permanent workers remained among the highest among its member states.[48]

Advances were also eventually made in Greece, especially in late 2011 and early 2012. Reforms shifted power to individual employers; as was the case in Spain, firms could now negotiate directly with their staff. Unions could no longer exploit an arbitration panel, which had routinely favoured them in disputes. Restrictions on working-time flexibility were eased and severance payments for white-collar workers were cut. Moreover, minimum wages were cut by over 20 per cent (more than 30 per cent for those under the age of twenty-five), which contributed to a big, if belated, reduction in labour costs.[49] The IMF reckoned in the spring of 2014 that nominal private-sector wages had fallen by 16 per cent since 2009.[50]

In Portugal, reforms were extensive, but still fell short of what had to be done to overhaul so rigid a labour market. Unemployment benefits, among the most generous in Europe for those covered by them, were trimmed. The exceptionally tough regime of employment protection was eased. Individual dismissals for economic reasons were facilitated, and severance pay was sharply reduced (though as was the case in Spain existing entitlements were preserved). Even after such changes, the EPL indicator measuring the protection enjoyed by permanent employees against individual dismissals remained the highest in the OECD in 2013, but it was no longer the outlier it had been before. However, some of this loosening (for example doing away with 'first in, last out' dismissal rules) was cast in doubt by an adverse ruling from the constitutional court in September 2013, although the government tried to retain as much of the enhanced flexibility as possible through a new law in 2014. The threshold above which firm-level bargaining was possible was lowered from 500 employees to 150, though union approval was still required above this new level. This left wage bargaining still mainly at sectoral level, with collective agreements reached by the largest firms and then administratively extended across whole industries.[51]

If Portugal's reforms remained inadequate because the starting point was so poor, those in Italy did not go far enough, leaving Renzi with unfinished work to do when he became prime minister in early 2014. Monti and his labour minister, Elsa Fornero, picked a quarrel over a right, set out in Article 18 of the workers' statute of 1970, that tied employers (other than small firms) in knots when trying to sack staff. The fight was totemic because trade unions had vehemently resisted previous attempts to alter the provision, which forced employers to reinstate workers who were unfairly dismissed. It was also courageous because a decade earlier terrorists had killed first Massimo D'Antona and then three years later Marco Biagi, both labour-law experts advising on reforms.[52]

The reform in 2012 sought to cut the time that the courts could take to consider appeals by streamlining procedures.[53] But Monti diluted the original proposal to end reinstatement, amending it to allow employees to reclaim their old jobs if they could prove that the economic grounds for dismissal were 'manifestly' lacking. The government's partial retreat was greeted with dismay by Emma Marcegaglia, the leader of Confindustria, the employers' confederation, who described the amended text as 'very bad'. Though she then toned down her criticism, Monti himself in effect later admitted that the reform had been fainthearted. After resigning as prime minister in December 2012, his manifesto for the election held in February 2013 called for 'drastic simplification' of labour market rules to tackle Italy's dual labour market – the very goal his reform had sought to achieve when he was in power.[54]

In fact, the record of Monti's government in overhauling the Italian labour market was in some respects rather better than usually depicted. This was because the earlier pension reform pushed through by Fornero in the desperate closing weeks of 2011 – a centrepiece of Monti's 'Save Italy' measures – was in itself a major labour market reform as well as a fiscal reform (although it still left public pension spending extraordinarily high in relation to GDP). All workers were switched into the 'notional' defined-contribution state pension system first established in 1995, which remained pay-as-you-go but created the same incentives, as a funded plan, for people to retire later as they lived longer. This bold move did away with an absurdly protracted transition (stretching to the 2030s) from the previous defined-benefits regime.[55] Fornero also yanked up the retirement age for women working in the private sector, from sixty to sixty-two, which was to be fully equalised with men's to sixty-six by 2018; the joint retirement age would then rise automatically in response to improving life expectancy. If the reform worked, it would bring about a sharp increase in the supply of labour over the coming decade as many more fifty-five- to sixty-four-year-olds stayed in the workforce.[56]

If anything, the overhaul undertaken in Greece especially in 2010 and also in 2012 went even further than the Italian one, yet that only went to highlight how absurdly generous the pension system had become. According to estimates from the OECD before the reforms, Greece's state pension commitments envisaged expenditure of close to 25 per cent of GDP by 2050.[57] These unaffordable promises were withdrawn by slashing the replacement rate – the value of the public pension in relation to prior earnings – from 96 per cent for average earners, the highest in the OECD, to 54 per cent in 2012 (though this was still higher than Germany's 42 per cent).[58] The statutory retirement age, which had previously been sixty-five for men and sixty for women was raised to sixty-seven in 2013. More important, the minimum retirement age was raised to sixty-two and the number of contributions entitling a pensioner to a full benefit went up from thirty-five to forty years. Pensions in payment were also cut sharply, for example by eliminating two annual bonuses.[59]

Yet this still left much unfinished business, manifest in the fact that Greek pension spending in 2013 was 16.2 per cent of GDP, above the share in Italy, traditionally the highest in Europe. Though the shrinkage of the economy contributed to this outcome, it also reflected the fact that there had been a surge in early retirement, long the bane of the Greek pension system and encouraged by the weak actuarial link between pension contributions and benefits. One indicator of this was that the employment rate among fifty-five- to sixty-four-year-olds in 2014 was only 34 per cent in Greece, lower even than Italy's 46 per cent, and far below the 66 per cent of Germans in that age-group who were still working; in Sweden, which had introduced a notional defined-contribution pension scheme shortly before Italy but with more dispatch and integrity, the rate was 74 per cent.[60]

Spain's starting point was less precarious, but a reform in the final year of Zapatero's government was a more modest affair than it was made out to be at the time. It raised the retirement age from sixty-five to sixty-seven, but over a long period, between 2013 and 2027.[61] Under Rajoy, there was a move away from price indexation of pensions to a formula aiming to ensure financial sustainability by taking into account increases in life expectancy and trends in pension contributions and spending, though arguably it was too complicated for its own good and might itself be unsustainable.[62] Portugal raised the retirement age from sixty-five to sixty-six, from 2014, after trying to hack away at pension spending by cutting two annual bonus payments for a majority of pensioners, a policy that had to be reversed following rulings by the constitutional court.[63] The bigger picture was that even after the reforms, southern Europe (along with Austria and France) still stood out for the disproportionate scale of public expenditure on pensioners.

As well as labour and pension reforms, overhauls of product markets were a priority. The aim of such reforms was broadly similar: reducing the power of insiders and increasing the scope for outsiders to enter markets. At root, the aim was to strengthen competitive pressures within economies, which would in turn raise productivity, as new and more efficient companies entered markets and forced out older and less productive firms. The potential dividends were high. In the case of Italy, for example, the estimates made by the IMF in 2012 envisaged labour market changes boosting the level of GDP by 1.1 per cent over five years. This was welcome but overshadowed by the gain from product-market reforms of 4.4 per cent, most of which would come from reducing the burden imposed by the protected sectors of the economy, 'network industries' such as energy and transport. (The fact that the total gain was a little higher, at 5.7 per cent, than the sum of the components represented a pay-off from combining the two sets of reforms.) This composition of the possible gains also held true for the long-term potential boost to GDP of 10.5 per cent through reforms.[64]

One particular target for the reforms was the professional and trading cartels. Dismantling them was a tough endeavour especially in Greece where their grip was particularly intense. A detailed scrutiny by the OECD in 2013 of four sectors making up a fifth of national output – food processing, retail trade, building materials and tourism – uncovered 555 regulatory restrictions that were impeding competition. Tackling 329 of them – some were warranted – would provide a gain for the Greek economy of around €5 billion, 2.5 per cent of GDP.[65] The troika did manage fairly early in the bail-out programme to get the government to deregulate the trucking industry. By early 2013, around three-quarters of the professions had been formally liberalised, though in an interview in November that year, Poul Thomsen, who headed the IMF staff team, pointed out that 'even where legal restrictions have been lifted, new administrative or other barriers often crop up'.[66] A tussle between the troika and the government over reforms contributed to a long delay in completing the usual quarterly inspection, which dragged on well into 2014.[67]

The gain from the reforms might be large but the political pain involved was intense. Greek politicians quailed at the prospect of confronting PPC, the power company that was 51 per cent publicly owned, and the militant workers who defended its monopoly. It took until the summer of 2014 for a decision to spin off and privatise 30 per cent of it by creating 'Small PPC' to become law; the long delay meant that the plan could be halted when Syriza won power in January 2015.[68] In Italy, attempts to tackle the intertwining monopolies at the heart of energy supply were similarly half-hearted even under Monti, in 2012. Eni, a partially state-owned energy group, was forced to divest Snam, the gas network it controlled through a 52.5 per cent holding. But the grid was not fully privatised since Eni sold a 30 per cent stake in it, to Cassa Depositi e Prestiti, a state-controlled bank.[69]

Despite the inherent complexity of seeking to gauge reforms in one country, let alone comparing them across states, both the OECD's product-market regulation indicator and a survey by the World Bank on the ease of doing business offered some insights into what had been achieved. The PMR gauge showed that between 2008 and 2013, Greece made the most progress among OECD member states in hacking away at unhelpful regulations, while Portugal had also achieved a lot. Despite its advances, Greece still had the highest score in 2013 among euro-zone members of the OECD, and was above the overall average (see Figure 14). Strikingly, however, Portugal as well as Italy were now below average, while Spain was not that much above it (along with Ireland, which had regressed). Judging by these scores, much of southern Europe appeared to have done enough to tackle rusty rules holding back growth.

This fitted in with earlier evidence, showing that both Italy and Portugal had done more than most to reduce the weight of burdensome regulations though with scant reward in their economic performance. Retail trade remained tightly controlled in Italy in 2013, while transport was heavily regulated in Portugal. But in both countries, barriers to entrepreneurship were especially low, while a measure of state control was average.[70] One explanation might be that the PMR indicator captured formal policy settings rather than how they were enforced, and did not take into account informal administrative guidelines. And it might in any case have been failing to pick up other important handicaps shackling businesses in southern Europe. Despite Portugal's below-average PMR score, the OECD noted in 2013 that competitive pressures in network industries, wholesale and retail trade, ports and professional services were still limited, while also highlighting relatively high prices for electricity and gas.[71]

Table 1 *Ease of doing business, rankings in 2008, 2013 and 2014*

|  | Mid 2008 (out of 181) | Mid 2013 (out of 189) | Mid 2014 (out of 189) |
|---|---|---|---|
| Singapore | 1 | 1 | 1 |
| United States | 3 | 4 | 7 |
| United Kingdom | 6 | 10 | 8 |
| Ireland | 7 | 15 | 13 |
| Germany | 25 | 21 | 14 |
| Portugal | 48 | 31 | 25 |
| France | 31 | 38 | 31 |
| Spain | 49 | 52 | 33 |
| Slovenia | 54 | 33 | 51 |
| Italy | 65 | 65 | 56 |
| Greece | 96 | 72 | 61 |

*Source:* World Bank

The global rankings of the World Bank's 'Doing Business' survey, headed by Singapore for the most business-friendly environment, provided another indicator of what had been achieved (see Table 1). Comparing the rankings in mid 2008, before the euro crisis, and mid 2014, when there were eight euro-zone states in the top thirty, showed a general picture of progress on the periphery.[72] Greece had risen from 96th to 61st, while Portugal moved up from 48th to 25th. Ireland had lost ground but remained among the top performers and was one place ahead of Germany. Despite Ireland's slippage, the rankings confirmed that having to comply with the conditions of a rescue spurred greater reform effort. Italy, which managed to avoid a bail-out, made a more limited advance from 65th to 56th. Spain did rather better thanks to a late spurt, rising from 49th to 33rd.

The survey had its limitations since Luxembourg, which prospered as a tax-friendly home for multinationals, scored 59th in 2014. But despite the improvements it charted on the periphery, the findings were only partially reassuring. On the one hand, there had been advances throughout southern Europe. Spain and Portugal in particular had made changes that seemed likely to pay dividends. A report by the OECD in 2013 estimated that the reforms in labour and product markets since 2008 were likely to boost the level of potential GDP in Portugal by around 3.5 per cent by 2020.[73] On the other hand, the World Bank's rankings of Greece (one ahead of Russia) and Italy (one better than Belarus) as places to do business were distinctly unflattering.[74]

The reforms undoubtedly got off to a bad start because they were introduced, whether at the behest of the troika or under the pressure of the markets, at the same time as tough fiscal consolidation. Ideally, the reforms should have come first, the austerity later. Such a sequencing might have allowed them to be deeper and bolder, in part because economic activity would have been stronger. As the supply side of economies improved, they would have been more resilient when austerity was subsequently imposed. However, this critique failed to acknowledge the political economy of both austerity and reforms, dictating that the opportunity to push through harsh measures was at a time of crisis, which was why Monti was able to act most boldly when the Italian state was close to the edge in the winter of 2011–12. But to the extent that the structural reforms were sown in frosty ground this might help to explain their lack of immediate success. A case in point was the deregulation of the Greek trucking industry, one of the early successes of the troika. In practice, very few new operators took advantage, discouraged by an economy in free fall.[75]

Did the reforms actually make things worse in the first instance, deepening the recession on the periphery? Before being appointed Italy's economy and finance minister by Renzi in February 2014, Pier Carlo Padoan, in his capacity as chief economist at the OECD, had tilted against the view that reforms might in the short term depress activity. In an editorial to *Going for Growth* published in 2012, he dismissed such fears as 'overblown', based on new research at the intergovernmental think-tank. Even so, he had to concede that some labour market reforms could be 'temporarily detrimental if implemented in bad times'. When economies were depressed, as was undoubtedly the case on the periphery of the euro area, weakening job protection for example would make it easier for firms to sack excess staff, but they would make no offsetting hires.[76]

Product-market reforms were less sensitive to the state of the economy, but along with labour market changes, they took a long time to bear fruit. The OECD research found that the full pay-off typically took five years to materialise though some gains appeared earlier. Another cautionary finding was that product-market reforms in network industries could depress investment in the short term as incumbent firms being shaken up cut capital spending.[77] In fact, a hallmark reform such as the shake-up of the UK's labour market in the 1980s was generally reckoned to have taken about a decade to pay dividends, notably after the economy recovered from the recession of the early 1990s. The Hartz reforms that came into force between 2003 and 2005 appeared to deliver an earlier harvest in Germany since the labour market behaved so well during the financial and euro crises, but if the genesis of that improvement lay rather in the threat to workers of moving production to eastern and central Europe dating back to the 1990s, the pay-off also took its time.

As Draghi pointed out, the make-up of austerity measures was also misjudged, with too much directed at public investment cutbacks and tax rises that sapped incentives to work and to invest, and not enough at reducing current spending.[78] Although the Italian pension reforms cut spending, the measures taken first by Berlusconi and then by Monti between July and December 2011 relied mainly on tax increases, which accounted for four-fifths of the fiscal retrenchment in 2012.[79] The Portuguese government kept on being foiled in its attempts to reconfigure consolidation away from revenue increases to spending cuts involving sensitive areas such as public wages and pensions because of their weight in overall public expenditure by adverse decisions taken by the constitutional court.[80]

As well as lightening an overheavy state, there was a strong case for tackling more fundamental flaws that were holding back economies in southern Europe. Foremost among these were poor education and skills, a handicap for countries trying to compete not just with northern but eastern Europe as well as the increasingly well educated workforces of Asia. A measure of educational performance was the proportion of the working-age population (twenty-five–sixty-four year-olds) without a high-school diploma. Across the mainly rich countries belonging to the OECD, this averaged 24 per cent in 2012; in Germany, Estonia and South Korea it was, respectively, 14, 10 and 18 per cent. By contrast, 62 per cent of the adult population in Portugal lacked such a qualification, virtually on a par with Mexico.[81] Small wonder that the OECD peppered its generally positive assessment of reforms in Portugal in 2013 with the observation that 'human capital remains the Achilles' heel of the Portuguese economy'.[82] Other countries in southern Europe were also well behind. In Italy and Spain, around 45 per cent of the adult population similarly lacked this basic educational grounding.

Yet in the short-to-medium term, the bigger worry was that young (and better-educated) people were turning their backs on their countries and emigrating. The balance of net migration swung negative in 2010 in Spain, which had attracted so many incomers in the boom years. In 2013, 550,000 people emigrated, 250,000 more than those immigrating to Spain. The outflows were concentrated among twenty– and thirty-year-olds. Although the emigrants were predominantly foreign nationals, they also included 80,000 Spanish citizens.[83] Portuguese emigration reached over 100,000 a year between 2011 and 2013. The exodus, in which younger people were also prominent, was on a similar scale given the fact that the population of Portugal was less than a quarter that of Spain.[84] In principle, greater labour mobility across borders was needed to make the currency union work better, but many of the emigrants were leaving the euro area entirely and their departure did not bode well for their countries' future.

Along with poor education and skills, the other obstacle to growth was the state itself. Embedded in the detail of the World Bank's survey on the ease of doing business were some telling findings for individual components of the index. Italy's poor overall ranking reflected particularly bad scores in three areas. In 2014, it ranked 141st for the tax burden on businesses; 147th for enforcing contracts; and 116th for dealing with construction permits. The first two – the tax burden and the problems in enforcing contracts – were core responsibilities of the state. A similar story emerged for Greece, which ranked 116th in the world as a place to register property and 155th for enforcing contracts. These were extraordinarily disappointing results for a country urgently requiring foreign direct investment by companies, to bring in both capital and expertise.[85] Greece still lacked a proper land registry and the objective of completing one by 2020 looked optimistic given past failures to put in place this basic building-block of any modern state.[86]

The malfunctioning of the Greek state might have been egregious but it was not unique. In Italy for example, there were not just the familiar three tiers of government – central, regional and local – but a fourth, provincial, level. Though this was essentially redundant – its role in functions such as roads and planning could easily be transferred to other tiers of government – provinces proved difficult to abolish. A reform by Renzi in April 2014 stripped them of their political authority – officials were no longer elected – but their administrative functions remained intact.[87]

More important, the Italian judicial system was notorious for its delays. An important reason for Italy's poor record in enforcing contracts was the time it took (1,185 days) to enforce a simple commercial contract – three times as long as in France and Germany (395 and 394 days, respectively).[88] Completing a civil case up to Supreme Court level took almost eight years, far longer than the average among rich countries of just over two years.[89] Probably the most serious shortcoming for employers of Article 18 in the workers' statute was that resolving any dispute with employees claiming they had been dismissed unfairly could last for years with little predictability about what the eventual outcome might be.

Even though Ireland's economic governance was generally superior to the regimes in southern Europe, its ruling politicians became too close to property developers in the 2000s, which contributed to the failure of supervisors to contain the reckless behaviour of its banks. An analysis of the Irish banking crisis by Blánaid Clarke and Niamh Hardiman of University College Dublin concluded that 'during a critical period in the 2000s, government priorities were more attentive to the interests of the bankers, the builders and property developers than they were to considerations of good governance'.[90] Such failings were greater still in both Italy and Spain where local politicians had secured too much power over banks. In the case of Italy, this influence was exerted through 'foundations' holding equity stakes in big banks, such as Banca Monte dei Paschi di Siena, the third largest. A financial-stability assessment by IMF staff in 2013 identified banks with a significant presence of such foundations among their shareholders as the 'weakest link' of the Italian banking system, along with cooperative banks.[91]

Increasingly and especially in Greece, the troika was drawn into tackling these broader weaknesses in governance, in particular by trying to shake up public administration. The Commission set up a task force for Greece led by Horst Reichenbach, an official with long experience in Brussels, whose remit was to provide technical assistance in carrying out the delivery of the measures required in the programme.[92] But externally driven reform kept on tripping up on obstacles embedded deep within Greek society and politics. Although public-sector payrolls fell under a policy of natural attrition (hiring far fewer new staff than those retiring), civil servants were virtually impossible to sack no matter how useless they were. Not until 2013 did the troika manage to make some progress on this front, and even this was fairly limited.[93]

A litmus test of Greece's willingness to reform was its privatisation programme. As well as providing an alternative source of finance to seemingly endless euro-zone rescue money, this could also bring in precious expertise that could help to modernise the Greek economy. Indeed, the IMF said in early 2013 that privatisation was 'a key element towards a decisive break with Greece's previous failed model of public sector led growth'.[94] The potential was particularly large for land sales, permitting up-market tourist developments and logistics hubs exploiting Greece's favourable location as an entry point for trade with south-eastern Europe. In 2011, a figure of €50 billion in potential privatisation proceeds was bandied about, but this was never attainable under any realistic timeframe.[95] By early 2013, the target had been slashed to half that amount by 2020. Yet even this more modest aim proved difficult to accomplish, with the programme already falling behind that year when the sale of DEPA, a gas supplier that dominated the Greek market, fell through.[96] Against this background the plan to renew the €50 billion target in July 2015 as one of the conditions for a third bail-out was unrealistic; as the IMF pointed out, Greece had achieved privatisation revenues of just €3 billion in the preceding five years.[97]

Syriza's victory had brought to power a party that wanted to tear up previous reforms rather than to press ahead with new ones. But even before this rebuff to modernisation, the impetus behind reform on the periphery was waning. As first Ireland in December 2013 and then Portugal in May 2014 exited their rescue programmes, the direct influence exercised by the troika on both countries ceased; although both the Commission and IMF continued to monitor developments closely. More important, the pressure from the markets had disappeared, with the exception of Greece as political worries mounted in late 2014. In many ways, this was the real test, and the results were generally discouraging. In Spain, Rajoy's government introduced a shake-up in the tax system, pushing down for example the corporate-income tax rate from 30 to 28 per cent in 2015, with a future reduction to 25 per cent due in 2016.[98] However, the steam had gone out of the government's reforming agenda. In Portugal, the modernising momentum was weakened by successive judgments of the constitutional court, the guardian of the outdated left-leaning constitution written in the 1970s.

Despite these setbacks in the smaller peripheral countries, it was the lack of progress in Italy and, increasingly, France that caused increasing anxiety among European policymakers and the German government. In Italy, Renzi made the right noises, which meant that Merkel was prepared to give him a chance, but hopes that he would be able to achieve a lot in a short time had evaporated. Indeed, in early 2015, a year after becoming prime minister, the only big structural reform he had achieved was an overhaul of the labour market that had gone further than Monti's. The Jobs Act scrapped the obligation to reinstate employees sacked for business reasons who were judged to be unfairly dismissed, but it was not exactly the 'Copernican revolution' proclaimed by Renzi since it applied only to new private-sector contracts and not at all within the public sector.[99]

If the fear about Italy was that Renzi would prove to be more bombast than delivery, the worry about France was that it had postponed reforms for far too long. Indeed, matters got worse initially under Hollande, who wasted his first eighteen months in office. The minimum retirement age, which had only recently been raised to a hardly oppressive sixty-two, was in effect moved back to sixty for workers who had started their careers early. Whatever the social case for this, it seemed to show that France was not serious about tackling its persistent fiscal deficits, given the scale of pension spending. Moreover, a swingeing tax was imposed on high earners that swiftly ran into legal difficulty and even after being amended had eventually to be dropped since it yielded little while damaging the image of France as a place to do business.[100] Hollande did make a sensible change in allowing firms to negotiate temporary wage and working-time reductions in exchange for employees keeping their jobs, but few firms took advantage.[101] Weighed down by excessive taxation, France continued to struggle even though it was spared the credit blight still afflicting firms in southern Europe. Its stagnating economy and repeated budgetary misses caused both anxiety and infuriation among Germany's governing elite who feared that its national 'morosity' and reluctance to change its ways would hold back the euro area.

Not before time, Hollande became the second socialist president to make an unceremonious U-turn. Thirty years after Mitterrand had jettisoned his left-wing programme, Hollande conceded that he too had to ditch his election promises and to make reforms. The change of course occurred in January 2014 when the French government announced a plan to cut spending by a cumulative €50 billion between 2015 and 2017 and to hand back most of that saving to businesses in lower payroll taxes. In fact, the spending cuts were less harsh than they appeared to a French public accustomed to never-ending deficits and ever-rising public expenditure. Even with the decreases in the planned budgets, spending would still increase in real terms by 0.2 per cent a year in 2015 and 2016.[102] But at least Hollande was no longer heading in the wrong direction.

Following a political shake-up of his government later that year, there was a belated concession to the need for structural reforms spelt out in France's poor performance on product markets and as a place to do business. Whereas the peripheral countries had generally made progress in the World Bank's rankings for ease of doing business between 2008 and 2014 France stayed at 31st (though this was better than in 2013 when it had slipped to 38th), a disappointing record which chimed with its poor performance on the OECD's PMR indicator and meagre improvement since 2008 (see Figure 14). France's gummed-up labour market, where there had also been minimal progress over the same period, was also in urgent need of repair; in March 2015, the OECD said that the country's 'key challenge' was to reform it to promote job growth.[103]

In late 2014, Emmanuel Macron, a former investment banker who had become the economy minister, set out a detailed plan to loosen up regulations. A laundry list of changes included opening up protected professions such as notaries, extending opportunities to shop on Sundays and deregulating the intercity coach industry. The proposals also sought to streamline labour tribunals, which would shorten often protracted unfair-dismissal procedures. The 'Macron law', which was controversially pushed through parliament without a vote in February 2015, was undoubtedly a step in the right direction. However, it fell short of its grand objective of modernising the French economy and taking the brakes off it. One glaring omission was a reform of the thirty-five-hour working week. And it had come late in the day as French politics soured on the European project.[104]

There were wider reasons, beyond the creation of the single currency, why its members were struggling. The rise of China had undermined industries and sectors that were vulnerable to low-cost competition, injuring particularly Portugal and Italy. Arguably that made structural reforms all the more necessary, certainly in the long term even though the acute phase of the euro crisis itself had been rooted in systemic rather than national deficiencies. Yet there was also a question over whether the euro area and Germany in particular placed too much faith in these reforms as a remedy, particularly as the ambition appeared to undergo 'mission creep', extending ever wider to embrace not just the core markets that needed an overhaul but the entire state. The ambition set for the third bail-out of Greece of 'capacity-building and depoliticising the Greek administration' would offer a test case in this respect. Whatever the case for reforms, they were a manifesto for long-term improvement in the supply-side of economies. And however impressive the putative benefits might appear in simulations of reforms, hard experience suggested that gains in raising potential growth would be small. Even if they did not make matters worse in the short term, it would take time for the changes to bear fruit. For all the attention paid to them, they were no miracle cure.

# 9 Debtors' prison

During 2013 and especially in the first half of 2014, the bond markets decided that the euro crisis was over. Government debt yields generally fell across the periphery in the first few months of 2013, shrugging off the eventful bail-out of Cyprus in March. When global yields rose generally in the 'taper tantrum' after the Fed aired in late May the possibility of phasing out its monthly bond purchases, euro-zone states were not immune; but, significantly, spreads between the periphery countries and Germany did not for the most part widen that much and before long started to close further. There were local flare-ups, but they did not persist or cause a wider conflagration. For example, yields spiked in Portugal during a summer political crisis, when the coalition government carrying out the painful measures required under the bail-out programme looked as if it might fall apart. They then subsided when the two governing parties coalesced again after Passos Coelho, the prime minister, gave Paulo Portas, the leader of the junior party, a bigger role.[1]

Politicians in both the core and peripheral countries were keen to declare the crisis over, even if this was imprudent. Ireland threw away its bail-out crutches in December 2013, making it the first crisis country to conclude its rescue programme on time. That 'clean exit' was in fact risky since both the Commission and the IMF as well as the ECB considered that Ireland would have done well to get a precautionary credit line with the ESM.[2] The main advantage this would have conferred was eligibility for OMT since such a precautionary programme would require conditionality. That eligibility would have lasted for up to two years because the credit line could be renewed twice for six months after the initial one-year term.[3] The counsel from the troika was disregarded for reasons both of Irish pride and of the German desire to wrap up the embarrassing rescues.

A similar alliance on the periphery and core helped Slovenia avoid the threat of a bail-out that had long hung over the country. Having seen the effects of such programmes elsewhere, the government led by Alenka Bratusek was doing its utmost to avoid becoming the sixth country to require a rescue. It was helped by the fact that Germany also wanted to avoid such an outcome. That saved the day for Slovenia, even though its three biggest banks were to all intents and purposes insolvent, able to continue only because of the promise of capital injections from the government. But when the hard numbers about the cost of bailing out the banks emerged in December 2013 following a thorough asset-quality review and stress tests, Slovenia was spared, not least because euro-zone leaders did not want to spoil their 'crisis over' narrative.[4]

A few months later, Portugal also benefited from a similar conjuncture of politics in the core and on the periphery to make a full exit from its bail-out programme. This had appeared virtually impossible as recently as the autumn of 2013 when Portuguese ten-year bond yields went above 7 per cent again. Then, much more than Ireland, Portugal seemed to require an extension of its official support through at least a precautionary credit line. Both economies were saddled with high private and public debt. But unlike Ireland, which had been rated below investment grade by only one of the three main agencies (which restored it a month after the exit), Portugal's credit rating had been deemed junk by all three of them and remained so in 2014.[5] The Portuguese economy also lacked the presence of multinationals in advanced sectors such as IT and pharmaceuticals that added lustre to an otherwise drab domestic economy in Ireland.

Yet by the spring of 2014, it was becoming clear that Portugal would follow where Ireland had led and also make a clean exit. The turnaround reflected a remarkable rally in euro-zone peripheral markets as investors decided that the once reviled sovereign debt of southern European members of the monetary union was the bargain of the year. The rally gathered force despite the Fed's tapering-away of its monthly asset purchases as bond markets in advanced countries generally did better than expected in a climate of low inflation. In that context, investors saw fresh attractions in peripheral debt in the single-currency club.[6] The euro-zone recovery that started in the spring of 2013 might be feeble but it was an improvement on the protracted double-dip recession from the third quarter of 2011 until the first quarter of 2013. And although the onset of lowflation was an ill tiding, since it made debt more burdensome, it added to the short-term attractions of purchasing peripheral bonds by increasing their real return; moreover, it shortened the odds on the ECB adopting QE, which would raise the prices of bonds still further.

It was the rally in the markets that gave Portugal its chance, by reopening its access to private financing. The crucial moment was in early January 2014 when the government's debt management agency raised €3.25 billion in five-year debt at a yield of 4.7 per cent in an issue attracting orders of over €11 billion.[7] The government then took a further leaf out of Ireland's book by using the favourable conditions to prefund its financing needs, building up a cash reserve that would enhance its ability to make a clean break later that spring.[8] That duly occurred, in May. But in a reminder of the internal opposition to the programme, another hostile ruling by the constitutional court on the government's fiscal measures, overturning public-sector pay cuts, which would have required the government to present alternative proposals to the troika, led Portugal to sidestep the final review and do without the final tranche of official financing.[9]

Although this cast a shadow over the Portuguese exit, such was the turnaround in market sentiment that it did not matter. The renewed investor confidence in peripheral Europe allowed Greece to return to the markets in April 2014, only two years after the biggest restructuring of debt on record. The government raised €3 billion in five-year debt at a yield of just under 5 per cent in a heavily oversubscribed issue. Although that yield was comparable to Portugal's in January, the rally had built upon itself to such an extent that Portuguese five-year notes were by then trading at 2.6 per cent.[10] The episode confounded those who feared that Greece would for long remain a pariah in the markets and seemed to mark a closure to the euro crisis. What was missing in that optimistic narrative was political risk in a country that had suffered an agonising economic reverse. The following month, Syriza topped the polls in the European election.

Yet, for investors and traders who looked ahead rather than back and focused typically on one story rather than several, the euro's existential crisis was ancient history. The capacity of bond markets to shake governments had defined the acute phase of the euro crisis. Led above all by the Fed, however, central banks had humbled the bond vigilantes by making massive interventions across the yield curve. In this new era, it was investors who now quailed at the power of central banks. Even though the ECB continued to desist from quantitative easing, preferring to brandish it as a possibility, markets were prepared to factor in an increasing likelihood that the policy would eventually be adopted.

As important, there was some substance to the sharp fall in bond yields across the periphery since there had been a notable improvement in the fiscal and economic imbalances that had contributed to the crisis. Underlying budgetary positions were improving markedly. Primary budget balances were in surplus in 2014 in Portugal and Greece (though the latter's was smaller than expected owing to a sharp fall in taxes late that year). Italy's had remained in the black throughout, apart from 2009.[11] Structural measures also showed substantial progress; for example, figures from the OECD for Ireland's structural primary budget balance, stripping out cyclical effects and one-offs as well as excluding interest payments, had gone from a deficit of 7.4 per cent of GDP in 2009 to zero by 2013.[12] That brightening picture dulled somewhat when attention was focused on the overall unadjusted budget balances, which included interest payments that were rising because of the increase in debt. For example, Portugal's budget deficit narrowed from 11.2 per cent of GDP in 2010 to 4.8 per cent in 2013, a smaller swing, of 6.4 percentage points, than the 8.3 points change over the same period on the primary budget.[13]

Despite its still extraordinarily high public debt, of 175 per cent of GDP in 2013, the Greek government's interest payments were manageable, at 4 per cent of national output, which was lower than in 2008, before the crisis, when they amounted to almost 5 per cent of GDP even though the debt burden then was much lower, at 109 per cent of output.[14] This reflected the fact that so much was now owed to euro area governments, which had long ago moved away from the early punitive rates of the first bail-out and were instead charging ultra-low interest rates. In cash terms, the interest burden was even lighter, at just 3 per cent of GDP, thanks to the decision taken by the Eurogroup in late 2012 to defer interest payments on most of the EFSF loans, amounting to about a third of total Greek public debt, for ten years.[15] Other rescued economies such as Ireland and Portugal also benefited from longer maturities and low interest rates, but their gain was smaller because their bail-outs had been much smaller and the share of the Irish and Portuguese bail-outs from the IMF, which had not offered similar concessions, was higher than its share of the two Greek rescues. Indeed, the Irish government used its ability to borrow more cheaply in the markets to repay early, in December 2014, €9 billion of its €22.5 billion loan from the IMF.[16]

The second component of the euro crisis – the chronic banking malaise – was also looking less menacing. The cure – big capital injections – had been mistimed. Whereas the US and UK had been swift to stuff capital into their weak banks, there were long delays in dealing with the capital shortfalls in the euro area. To varying degrees, bail-out money in the five rescues was directed towards troubled banking sectors. Greece and Spain each spent around €40 billion of the official financing on their banks. Even in Cyprus where most of the recapitalisation occurred through a bail-in of creditors, some of the official rescue finance went to support the cooperative banks which were regarded as worthier of help although many had lent recklessly; €1.5 billion of the total €9 billion from the ESM was used for this purpose.[17]

Elsewhere, a variety of methods were used to fill the capital holes. In Slovenia, the government stumped up the money required to deal with its three bust banks. In Italy, the central bank pressured banks to shore up their capital positions by selling unessential assets and curbing bonuses and dividends.[18] More generally, banks everywhere sought to improve their capital ratios by reducing their risk-weighted assets, cutting the overall size of balance sheets and changing their composition to less risky claims. Finally, the ECB's year-long comprehensive assessment was supposed to have drawn a line under the banking crisis, although there was a degree of scepticism about its findings, which revealed only shallow capital holes.

There were also encouraging signs of improvement in the third dimension to the crisis – the macroeconomic imbalances that had emerged within the euro area. In his book, *The Euro Trap,* Sinn was gloomy about whether some economies in southern Europe, particularly those of Greece, Portugal and Spain, could claw back competitiveness within the monetary union. He suggested that distressed countries should make a temporary exit and devalue their new currencies with the option of rejoining at some later stage.[19] Quite apart from the disruption that would cause, the diagnosis was questionable since measures of competitiveness based on unit labour costs rather than his preferred measure of prices suggested substantial improvement on the periphery. In the spring of 2014, the IMF estimated for example that the Greek real effective exchange rate was still overvalued using consumer prices by about 10 per cent, but had fallen below its level in 2000 using a gauge based on unit labour costs.[20]

Indeed, there was particularly striking progress in tackling the big current-account deficits that had emerged before the crisis among peripheral economies (see Figure 4). Ireland led the way, turning a deficit of nearly 6 per cent of GDP in 2008 to a surplus as early as 2010. The improvement was especially notable for Spain and Portugal, which moved from deficits of around 9.5 and 12 per cent of GDP, respectively, at their highest (in 2007 and 2008), to surpluses by 2013. The Greek current account switched from an extraordinary deficit of 14 per cent or more of GDP in 2007–8 to a small surplus in 2013. The Italian balance of payments also improved, though in a more modest fashion, moving from a deficit of 3.5 per cent of GDP in 2010 to a surplus of 1 per cent three years later.

The nature of the rebalancing varied. At first, it appeared that peripheral current accounts were improving primarily because imports were contracting sharply as domestic demand slumped, casting doubt over the sustainability of the adjustment once a recovery got under way. This story continued to hold broadly true for Greece. Although tourism eventually bounced back in 2013 and 2014, a prolonged slump in global shipping was unhelpful for an economy that relied heavily on this sector to bolster its balance of payments. But the biggest disappointment was that Greece's admittedly small goods exporting sector took so little advantage of gains in competitiveness when its labour costs eventually fell sharply, although belatedly there was a jump in overall exports in 2014, which grew by 9 per cent in real terms.[21]

The picture was more encouraging outside Greece. Irish export performance was helped by the fact that it was a base for multinationals making technologically advanced products like pharmaceuticals and providing services such as those related to information technology. In fact, the concentration of drugs firms became a disadvantage from the middle of 2012, as a number of products made in Ireland fell out of patent, sharply reducing their value. After slowing to a crawl in 2013, however, exports of goods and services rebounded in 2014.[22] A robust export recovery in Spain was also consistent with its record in the first decade of the euro, in which its exporters were surprisingly effective in defending their market shares, which fell overall relatively modestly given the country's sharply deteriorating competitiveness, a phenomenon dubbed the 'Spanish paradox'. One explanation, according to economists at BBVA, one of Spain's two big banks, was that firms were pursuing strategies for international markets that produced offsetting non-price improvements in their export performance.[23]

The most unexpected turnaround came in Portugal, which had been hurt before the crisis by the impact of low-cost producers in Asia on its textile industries. A boom in fuel exports as refinery production expanded did not make much difference to the balance of payments since the oil was imported. Yet excluding energy products from both exports and imports, the improvement in the goods balance between 2010 (when the overall current-account deficit was still 10 per cent of GDP) and 2013 came more from higher exports than lower imports while the services balance was boosted by higher tourism. Another encouraging feature of the Portuguese performance was that much of the rise in non-fuel goods exports was through trading with countries outside the EU.[24]

Although France ran a modest current-account deficit, averaging less than 1.5 per cent of GDP between 2011 and 2013, other countries in the core, especially Germany and the Netherlands continued to pile up big surpluses.[25] Because of its economic weight, the German surplus, which averaged over 6 per cent of GDP between 2007 and 2013, was the one that mattered. The continuing surpluses sparked sharp criticism from the US Treasury in October 2013, which argued that Germany was contributing to 'a deflationary bias' for the euro area and the global economy.[26] The surpluses also prompted an investigation by the Commission. Under its new macroeconomic monitoring regime, sustained big current-account imbalances were a cause for concern though the threshold for surpluses (6 per cent of GDP on average over a three-year period) was higher than that for deficits (4 per cent). In the event, Germany got no more than a mild ticking-off about the need to raise both business and public investment when the report was published in the spring of 2014.[27]

Yet the easing in the three crises – sovereign debt, banking and macroeconomic – was only partial. Although flows – the budget and current-account balances – were improving, stocks had risen to unsustainably high levels. Government debt as a share of GDP was far higher in 2013 than in 2007 (see Figure 7). At 175 per cent of GDP, Greece's debt was the most eyecatching (though that figure exaggerated the burden because of covert forms of relief such as extended maturities and ultralow interest rates on official loans), but debt was also oppressively high in Italy and Portugal where it was around 130 per cent of GDP. Irish debt peaked at over 120 per cent of GDP in 2013, but that measure flattered its position; measured against GNP, which stripped out the profits made by low-taxed foreign multinationals and was a better gauge of the taxable capacity of the Irish economy, it had peaked at almost 150 per cent in 2012.[28] Even such figures did not portray the full extent of state indebtedness as they did not include contingent liabilities that could end up on the public books if things went wrong. These were a particular worry for Portugal given its extensive public-private partnerships and state-owned enterprises.[29]

The banking system might have been cleaned up and recapitalised, but doubts about hidden bad loans lingered despite the efforts made by the ECB to quell them in its year-long assessment of their books. The collapse of Banco Espírito Santo in the summer of 2014, showed that euro-zone banks retained dark secrets. Whatever the true state of their balance sheets, as businesses they remained part of the problem rather than the solution. There were still too many banks and too great a reliance upon them. The underlying trend was still for banks to retrench, yet the euro area lacked a viable alternative in the form of sufficient market-based finance, a deficiency only starting to be tackled through the goal of a 'capital-markets union' set out by Juncker in the summer of 2014, before he took over as president of the Commission later that year.[30]

The macroeconomic improvement within the euro area was also less impressive than it appeared. Despite the turnaround in the balance of payments on the periphery, Germany continued to run a current-account surplus with the rest of the euro zone, although it had shrunk from the peak of over 4 per cent of GDP in 2007 to less than 2 cent in 2013.[31] In a report in December 2014, Moritz Kraemer, an analyst at Standard & Poor's, suggested that the rebalancing within the euro zone that had got under way in

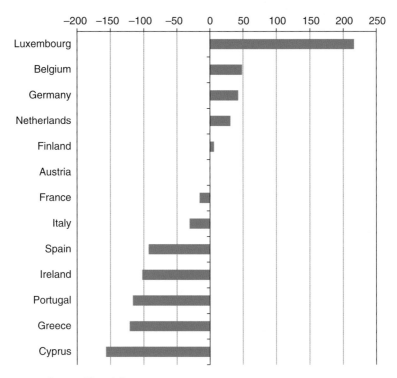

Source: Eurostat

FIGURE 15  Net international investment position, per cent of
GDP, 2013

2008 was stalling.[32] And, although current accounts might have
returned to surplus around the periphery (with the exception of
Cyprus), helped by demand from outside the euro area, the preceding deficits had left a pile of external debt. As a result, the net
international investment position – the balance of foreign assets
owned by a country's residents less their liabilities to foreigners –
was deeply in the red on the periphery (see Figure 15). In all five
countries that had been rescued, their external balance sheets were
negative, to as much as 100 per cent or more of GDP, far above the
threshold of 35 per cent identified by the Commission as a cause
for concern. Italy scored better since its shortfall was only around

30 per cent. For the economies such as Portugal, where the gap was so much larger, this left them worryingly vulnerable if international investors took fright again (though Greece was less exposed in this respect because it was mainly beholden to official creditors).

Related to these big net external liabilities, the fourth crisis – excessive private debt – remained stubbornly difficult to resolve. Debt levels as a share of GDP were higher in 2013 than in 2007 for the euro area and generally in the periphery, although Spain was making some progress in reducing this burden (see Figure 6). Luigi Buttiglione, Philip Lane, Lucrezia Reichlin and Vincent Reinhart highlighted the plight of the euro-zone periphery in a report, 'Deleveraging? What deleveraging?', published in the autumn of 2014. The four economists said that the debt overhangs represented 'a substantial drag on the potential growth performance' of this group of countries.[33] The fundamental problem besetting the single-currency area was that large parts of it, especially in southern Europe, were caught in a debt trap, in which indebtedness, both public and private, was too high and growth too low to break free.

The onset of lowflation and then outright deflation made that trap even harder to escape, kindling fears that the euro area was 'turning Japanese'. This would see the currency club caught in the clutches of persistent deflation, an outlook made more likely by the fact that Germany in particular had a similar demographic signature to Japan, vying with it for the intensity of population ageing in coming decades. Draghi resisted the troubling analogy, arguing in late 2013 and early 2014 that among other things European monetary policy was more preemptive and the euro area was confronting its banking problems more decisively than Japan when deflation started there in the late 1990s.[34] Yet there was a case for worrying that the euro zone might be even more vulnerable. One reason why Japan had been able to withstand the destructive effect of deflation on demand was through government borrowing, pushing up its public debt to around 245 per cent of GDP in 2014 (the net figure was much lower but still worryingly high at almost 130 per cent).[35] Whereas this escape route was possible in Japan, where most of the debt was domestically held, giving recourse to future generations of taxpayers, it was not feasible in the euro area, where foreign holdings were much more prominent.[36] Furthermore, the fiscal rules did not permit this and even if they were relaxed, foreign creditors would prove sterner taskmasters than the compliant Japanese population.

Despite the worries about the still sickly state of the euro area, European policymakers, especially in Germany, believed that the currency club could muddle through once the acute phase of the crisis was over. The worst afflicted economies, those that had required bail-out loans, would be helped through a covert form of debt forgiveness. Rather than outright writedowns of debt, which would have enraged electorates (and on any straightforward interpretation would have definitively breached the no-bail-out clause of the Maastricht Treaty), the euro area would assist through charging rock-bottom interest rates and by lengthening the term of the loans. In effect, it was a 'pretend and extend' strategy that delivered a present-value reduction in debt through low rates and longer maturities, even if face values remained the same.

Such help could not be offered to Italy, whose onerous sovereign debt (as a share of GDP) posed an ominous threat given the size of the Italian economy. But in *Managing the Euro Area Debt Crisis*, published in 2014, William Cline, an economist at the Peterson Institute for International Economics in Washington, argued that Italian public debt could nonetheless be brought back under control. Even though the starting point was already so high, at over 130 per cent of GDP, which meant that interest payments were also high, Cline forecast that by 2020 it would be less than 120 per cent, a level he judged to be sustainable given plausible growth and interest rate conditions. His debt forecasting model, encompassing favourable and unfavourable scenarios as well as central projections and taking into account privatisation revenues and debt that might emerge from the woodwork, produced this reassuring result mainly because Italy would run big enough primary surpluses over that period to more than offset the prospective increase in the debt burden (as a share of GDP) arising from interest on the existing stock of debt and weak growth prospects. Using the same approach, he was also confident about the underlying solvency of Ireland, Portugal and Spain, although Greece was likely to require further official debt relief.[37]

Cline argued that the euro area had much to gain by avoiding any further restructuring and much to lose by going down that path again. Europe should stick by the unwritten rule before the Greek default that developed economies do not renege upon their debt. Greece should remain the exception that the governments of the euro zone had said it was in 2011. He argued that the 'immaculate haircut' – one imposed without long-term harm – did not exist.[38] In fact, Greece's own return to the markets in April 2014, just two years after its restructuring, seemed to show that it was possible to kneecap investors without putting new ones off for good. An alternative view was that the euro area would need to confront both its sovereign and its private debt crises through more writedowns.

But even more important than debt reductions was a restoration of growth, which would make it easier to deal with any given level of debt. Although interest rates had fallen to record lows, those arguing that this would ease the pain of high debt were being too optimistic because what determined debt dynamics – the evolution of debt over time – was the differential between interest rates and growth, together with the primary budget balance. Even if nominal interest rates were very low, debt as a share of GDP would still increase if nominal growth were still lower or negative unless constrained by a primary surplus. And such a surplus would be harder to achieve if growth was lacking.

A recovery did get under way in the euro area after the protracted double-dip recession, but it was a feeble affair. It began in the spring of 2013 with a quarterly expansion of 0.4 per cent. Dispiritingly, this was as good as it got until the end of 2014. There were some bright spots, notably recoveries in Portugal and Spain. But the euro area was

blighted by its poorly performing second- and third-biggest economies. France was stuck in a rut while output continued to slide or at
best to stagnate in Italy. That left the upturn over-reliant on Germany;
and when its economy suffered a setback in the second quarter of
2014, the euro-zone recovery stalled.[39] The release of this information
in August was a moment of truth revealing the continuing frailty of
the euro area. Although subsequent revisions showed that GDP had
expanded in the spring (though only by 0.1 per cent), growth remained
barely discernible until the final three months of the year, when output increased once again by 0.4 per cent.[40]

So weak and faltering was the recovery that European economists, using a similar approach to that of the National Bureau of
Economic Research in the US for dating business cycles, argued in
the middle of 2014 that it was not worthy of the name. They preferred
instead to call it 'a prolonged pause in the recession' that had started in
2011.[41] Whatever it was called, so feeble an upturn was something the
euro area could ill afford. In Italy, for example, the chronic weakness of
the economy made for troubling debt dynamics. Since Italian GDP
was continuing to shrink in real terms though more moderately than
before (by 0.4 per cent in 2014) and inflation was very low, the sovereign debt burden would carry on rising even though the government
was running a primary surplus of nearly 2 per cent of GDP.[42]

If the euro area had been a genuinely integrated single economy
with a federal government, the diagnosis and remedy would have been
relatively simple. Clearly, it was suffering from deficient demand. Put
another way, there was a big output gap; in its economic forecast in
late 2014, the Commission estimated that GDP that year was 2.8 per
cent below its potential.[43] Draghi's speech at Jackson Hole in August
2014 drew attention because by highlighting a sharp fall in longer term
inflation expectations, he appeared to signal a new urgency in providing extra monetary stimulus. But his speech, which was actually
about unemployment in the euro area, had another message to con-
vey: getting people back to work required not just structural reforms
to tackle poorly functioning labour markets but also a concerted effort

by national governments through fiscal policy as well as by the ECB through monetary policy to boost demand. When Draghi said, tactfully, that it might be 'useful to have a discussion on the overall fiscal stance of the euro area', this was a plea for euro-zone leaders, and above all Merkel, to raise their eyes above their national parapets and to act as if they were collectively responsible for the monetary union's economy as a whole. Since the German government had the most room for fiscal manoeuvre among the big economies, this could be interpreted as a call for Merkel to loosen the budgetary reins.[44]

Instead of such a concerted fiscal effort to foster a genuine recovery, the euro area found itself in a typical impasse in the autumn of 2014. Merkel and Schäuble made a small concession to spend more on public works, but they stuck to their objective of balancing the German federal budget in 2015 – known as the 'black zero' (in the event achieved a year early, in 2014); higher spending on infrastructure between 2016 and 2018 would amount altogether to only €10 billion.[45] The German government was hostile to any slackening in fiscal effort in France and Italy. There was dismay in Berlin when following the disappointing second quarter in which the French economy floundered again, Michel Sapin, the finance minister, peremptorily declared that France would be unable to meet its fiscal objective for 2015.[46] This after all was a target to lower the budget deficit to within the Maastricht limit of 3 per cent of GDP whose deadline had already been extended by two years in May 2013. Merkel was also at odds with Renzi over his budgetary plans for 2015, which would keep the deficit close to the Maastricht limit.[47]

The tension between Germany on the one hand and France and Italy on the other reflected continuing flaws in the governance of the euro zone, despite the efforts to resolve this fifth and most serious dimension to the euro crisis. A permanent rescue fund had been created in the shape of the ESM. But as De Witte pointed out, this new regime was 'marked by a high degree of intergovernmentalism'.[48] Similarly, the Single Resolution Fund, a crucial component in the banking union, was based on an intergovernmental agreement during the eight-year period when national funds from bank levies were being transferred to a common pool and progressively mutualised.[49]

Other reforms had strengthened the hand of the Commission in conducting both economic and fiscal surveillance, through the 'six-pack', which came into force in December 2011.[50] Sounding rather more muscular than it really was – five regulations (applying directly) and one directive (requiring national legislation to take effect) – the six-pack gave the Commission new powers to monitor the European economy for emerging economic imbalances, allowing for example its probe into Germany's big current-account surplus. The six-pack also strengthened the stability pact by allowing action to tackle excessive debt as well as deficits and by introducing 'reverse' qualified majority voting on proposed punishment of miscreant euro-zone states. The voting arrangement meant that instead of a majority being required to impose sanctions one was needed to block most of them, making the process more automatic and strengthening the hand of a reformed sinner like Germany in getting the rules enforced. Tellingly, however, the fiscal compact, so dear to Merkel's heart, was specifically designed to enforce budgetary responsibility at a national rather than euro-zone level.

A follow-up 'two-pack' (in this case, two regulations), which came into force in May 2013 and applied only to the euro area states, strengthened fiscal surveillance, in particular by requiring countries to submit their draft budgets to the Commission.[51] This process started in the autumn of 2013, when thirteen out of the seventeen states notified their plans (including Spain but not the four countries that had received full bail-outs and were already being intensively monitored).[52] Although authority for budget-making remained with the national parliaments, this gave the Commission (along with the Eurogroup) an opportunity to influence fiscal policies earlier than before.

The reforms took the Maastricht model of independent fiscal states binding themselves to common rules and central monitoring to its limit, according to one senior official in Brussels. That limit included comprehension. In a report on euro area policies in July 2014, the IMF said that the rules of the stability pact had become 'exceedingly complex', illustrating its critique pointedly with a diagram showing the various constraints (eight or nine depending upon whether or not the fiscal compact national rule was included) and measures of performance (six) that resembled a cat's cradle. The Fund also pointed out that sanctions and corrective actions were 'mild' compared with existing federations.[53] But their main flaw was that they left an economic policy vacuum, which was particularly hazardous when conventional monetary policies had been exhausted, requiring the ECB eventually to adopt QE, even though this was much trickier for a diverse monetary union than for countries retaining their own currencies and autonomous central banks.

The steps taken to create a banking union, in particular the creation of a single supervisor, undoubtedly marked an important advance though it remained half-built, in large part reflecting the reluctance to provide a fiscal backstop. That was if nothing else in keeping with the wider framework of governance for the currency union, which was also a construction site where the workers had downed tools. For all the institutional changes, such as the ESM, and the attempts to strengthen fiscal surveillance, the euro area was far from being a federal state. The ECB might have sweeping new supervisory powers but it remained a unique body, a central bank without a state. The euro zone had no budget of its own and no fiscal authority.

In one of Trichet's parting shots, speaking in Aachen in June 2011 when accepting the Charlemagne prize for fostering European unity (previous prizewinners included the euro), he asked rhetorically whether it would be 'too bold' for Europe eventually to have its own finance ministry, though not necessarily one with a big budget.[54] By December 2012, the leisurely timetable envisaged by Trichet had been superseded by a more urgent call to arms, in a report from the 'four presidents', Herman Van Rompuy, of the European Council, together with Barroso, Draghi and Juncker, as head of the Eurogroup. *Towards a Genuine Economic and Monetary Union* – the title was a confession in itself – made the case for yet another three-stage process of deeper integration, including more coordinated efforts to promote structural reforms, in which the third stage, after 2014, would feature the creation of 'a well-defined and limited fiscal capacity' in order to provide a means of cushioning shocks hurting specific countries.[55]

The four presidents did not get their way since the crisis was by then ebbing. The bevy of chiefs inadvertently revealed the dysfunctional nature of Europe's decision-making processes; by the time of a subsequent report in June 2015 urging more integration within the euro area there were five, as the head of the European Parliament joined the deliberations. Still, Draghi continued to urge further institutional strengthening, understandably since the ECB remained in a lonely position. His address at Jackson Hole in 2014 came shortly after an even more overtly integrationist call for action in London two years after his 'whatever it takes' intervention. Whereas his remarks in the US suggested that European leaders should use the existing system of budgetary responsibilities to work more closely together in forging a collective fiscal stance, his speech in London pressed the case for 'some form of common governance over structural reforms'.[56] This demand went beyond the 'intense dialogue' between states and European institutions and contractual arrangements (involving financial incentives) that the four presidents had advocated in 2012; even though these were to be mandatory for euro-zone states they had acknowledged that 'national ownership is pivotal to implementation of structural reforms'.[57] Draghi said that the common interest in them was such that they should be 'made subject to discipline at the community level'. And he spelt out bluntly what this would mean: national debates would centre not on whether reforms should take place, but how they should be implemented.

If European leaders were to accept this centralising agenda, it would take integration into the very heart of domestic politics since structural reform increasingly strayed into the most sensitive areas of national life, such as the design of pension systems. Draghi's case for this further encroachment on national sovereignty rested on the fact that the euro area was not a transfer union, and hence each economy had in the longer term 'to stand on its own feet'. Structural reforms were needed to avoid permanent imbalances. In a similar vein, speaking on the same day in Athens, Benoît Cœuré, the French member of the ECB's executive board, likened membership of the euro zone to taking part in a 'political triathlon' composed of fiscal, economic and financial policies.[58] The most important lesson of the crisis, he argued, was that the euro-zone 'team' could be strong only if every participant did well in all three disciplines. This was a remarkable claim to make, as if the economic fate of the US, a monetary union that worked, were to depend on its worst-performing state, Mississippi.[59]

Yet there was a compelling logic behind the central bankers' demands for further integration, as the renewed Greek crisis in 2015 illustrated. Even more than in 2012, the German government made clear that there were limits to German patience in the face of Greek recalcitrance. Already in a warning shot ahead of the election in January that brought a Syriza-led government to power, Merkel was reportedly prepared to let Greece go, in contrast to the stance she had eventually taken in 2012.[60] That threat of an enforced departure – supposedly a 'time out' of at least five years – was brandished openly in the harsh negotiations of mid July. But although creditor nations needed to be able to threaten such an exit to avoid blackmail from debtor countries, it remained the case, as in 2012, that a departure would undermine the principle that euro zone membership was irrevocable, undermining long-term confidence in the project. Given this continuing risk, there had to be an alternative method of keeping unruly members of the currency club in line.

Without such an extension of euro-wide control, the continuing expansion of the single currency's reach was less welcome than it appeared to be. The adoption of the euro, by Latvia in 2014 and Lithuania in 2015, was naturally greeted as an endorsement of the single currency. Instead of fragmenting as had been feared during the acute phase of the crisis, the monetary union continued to attract new members. Yet the expansion raised the risk that at some point another country would get into trouble and come under pressure to leave. The construction of the euro zone remained structurally fragile since its viability remained as strong as the weakest link.

The continuing expansion of the euro was in any case less impressive in terms of population. The number of people in the seven states that joined after Greece in 2001 was just 15 million out of a total population of 340 million in the 19-strong union in 2015.[61] Joining the club was also driven increasingly by strategic rather than economic priorities. For Latvia, membership of the euro provided a further bulwark of European solidarity for small states previously under the Soviet yoke. It was this strategic case for adopting the euro that led the prime minister, Valdis Dombrovskis, to brush aside public opposition, even though a majority of Latvians opposed membership. The Latvian foreign minister stressed in 2013 that joining the euro was above all 'a geopolitical choice'.[62] By contrast, countries in northern Europe that were far closer to the core euro-zone members historically, economically and politically continued to stand apart. This was not just a matter of British exceptionalism. Denmark, which had joined the European community along with Ireland and the UK in 1973, preferred to stay outside even though it retained a firm peg to the euro, just as it had done before with the deutsche mark since 1982.[63] And Sweden, which had joined the EU in 1995, also stayed aloof even though it did not have a legal opt-out right. In both countries, public opposition ruled out membership.

The advent of the new members added to the cumbersome decision-making processes of the ECB. Each new state, however small it might be, brought a new central bank governor with a seat on the governing council. The arrival of Lithuania in 2015, taking the total size of the council to twenty-five, triggered a new voting system to deal with the surfeit of chiefs, in which the number of voting rights would be limited to twenty-one, of which the board would hold six permanently while the remaining fifteen would be divided between the central bank governors. The reform, which had been planned over a decade earlier when the EU was due to expand from fifteen to twenty-five states in 2004, meant that the five central bank governors from countries with the biggest economies and banking sectors (Germany, France, Italy, Spain and the Netherlands) would share four votes, meaning that every fifth month Weidmann would for example lose his vote; the other fourteen governors would share eleven voting rights.[64] Making matters still more complicated, the introduction of the new rotation system coincided with a reduction in the number of monetary-policy meetings from twelve to eight, so that the monthly rotation of votes meant that governors could lose their vote in a month when there was no meeting anyway. For example, although Weidmann lost his vote in May 2015 that did not affect him because it was one of the four months when there was no meeting; however, when he next lost his vote, in October, there was one.[65]

As this implication of the impending Lithuanian membership dawned upon Germans in 2014, the move was greeted in some quarters with dismay; conservative politicians criticised a system that would mean the intermittent disenfranchisement of the Bundesbank president.[66] In fact, the new voting arrangements changed little since Weidmann could be outvoted at any meeting and he would still be present and able to participate in discussions. If anything, a decision that he opposed would be less likely to be pushed through at a meeting when he was unable to vote. What the complex shake-up of the council's procedures highlighted was the half-hearted integration of the ECB itself, since if its governance had been truly European, it would have emulated the Fed's structure, with a few regional central banks each straddling more than one country; alternatively, the NCBs could all be turned into branches, as Marsh advocated in his book, *Europe's Deadlock*.[67]

The sour response of Germans to the reconfiguration of the ECB council's voting system nonetheless bore witness to the limits of reform. In a speech in Helsinki in November 2014, Draghi went further than his predecessor, Trichet, and beyond the more modest proposal of the four presidents' report in arguing the case for a fiscal union, saying that doubts over the viability of the monetary union would be fully removed only through achieving an economic and fiscal union. The head of the ECB made clear that he did not envisage a transfer union, but he argued that for budgetary policy to be available to help stabilise the business cycle there needed to be 'a decisive step towards closer fiscal union'. More generally, the euro's ultimate success depended on acknowledging that 'sharing a single currency *is* political union, and following through with the consequences'.[68]

At the height of the crisis, Merkel had toyed with the idea of moving towards a genuine fiscal and political union.[69] But such an initiative, which was in any case couched in no more than vague terms, would have been extraordinarily difficult to sell to German voters and indeed to other European leaders even during the emergency. Once things calmed down, it was quietly set on one side, no matter what Draghi might urge. From a national perspective, there was no need to do more. Although the German economy was hurt more than expected in the middle of 2014 by the Ukraine crisis and the impact of sanctions against Russia, its underlying health remained robust with employment at its highest since unification; indeed it sprang back into unexpectedly strong growth in the final quarter of the year. Moreover, the emergence of the euro-sceptic AfD made it harder for Merkel to make further concessions in the European cause.

If the euro area could not progress towards a fiscal union, then it was vital to restore the balance between liability and control, argued Weidmann in a speech staking out the Bundesbank's position on the way forward for the currency bloc, which he delivered in Amsterdam in April 2014.[70] That balance was essential for the stability of the monetary union: 'you would certainly not want to share your bank account with your neighbour if you were unable to control his or her spending'. But it had become 'lopsided' owing to the various rescues during the crisis. Given the reluctance of the euro-zone states to relinquish fiscal sovereignty, 'the principle of individual responsibility' had to be restored. As well as getting investors to shoulder their duties through effective bail-in procedures for creditors, national governments would have to deliver on their pledges to keep their public finances shipshape. In effect, Weidmann was calling for the reinforcement of the original Maastricht template. But since that could involve debt restructuring – 'if the fiscal limit has been reached for real, public debt needs to be restructured without posing a systemic threat to financial stability' – his was an uncomfortable message for European leaders who had been scarred by their experience in enforcing that in Greece.

The continuing disjuncture between the deeper integration needed to make the monetary union really work, and the political impossibility of bringing that about in a Europe that feared any close encounter with voters, above all in possible referendums on new treaties, meant that the institutional framework of the monetary union remained an unsatisfactory halfway-house. As Weidmann also pointed out in Amsterdam, a genuine fiscal union would require changes to the European treaties and national constitutions. 'But judging by the reluctance of governments and electorates to let Brussels have a say on fiscal matters', he went on to say, 'this avenue seems blocked, at least for the foreseeable future'. The terror that the notion of treaty change inspired in European leaders, most of all in France following the rebuff by voters in the referendum of 2005 on the proposed European constitution (which was then essentially repackaged as the Lisbon Treaty), left the euro area in a legal limbo. Indeed, one reason why the single resolution mechanism and the fund underpinning it were such a messy compromise was legal concern on the part of Schäuble about whether they could be put in place without treaty change, leading him to argue that this meant that the banking union would have to be 'timber-framed' rather than 'steel-framed'.[71]

One source of strength was that the euro was surprisingly popular. Regular opinion surveys conducted for the Commission suggested a firm bedrock of support for the single currency. According to one published in October 2014, 57 per cent of people in the euro area thought that the euro was good for their country, whereas 33 per cent thought it was bad.[72] Remarkably, support for it across the bloc had increased since 2007, before the financial crisis, when 45 per cent had judged it good and 42 per cent bad.[73] Unsurprisingly, scepticism was greatest in southern Europe, with narrow majorities of Cypriots and Italians believing that the euro hurt rather than benefited their nation. On the other hand, despite their arduous bail-out programme, the Irish were the strongest backers of the single currency. And for all the hardship they had endured during the crisis, many more Greeks considered the euro good (59 per cent) rather than bad (28 per cent); this was all the more remarkable given the fact that in 2007 the Greeks were least keen on the euro, with a big majority thinking it was a bad thing for their country.

But backing for the euro did not protect it from the vagaries and contradictions of national politics, both in the south and in the north, and the uncertainty this created – the sixth dimension to the crisis. Despite the Greek public's support for the euro, Syriza prevailed in the election of January 2015 even though its policies were bound to antagonise the rest of the euro zone, calling into question Greece's membership of the currency club. The resulting crisis meant that for the second time in the brief history of the euro (the first being in Cyprus in 2013), banks were closed for weeks and capital controls introduced for much longer, an indictment of a monetary union conceived in part as a solution to the free movement of capital. Once again, the underlying fragility of the euro area was revealed as frantic rounds of emergency meetings by its leaders were required to sort out the Greek imbroglio.

The biggest loser was Greece, in large measure owing to the damaging policies pursued by the Syriza-dominated government. By pursuing an adversarial attempt to rewrite the terms of its relationship with the rest of the euro area, confidence was sapped, causing the persistent drain of deposits and increasing reliance on emergency central bank lending that hampered the banks from providing credit to businesses. Moreover, the government's strategy of stringing out the talks meant that it ran so short of money that commercial creditors were not paid, who in turn were unable to pay their suppliers, adding to the overall liquidity squeeze on the economy. The self-harm was magnified by the imposition of capital controls at the end of June and the closure of banks for three weeks. Instead of growing by almost 3 per cent in 2015, as the European Commission had forecast in November 2014, the economy looked set to contract by nearly as much; for example, economists at Barclays forecast a decline in GDP of 2.1 per cent.[74]

The crisis also destroyed hopes that Greek public debt might be brought to a sustainable level over the next few years. In November 2012, euro-zone governments had agreed with the IMF upon a goal for the debt to be 'substantially below' 110 per cent of GDP by 2022 and said that they would consider further measures to bring this about, provided that Greece complied with the conditions of the programme. In an analysis just before the escalation of the crisis when Tsipras called the referendum, the IMF said that by the late summer of 2014 that objective had become attainable, mainly because of lower interest rates. Whereas the Fund's projection in May 2014 was for debt to reach 117 per cent in 2022, the improved outlook had changed that to 104 per cent, putting it on a sustainable path without more help. All that had been thrown away since the new projection showed debt at around 140 per cent in 2022.

Three weeks later the IMF published an even bleaker update, in which it forecast that debt would peak at close to 200 per cent of GDP in the next two years rather than at 177 per cent in 2014 as previously expected; and it was projected to be 170 per cent in 2022. Greek debt could be made sustainable only by providing relief that went 'far beyond what Europe has been willing to consider so far', whether through deep reductions in its face value or an extended moratorium of as long as 30 years on any repayments of principal (which already benefited from a 'grace period' of ten years until the end of 2022).[75]

The IMF's judgement showed once again the old truth that a debtor in trouble passes the problem back to the creditor. Even if Greece had lost most in the crisis of 2015, northern creditor nations in the euro area would also suffer. But the collateral damage of the

Greek crisis was more worrying still. The euro was after all conceived primarily in political terms as a means of binding the peoples of European nations together. Instead, it had become a means of tearing them apart as the crude caricatures of feckless Greeks in Germany and of bullying Germans in Greece which came to the fore demonstrated. Even if a typical eleventh-hour deal had kept the euro together, a venture subject to such political rifts and ill-feeling remained inherently flawed.

Further political tensions seemed likely if the currency union's dismal economic performance continued (see Table 2). The euro might have celebrated its fifteenth anniversary at the start of 2014, but there was little to toast in its economic performance. Growth in living standards (measured by GDP per person) between 1999 and 2014 was a spartan 11 per cent (0.7 per cent a year) across the 12-strong euro zone (the eleven founders together with Greece). This compared with 13 per cent in Japan, usually dismissed as a deflationary loser, 17 per cent in the US and 19.5 per cent in the UK, even though the latter in particular had taken a beating from the financial crisis. Sweden, also outside the euro area, had done particularly well.

Despite its setback during the crisis, the Irish economy grew the fastest within the euro area over the period, a tribute to its rapid expansion until 2007 and a recovery that took wings in 2014, when GDP expanded by nearly 5 per cent. However, the scars of the crisis were visible in the labour market where its jobless rate of 11.3 per cent in 2014 was double that in 1999. The performance of southern Europe, suffering from mass unemployment and lost output on an epic scale, was bleak. In Portugal, living standards had improved by 3 per cent over fifteen years; in Greece, by 1 per cent. Italians were actually 3 per cent poorer in 2014 than they had been in 1999. The record on unemployment was also dismal. The Portuguese jobless rate had fallen from its high during the crisis but at 14 per cent in 2014 was far higher than in 1999, when it was less than 6 per cent. Southern nations had long been enthusiastic supporters of the European project because they saw it as a means of catching

Table 2 *Per cent change in GDP per person in euro area and other advanced countries between 1999 and 2014, unemployment in 1999 and 2014*

| | GDP per person, 1999–2014,% change | Unemployment rate,% | |
|---|---|---|---|
| | | 1999 | 2014 |
| Euro area (12) | 11.1 | 9.5 | 11.6 |
| Ireland | 22.0 | 5.7 | 11.3 |
| Germany | 21.2 | 8.6 | 5 |
| Austria | 17.7 | 4.2 | 5.6 |
| Finland | 17.6 | 10.2 | 8.7 |
| Luxembourg | 17.1 | 2.4 | 6 |
| Belgium | 13.0 | 8.5 | 8.5 |
| Netherlands | 12.3 | 4.2 | 7.4 |
| France | 10.5 | 10 | 10.2 |
| Spain | 9.6 | 13.6 | 24.5 |
| Portugal | 2.7 | 5.5 | 14.1 |
| Greece | 0.9 | 12 | 26.5 |
| Italy | –2.8 | 10.9 | 12.7 |
| **Non-euro area countries** | | | |
| Sweden | 24.2 | 6.7 | 7.9 |
| United Kingdom | 19.5 | 5.9 | 6.1 |
| United States | 16.7 | 4.2 | 6.2 |
| Japan | 13.1 | 4.7 | 3.6 |

*Sources:* IMF; Eurostat

up with prosperous northern countries. Instead, that general process of convergence had given way to divergence.

That unfortunate outcome might prove temporary if the promising signs of revival in Portugal and Spain augured better prospects throughout the euro area, helped by QE. In early 2015, there were increasing signs that the euro zone might at long last be experiencing a recovery worthy of the name. Equity markets were buoyant and business and particularly consumer sentiment improved markedly. The jury was still out, however, on whether this was a cyclical upturn, driven in particular by the temporary impact of the fall in the oil price in the second half of 2014, which worked like a tax cut for both businesses and consumers, or something that would take root and flourish allowing at least some of the lost ground in the prolonged period of weakness since the financial crisis to be regained.

In one of the many paradoxes of the euro experiment, the single currency that was once supposed to boost growth now itself needed growth if it was to continue in the long run. For although the euro area had fended off the threats that loomed so large in the acute phase, it remained vulnerable to political risk if economies within the club continued to do so badly. In late 2014, shortly before the Greek crisis flared up again, Draghi conceded this point in his speech in Helsinki saying that member states had to be better off inside than they would be outside since 'if there are parts of the euro area that are worse off inside the union doubts may grow about whether they might ultimately have to leave'; this would create 'a replicable precedent for all countries'. In 2013, Nicholas Crafts, an economic historian at Warwick University, pointed out that the euro had in practice been harder to leave than the gold standard, with which it bore several disconcerting resemblances. But the currency club's success in holding together might turn out to be a Pyrrhic victory, since countries leaving the gold standard in the 1930s did better than those who stayed on it. The long-term growth prospects of the euro zone, he argued, were poor because of the big overhang of public debt. His gloomy conclusion was that saving the euro had come 'at a very high price', resulting in what might well be a lost decade for southern Europe.[76]

Another paradox in the story of the euro's survival was the fact that Germany had done particularly well despite all the angst about the rescue packages. In the story of the euro's survival, Germans cast themselves in the role of the reluctant and put-upon saviour. Each successive bail-out had to win approval from the Bundestag, which could not be taken for granted. Other steps to make the currency union more stable also encountered resistance. The Bundesbank, in particular, got a bloody nose after it failed to block Draghi from pushing the bond-purchasing pledge in September 2012, but was then handed a helping hand by the constitutional court. The German government fought a dogged rearguard battle to restrict the banking union that Merkel had accepted in June 2012.

Yet, in economic terms, the Germans were the clear winners from the currency union. In part owing to a stagnant population, the improvement in their living standards was second-biggest among the founder members of the monetary union, rising by 21 per cent between 1999 and 2014, easily outstripping the gain in France whose GDP per person increased by 10.5 per cent, in line with the euro-zone average. Moreover, the unemployment rate in Germany was just 5 per cent in 2014 compared with 8.6 per cent in 1999. And although consumers would have fared better still with a stronger currency, as would have been the case had they retained the deutsche mark, exporters were buoyed by a currency that became undervalued for Germany. During the crisis, the German economy benefited as a haven for capital, which pushed interest rates down. The economic gains from the euro were reflected in public support for the euro, which was lacking in the early years of the single currency.[77] Whereas more Germans thought it bad rather than good for their country in 2007 – ironically, they were only a little less hostile than the Greeks – their attitudes also changed. In 2014, as many as 65 per cent said the euro benefited Germany and only 24 per cent thought it was bad for the country.

In a broader geopolitical sense, the Germans also prevailed. A currency designed to wrest economic power away from Germany did exactly the opposite. In Frankfurt, the Bundesbank might play second fiddle to the ECB, but more generally it was Berlin rather than Brussels that now held sway. Merkel might be mild-mannered but she had become the unofficial leader not just of the euro area but of Europe, even though the power was thrust upon her through events and Germany's underlying economic and fiscal weight in the monetary union. The euro was supposed to create a European Germany, and to the extent that Germany did lead the rescues of the peripheral countries, maybe it was doing that. But what was indisputable was that it was creating a German Europe. The price of German support to countries in southern Europe was for them to become more Prussian than Germany itself in binding themselves to strict fiscal targets and accepting harsh structural reforms, a price that became even more galling when Merkel's coalition government formed in late 2013 relaxed its own stance.

In the most painful paradox of all, the currency that was supposed to secure the European project was instead generating rancour and instability. Extremist politics made a breakthrough both at national and European levels. The populist backlash against Europe in the elections of May 2014 should not have come as a surprise. For decades, governments had blamed unpleasant measures on the demands of Europe, which had become a convenient whipping-boy for politicians seeking to displace national pain. This poisonous habit of buckpassing was possible because no one any longer seemed to be fully in control owing to the incomplete and haphazard process of European integration, of which the euro was the flagship even if voters chose to focus on other institutions for their discontent. The biggest threat to the euro remained the lack of a corresponding federal state. A currency spanning national borders and run by a supranational institution lacked legitimacy. Occasional hearings of Draghi at the European Parliament could not rectify the imbalance between the ECB, a power not just within the euro area but on the global stage, and weak democratic institutions.

From the beginning, the euro was an extraordinary venture. That it had survived the economic and financial equivalent of a life-threatening illness was testimony to an underlying resilience. But that episode of acute crisis had weakened it and the measures undertaken in response had in large measure been grudging attempts to restore the spirit of the original design even though it had failed so dismally. Manifestly, it had been unwise to create a single money first and then to try to create, if not a federal state, a more secure set of common institutions. Yet retreat appeared to be harder than advance. Judged by economic performance and political cohesion, the experiment had failed. But judged by survival, it had succeeded although Greece's place within the monetary union still looked precarious. Survival was not enough. But it gave the euro further time to redeem itself, leaving the final outcome of the experiment still to be determined.

# Notes

I   A QUESTION OF SURVIVAL

1. Jean-Claude Trichet, interview with *Le Figaro* (23 January 2009).

2. European Commission (EC), 'Communication from the Commission', in *EMU@10: Successes and Challenges after Ten Years of Economic and Monetary Union* (May 2008), p. 3.

3. Lars Jonung and Eoin Drea, 'The euro: it can't happen. It's a bad idea. It won't last. US economists on the EMU 1989–2002', Economic paper 395 (EC, December 2009), pp. 4, 12, 28.

4. Martin Feldstein, 'EMU and international conflict' (*Foreign Affairs*, November–December 1997).

5. Deutsche Bank Markets Research, 'Bonds: the final bubble frontier?' Long-term asset return study (10 September 2014), pp. 8–10.

6. 'Statement by President Barroso following the College visit to Athens for the start of the Greek presidency' (EC, 8 January 2014).

7. 'President Sarkozy's press conference in Brussels' (2 March 2012).

8. Christine Lagarde, 'The road to sustainable global growth – the policy agenda' (IMF, 2 April 2014).

9. IMF, *World Economic Outlook* (October 2014), p. 14, Figure 1.12.

10. US Bureau of Labour Statistics, data.bls.gov/timeseries/LNS14000000; Eurostat, press release on unemployment (31 March 2015); Eurostat (statistics explained) ec.europa.eu/eurostat/statistics-explained/index.php/Unemployment_statistics.

11. Jay C. Shambaugh, 'The euro's three crises' (*Brookings Papers on Economic Activity*, Spring 2012), pp. 158–9.

12. German Council of Economic Experts, *Annual Report 2012/13* (November 2012), English translation, Chapter 2, pp. 2–3.

13. IMF, *World Economic Outlook* database (April 2015), current-account balances in dollars, imf.org/external/pubs/ft/weo/2015/01/weodata/index.aspx.

14. Carmen M. Reinhart and Kenneth S. Rogoff, *This Time Is Different* (Princeton University Press, 2009), pp. 98–9.
15. Paul De Grauwe, 'Managing a fragile euro zone' (VoxEU, 10 May 2011); 'The European Central Bank as a lender of last resort' (VoxEU, 18 August 2011).
16. Charles Wyplosz, 'ECB's outright monetary transactions' (*European Parliament*, October 2012), pp. 4–8; Marcus Miller and Lei Zhang, 'Saving the euro: self-fulfilling crisis and the "Draghi put"' (VoxEU, 26 June 2014).
17. EC, *Statistical Annex of European Economy* (May 2015), Table 78, p. 164.
18. 'Italy's Grillo pushes euro referendum campaign in Brussels' (*EurActiv*, 13 November 2014).
19. 'François Hollande becomes most unpopular French president ever' (*The Guardian*, 29 October 2013).
20. 'Spanish upstart party challenges status quo' (*Financial Times*, 22 November 2014).
21. European Parliament, 'Results of the 2014 European elections'; 'Merkel's right wingers suffer jitters over eurosceptic threat' (*Financial Times*, 17 September 2014): 10.6 per cent in Thuringia and 12.2 per cent in Brandenburg.
22. 'Euro zone warns on fiscal rules' (*Financial Times*, 13 September 2014).
23. 'Greece's economy: running on empty' (*The Economist*, 7 March 2015).
24. 'Euro summit statement' (12 July 2015).
25. 'Greek leftist widens poll lead, says to end "humiliation"' (*Reuters*, 22 January 2015).
26. Thomas Mayer, *Europe's Unfinished Currency* (Anthem Press, 2012); David Marsh, *Europe's Deadlock* (Yale University Press, 2013); Jean Pisani-Ferry, *The Euro Crisis and Its Aftermath* (Oxford University Press, 2014); Hans-Werner Sinn, *The Euro Trap* (Oxford University Press, 2014); John Peet and Anton La Guardia, *Unhappy Union* (Profile Books, 2014).
27. Mario Draghi, 'A consistent strategy for a sustained recovery' (ECB, 25 March 2014).
28. EC, *EMU@10*, p. 4.

## 2 DEFECTIVE DESIGN

1. EC, *Statistical Annex* (November 2014), Table 1, p. 10.
2. 'Schröder nennt Euro "kränkelnde Frühgeburt"' (Berliner Zeitung, 27 March 1998).

3. ECB, 'The accountability of the ECB' (*Monthly Bulletin*, November 2002), p. 48.

4. Jeffrey Frankel and Andrew Rose, 'The endogeneity of the optimum currency area criteria', Working paper 5700 (NBER, August 1996), p. 22.

5. 'Robert A. Mundell – facts' (nobelprize.org).

6. Robert A. Mundell, 'A theory of optimum currency areas' (*American Economic Review*, September 1961), Vol. 51, No. 4, pp. 657–65.

7. Harold James, 'Monetary and fiscal unification in nineteenth-century Germany: what can Kohl learn from Bismarck?', *Essays in International Finance*, 202 (Princeton University, March 1997), pp. 3–4.

8. Charles Kindleberger, *A Financial History of Western Europe* (George Allen & Unwin, 1984), p. 117.

9. James, 'Monetary and fiscal unification in nineteenth-century Germany', pp. 9–10.

10. National Monetary Commission, *The Reichsbank: 1876–1900* (Washington, DC, Government Printing Office, 1910), pp. 15–17, 21, 35–6.

11. Deutsche Bundesbank, 'Circulation of the deutsche mark – from currency reform to European monetary union' (*Monthly Report*, March 2002), pp. 19–20; Kindleberger, *A Financial History of Western Europe*, p. 301.

12. Avi Shlaim, *The United States and the Berlin Blockade, 1948–1949: A Study in Crisis Decision-Making* (University of California Press, 1983), pp. 151–62.

13. Francesco Paolo Mongelli, 'The OCA theory and the path to EMU', in Marco Buti, Servaas Deroose, Vítor Gaspar and João Nogueira Martins (eds.), *The Euro: The First Decade* (Cambridge University Press, 2010), pp. 115–22, summarises some main findings.

14. EC, *Statistical Annex* (November 2014), Table 5, p. 18. In 1999, German and French output made up 54 per cent of that of the original 11-country euro area.

15. HM Treasury, *UK Membership of the Single Currency: An Assessment of the Five Economic Tests* (October 1997), pp. 5–7.

16. Milton Friedman, 'The case for flexible exchange rates', *Essays in Positive Economics* (University of Chicago Press, 1953), p. 173.

17. Barry Eichengreen and Charles Wyplosz, 'Kenen on the euro' (VoxEU, 21 December 2012).

18. Xavier Sala-i-Martin and Jeffrey Sachs, 'Fiscal federalism and optimum currency areas: evidence for Europe from the United States', Working paper 3855 (NBER, October 1991), pp. 19–20, 28.

19. EC, *One Market, One Money* (October 1990), pp. 269–79, Annex B, examining links between the Netherlands and Germany.

20. Michael Artis, 'Analysis of European and UK business cycles and shocks', EMU study (HM Treasury, June 2003), pp. 21–2.

21. EC, *Statistical Annex* (November 2014), Table 36, p. 80, shows exports worth 25.7 per cent of GDP in France in 1999 compared with 64 and 61.5 per cent in Belgium and the Netherlands.

22. Rüdiger Soltwedel, Dirk Dohse and Christiane Krieger-Boden, 'EMU challenges European labour markets', Working paper 99/131 (IMF, September 1999), p. 9, Table 3, p. 42; 'Law on the 35-hour week is in force' (European Observatory of Working Life, 27 January 2000): the 35-hour working week came into effect in 2000 for companies with more than 20 employees and 2002 for those with 20 or fewer employees.

23. David Marsh, *The Euro* (Yale University Press, 2010), pp. 162–3.

24. EC, *Statistical Annex* (November 2014), Table 36. In 1999, exports were 19.2 per cent of GDP in Greece, 26.5 per cent in Portugal; by contrast, 37.6 per cent in Finland, a similar-sized economy.

25. ECB, 'Housing finance in the euro area' (March 2009), pp. 25–6; 'Structural factors in the EU housing markets' (March 2003), Table 5.1, pp. 50–1.

26. Marsh, *The Euro*, pp. 193–4, 204–5; Claudio Radaelli, 'The Italian state and the euro', in Kenneth Dyson (ed.), *European States and the Euro* (Oxford University Press, 2002), p. 227.

27. John Williamson, 'What role for currency boards?' (Institute for International Economics, September 1995), p. 7.

28. David Marsh, *The Bundesbank: The Bank that Rules Europe* (Mandarin Paperbacks, 1993), pp. 206–16.

29. Jacques Rueff, 'L'Europe se fera par la monnaie ou ne se fera pas' (*Synthèses*, 1950), No. 45, republished in *Commentaire* (1978).

30. EC, *Werner Report* (October 1970), pp. 10–14, 26–9.

31. Gianni Toniolo, *Central Bank Cooperation at the Bank for International Settlements, 1930–1973* (Cambridge University Press, 2005), pp. 446–8.

32. Toniolo, *Central Bank Cooperation*, pp. 448, 432–5.

33. Ben Bernanke and Harold James, 'The gold standard, deflation, and financial crisis in the great depression: an international comparison', in

R. Glenn Hubbard (ed.), *Financial Markets and Financial Crises* (NBER, January 1991), p. 37, Table 2.1, p. 42, p. 45, Table 2.4.

34. Harold James, *Making the European Monetary Union* (Harvard University Press, 2012), pp. 2–5, 14–15, 20–7, 383.

35. Toniolo, *Central Bank Cooperation*, pp. 33–9.

36. EC, *Report on Economic and Monetary Union in the European Community (Delors Report)* (April 1989), p. 37.

37. Peter Bofinger, 'The European Monetary System: achievements, flaws and applicability to other regions of the world', p. 34, Table 2 (UN Economic Commission for Europe, December 2000).

38. Horst Ungerer, Jouko Hauvonen, Augusto Lopez-Claros and Thomas Mayer, 'The European monetary system: developments and perspectives', Occasional paper 73 (IMF, 1990), pp. 2–8.

39. Marsh, *The Euro*, pp. 114–15.

40. *Delors Report*, pp. 3, 39, on the terms of reference set by the Hanover summit in June 1988; Marsh, *The Euro*, pp. 116–19.

41. James, *Making the European Monetary Union*, pp. 232–6.

42. *Delors Report*, pp. 21–3, 28, 30–5.

43. James, *Making the European Monetary Union*, pp. 213–14; *Delors Report*, pp. 11–12.

44. EC, *One Market, One Money*, pp. 65–6.

45. EC, *One Market, One Money*, pp. 9–11, 20–30, 63, 68.

46. EC, *One Market, One Money*, pp. 63, 83; EC, *Statistical Annex* (November 2014), Table 19, p. 46.

47. EC, *One Market, One Money*, p. 9.

48. *Delors Report*, p. 18.

49. Cited in Timothy Garton Ash, 'The crisis of Europe: how the union came together and why it's falling apart' (*Foreign Affairs*, September–October 2012).

50. Maastricht Treaty (*Official Journal of the European Communities*, 31 August 1992): Articles 2, 104 (c), and 109 (j); Protocols on the excessive-deficit procedure and the convergence criteria.

51. EC, *EMU@10*, p. 17, footnote 3.

52. EC, *Convergence Report 2013 on Latvia* (2013), pp. 3–5, 15–22.

53. Eric T. Swanson, 'Convergence of long-term bond yields in the euro area' (*FRBSF Economic Letter*, November 2008).

54. European Council, Presidency conclusions, Madrid (15–16 December 1995).

55. Robert Anderton, Richard Baldwin and Daria Taglioni, 'The impact of monetary union on trade prices', Working paper 238 (ECB, June 2003), p. 14.

56. 'Chancellor's right-hand man packs his case for Commons' (*Financial Times*, 2 July 2004).

57. HM Treasury, *UK Membership of the Single Currency: An Assessment of the Five Economic Tests* (October 1997), p. 5.

58. *Werner Report*, p. 12.

59. *Report of the Study Group on the Role of Public Finance in European Integration* (*MacDougall Report*) (April 1977), p. 14, available at cvce.eu.

60. Dick Leonard, *The Economist Guide to the European Union* (Hamish Hamilton, 1994), pp. 74–5; EC, 'The budget explained', ec.europa.eu/budget/explained/index_en.cfm.

61. Maastricht Treaty, Article 104 (c) 2, and Protocol on the excessive-deficit procedure, Article 1.

62. Willem Buiter, Giancarlo Corsetti and Nouriel Roubini, '"Excessive deficits": sense and nonsense in the Treaty of Maastricht', Discussion paper 750 (CEPR, December 1992), summary and pp. 59–61.

63. Buiter *et al.*, 'Excessive deficits', Table II.2, p. 72: on the vintage of public debt-to-GDP figures available in the early 1990s Ireland was also above 100 per cent, though it was falling.

64. Marsh, *The Euro*, pp. 191, 195–6.

65. European Council, 'Resolution on the stability and growth pact' (17 June 1997).

66. Marco Buti and Gabriele Giudice, 'Maastricht's fiscal rules at ten: an assessment' (*Journal of Common Market Studies*, 2002), p. 839.

67. Regulations 1466 and 1467 of 7 July 1997 on strengthening budgetary surveillance and speeding up the excessive deficit procedure.

68. R. Morris, H. Ongena and L. Schuknecht, 'The reform and implementation of the stability and growth pact', Occasional paper 47 (ECB, June 2006), p. 16.

69. 'Farewell to the stupidity pact?' (*The Economist*, 22 October 2002).

70. 'Germany escapes an EU reprimand for its big budget deficit' (*The Economist*, 14 February 2002).

71. Morris *et al.*, 'Reform and implementation of the SGP', pp. 17–19.

72. Regulations 1055 and 1056 of 27 June 2005 amending the original ones in 1997.

73. Morris *et al.*, 'Reform and implementation of the SGP', pp. 19–23.

74. Willem Buiter, 'The "sense and nonsense of Maastricht" revisited: what have we learnt about stabilisation in EMU?' (October 2005), p. 10.

75. HM Treasury, *An Assessment of the Five Economic Tests* (June 2003), pp. 8, 129–34; 'Fiscal stabilisation and EMU', Discussion paper (June 2003).

76. Otmar Issing, speech in Mexico City, 'The role of fiscal and monetary policies in the stabilisation of the economic cycle' (ECB, 14 November 2005).

77. Buiter, 'The 'sense and nonsense of Maastricht' revisited', p. 15.

78. Maastricht Treaty, Articles 107 and 108.

79. H.V. Bowen, 'The Bank of England during the long eighteenth century, 1694–1820', in Richard Roberts and David Kynaston (eds.), *The Bank of England: Money, Power and Influence 1694–1994* (Oxford University Press, 1995), pp. 2–5.

80. Maurice Obstfeld, 'Europe's gamble' (*Brookings Papers on Economic Activity*, 2: 1997), p. 242.

81. Peter M. Garber, 'The target mechanism: will it propagate or stifle a Stage III crisis?', *Carnegie-Rochester Conference Series on Public Policy*, 51 (Elsevier, 1999).

82. HM Treasury, 'Policy frameworks in the UK and EMU', EMU study (June 2003), p. 52.

83. HM Treasury, *Assessment of the Five Tests* (June 2003), pp. 4–6; pp. 183–93 for main findings from the 'Policy frameworks' study.

84. OECD, *Euro Area Economic Survey* (January 2009), pp. 23–4.

85. Pierfederico Asdrubali, Bent Sørensen and Oved Yosha, 'Channels of interstate risk sharing: US 1963–1990' (*Quarterly Journal of Economics*, November 1996), pp. 1082, 1092.

86. Vincent Duwicquet and Etienne Farvaque, 'US interstate risk sharing: a post-crisis examination' (February 2013).

87. Michael Bordo and Harold James, 'The European crisis in the context of the history of previous financial crises', Working paper 19112 (NBER, June 2013).

88. Nicholas Crafts, 'Saving the euro: a pyrrhic victory?', *CAGE-Chatham House Series No. 11* (November 2013), p. 5.

89. Barry Eichengreen, 'The euro: love it or leave it?' (VoxEU, 17 November 2007).

## 3   FRAGILE STRENGTH

1. Eurostat GDP figures, ec.europa.eu/eurostat/data/database GDP figures (accessed May 2015): the euro area including Greece (EA-12), big three economies, and other nine, grew by 1.8, 1.4 and 2.7 per cent a year respectively between 1999 and 2003.

2. Willem Buiter, 'How likely is a sterling crisis or: is London really Reykjavik-on-Thames?' (*Financial Times* blog, 13 November 2008).

3. Eurostat, 'Annex: euro changeover effects' in 'Euro-zone annual inflation down to 1.9%', news release 69/2003 (18 June 2003).

4. ECB, map showing the spread of the euro, ecb.europa.eu/euro/intro/html/map.en.html.

5. DeAnne Julius, 'Back to the future of low global inflation' (Bank of England, 20 October 1999), pp. 4–14; EC, *EMU@10*, pp. 29–30; IMF, 'Commodity price swings and commodity exporters', *World Economic Outlook* (April 2012), p. 125, Figure 4.1.

6. Marsh, *The Euro*, p. 185.

7. 'Commission recommends 11 member states for EMU' (25 March 1998), based on the fiscal figures used in the assessment.

8. OECD, *Euro Area Economic Survey* (September 2005), p. 90, Table 3.2.

9. Fabrizio Balassone *et al.*, 'Italy: fiscal consolidation and its legacy' (Bank of Italy, March 2002), p. 787; James Walsh, 'The uncertain path to monetary union', in Luciano Bardi and Martin Rhodes (eds.), *Italian Politics: Mapping the Future* (Westview Press, 1998), pp. 100–1.

10. 'Italy's chances for euro improve: creative accounting gets EU's approval' (*New York Times*, 22 February 1997).

11. Laurent Paul and Christophe Schalck, 'Transfers to the government of public corporation pension liabilities: the French case study' (Magyar Nemzeti Bank, 2007), pp. 72–6, 80; IMF, *Staff Report on Portugal* (June 2011), p. 6.

12. Mark Duckenfield, 'The Goldkrieg: revaluing the Bundesbank's reserves and the politics of EMU' (Harvard University, September 1998).

13. ' "Euro to sink below dollar" by 2000' (*The Observer*, 7 March 1999); Michael R. Rosenberg, 'The dollar's equilibrium exchange rate: a market view', in C. Fred Bergsten and John Williamson (eds.), *Dollar Overvaluation and the World Economy* (Institute for International Economics, 2003), pp. 40–5.

14. Willem Duisenberg, 'ECB press conference: introductory statement' (9 June 1998).

15. Deutsche Bundesbank, 'Understanding the capital key' (16 January 2014); Martin Handig and Robert Holzfeind, 'Euro banknotes in circulation and the allocation of monetary income within the Eurosystem', in *Monetary Policy and the Economy Q1/07* (Oesterreichische Nationalbank, 2007), pp. 151–2, 162, Table 5.

16. ECB, 'Key for the ECB's capital' (1 December 1998): the figures cited are for the notional capital if all 15 member states participated; Germany's share was 24.5 per cent on this basis, corresponding to an adjusted 31 per cent among the 11 states actually joining the euro.

17. Maastricht Treaty, ECB Protocol, Articles 10.3, 28–30, 32–3.

18. Maastricht Treaty, ECB Protocol: Article 11.2, stated 'common accord'; this was revised in the Lisbon Treaty to 'qualified majority'.

19. Jean-Claude Trichet, interview with *l'Express* (conducted 29 September 2004); he also termed the ECB 'a very effective shield' on this occasion.

20. Mario Draghi, speaking at press conference (ECB, 8 March 2012).

21. 'The European monetary institute' (EMI, 1997), pp. 7–9, 38; Marsh, *The Euro*, pp. 201–3; statement by Tony Blair to the House of Commons (*Hansard*, 5 May 1998).

22. 'Seventeen characters in search of a central banker' (*The Economist*, 12 February 2011).

23. Maastricht Treaty, Article 105.1; Federal Reserve Act, Section 2A, Monetary-policy objectives.

24. Gill Hammond, 'State of the art of inflation targeting – 2012', CCBS Handbook 29 (Bank of England, February 2012), pp. 7–8.

25. Federal Reserve, press release (25 January 2012).

26. Willem Duisenberg, speaking at press conference (ECB, 13 October 1998); on introduction of press conferences, see Otmar Issing, 'Communication, transparency, accountability: monetary policy in the twenty-first century' (*Federal Reserve Bank of St Louis Review*, March/April 2005), pp. 72–3, 80–3.

27. Press release, 'The ECB's monetary-policy strategy' (8 May 2003); Otmar Issing, speaking at press seminar (8 May 2003); 'The outcome of the ECB's evaluation of its monetary-policy strategy' (*Monthly Bulletin*, June 2003), pp. 79–92.

28. Jean-Claude Trichet, interview with *Le Figaro, FAZ, Irish Times* and *Jornal de Negócios* (conducted 11 July 2008), answer to second question.

29. Willem Duisenberg, speaking at press conference (ECB, 8 May 2003).

30. Draghi's opening statements to the monthly press conferences in 2014 until August said that inflation expectations over the medium to long term were 'firmly anchored'; the wording changed in September to measures being adopted 'with a view to underpinning the firm anchoring of medium to long-term inflation expectations'.

31. ECB, 'Monetary policy implementation' in *The Monetary Policy of the ECB* (2004), pp. 71–9.

32. ECB, 'The collateral framework of the Eurosystem' (*Monthly Bulletin*, April 2001), pp. 49–57.

33. ECB, 'The single list in the collateral framework of the Eurosystem' (*Monthly Bulletin*, May 2006), pp. 75–6, 81–7; Bank of England, *The Red Book* (November 2006), p. 23.

34. Jean-Claude Trichet, speaking at press conference (ECB, 8 September 2011).

35. Jean-Claude Trichet, 'Two continents compared' (ECB, 10 June 2011); and p. 4 of charts.

36. EC, *EMU@10*, p. 78.

37. OECD, *Statistical Annex* (November 2014), Table 12; see also EC, *EMU@10*, p. 19.

38. EC, *EMU@10*, pp. 80–3, 170.

39. EC, *Statistical Annex* (November 2014), Table 78, p. 164.

40. EC, *Statistical Annex of European Economy* (November 2010), Table 76, p. 180.

41. OECD, *Euro Area Economic Surveys* (December 2010), pp. 54–5; (September 2004), Figure 4.3, p. 104.

42. OECD, *Euro Area Economic Survey* (2004), p. 110, Figure 4.5.

43. National sources, BIS residential property price, bis.org/statistics/pp.htm; OECD, *Statistical Annex* (November 2014), Table 59.

44. Daniel Gros and Cinzia Alcidi, 'Country adjustment to a "sudden stop": does the euro make a difference?', Economic paper 492 (EC, April 2013), p. 15.

45. OECD, *Ireland Economic Survey* (November 2009), pp. 19, 22; Irish Department of Finance, 'The Irish economy in perspective' (June 2011), p. 9.

46. Karl Whelan, 'Policy lessons from Ireland's latest depression', Working paper 09/14 (University College Dublin, October 2009), pp. 2–7; and Figure 1.

47. IMF, *World Economic Outlook* database (April 2015), EA-12, imf.org/external/pubs/ft/weo/2015/01/weodata/index.aspx.

48. OECD, *Spain Economic Survey* (November 2012), p. 52, Figure 1.4c, showing housing and construction investment as a share of GDP from 1970; 'Newly built ghost towns haunt banks in Spain' (*New York Times*, 17 December 2010).

49. Eurostat GDP figures, euro area figures are for the EA-12, ec.europa.eu/eurostat/data/database (accessed May 2015).

50. EC, *EMU@10*, pp. 31, 115.

51. OECD, *Statistical Annex* (November 2014), Tables 11 and 12: both compensation per employee and labour productivity grew on average by 1.1 per cent a year in 1999–2007; they had risen at an annual rate of 3.8 and 2.0 per cent respectively between 1987 and 1997.

52. Trichet, opening statement and answers at press conference (ECB, 6 October 2005); ECB, press notice, 'Schedules for the meetings of the governing council and general council of the ECB and related press conferences in 2000' (17 June 1999).

53. Deutsche Bundesbank (February 2015); see also 'Europe's economic rules: Brussels v Berlin' (*The Economist*, 16 November 2013).

54. OECD, *Euro Area Economic Survey* (2010), p. 47.

55. 'Briefing: the European Central Bank' (*The Economist*, 22 October 2011); *Werner Report*, p. 10.

56. EC, *Alert Mechanism Report* (February 2012), Table 1, p. 3.

57. OECD, *Euro Area Economic Survey* (2010), pp. 122–3, Figure 4.1; *Ireland Economic Survey* (2009), p. 19.

58. OECD, *Euro Area Economic Survey* (2009), p. 57, Figure 2.4.

59. OECD, *Euro Area Economic Survey* (2010), pp. 125–30.

60. Stephen Cecchetti, M. S. Mohanty and Fabrizio Zampolli, 'The real effects of debt', Working paper 352 (BIS, September 2011), pp. 1, 21–2.

61. OECD, *Slovenia Economic Survey* (April 2013), p. 15, Figure 2A.

62. EC, *Statistical Annex* (November 2014), Tables 77 and 78, pp. 162 and 164.

63. Otmar Issing, 'Get your finances in order and stop blaming Germany' (*Financial Times*, 26 March 2014).

64. IMF, *Greece: Ex-Post Evaluation* (June 2013), pp. 5–6.

65. EC, *Statistical Annex* (November 2014), Table 78, p. 164 for debt; *Statistical Annex of European Economy* (November 2013), Table 77, p. 182 for Belgian primary balances.

66. Isabelle Joumard and Christophe André, 'Revenue buoyancy and its fiscal-policy implications', Working paper 598 (OECD, 2008), p. 8.
67. Paul Krugman, 'Europe's economic suicide' (*New York Times*, 15 April 2012).
68. 'Council decision of 17 December 1999 abrogating the decision on the existence of an excessive deficit in Greece', 2000/33/EC (*Official Journal of the European Communities*, 18 January 2000).
69. 'Report by Eurostat on the revision of the Greek government deficit and debt figures' (22 November 2004), pp. 3–5, 15–18, 27–33.
70. IMF, *Staff Report on Portugal* (December 2011), pp. 42–3.
71. OECD, *Euro Area Economic Survey* (January 2007), p. 110. In late 2006, Greece was rated A, Italy A+ and Portugal AA–, by Standard & Poor's.
72. Willem Buiter and Anne Sibert, 'How the Eurosystem's treatment of collateral in its open market operations weakens fiscal discipline in the euro zone (and what to do about it)' (London School of Economics, December 2005), especially pp. 6–12.
73. ECB, *Implementation of monetary policy* (February 2005), pp. 46–7, Box 10.
74. *Delors Report*, p. 20.
75. BNP Paribas, press release (9 August 2007).
76. José Manuel González-Páramo, 'The ECB's monetary policy during the crisis' (ECB, 21 October 2011).
77. Daily ten-year government bond yields.
78. Bank of England (March 2015), exchange-rate data, monthly averages, bankofengland.co.uk/boeapps/iadb/NewInterMed.asp?Travel=NixIRx; monthly averages.
79. Gros and Alcidi, 'Country adjustment to a "sudden stop"', p. 30, Figure 18.
80. 'Germany ready to help euro-zone members' (*Financial Times*, 18 February 2009).
81. 'Euro zone has bail-out solution for members – Almunia' (*Reuters*, 3 March 2009).
82. OECD, *Euro Area Economic Survey* (2010), p. 22, Figure 1.2.
83. Timothy W. Guinnane, 'Financial Vergangenheitsbewältigung: The 1953 London debt agreement', *Economic Growth Centre discussion paper 880* (Yale University, January 2004), pp. 27–30, 43.

84. Carlo Cottarelli, Lorenzo Forni, Jan Gottschalk and Paolo Mauro, Staff position note 10/12, 'Default in today's advanced economies: unnecessary, undesirable and unlikely' (IMF, September 2010).

## 4   GREEKS BEARING DEBTS

1. 'Revised Greek deficit figures cause outrage' (*EUobserver*, 20 October 2009); EC, *Report on Greek Government Deficit and Debt Statistics* (8 January 2010), p. 3.
2. EC, *Statistical Annex* (November 2014), Table 76, p. 160.
3. 'Greece raises $6.7 billion in bond sale' (*New York Times*, 29 March 2010).
4. IMF, *Greece: Ex-Post Evaluation*, pp. 7–8.
5. EC, 'Statement on the support to Greece by euro area member states' (11 April 2010); 'IMF reaches staff-level agreement with Greece on €30 billion stand-by arrangement', press release 10/176 (IMF, 2 May 2010).
6. EC, *Statistical Annex* (November 2014), Table 5, p. 18: Greek GDP was €237 billion at current prices in 2009.
7. IMF, 'Factsheet on IMF quotas' (October 2014); *Greece: Ex-Post Evaluation*, pp. 9, 29.
8. 'IMF executive board approves $47 billion arrangement for Mexico under the flexible credit line' (IMF, 17 April 2009).
9. IMF, *Staff Report on Greece* (May 2010), pp. 19–20.
10. IMF, *Greece: Ex-Post Evaluation*, pp. 28–9.
11. EC, 'Economic adjustment programme for Greece', Occasional paper 61 (May 2010), p. 26, Box 8.
12. 'Slovakia rejects its share of Greek bail-out' (*New York Times*, 12 August 2010); EC, 'Financial assistance to Greece, first economic adjustment programme', ec.europa.eu/economy_finance/assistance_eu_ms/greek_loan_facility/index_en.htm.
13. IMF, *Staff Report on Greece* (January 2013), Table 19, p. 62.
14. 'Statement by the heads of state or government of the euro area' (7 May 2010), in *The European Council in 2010* (EU, January 2011), p. 29.
15. Ecofin council meeting 9/10 May, press release, 9596/10 (9 May 2010).
16. 'Decision of the ECB of 14 May 2010 establishing a securities markets programme' (*Official Journal of the European Union*, 20 May 2014): the actual decision was taken and announced on 9 May.

17. Axel Weber, interview with *Börsen-Zeitung* (Bundesbank, 11 May 2010); 'Brandbrief: Ex-Währungshüter Stark attackiert EZB-Kurs' (*Der Spiegel*, 14 January 2012).
18. 'Towards a United States of Europe' (*Wall Street Journal*, 17 December 2010).
19. European Council, '16–17 December 2010 conclusions' (25 January 2011).
20. IMF, *Staff Report on Greece* (January 2013), Table 19, p. 62; ESM, 'FAQ document on Greece' (3 July 2015); IMF, *Staff Reports on Greece* (January, May and July 2013, June 2014).
21. Jeromin Zettelmeyer, Christoph Trebesch and Mitu Gulati, 'The Greek debt restructuring: an autopsy' (July 2013), p. 13.
22. IMF, *Staff Report on Greece* (January 2013), pp. 31–4, Box 4, p. 84; Letter from Mario Draghi to Liêm Hoang Ngoc, member of the European Parliament (12 March 2013); Zettelmeyer *et al.*, 'The Greek debt restructuring: an autopsy', p. 10.
23. Banca d'Italia, *Economic Bulletin Statistical Appendix* (October 2012), Table 2.21, p. 66.
24. 'Economic and financial affairs, policy and surveillance, the EU as a borrower', ec.europa.eu/economy_finance/eu_borrower/index_en.htm.
25. 'Decision of the representatives of the governments of the euro area member states meeting within the Council of the European Union', 9614/10 (10 May 2010).
26. Treaty on the Functioning of the European Union (TFEU), Article 122.2; Bruno De Witte, 'Using international law in the euro crisis: causes and consequences', Working paper 4 (University of Oslo, Arena Centre for European Studies, June 2013), p. 6.
27. EC, 'Investor presentation' (January 2015), p. 4; Council of the EU, 'EFSM: Council approves €7bn bridge loan to Greece' (17 July 2015).
28. De Witte, 'Using international law in the euro crisis', pp. 1, 4–5.
29. EFSF framework agreement (7 June 2010); 'EFSF places inaugural benchmark issue' (25 January 2011); 'Frequently asked questions' (2 February 2011), answers to questions A1, A10 and A12.
30. EFSF, Newsletters 2 and 3 (July and November 2011): under the amended scheme total guarantees amounted to €780 billion; excluding Greece, Ireland and Portugal, to €726 billion.
31. EFSF Framework agreement, Articles 2.5, 2.10, 11.
32. De Witte, 'Using international law in the euro crisis', pp. 5–7.

33. EFSF, Newsletter 4 (February 2012); ESM, *2012 Annual Report* (June 2013), pp. 7–8, 13, 15; EFSF and ESM, 'Investor presentation' (January 2015), pp. 3–9; 'Lending operations', www.efsf.europa.eu/about/operations/.

34. IMF, *Staff Report on Greece* (May 2010), Table 3, p. 28; *Staff Report on Greece* (January 2013), Table 19, p. 62; 'Financial Activities Update' (26 December 2014): amount outstanding in SDRs.

35. IMF, press release 13/103 (3 April 2013).

36. Holger Bonin, '15 years of pension reform in Germany: old successes and new threats', Discussion paper 09–035 (ZEW, 2009), p. 8; IMF, *Staff Report on Greece* (May 2010), p. 40.

37. 'Finland's election: truly amazing' (*The Economist*, 18 April 2011).

38. 'Revisiting the collateral deal with Greece' (Yle news, 1 August 2012).

39. EFSF framework agreement, Articles 2.1, 10; ESM, *2012 Annual Report*, pp. 19–23.

40. Jens Weidmann, interview with *Der Spiegel* (19 September 2011).

41. 'Letter of the European Central Bank to Silvio Berlusconi' (5 August 2011), leaked to *Corriere della Sera*, which published it on 29 September 2011, available on voltairenet.org.

42. 'Outcry over Berlusconi budget reversal' (*Financial Times*, 30 August 2011); 'Berlusconi backtracks on wealth tax, sparks criticism' (EurActiv. com, 31 August 2011).

43. EFSF, Newsletter 4 (February 2012); FAQ (January 2013), pp. 11–12.

44. Daniel Gros, 'Eurobonds: wrong solution for legal, political and economic reasons' (VoxEU, 24 August 2011).

45. Bundesverfassungsgericht, judgment 1390/12 (12 September 2012), para. 113.

46. IMF, *Fiscal Monitor* (October 2014), Tables 1 and 7, pp. 65 and 71.

47. Jacques Delpla and Jakob von Weizsäcker, 'The blue bond proposal' (Bruegel, May 2010).

48. Gros, 'Eurobonds: wrong solution for legal, political and economic reasons'.

49. Wim Boonstra, 'The ELEC temporary euro T-bill facility' (Rabobank, 6 March 2012).

50. German council of economic experts, *Annual Report*, Chapter 1 (2011/12), pp. 3–6.

51. John Muellbauer, 'Resolving the euro-zone crisis: time for conditional eurobonds', Policy Insight 59 (CEPR, October 2011); 'Time for eurobonds – but with conditions' (VoxEu, 12 October 2011).

52. 'Merkel presents election platform' (*Deutsche Welle*, 24 June 2013).

53. 'Treaty on stability, coordination and governance' (Fiscal compact), p. 7.

54. Fiscal compact, Article 3, pp. 11–13.

55. Heiko Burret and Jan Schnellenbach, 'Implementation of the fiscal compact in the euro area member states', Working paper 08/2013 (German council of economic experts, January 2014), p. 10; Deutsche Bundesbank, 'The debt brake in Germany' (*Monthly Report*, October 2011).

56. De Witte, 'Using international law in the euro crisis', pp. 8–9.

57. EC, *Autumn Forecast 2014* (November 2014), Table 41, p. 164.

58. Olivier Blanchard and Daniel Leigh, 'Are we underestimating short-term fiscal multipliers?', in *World Economic Outlook* (IMF, October 2012), Box 1.1, pp. 41–3; 'Growth forecast errors and fiscal multipliers', IMF working paper 13/1 (January 2013).

59. The letter was dated 13 February 2013.

60. 'Commission takes steps under the excessive deficit procedure' (EC, 29 May 2013): the deadline for Spain was extended from 2014 to 2016; for France and Slovenia from 2013 to 2015; for the Netherlands from 2013 to 2014; and for Portugal from 2014 to 2015.

61. Quarterly GDP (ESA-2010), ec.europa.eu/eurostat/data/database; EC, *Autumn Forecast 2014*, Table 41, p. 164.

62. 'Franco-German declaration', Deauville (18 October 2010).

63. European Council conclusions of 24/25 March 2011 (20 April 2011), Annex II.

64. Statement by the Eurogroup (28 November 2010); Michael Bradley and Mitu Gulati, 'Collective-action clauses for the euro zone' (*Review of Finance*, December 2013), pp. 1–7.

65. EC, *Economic Adjustment Programme for Greece* (May 2010), pp. 26–7.

66. IMF, *Staff Report on Greece* (December 2010), pp. 22, 35.

67. Lee Buchheit and Mitu Gulati, 'Greek debt: the endgame scenarios', in Franklin Allen, Elena Carletti and Giancarlo Corsetti (eds.), *Life in the Euro Zone With or Without Sovereign Default?* (European University Institute and Wharton Financial Institutions Centre, 2011), pp. 83–95; 'The governments' man when creditors bay' (*Reuters*, 23 May 2012).

68. 'The never-ending crisis: Greek debt restructuring looks inevitable' (*Der Spiegel*, 11 April 2011).

69. 'Statement by heads of state or government of the euro area and EU institutions' (21 July 2011); 'IIF financing offer' (Institute of International Finance, 21 July 2011).

70. Zettelmeyer *et al.*, 'Greek debt restructuring', pp. 5–8, especially Table 1.

71. Zettelmeyer *et al.*, 'Greek debt restructuring', pp. 10–14, 51.

72. Zettelmeyer *et al.*, 'Greek debt restructuring', pp. 17–21.

73. IMF, *Article IV Staff Report on Argentina* (July 2003), p. 31.

74. 'Lending operations', www.efsf.europa.eu/about/operations/; IMF, *Staff Report on Greece* (May 2010), p. 17.

75. Hellenic Financial Stability Fund, *Annual Report 2013* (June 2014), pp. 5–6; *Interim Financial Statements for the Nine-Month Period Ended 30/09/2014* (December 2014), p. 14; as well as the €13.5 billion 'funding gap' showing there were additional resolution costs of around €2 billion.

76. Hellenic Statistical Authority, *Quarterly National Accounts* (14 November 2014).

77. 'Quarterly GDP figures', ESA 2010,ec.europa.eu/eurostat/data/database (accessed May 2015).

78. Factsheet on treaty establishing ESM (EC, 2 February 2012).

## 5   BAD BANKS

1. IMF, *Article IV Staff Report on Portugal* (January 2010), pp. 7, 16–18.

2. Euro area summit statement (29 June 2012).

3. National Treasury Management Agency, 'Ireland regaining creditworthiness' (December 2012), p. 68 gave the figure of €64 billion, equivalent to 41 per cent of 2011 GDP (pre-ESA 2010 revisions made in late 2014).

4. Hyun Song Shin, 'Global banking glut and loan risk premium' (Princeton University, January 2012), p. 16, Figure 10, and p. 17; OECD, *Euro Area Economic Survey* (2010), p. 125.

5. Charles Goodhart, Westminster Economics Forum, held at National Institute of Economic and Social Research (26 October 2009).

6. Andrew Haldane, 'Constraining discretion in bank regulation' (Bank of England, 9 April 2013), pp. 3–6, 15, Charts 1 and 2.

7. Ben Bernanke, 'The global saving glut and the US current-account deficit' (Federal Reserve, 10 March 2005).

8. OECD, *Statistical Annex* (November 2014), Table 51, p. 267.

9. Shin, 'Global banking glut and loan risk premium', especially pp. 2–22, 39–42.

10. IMF, *Global Financial Stability Report* (October 2013), pp. 107–14.

11. EC, 'Aid in the context of the financial and economic crisis' (State aid scoreboard, 2014).

12. 'Ireland guarantees six banks' deposits' (*Financial Times*, 30 September 2008); Department of Finance, 'List of covered institutions' (6 November 2008).

13. Joe Peek and Eric Rosengren, 'Unnatural selection: perverse incentives and the misallocation of credit in Japan', Working paper 9643 (NBER, April 2003), p. 1 describes this practice in the Japanese banking crisis.

14. Claudio Borio and William White, 'Whither monetary and financial stability: the implications of evolving policy regimes', Working paper 147 (BIS, February 2004, presented at Jackson Hole, August 2003), especially pp. 5–6, 12–24, 32–3.

15. ECB, *Financial Stability Review* (December 2004), pp. 7–8.

16. ECB, 'The role of central banks in prudential supervision' (March 2001): ten of the twelve NCBs were 'either directly responsible for prudential supervision or strongly involved in this activity'.

17. Report of Advisory Scientific Committee to the European Systemic Risk Board, 'Is Europe Overbanked?' (ESRB, June 2014), pp. 38–40.

18. ECB, *Financial Integration in Europe* (May 2011), pp. 12–14, Chart 2, statistical annex, p. 3.

19. Bank of England and ECB, 'The case for a better functioning securitisation market in the European Union' (May 2014), pp. 10–12.

20. Association for Financial Markets in Europe, 'Funding the EU economy: the role of banks and financial markets' (2014), p. 3.

21. Standard & Poor's, 'Credit shift: as global corporate borrowers seek $60 trillion, Asia-Pacific debt will overtake US and Europe combined' (15 June 2014), Chart 4 and Table 2A.

22. EC, 'Recommendation concerning the definition of micro, small and medium-sized enterprises' (6 May 2003), Annex, Article 2.

23. OECD, *Entrepreneurship at a glance* (2014), Table 2.3, p. 33.

24. ECB, 'Changes in bank financing patterns' (April 2012), pp. 10, 16–17, Chart 11; unweighted average across euro area countries for loans to and deposits from private non-financial customers.

25. Banco de Portugal, *Financial Stability Report* (November 2013), pp. 40–1.

26. IMF, *Ireland: Ex-Post Evaluation* (January 2015), p. 19.

27. ECB, *Financial Integration in Europe* (March 2007), pp. 17–18; Shin, 'Global banking glut and loan risk premium', pp. 40–1.

28. Jean-Claude Trichet, 'The state of European financial integration', speech in Paris (ECB, 28 November 2005); ECB, *Indicators of Financial Integration in the Euro Area* (September 2005), pp. 6, 9–10.

29. 'What is ERM II?', http://ec.europa.eu/economy_finance/euro/adoption/erm2/index_en.htm.

30. Eva Banincova, 'Developments in banking sectors of central and eastern Europe and three Baltic states after the global financial crisis and European debt crisis' (*Kobe University Economic Review*, 2012), pp. 39–51; Dirk Schoenmaker and Wolf Wagner, 'The impact of cross-border banking on financial stability', Discussion paper 11–054 (Tinbergen Institute, February 2011), p. 4.

31. 'Crédit Agricole successfully completes the public offer for Emporiki', press release (9 August 2006); 'Crédit Agricole exits Greece taking profit hit on unit' (*Bloomberg News*, 17 October 2012); OECD, *Competition, Concentration and Stability in the Banking Sector* (2010), p. 126.

32. OECD, *Ireland Economic Survey* (2009), p. 30; Blánaid Clarke and Niamh Hardiman, 'Crisis in the Irish banking system', Working paper 2012/03 (University College Dublin Geary Institute, February 2012), p. 8.

33. OECD, *Ireland Economic Survey* (2009), pp. 9–11, 19, 28–36; HM Treasury, *RBS and the Case for a Bad Bank: The Government's Review* (November 2013), pp. 32, 50–1.

34. Bank of England, *Financial Stability Report* (October 2008), pp. 44–5.

35. Sir John Gieve, 'The credit crunch and the UK economy' (22 September 2008).

36. 'Banks in Latin America: "Reconquest" of New World is lifeline as profits suffer at home' (*Financial Times*, 29 November 2012).

37. Santander UK, 'The history of Santander in the UK', www.santander.co.uk/uk/about-santander-uk/about-us/our-history; 'Takeover move sends Abbey shares soaring' (*The Guardian*, 23 July 2004); Kevin Ryan, 'Building society conversions', in *Financial Stability Review* (Bank of England, Autumn 1996), pp. 12–13.

38. IMF, 'The reform of Spanish savings banks: technical note' (June 2012), pp. 9–12.

39. Luis Garicano, 'Five lessons from the Spanish *cajas* debacle for a new euro-wide supervisor' (VoxEU, 16 October 2012).

40. OECD, *Spain Economic Survey* (November 2012), pp. 61–5.

41. 'The Spanish bail-out: going to extra time' (*The Economist*, 16 June 2012); 'Bankia posts record loss' (*Wall Street Journal*, 28 February 2013); 'A turbulent history of Madrid's towers of crisis' (*Iberosphere*, 15 June 2012).

42. IMF, *Greece: Ex-Post Evaluation*, pp. 18–19.

43. EC, 'Macroeconomic imbalances: Italy 2014', Occasional paper 182 (March 2014), p. 19; IMF, *Article IV Staff Report on Italy* (May 2010), pp. 3–5.

44. EC, *Macroeconomic Imbalances: Italy 2014*, p. 19.

45. IMF, *Staff Reports on Portugal* (June 2011), p. 14; (February 2014), p. 17.

46. 'State aid: Commission approves resolution aid for Portuguese Banco Espírito Santo' (EC, 4 August 2014); 'Banco Espírito Santo: sharing the pain' (*The Economist*, 9 August 2014).

47. EC, *Statistical Annex* (November 2014), Table 10, p. 28.

48. IMF, *Article IV Staff Report on Slovenia* (May 2011), pp. 12–13, 27, 34.

49. 'Slovenia's financial crisis: stressed out' (*The Economist*, 30 November 2013).

50. Henri Maurer and Patrick Grussenmeyer, 'Financial assistance measures in the euro area from 2008 to 2013: statistical framework and fiscal impact', Statistics paper 7 (ECB, April 2015), p. 19.

51. Independent Commission on the Future of the Cyprus Banking Sector (Cyprus Banking-Sector Commission), *Final Report and Recommendations* (October 2013), pp. 21–2, gave a figure of nine times GDP, but national-account revisions in 2014 raised the level of GDP for 2009 by 9.3 per cent; see Cystat, 'Explanatory note for the revision of national accounts 1995–2013' (15 October 2014).

52. IMF, *Article IV Staff Report on Cyprus* (November 2011), pp 14–17; EC, *Economic Adjustment Programme for Cyprus* (May 2013), Box 2, p. 31; Cyprus Banking-Sector Commission, pp. 3–5.

53. Jaime Caruana and Adrian Van Rixtel, 'International financial markets and bank funding in the euro area: dynamics and participants' (BIS, February 2013), pp. 2, 6–7, Chart 4.

54. ECB, *Financial Integration in Europe* (May 2011), p. 66, Chart 54.

55. Cyprus Banking-Sector Commission, p. 4.

56. ECB, *Financial Stability Review* (May 2014), Chart 9, p. 14.

57. Adrian Van Rixtel and Gabriele Gasperini, 'Financial crises and bank funding: recent experience in the euro area', Working paper 406 (BIS, March 2013), p. 22.

58. 'Exclusive – ECB limits bond buying, euro zone looks to banks' (*Reuters*, 9 December 2011).

59. 'How big could the Sarko trade go?' (*Financial Times*, 15 December 2011).

60. EC, *Macroeconomic Imbalances: Italy 2014*, p. 21.

61. IMF, *Global Financial Stability Report* (October 2013), pp. 32, 34, Figure 1.45.

62. Same source as Figure 5; see also ECB, *Financial Stability Review* (May 2014), p. 12.

63. European Banking Federation, 'International comparison of banking sectors' (March 2014).

64. ECB, *Financial Stability Review* (May 2014), pp. 12, 69, Chart 3.10.

65. ECB, *Financial Stability Review* (May 2014), p. 74, Chart 3.16.

66. 'EU business rivals divided by rates' (*Financial Times*, 29 July 2012).

67. ECB, *Bank Lending Surveys* (January, April and July 2013).

68. Mario Draghi, 'Monetary policy in a prolonged period of low inflation', speech in Sintra (ECB, 26 May 2014).

69. IMF, *World Economic Outlook* (April 2009), pp. 122–3; Stijn Claessens *et al.* (eds.), *Financial Crises: Causes, Consequences and Policy Responses* (IMF, 2014), pp. 477–9.

70. Maurer and Grussenmeyer, 'Financial assistance measures in the euro area from 2008 to 2013', p. 19.

71. Robert Weber, 'A theory for deliberation-oriented stress testing regulation' (*Minnesota Law Review*, 2014), pp. 2237–50.

72. Federal Reserve, 'The supervisory capital assessment programme (SCAP): design and implementation' (April 2009), pp. 1–2; 'SCAP: overview of results' (May 2009);Timothy Geithner, *Stress Test* (Random House, 2014), pp. 235–9; US Treasury, 'Troubled asset relief programme', transactions report for period ending 31 December 2008.

73. Li Lian Ong and Ceyla Pazarbasioglu, 'Credibility and crisis stress testing', Working paper 13/178 (IMF, August 2013), pp. 6–8, 13.

74. CEBS, 'The results of the EU-wide stress testing exercise', press release (1 October 2009); Ong and Pazarbasioglu, 'Credibility and crisis stress testing', pp. 11, 14.

75. CEBS, *Annual Report 2010*, p. 3.

76. CEBS, 'Aggregate outcome of the 2010 EU-wide stress test exercise' (23 July 2010); summary of 91 bank-by-bank results, by country.

77. CEBS, *Annual Report 2010*, p. 4; EBA, *The Single Rulebook*. www.eba. europa.eu/regulation-and-policy/single-rulebook.

78. Willem Pieter de Groen, 'A closer look at Dexia: the case of the misleading capital ratios' (CEPS, 19 October 2011); 'European banks: Dexia the latest to be bailed out' (*The Guardian*, 30 September 2008); 'Fresh bail-out for Dexia' (*Financial Times*, 8 November 2012).

79. Geithner, *Stress Test*, pp. 286–8, 323, 345–55.

80. 'European parliament approves the single supervisory mechanism' (Institute of International and European Affairs, 24 September 2013).

81. Council regulation 1024/2013 of 15 October 2013 (*Official Journal of the European Union*, 29 October 2013), Articles 6, 33.2 and 33.4; ECB, 'Note: comprehensive assessment' (October 2013).

82. Ong and Pazarbasioglu, 'Credibility and crisis stress testing', pp. 10–18, 24–5; 'Bank of Slovenia and Slovenian government announce results of stress tests' (Bank of Slovenia, 12 December 2013).

83. ECB, *Aggregate Report on the Comprehensive Assessment* (October 2014), pp. 2–5.

84. 'EBA/SSM stress test: the macroeconomic adverse scenario' (ESRB, 17 April 2014), Table 9, p. 13; 'General features of the baseline macroeconomic scenario' (EBA, 18 March 2011) and 'Macreconomic adverse scenario for the 2011 EU-wide stress test' (ECB, 18 March 2011), Tables 1 and 3.

85. EBA, 'Overview of the EBA 2011 banking EU-wide stress test' (18 March 2011), p. 8; 'Results of 2014 EU-wide stress test' (October 2014), p. 14.

86. ECB, *Aggregate Report*, pp. 6–9, Table 1, p. 10.

87. Viral Acharya and Sascha Steffen, 'Making sense of the comprehensive assessment' (VoxEU, 29 October 2014). The official exercise revealed a small capital shortfall at one French bank, but it was not included in the sample of 39 banks used by Acharya and Steffen (see their Appendix 1).

88. Willem Buiter, 'How to avoid secular stagnation after AQR and stress-test fudge' (*Financial Times*, 31 October 2014).

89. ECB, *Financial Stability Review* (May 2014), p. 7, Chart 2.

90. Finland finance ministry, 'Joint statement of the ministers of finance of Germany, the Netherlands and Finland' (25 September 2012).

91. FDIC, 'When a bank fails: facts for depositors, creditors and borrowers'.

92. EU Council, 'Single resolution mechanism: council confirms deal with European Parliament' (27 March 2014); 'Agreement on the transfer and mutualisation of contributions to the single resolution fund' (14 May 2014); Single Resolution Board, press release (25 March 2015).

93. IMF, *Article IV Staff Report on Euro Area Policies* (July 2014), p. 15.

94. IMF, *Cyprus Selected Issues* (November 2011), p. 4; Cystat, 'Explanatory note for the revision of national accounts 1995–2013'.

95. Council of Europe, 'Special assessment of the effectiveness of customer due diligence measures in the banking sector in Cyprus' (April 2013), pp. 19–23.

96. IMF, *Ireland: Ex-Post Evaluation* (January 2015), pp. 27–9.

97. EC, *Statistical Annex* (May 2015), Table 10, p. 28.

98. 'European banking tests: exam nerves' (*The Economist*, 9 August 2014); ECB, *Aggregate Report on the Comprehensive Assessment*, Table 1, p. 10.

99. Bank of Cyprus, 'Preliminary Financial Results for the year ended 31 December 2013', pp. 13, 17; 'Cyprus one year on: injured island' (*The Economist*, 8 March 2014).

100. 'Cyprus lifts last capital controls after two years' (*EUobserver*, 7 April 2015).

101. 'Concerns grow over Denmark's bail-in rules' (*Financial Times*, 23 May 2011); 'Danish bail-in trauma consigned to history in merger wave' (*Bloomberg News*, 27 April 2012).

102. S&P, 'The rating implications of the emerging bank resolution frameworks in the UK, Germany, Austria and Switzerland' (3 February 2015).

103. Financial Stability Board, 'Adequacy of loss-absorbing capacity of global systemically important banks in resolution', Consultative document (10 November 2014); 'Banks face 25% loss buffer as FSB fight too-big-to-fail' (*Bloomberg News*, 10 November 2014).

104. ESM, 'FAQ on the ESM direct recapitalisation instrument' (8 December 2014).

## 6   THE EXISTENTIAL CRISIS

1. Andrew Rose, 'Checking out: exits from currency unions', *Discussion paper 6254* (CEPR, April 2007), pp. 1–2, 14.

2. Guido Thiemeyer, 'The "forces profondes" of internationalism in the late nineteenth century: politics, economy and culture', in Isabella Löhr and Roland Wenzlhuemer (eds.), *The Nation State and Beyond* (Springer, 2013), pp. 28–9.

3. Luca Einaudi, '1,000 years of monetary union in Europe' (*National Institute Economic Review*, April 2000), pp. 95–7; 'From the Franc to the "Europe": the attempted transformation of the Latin Monetary Union into a European Monetary Union (1865–1873)' (*Economic History Review*, May 2000), pp. 284–308; Dickson H. Leavens, *Silver Money* (Principia Press, 1939), pp. 28–9.

4. H.P. Willis, *A History of the Latin Monetary Union* (University of Chicago Press, 1901), pp. 55–9; Thiemeyer, 'The "forces profondes" of internationalism in the nineteenth century', pp. 33–5.

5. Kindleberger, *A Financial History of Western Europe*, pp. 65–7.

6. Einaudi, '1,000 years of monetary union', pp. 96–7; Leavens, *Silver Money*, pp. 32–3.

7. Mayer, *Europe's Unfinished Currency*, pp. 43–6.

8. Willis, *A History of the Latin Monetary Union*, p. 81.

9. Willis, *A History of the Latin Monetary Union*, pp. 253–67.

10. Einaudi, '1,000 years of monetary union', pp. 95, 97.

11. Krim Talia, 'The Scandinavian currency union 1873–1924', Ph.D. thesis (Stockholm School of Economics, 2004), especially pp. 17, 31–3, 82–6, 100–18, 124, 129–30; U. Michael Bergman and Lars Jonung, 'Business cycle synchronisation in Europe: evidence from the Scandinavian currency union', *Economic paper 402* (EC, February 2010), pp. 5–10.

12. Einaudi, '1,000 years of monetary union', pp. 97–8.

13. Talia, 'The Scandinavian currency union', pp. 166–79.

14. Peter Garber and Michael Spencer, 'The dissolution of the Austro-Hungarian empire: lessons for currency reform', *Essays in International Finance*, 191 (Princeton University, February 1994), especially pp. 1–18, 24–8.

15. Roberts and Kynaston (eds.), *The Bank of England 1694–1994*, pp. 45–6, 60–1, 177–8; Andrew Haldane, 'The Bank and the banks', speech at Queen's University, Belfast (18 October 2012), pp. 1–5.

16. Steve Hanke and Nicholas Krus, 'World hyperinflations' (Cato Institute, August 2012), pp. 12–13.

17. Patrick Conway, 'Currency proliferation: the monetary legacy of the Soviet Union', *Essays in International Finance*, 197 (Princeton

University, June 1995), pp. 1, 41–2; C. Melliss and M. Cornelius, 'New currencies in the former Soviet Union: a recipe for hyperinflation or the path to price stability?' (Bank of England, 1994), p. 3; IMF, *Staff Report on Belarus* (December 1999), pp. 97–8.

18. Jan Fidrmuc, Julius Horvath and Jarko Fidrmuc, 'The stability of monetary unions: lessons from the break-up of Czechoslovakia' (*Journal of Comparative Economics*, 1999), p. 754.

19. The Maastricht Council was held on 9–10 December; the crucial meeting when the leaders of Russia, Ukraine and Belarus agreed upon the dissolution of the Soviet Union and its replacement by the Commonwealth of Independent States was held on 8 December and the Soviet Union formally ended on 25 December.

20. Conway, 'Currency proliferation', pp. 33, 41–2.

21. Melliss and Cornelius, 'New currencies in the former Soviet Union', pp. 14–17, 20–1, 26–9; Conway, 'Currency proliferation', pp. 2, 17, 19, 44–8.

22. IMF, 'Germany: technical note on crisis-management arrangements' (December 2011), p. 5.

23. ECB, 'ELA procedures' (February 2014).

24. Karl Whelan, 'The ECB's collateral policy and its future as lender of last resort' (European Parliament, November 2014), pp. 12–18.

25. ECB, 'Eligibility of Greek bonds used as collateral in Eurosystem monetary policy operations' (4 February 2015); 'ELA to Greek banks maintained at its current level' (28 June 2015).

26. 'ECB announces measures to support bank lending and money market activity' (8 December 2011); 'ECB's governing council approves eligibility criteria for additional credit claims' (9 February 2012); Mario Draghi, speaking at press conference (9 February 2012): the seven NCBs were those of Austria, Cyprus, France, Ireland, Italy, Portugal and Spain.

27. 'Is the euro zone at risk of turning into the rouble zone?' (Citigroup, 13 February 2012).

28. Rose, 'Checking out', pp. 5–9, 16.

29. Reuven Glick and Andrew Rose, 'Does a currency union affect trade?' (*European Economic Review*, 2002), pp. 1135–8.

30. Rodney Thom and Brendan Walsh, 'The effect of a common currency on trade: Ireland before and after the sterling link', *Working paper 01/10* (University College Dublin, May 2001), pp. 16, 22–3.

31. Richard Baldwin, 'In or out: does it make a difference? An evidence-based analysis of the trade effects of the euro' (CEPR, May 2006), pp. 1–3.

32. Fidrmuc *et al.*, 'The stability of monetary unions', pp. 774–9.

33. Wolfgang Schäuble, 'Why Europe's monetary union faces its biggest crisis' (*Financial Times*, 11 March 2010); 'Pleite-Länder notfalls raus aus dem Euro!' (*Bild*, 15 March 2010).

34. 'Merkel – need scope to exclude countries from euro' (*Reuters*, 17 March 2010).

35. 'Euro is facing "existential crisis", Merkel says' (*EU Observer*, 19 May 2010); 'European debt crisis: markets fall as Germany bans "naked short-selling"' (*The Guardian*, 19 May 2010).

36. Dagmar Hartwig Lojsch, Marta Rodríguez-Vives and Michal Slavík, 'The size and composition of government debt in the euro area', *Occasional paper 132* (ECB, October 2011), pp. 33–4, 36, Table 13.

37. Bank of Italy data for non-residents' share of total general government securities

38. Bank of England, *Financial Stability Reports* (December 2010), pp. 6–7, Chart 6; (June 2012), p. 17, Table 2.A, p.18, chart 2.2.

39. IMF, 'Currency composition of official foreign-exchange reserves' (2014).

40. 'Euro notes cash in to overtake dollar' (*Financial Times*, 27 December 2006); ECB, *Monthly Bulletin* (December 2006), p. 78; *Monthly Bulletin: Tenth Anniversary of the ECB* (June 2008), p. 142.

41. Hans-Olaf Henkel, 'Germany needs to resist the euro's sweet-smelling poison' (*The Guardian*, 13 March 2011); 'A sceptic's solution: a breakaway currency' (*Financial Times*, 29 August 2011).

42. UBS Investment Research, 'Euro break-up: the consequences' (6 September 2011), cited in 'The cost of break-up: after the fall' (*The Economist*, 17 September 2011).

43. IMF, 'Greece: potential economic impact of euro exit', in *Staff Report on Greece* (March 2012), Box 2, pp. 46–7, 67 for baseline GDP decline; 'Greece as a source of contagion', in *Staff Report on Greece* (January 2013), Box 2, pp. 78–80.

44. Daniel Gros, 'Contribution to debate on the future of the euro area' (*The Economist*, 31 May 2010).

45. Stephen Cecchetti, Robert McCauley and Patrick McGuire, 'Intepreting Target2 balances', *Working paper 393* (BIS, December 2012), p. 8.

46. Norton Rose Fulbright, 'Redenomination risk' (August 2012).

47. Allen & Overy, 'The euro and currency unions' (October 2011), p. 9.
48. Charles Proctor, 'The euro: fragmentation and the financial markets' (*Capital Markets Law Journal*, 2011), Vol. 6, No. 1, pp. 16–28.
49. Briefing in London (July 2013).
50. Allen & Overy, 'The euro and currency unions', p. 17.
51. 'Germany faces a machine from hell' (*Financial Times*, 13 February 2012).
52. ECB, 'Determination of the euro conversion rates' (31 December 1998).
53. Phoebus Athanassiou, 'Withdrawal and expulsion from the EU and EMU: some reflections', *Legal working paper 10* (ECB, December 2009), p. 7.
54. Proctor, 'The euro: fragmentation and the financial markets', pp. 8–10.
55. 'The euro area's debt crisis: sovereign remedies' (*The Economist*, 5 March 2011).
56. 'Ireland's referendum on the fiscal compact: Irish ayes' (*The Economist*, 2 June 2012).
57. Based on briefings in Portugal on 28 April 2011.
58. IMF, *Staff Report on Portugal* (June 2011), p. 10; Eurostat database for GDP May 2015 and annual and monthly unemployment rate, ec.europa.eu/eu rostat/data/database.
59. 'Berlusconi says Italy may be forced to leave the euro zone' (*Reuters*, 18 December 2012).
60. 'Italy floated plans to leave the euro in 2011, says ECB insider' (*Daily Telegraph*, 12 September 2013).
61. 'From ceremonial figure to Italy's quiet power broker' (*New York Times*, 2 December 2011).
62. 'EU leaders tell Italy: stop the rot and get your house in order' (*The Guardian*, 23 October 2011); 'Berlusconi under pressure at G20 and in Rome' (*Financial Times*, 3 November 2011).
63. Francesco Marangoni, 'Technocrats in government: the composition and legislative initiatives of the Monti government eight months into its term of office' (*Bulletin of Italian Politics*, 2012), pp. 135–8.
64. 'Euro summit statement' (26 October 2011).
65. 'How the euro was saved' (*Financial Times*, 12 May 2014).
66. 'The euro crisis: there are all too many alternatives' (*The Economist*, 12 May 2012).
67. 'How the euro was saved: inside Europe's plan Z' (*Financial Times*, 15 May 2014); Mario Draghi speaking at press conference (ECB, 16 July 2015).
68. 'Leaving the euro: my big fat Greek divorce' (*The Economist*, 9 June 2012).

69. Capital Economics, 'Leaving the euro: a practical guide' (June 2012), pp. 42–5.
70. Williamson, 'What role for currency boards?', pp. 2–4, 7–9.
71. Luis Catão and Marco Terrones, 'Determinants of dollarisation: the banking side', *Working paper 00/146* (IMF, August 2000), pp. 3–4, Figure 1.
72. J. F. Hornbeck, 'Argentina's defaulted sovereign debt: dealing with the "holdouts"' (Congressional Research Service, 6 February 2013), p. 1.
73. IMF, *Article IV Staff Report on Argentina* (July 2005), p. 38.
74. John Baffes and Tassos Haniotis, 'Placing the 2006/08 commodity price boom into perspective', *Policy research working paper 5371* (World Bank, July 2010), p. 3 and Figure 4, p. 28; Sergio Lence, 'The agricultural sector in Argentina: major trends and recent developments', in Julian Alston, Bruce Babcock and Philip Pardey (eds.), *The Shifting Patterns of Agricultural Production and Productivity Worldwide* (Iowa State University, 2010), pp. 409–10, 420–2.
75. Hornbeck, 'Argentina's defaulted sovereign debt', pp. 1, 14.
76. 'Argentina devaluation sends currency tumbling most in 12 years' (*Bloomberg News*, 23 January 2014).
77. 'Argentina defaults for second time' (*BBC News*, 31 July 2014).
78. 'Greek coalition proposes easing bail-out terms' (*BBC News*, 23 June 2012).
79. Briefings in Berlin, June 2014; 'An unexpected U-turn: why Merkel wants to keep Greece in the euro zone' (*Der Spiegel*, 10 September 2012); Peet and La Guardia, *Unhappy Union*, pp. 81–2.
80. 'Greece in talks for third bail-out of up to €50 billion, Spain says' (*Financial Times*, 2 March 2015).
81. IMF, *Global Financial Stability Report* (October 2012), p. 27.

## 7    DEFENDER OF LAST RESORT

1. Jens Weidmann, 'Money creation and responsibility', speech in Frankfurt (18 September 2012).
2. 'Mario Draghi: "Alle sollten dem deutschen Beispiel folgen"' (*Frankfurter Allgemeine Zeitung*, 15 February 2011); ECB press conference (3 November 2011).
3. 'Seventeen characters in search of a central banker' (*The Economist*, 12 February 2011); 'So deutsch ist der neue EZB-chef' (*Bild*, 29 April 2011).

4. 'The European Central Bank: German shepherding' (*The Economist*, 18 February 2010).

5. Brief details of Mario Draghi's career are available on the Bank of Italy's website, www.bancaditalia.it/chi-siamo/storia/governatori-direttori-gen erali/governatori/mario-draghi/index.html; European Parliament, 'Draft report on the council recommendation on the appointment of the president of the ECB' (1 June 2011).

6. European Council, 'Jörg Asmussen is appointed to the executive board of the European Central Bank' (23 October 2011).

7. 'Draghi reshuffles ECB board' (*Financial Times*, 4 January 2012).

8. 'ECB's Bini Smaghi resignation raises doubts over independence' (*Reuters*, 11 November 2011).

9. Protocol of the ESCB and of the ECB, Articles 18.1 (open-market and credit operations) and 21.1 (prohibition of monetary financing).

10. ECB, *Annual Report 2010* (May 2011), pp. 92–3, 100; Willem Buiter, 'Looking into the deep pockets of the ECB' (Citigroup, 27 February 2012), p. 34, called this 'semantic sterilisation'.

11. ECB, 'Decision of 14 May 2010 establishing a securities markets programme'.

12. Buiter, 'Looking into the deep pockets of the ECB', p. 19.

13. Ulrich Bindseil, *Monetary Policy Implementation: Theory, Past and Present* (Oxford University Press, 2004), pp. 151–2.

14. ECB, *Annual Report 2012* (April 2013), pp. 82, 190; press release, 'Details on securities holdings acquired under the Securities Markets Programme' (21 February 2013); Fabian Eser and Bernd Schwaab, 'Assessing asset purchases within the ECB's SMP', Working paper 1587 (September 2013), p. 12, Figure 2.

15. Guillermo Calvo and Carmen Reinhart, 'When capital inflows come to a sudden stop: consequences and policy options' (University of Maryland, June 1999); Dick Nanto, 'The 1997–98 Asian financial crisis' (Congressional Research Service, 6 February 1998).

16. Galina Hale, 'Balance of payments in the European periphery' (*FRBSF Economic Letter*, 14 January 2013).

17. 'Target2 project and go-live', www.ecb.europa.eu/paym/t2/target/html/index.en.html; Target stands for 'trans-European automated real-time gross-settlement express transfer'.

18. The Finnish central bank's balance peaked in March 2012 at €73 billion, or 37 per cent of Finland's GDP; the Bundesbank's peaked at €751 billion in August 2012, or 27 per cent of German GDP.

19. Hans-Werner Sinn and Timo Wollmershäuser, 'Target loans, current-account balances and capital flows: the ECB's rescue facility', Working paper 3500 (CESIfo, June 2011), pp. 3, 31–5.

20. Cecchetti *et al.*, 'Intepreting Target2 balances'.

21. Willem Buiter, Ebrahim Rahbari and Juergen Michels, 'The implications of intra-euro area imbalances in credit flows', *Policy Insight 57* (CEPR, August 2011), pp. 4–7; Ulrich Bindseil and Philipp Johann König, 'The economics of Target2 balances', *SFB discussion paper 649* (Humboldt University, June 2011), pp. 20–3.

22. Protocol of the ESCB and of the ECB, Article 14.4.

23. ECB, 'The accountability of the ECB', pp. 51–2.

24. Forward by Jaime Caruana to David Archer and Paul Moser-Boehm, 'Central bank finances', BIS paper 71 (BIS, April 2013), pp. 1–2.

25. Eurostat, NIIP as per cent of GDP, ec.europa.eu/eurostat/tgm/printTable.do?tab=table&plugin=1&language=en&pcode=tipsii10&printPreview=true; IMF, *Staff Report on Ireland* (May 2011), p. 38.

26. Deutsche Bundesbank, 'Germany's international investment position at the end of 2013' (30 September 2014), figures for Q4 2012; EC, *Statistical Annex* (November 2014) for GDP figures.

27. ECB, 'The Eurosystem collateral framework throughout the crisis' (*Monthly Bulletin*, July 2013), pp. 73–5, 82–6; 'ECB announces measures to support bank lending and money-market activity' (8 December 2011); 'ECB takes further measures to increase collateral availability for counterparties' (22 June 2012).

28. ECB, 'The ECB increases its capital' (16 December 2010); 'Adjustments to the ECB's capital subscription key and the contribution paid by Latvijas Banka' (1 January 2014); and update to capital subscription (1 January 2015): the Bundesbank's share of paid-up capital was 27 per cent during the crisis between 2010 and 2013, falling to 26 per cent in 2014 and 2015.

29. Mario Draghi, speaking at press conferences (ECB, 9 February 2012 and 6 June 2012).

30. History of all ECB open market operations, LTROs and MROs, www.ecb.europa.eu/mopo/implement/omo/html/top_history.en.html.

31. 'ECB announces details of refinancing operations from October 2011 to 10 July 2012' (6 October 2011).

32. 'ECB announces measures' (8 December 2011).

33. ECB, Consolidated financial statements of the Eurosystem, as at 16 December 2011 and 9 March 2012 show an increase in the Eurosystem's balance-sheet from €2,494 billion to €3,006 billion; see also Mario Draghi at Global Investment Conference in London (ECB, 26 July 2012).

34. Van Rixtel and Gasperini, 'Financial crises and bank funding', p. 21.

35. EC, *Statistical Annex* (November 2014), Table 76, p. 160.

36. IMF, *Fiscal Monitor* (April 2012), Table 1, p. 61; (October 2012), Figure 1, p. 3, Table 1, p. 77.

37. Eurostat, NIIP as per cent of GDP, accessed March 2015.

38. 'Spain and the markets: the Spanish patient' (*The Economist*, 28 July 2012).

39. Mario Draghi, remarks at Global Investment Conference in London (ECB, 26 July 2012).

40. Mario Draghi, speaking at press conference (ECB, 2 August 2012).

41. EC, *Statistical Annex* (November 2014), Table 78, p. 164.

42. De Grauwe, 'The European Central Bank as a lender of last resort'.

43. Mario Draghi, speaking at press conference; press release, 'Technical features of outright monetary transactions' (ECB, 6 September 2012).

44. 'Statement by the heads of state or government of the euro area and EU institutions' (21 July 2011); EFSF guideline on precautionary programmes (29 November 2011).

45. Bundesbank, '55 years for stability', interview with Jens Weidmann and Helmut Schlesinger (27 July 2012).

46. Mario Draghi, speaking at press conference (ECB, 4 October 2012).

47. 'The ECB's unfired weapon: waiting for Rajoy' (*The Economist*, 4 October 2012).

48. Deutsche Bundesbank, 'Stellungnahme gegenüber dem Bundesverfassungsgericht' (21 December 2012), p. 9; 'The European Central Bank's deterrent: bench press' (*The Economist*, 8 June 2013).

49. Helmut Siekmann and Volker Wieland, 'The question before the court' (*The Economist*, 18 June 2013).

50. 'Germany and the euro: the ja and nein of euro rescues' (*The Economist*, 15 June 2013).

51. Sebastian Recker, 'Casenote – euro rescue package case: the German federal constitutional court protects the principle of parliamentary budget' (*German Law Journal*, 2011), pp. 2071–5.

52. Bundesverfassungsgericht, press release 9/2014 (7 February 2014); 'The German court and the European Central Bank' (*The Economist*, 7 February 2014).

53. Jörg Asmussen, 'Introductory statement by the ECB in the proceedings before the Federal Constitutional Court' (11 June 2013).

54. ECJ, press release No. 2/15, 'Advocate general's opinion in case C-62/14' (14 January 2015).

55. 'The German court and the ECB: it isn't over' (*The Economist*, 15 February 2014).

56. ECJ, Opinion of advocate general in case C-62/14 (14 January 2015), especially paras. 150–1, 182–4, 252–4; 'A preliminary judgment from the European Court of Justice rules in favour of bond purchases – but with strings attached' (*The Economist*, 14 January 2015).

57. Frank Schorkopf, 'Stellungnahme Europäische Zentralbank' (16 January 2013), p. 34.

58. Federal Reserve, press release (13 September 2012); 'The Federal Reserve launches QE3' (*The Economist*, 13 September 2012).

59. ECB, 'Eurosystem staff macroeconomic projections for the euro area' (*Monthly Bulletin*, June 2013), pp. 94–6.

60. Eurostat, 'Euro area annual inflation stable at 0.4%' (17 September 2014).

61. Paul De Grauwe, 'Should we worry about deflation?' (*The Economist*, 16 January 2014).

62. Mario Draghi, speaking at press conference (ECB, 4 December 2014).

63. Yves Mersch, 'Euro area monetary policy: where we stand' (9 December 2013).

64. Danmarks Nationalbank, *Monetary Review* (3rd quarter 2012), pp. 59–72.

65. Mario Draghi, speaking at press conferences (8 March 2012, 10 January 2013, 7 March 2013).

66. Mersch, 'Euro area monetary policy: where we stand'.

67. Mario Draghi, speaking at press conference (7 August 2014); Federal Reserve, press release (29 October 2014).

68. Bank of England, 'The funding for lending scheme' (*Quarterly Bulletin*, 2012 Q4), pp. 306–10.

69. ECB, press releases on TLTROs (5 June and 3 July 2014).

70. ECB, 'TLTROs: updated modalities' (29 July 2014), see especially chart 2, p. 4; Mario Draghi, introductory statement to press conference (22 January 2015).

71. The ECB lent €82.6 billion in September 2014 and €129.8 billion in December of that year.

72. Mario Draghi, introductory statement at press conference (ECB, 4 September 2014); ECB, 'Purchase programme for covered bonds' (4 June 2009); 'ECB announces details of its new covered bond purchase programme' (3 November 2011).

73. ECB, 'Covered bonds in the EU financial system' (December 2008), pp. 6–9.

74. Bank of England and ECB, 'The case for a better functioning securitisation market', p. 3.

75. Hans-Werner Sinn, 'Merkel has a duty to stop Draghi's illegal fiscal meddling' (*Financial Times*, 1 October 2014).

76. Bank of England and ECB, 'The case for a better functioning securitisation market', p. 10.

77. Open letter from Mervyn King, governor of the Bank of England, to George Osborne, chancellor of the exchequer (14 February 2011).

78. OECD, Main economic indicators (MEI), consumer prices, stats.oecd.org/ Index.aspx?DatasetCode=MEI_PRICES.

79. For example, Michael Joyce, Matthew Tong and Robert Woods, 'The UK's quantitative easing policy: design, operation and impact' (Bank of England *Quarterly Bulletin*, 2011 Q3), pp. 204–11.

80. 'QE in the euro zone' (*The Economist*, 20 January 2015), chart 2; 'S&P cuts Italy's rating to just above junk in blow to PM Renzi' (*Reuters*, 5 December 2014).

81. ECB, Introductory statement to press conference, and press notice, 'ECB announces expanded asset purchase programme' (22 January 2015); 'Decision of 4 March 2015 on a secondary markets public sector asset purchase programme'.

82. EC, *Economic Sentiment Indicator* (30 March 2015); Eurostat, 'GDP up by 0.4% in the euro area and the EU' (13 May 2015).

83. ECB, 'Q&A on the public-sector purchase programme'; 'The ECB makes its mind up' (*The Economist*, 22 January 2015).

84. 'Merkel refrains from criticising ECB but presses need for reform' (*Financial Times*, 22 January 2015).

## 8 SOVEREIGN REMEDIES

1. Lisbon European Council conclusions (23 and 24 March 2000).

2. OECD, *The OECD Jobs Study* (1994); Anita Wölfl *et al.*, 'Ten years of product-market reform in OECD countries', Working paper 695 (April 2009); 'Employment protection and labour market performance', in *Employment Outlook* (1999), Chapter 2; *Economic Policy Reforms: Going for Growth* (2005).

3. OECD, *Going for Growth* (2005), pp. 12, 37–55; *Going for Growth* (2014), pp. 9, 91–118.

4. 'Pact for competitiveness' (3 February 2011); European Council conclusions (24–25 March 2011), annex 1, pp. 13–20.

5. European Council conclusions (20 December 2013), pp. 17–20; 'The battle for euro-zone reforms: Angela all alone' (*The Economist*, 20 December 2013).

6. 'The sick man of the euro' (*The Economist*, 3 June 1999).

7. Lena Jacobi and Jochen Kluve, 'Before and after the Hartz reforms: the performance of active labour market policy in Germany', Discussion paper 2100 (IZA, April 2006), pp. 2–13, 25–7.

8. 'Schröder urges loosening of fiscal rules in EU states' (*Financial Times*, 17 January 2005).

9. Christian Dustmann, Bernd Fitzenberger, Uta Schönberg and Alexandra Spitz-Oener, 'From sick man of Europe to economic superstar: Germany's resurgent economy' (*Journal of Economic Perspectives*, 2014), Vol. 28, No. 1, pp. 168, 181–4.

10. Germany surpassed its pre-crisis peak in the first quarter of 2011; the US in the third quarter of 2011 (Eurostat and FRED, April 2015, ec.europa. eu/eurostat/data/database research.stlouisfed.org/fred2/series/GDPC1).

11. OECD, *Economic Survey of Germany* (May 2014), p. 31.

12. EC, *Statistical Annex* (November 2014), Table 8, p. 24, GDP at current prices per person in 1999.

13. Nicholas Crafts and Gianni Toniolo (eds.), *Economic Growth in Europe since 1945* (Cambridge University Press, 1996), pp. 5–8; UN Economic Commission for Europe, 'Catching up and falling behind: economic convergence in Europe' in *Economic Survey of Europe 2000*, No. 1, Chapter 5, pp. 156–70; EC, *Statistical Annex* (November 2014), Table 10, p. 28.

14. EC, *EMU@10*, pp. 88–93.

15. Charles R. Bean, 'The interaction of aggregate-demand policies and labour market reform' (*Swedish Economic Policy Review*, 1998), pp. 375–80.

16. OECD, 'Calculating summary indicators of EPL strictness: methodology'.

17. OECD, *Italy Economic Survey* (May 2013), p. 24.

18. Florence Jaumotte, 'The Spanish labour market in a cross-country perspective', Working paper 11/11 (IMF, January 2011), p. 9; Anita Wölfl and Juan Mora-Sanguinetti, 'Reforming the labour market in Spain', Working paper 845 (OECD, February 2011), pp. 11–12.

19. Eurostat, temporary employees as per cent of all employees, April 2015, ec.europa.eu/eurostat/data/database.

20. Kristian Orsini and Sonia Vila Núñez, 'The impact of the Spanish labour market reform on the on-the-job search rate', Country Focus (EC, June 2014), p. 2.

21. EC, *Macroeconomic imbalances: Italy 2014*, pp. 9, 35.

22. Jaumotte, 'The Spanish labour market', pp. 6–9, 30; OECD, *The 2012 Labour Market Reform in Spain: A Preliminary Assessment* (OECD, 2014), pp. 13–16.

23. Luis Díez Catalán and Ernesto Villanueva, 'Collective bargaining and unemployment during the great recession: evidence for Spain' (IZA, 15 February 2014), pp. 1–6, 10.

24. Banco de España, 'Wage adjustment to shocks in Spain' (*Economic Bulletin*, April 2011), pp. 146–7, 152–3; Jaumotte, 'The Spanish labour market', Table 2, p. 43.

25. OECD figures for real earnings consistent with *Employment Outlook* (September 2014); EC, *Statistical Annex* (November 2014), Table 10, p. 28.

26. BIS, *Annual Report* (June 2014), p. 62; ESA 2010 revisions did not materially affect the GDP figures cited in this report.

27. Wölfl et al., 'Ten years of product-market reform in OECD countries', p. 7; Tito Boeri, 'Reforming labour and product markets: some lessons from two decades of experiments in Europe', Working paper 05/97 (IMF, May 2005), pp. 3, 21, Figure 1, p. 26.

28. OECD, *Going for Growth* (2014), pp. 66–8; Wölfl et al., 'Ten years of product-market reform in OECD countries', p. 9.

29. The OECD-25 average were the 30 states before 2010, excluding Iceland, Luxembourg, Mexico, Slovakia and Turkey.

30. OECD, *Germany Economic Survey* (May 2014), p. 80.

31. OECD, *Greece Economic Survey* (November 2013), p. 31.

32. 'Structural reform in southern Europe: patchy progress' (*The Economist*, 19 April 2014).

33. IMF, *Article IV Staff Report on Italy* (July 2012), p. 17; *Italy: Selected Issues* (July 2012), p. 8.

34. Rankings downloaded from www.govindicators.org in February 2015.

35. Alexander Hijzen, Leopoldo Mondauto and Stefano Scarpetta, 'The perverse effects of job-security provisions on job security in Italy', Discussion paper 7594 (IZA, August 2013), pp. 4–7.

36. Uwe Böwer, Vasiliki Michou and Christoph Ungerer, 'The puzzle of the missing Greek exports', Economic paper 518 (EC, June 2014), pp. 2–3, 15–20.

37. Eurostat Pocketbooks, *Labour Market Statistics* (2011), Table 2.5, p. 29; for 15- to 64-year-olds.

38. Michael Porter, *The Competitive Advantage of Nations* (Macmillan Press, 1990), pp. 421–53.

39. Bill Emmott, *Good Italy, Bad Italy* (Yale University Press, 2012), pp. 187–202, 231–4.

40. IMF, *Article IV Staff Report on Italy* (2012), p. 16; *Italy: Selected Issues* (2012), pp. 6, 28–30.

41. Derek Anderson, Bergljot Barkbu, Lusine Lusinyan and Dirk Muir, 'Assessing the gains from structural reforms for jobs and growth', in IMF, *Jobs and Growth: Supporting the European Recovery* (IMF, April 2014), Chapter 7, pp. 2–4; 14–15, Table 7.4.

42. OECD, *Going for Growth* (2014), pp. 16–20 and especially Figure 1.11, p. 45; Group 1 comprised Greece, Italy, Portugal, Slovenia and Spain and the indicator measured the extent to which countries carried out previous OECD recommendations for structural reforms.

43. OECD, *Going for Growth* (2013), pp. 17–20.

44. 'Portugal's bail-out: final call' (*The Economist*, 22 March 2014).

45. Wölfl and Mora-Sanguinetti, 'Reforming the labour market in Spain', pp. 13–19; Samuel Bentolila, Juan Dolado and Juan Jimeno, *Reforming an Insider–Outsider Labour Market: The Spanish Experience* (Bank of England, March 2012), pp. 19–20.

46. OECD, *Spain Economic Survey* (November 2012), pp. 34–6; Bentolila *et al.*, 'Reforming an insider–outsider labour market', pp. 31–3.

47. 'Spain's economy: Iberian dawn' (*The Economist*, 2 August 2014).

48. OECD, *The 2012 Labour Market Reform in Spain: A Preliminary Assessment* (2014), pp. 6–8, 10–12.

49. OECD, *Greece Economic Survey* (November 2013), pp. 50, 88–90; IMF, *Staff Report on Greece* (March 2012), pp. 12, 51; Greek finance ministry, 'Hellenic national reform programme 2012–15' (April 2012), pp. 6–7.

50. IMF, *Staff Report on Greece* (June 2014), p. 4.

51. OECD, 'Portugal: reforming the state to promote growth' (May 2013), pp. 34–7; IMF, *Staff Report on Portugal* (February 2014), Box 4, p. 31.

52. 'Labour reform in Italy: dangermen' (*The Economist*, 18 February 2012); 'Italy: murder and the labour market' (*The Economist*, 21 March 2002).

53. OECD, *Italy Economic Survey* (May 2013), pp. 75–6, 79–80.

54. 'Employers attack Italy's labour reforms' (*Financial Times*, 5 April 2012); 'Italy employers' head now supports labour reform' (*Reuters*, 12 April 2012); 'Six months on, Monti's labour reform has changed little' (*Reuters*, 2 January 2013).

55. Daniele Franco and Nicola Sartor, 'NDCs in Italy: unsatisfactory present, uncertain future', in Robert Holzmann and Edward Palmer (eds.), *Pension Reform: Issues and Prospects for Non-Financial Defined Contribution (NDC) Schemes* (World Bank, 2006), pp. 467–76: the new system applied in full only to those entering work after 1995.

56. OECD, *Pensions at a Glance 2013* (November 2013), pp. 23, 33, 284–8; *Italy Economic Survey* (May 2013), pp. 54–5, 73.

57. OECD, *Pensions at a Glance* (March 2011), p. 159.

58. OECD, *Pensions at a Glance* (2011), pp. 116, 119–21; *Pensions at a Glance* (November 2013), pp. 132–7; Iceland's overall replacement rate was a little higher than Greece's in 2008, the year covered by the 2011 publication, but this included mandatory private provision.

59. OECD, *Pensions at a Glance* (2013), pp. 260–62; *Greece Economic Survey* (August 2011), pp. 95–9; *Pensions Outlook* (December 2014), pp. 65, 75; Georgios Symeonidis, 'The Greek pension reform strategy 2010–2013', Hellenic Actuarial Authority (November 2013).

60. EC, *The 2015 Ageing Report* (May 2015), p. 74; OECD, *Employment Outlook* (July 2015), p. 267.

61. OECD, *Pensions at a Glance* (2013), pp. 38, 340–2.

62. OECD, *Pensions Outlook* (December 2014), pp. 65, 80; Rafael Doménech and Victor Pérez-Díaz, 'The new sustainability factor of the public pension system in Spain' (VoxEU, 11 December 2013).

63. IMF, *Staff Reports on Portugal* (April 2012), pp. 85–6; (October 2012), pp. 7, 15–18; (June 2013), p. 10; OECD, *Pensions Outlook* (2014), pp. 63–4, 79.

64. IMF, *Italy: Selected Issues* (2012), pp. 6–7, 28–30.

65. OECD, *Competition Assessment Reviews: Greece* (2014), pp. 21–3, 29–31.

66. IMF, *Staff Report on Greece* (December 2010), p. 68; OECD, *Going for Growth* (2014), p. 18; 'Greece needs new targeted measures, says IMF's Poul Thomsen', *Interview with Kathimerini* (IMF, 24 November 2013).

67. IMF, *Staff Report on Greece* (July 2013), p. 59, showed schedule for the next review by the end of September; it was completed in May 2014.

68. Norton Rose Fulbright, 'Law 4273/2014: the privatisation of the not-so-Small PPC' (July 2014); 'Greek shares hit by privatisation freeze' (*Reuters*, 28 January 2015).

69. Snam, 'The Snam shareholder' (December 2013), p. 17; Cassa Depositi e Prestiti, *2012 Annual Report*, pp. 19–20, 322, 407.

70. OECD, *Going for Growth* (2014), Figures 2.2, 2.3, 2.7 and 2.9, pp. 70–8.

71. OECD, *Portugal: Reforming the State to Promote Growth*, p. 10.

72. Nine including Lithuania, which joined the euro at the start of 2015.

73. OECD, *Portugal: Reforming the State to Promote Growth*, pp. 3–6.

74. World Bank, *Doing Business 2015* (2014), Table 1.1, p. 4.

75. OECD, *Greece Economic Survey* (November 2013), p. 32.

76. OECD, *Going for Growth* (2012), pp. 4–5, 176–7; Romain Bouis *et al.*, 'The short-term effects of structural reforms: an empirical analysis', Working paper 949 (OECD, March 2012), pp. 30–3.

77. OECD, *Going for Growth* (2012), p. 175; Bouis *et al.*, 'The short-term effects of structural reforms', pp. 5–7, 21, 29–30.

78. Mario Draghi, speaking at press conference in Barcelona (ECB, 3 May 2012).

79. IMF, *Article IV Staff Report on Italy* (2012), Box 4, p. 21.

80. IMF, *Staff Report on Portugal* (June 2013), pp. 10–11; *Staff Report on Portugal* (February 2014), p. 9.

81. OECD, *Education at a Glance* (September 2014), Table A.1.4a, pp. 45–6.

82. OECD, *Portugal: Reforming the State to Promote Growth*, p. 6.

83. INE, press release on migration statistics for 2013 (30 June 2014).

84. ILO, *Tackling the Jobs Crisis in Portugal* (2014), pp. 14–15, especially Figure 1.4, for 2011–12; INE Provisional estimates of resident population

(16 June 2014), Table 11 for permanent outflows in 2013; temporary outflows in 2013 assumed to be the average of 2011–12; EC, *Statistical Annex* (November 2014), Table 1, p. 10.

85. World Bank, *Doing business 2015* (2014), pp. 188, 194.

86. EC, Task force for Greece, 'Second quarterly report' (March 2012), p. 27; 'Greece's economic woes: the labours of austerity' (*The Economist*, 9 April 2011).

87. 'Italy's Renzi cuts local government in first step of ambitious agenda' (*Reuters*, 3 April 2014); Tito Boeri, 'Purtroppo rimarremo provinciali' (lavoce.info, 28 March 2014); role of provinces is set out at Committee of the Regions, cor.europa.eu.

88. World Bank, *Doing business 2015*, pp. 137–8, 186–7, 194.

89. Gianluca Esposito, Sergi Lanau and Sebastiaan Pompe, 'Judicial system reform in Italy – a key to growth', Working paper 14/32 (IMF, February 2014), p. 3.

90. Clarke and Hardiman, 'Crisis in the Irish banking system', p. 39.

91. IMF, *Italy: Financial System Stability Assessment* (September 2013), pp. 15, 30, 39–41.

92. EC, 'Questions and answers on the task force for Greece', MEMO 11/599 (13 September 2011).

93. OECD, *Greece: Review of the Central Administration* (2011), p. 42; IMF, *Staff Report on Greece* (July 2013), pp. 14–15; *Staff Report on Greece* (June 2014), pp. 1, 8.

94. IMF, *Staff Report on Greece* (January 2013), p. 18.

95. IMF, *Staff Reports on Greece* (March 2011), pp. 13–14; (January 2013), p. 20.

96. IMF, *Staff Report on Greece* (January 2013), p. 20; 'Renewed Greek troubles: darkness at midnight' (*The Economist*, 15 June 2013).

97. 'Euro summit statement' (12 July 2015); IMF, 'Greece: preliminary draft debt sustainability analysis' (26 June 2015), p. 4.

98. OECD, *Spain Economic Survey* (September 2014), p. 29; Ernst & Young, 'Global tax alert: Spain enacts tax reform' (4 December 2014).

99. OECD, *Italy Economic Survey* (February 2015), p. 65; 'Italy Cabinet approves first planks of Renzi's labour reform' (*Reuters*, 24 December 2014); 'Italy's labour market: marching to a different tune' (*The Economist*, 28 February 2015).

100. OECD, *Pensions Outlook* (December 2014), pp. 67, 75; 'France forced to drop 75 per cent supertax after meagre returns' (*The Guardian*, 31 December 2014).

101. OECD, *Going for Growth* (2014), p. 31; *France Economic Survey* (March 2015), pp. 34–5.

102. Cour des Comptes, *Rapport Public Annuel*, Part 1 (February 2014), p. 49; 'French employers reject jobs targets' (*Reuters*, 21 January 2014).

103. OECD, *France Economic Survey* (March 2015), p. 12.

104. Projet de loi pour la croissance et l'activité presented to National Assembly (11 December 2014); OECD, *France Economic Survey* (2015), p. 106; 'French PM skips parliament vote to push through reforms' (*Reuters*, 17 February 2015).

## 9   DEBTORS' PRISON

1. 'Portugal's woes: on the rocks' (*The Economist*, 6 July 2013); 'Portugal political crisis a catalogue of missteps' (*Reuters*, 24 July 2013).

2. Mario Draghi, speaking at press conference (7 November 2013).

3. ESM, 'Guideline on precautionary financial assistance', Article 2.

4. 'Slovenia's financial crisis: stressed out' (*The Economist*, 30 November 2013); 'After the stress tests: Slovenia remains vulnerable' (*The Economist*, 12 December 2013).

5. 'Ireland regains investment grade rating from Moody's' (*Bloomberg News*, 18 January 2014); 'Moody's raises Portugal's rating to Ba2' (*Wall Street Journal*, 9 May 2014).

6. 'Sovereign debt markets: following a new script' (*The Economist*, 18 January 2014); US Federal Reserve, press release (18 December 2013).

7. IGCP, press release (9 January 2014).

8. IMF, *Staff Report on Portugal* (April 2014), p. 19.

9. Statement by the EC, ECB and IMF on Portugal (IMF, 12 June 2014); 'Portugal to do without final bail-out payment' (*Reuters*, 12 June 2014); 'Portugal court ruling on austerity measures threatens tax rises' (*Financial Times*, 1 June 2014).

10. 'Greece's return to the markets: the prodigal son' (*The Economist*, 12 April 2014).

11. EC, *Statistical Annex* (May 2015), Table 77, p. 162.

12. OECD, *Statistical Annex* (November 2014), Table 30, p. 246.

13. EC, *Statistical Annex* (May 2015), Tables 76 and 77, pp. 160 and 162.

14. EC, *Statistical Annex* (May 2015), Tables 66 and 78, pp. 140 and 164.

15. 'Greece's election: beware Greeks voting for gifts' (*The Economist*, 31 January 2015); EFSF, 'FAQ: new disbursement of financial assistance to Greece' (20 December 2012): the deferral of interest payments was on disbursements of €96 billion of EFSF lending, Greek public debt was €317 billion in 2014.

16. National Treasury Management Agency, 'NTMA completes first tranche of early repayment of IMF loan facility' (19 December 2014).

17. EC, *Cyprus Economic Adjustment Programme: Third Review* (March 2014), p. 39; Cyprus Banking-Sector Commission, p. 22.

18. 'Bank of Italy tells banks in the red not to pay bonuses, dividends' (*Reuters*, 14 March 2013); 'Italy banks' bad loans underline southern Europe malaise' (*Bloomberg News*, 1 August 2013).

19. Sinn, *The Euro Trap*, pp. 7, 112–26, 346–8.

20. IMF, *Staff Report on Greece* (June 2014), pp. 4–5.

21. EC, 'Greece second economic adjustment programme: fourth review', Occasional paper 192 (April 2014), pp. 11–15; EC, *Statistical Annex* (May 2015), Table 37, p. 82.

22. IMF, *Staff Report on Ireland* (December 2013), p. 29; Shane Enright and Mary Dalton, 'The impact of the patent cliff on pharma-chem output in Ireland' (Department of Finance, 2013), pp. 1–12; EC, *Statistical Annex* (May 2015), Table 37, p. 82.

23. OECD, *Spain Economic Survey* (December 2010), pp. 28–31; Miguel Cardoso, Mónica Correa-López and Rafael Doménech, 'Export shares, price competitiveness and the "Spanish paradox"' (VoxEU, 24 November 2012).

24. Banco de Portugal, trade in goods figures; 'Portugal's bail-out: final call' (*The Economist*, 22 March 2014).

25. OECD, *Statistical Annex* (November 2014), Table 51, p. 267.

26. US Treasury, *Report to Congress on International Economic and Exchange-Rate Policies* (30 October 2013), pp. 3, 25.

27. EC, '*Macroeconomic imbalances: Germany 2014*', Occasional paper 174 (March 2014), pp. 11–14.

28. CSO, 'Quarterly national accounts release' (11 December 2014), Table 2; Eurostat, 'Release on deficits and debt' (21 October 2014).

29. IMF, *Staff Report on Portugal* (April 2012), pp. 18, 54–6.

30. Jean-Claude Juncker, 'A new start for Europe' (15 July 2014), p. 7.

31. Figures from Deutsche Bundesbank, February 2015.

32. Moritz Kraemer, 'Rebalancing within the eurozone is grinding to a halt' (Standard & Poor's, 15 December 2014).

33. Luigi Buttiglione, Philip R. Lane, Lucrezia Reichlin and Vincent Reinhart, 'Deleveraging? What deleveraging?', Geneva report on the world economy 16 (CEPR, September 2014), pp. 58–64.

34. Mario Draghi, speaking at press conferences between November 2013 and March 2014.

35. IMF, *Fiscal Monitor* (April 2015), Tables A7 and A8, pp. 71–2.

36. Charles Horioka, Takaaki Nomoto and Akiko Terada-Hagiwara, 'Why hasn't Japan's massive government debt wreaked havoc (yet)?' (VoxEU, 21 January 2014); Lojsch *et al.*, 'The size and composition of government debt in the euro area', p. 36; S. M. Ali Abbas *et al.*, 'Sovereign debt composition in advanced economies: a historical perspective', Working paper 14/162 (IMF, 2014), Table 4, p. 22.

37. William R. Cline, *Managing the Euro Area Debt Crisis* (Peterson Institute for International Economics, 2014), pp. 4–5, 17–20, 194–5.

38. In remarks when presenting his paper at the National Institute of Economic and Social Research in London on 22 September 2014.

39. Eurostat, 'GDP stable in the euro area' (14 August 2014).

40. Eurostat, 'GDP up 0.4 per cent in both the euro area and the EU28' (9 June 2015).

41. CEPR, Euro Area Business Cycle Dating Committee, 'Euro area mired in recession pause' (16 June 2014); 'The CEPR and NBER approaches' (2015).

42. EC, *Statistical Annex* (May 2015), Tables 10, 24, 77 and 78, pp. 28, 56, 162, 164, for GDP, deflator, primary balance and government debt.

43. EC, *Autumn Forecast* (November 2014), Table 14, p. 150.

44. Mario Draghi, 'Unemployment in the euro area', speech at Jackson Hole (22 August 2014).

45. EC, *Country Report: Germany 2015* (March 2015), p. 30; 'German cabinet approves plans to approve mid-term spending' (*Reuters*, 18 March 2015).

46. 'France drops growth outlook, will miss deficit target' (*Wall Street Journal*, 10 September 2014); 'Paris pfeift auf EU-Defizitvorgaben' (*Tageschau*, 10 September 2014).

47. 'Merkel defends fiscal rules as Paris and Rome put growth first' (*Financial Times*, 16 October 2014); EC, *Country Report Italy 2015* (March 2015), p. 8.

48. De Witte, 'Using international law in the euro crisis', p. 22.

49. Council of the EU, 'Agreement on the transfer and mutualisation of contributions to the single resolution fund' (14 May 2014), Recitals 7 and 20; 'Member states sign agreement on bank resolution fund' (21 May 2014).

50. EC, 'EU economic governance "six-pack" enters into force' (12 December 2011).

51. EC, ' "Two-pack" enters into force' (27 May 2013).

52. EC, 'Communication: 2014 draft budgetary plans of the euro area' (15 November 2013); 'Remarks by Olli Rehn at the Eurogroup press conference' (22 November 2013).

53. IMF, *Euro Area Policies Report* (July 2014), p. 12.

54. Jean-Claude Trichet, 'Building Europe, building institutions', speech at Aachen (ECB, 2 June 2011).

55. Herman Van Rompuy, *Towards a Genuine Economic and Monetary Union* (5 December 2012), pp. 4–5, 9–12.

56. Mario Draghi, 'Memorial lecture in honour of Tommaso Padoa-Schioppa', London (9 July 2014).

57. Rompuy, *Towards a Genuine Economic and Monetary Union*, pp. 14–16.

58. Benoît Cœuré, 'Investing in Europe: towards a new convergence process' (9 July 2014).

59. 'Ranked: the fifty US state economies from worst to best' (*Business Insider*, 3 March 2015).

60. 'Grexit grumblings: Germany open to possible Greek euro-zone exit' (*Der Spiegel*, 5 January 2015).

61. EC, *Statistical Annex* (November 2014), Table 1, p. 10.

62. 'Latvia: reaching for the euro' (*Financial Times*, 23 April 2013).

63. Morten Spange and Martin Wagner Toftdahl, 'Fixed exchange-rate policy in Denmark' (Danmarks Nationalbank, *Monetary Review*, First Quarter 2014), pp. 49–60.

64. 'Voting rights at the ECB: new club rules' (*The Economist*, 14 December 2013); ECB, 'Rotation of voting rights in the governing council of the ECB' (*Monthly Bulletin*, July 2009), pp. 91–9.

65. ECB, 'ECB announces first list of governors subject to voting rotation' (18 September 2014).
66. 'Weidmann muss aussetzen' (*Handelsblatt*, 18 September 2014).
67. David Marsh, *Europe's Deadlock*, p. 118.
68. Mario Draghi, 'Stability and prosperity in monetary union', speech at the University of Helsinki (27 November 2014).
69. 'Merkel calls for "political union" to save the euro' (EurActiv.com, 8 June 2012); 'Analysis: Merkel's "fiscal union" drive faces major obstacles' (*Reuters*, 20 June 2012).
70. Jens Weidmann, 'Monetary union as a stability union', speech in Amsterdam (Bundesbank, 7 April 2014).
71. Wolfgang Schäuble, 'Banking union must be built on firm foundations' (*Financial Times*, 12 May 2013).
72. *Eurobarometer*, No. 405 (October 2014), pp. 7–8.
73. *Eurobarometer*, No. 216 (September 2007), pp. 8–9.
74. EC, *Statistical Annex* (November 2014), Table 10, p. 28; Barclays Economics Research, *Greece Quarterly Focus* (22 July 2015).
75. IMF, 'Greece: preliminary draft debt sustainability analysis' (26 June, 2015); 'An update of IMF staff's preliminary public debt sustainability analysis' (14 July 2015).
76. Crafts, 'Saving the euro: a pyrrhic victory?'.
77. *Eurobarometer*, No. 139 (November 2002), p. 66.

# Index

ABSs (asset-backed securities), 184, 202–3, 204–5
Acharya, Viral, 137–8
additional credit claims, 150–1
adverse scenario, stress testing, 133–5
AfD (Alternative für Deutschland) party, 19–20
Almunia, Joaquín, 85
Alpha Bank, 112, 124
Argentina
    currency crisis, 167, 168, 169–70
    sovereign debt, 112
Asian financial crisis (1997–8), 181
Asmussen, Jörg, 176–7, 191, 194, 195–6
assets denationalisation, 153
Athanassiou, Phoebus, 162–3
Attali, Jacques, 40–1
austerity fatigue, 9
austerity measures, 208
    acceptance of, 163
    controversy over impact, 107–8
    and double-dip recession, 107–8
    make-up of, 232
    and sovereign debt, 8–9, 26–7, 89
Austria
    bail-in policy, 141–2
    bank recapitalisation, 120
    exchange-rate test, 45–6
    price-stability test, 45
Austro-Hungarian empire, 146–7
automatic stabilisers, 50

bail-in policy, 139–42
balance of payments, 10–11, 17, 26–7, 46, 74–7, 180, 181–2, 245–6
Balassa–Samuelson effect, 70
Baldwin, Richard, 152
Balls, Ed, 46
Banca Monte dei Paschi di Siena, 126, 234–5
Banco Espírito Santo, 127, 248

bank/government vicious circle, 10–11, 139–40
bank credit, 121–2
Bank of Cyprus, 129, 139–40, 141
Bank of England, ix, x, 1, 28, 53–4, 64–6, 67–8, 84, 121, 125, 147, 178, 200–1, 203, 205
bank-funding markets, 14–15
Bankia, 125–6
banking crises, 27
    systemic characteristics, 128–9
banking union, ix, 17, 24, 27, 55, 116, 138–9, 142, 254–6
banking union pillars, 138–9
banks
    assets, 76–7, 131
    bad loans, 117, 248
    Baltic, 123–4
    banking foundations weakness, 14
    business lending restrictions, 10–11
    capital injections, 244
    cross-border lending, 119, 123
    debt financing, 121–2
    ECB assessment of, 136–9
    ECB long-term lending to, 200–1
    failing banks resolution, 17–18, 138–9
    and government, 129–30
    and international credit boom, 118–19
    loan-to-deposit ratios, 122–3
    national banking systems weakness, 7
    peripheral-countries vulnerability, 122–3
    recapitalisation, 120
    reliance on central bank funding, 129
    Southern Europe problems, 120–1
    sovereign bond holdings, 130–1
    and sovereign-debt crisis, 117, 129–30
    SRM (Single Resolution Mechanism), 138–9
    stress testing, 133–5, 137
    and sub-prime mortgage crisis, 117–18
    supervision
        by ECB, 17–18, 27, 29
    weaknesses, 9, 27, 31

315

banks (cont.)
  weaknesses, 116
  zombie banks, 137–8
  see also individual countries;
    NCBs
Baring Brothers, 147
Barroso, José Manuel, 3–5, 165, 256–7
Basel framework, 117–18
baseline scenario, stress testing, 133–5
BBVA, 125
Bean, Charles, 214
Belgium
  bank recapitalisation, 120
  debt test, 60–1
  exchange-rate test, 45–6
  sovereign debt, 79–81
Berlusconi, Silvio, 17, 100–1, 104, 164–5,
    222, 232
Bernanke, Ben, 65, 118–19
Biagi, Marco, 225
Bini Smaghi, Lorenzo, 177–8
BIS (Bank for International Settlements), 40–1
Blanchard, Oliver, 107
blue sovereign debt, 103
BNP Paribas, 84
bond investors, 82–3
bond markets, 3, 14–16, 22–3, 26–7, 28, 60, 83,
    84–5, 90–1, 94, 100, 101, 108, 111, 123,
    129–30, 137, 178–80, 188–9, 191–2,
    202, 240, 241–3
  penalising of, 129–30
  see also eurobonds
Boonstra, Wim, 103–4
Bootle, Roger, 169
Bordo, Michael, 56
Borio, Claudio, 121
Bratusek, Alenka, 241
Bretton Woods system, 39–40, 45–6
Brown, Gordon, 46
BRRD (Bank Recovery and Resolution
    Directive), 140
Bruegel think-tank, 23, 103
Buchheit, Lee, 109–10
Buiter, Willem, 48, 51, 52, 58, 83, 137–8,
    151, 179
Bundesbank, 15–16, 35–6, 38, 41, 44, 52–3, 54,
    59, 63–4, 65, 67–9, 149–50, 159, 176–7,
    179–80, 181, 182–4, 191, 192–3, 261–2,
    267–9
Buttiglione, Luigi, 250–1

capital flight, 180, 181–2
capital keys, 63
carry trade, 130
cartels, 218–19, 228
Caruana, Jaime, 128–9
Cassa Depositi e Prestiti, 228–9
CEBS (Committee of European Banking
    Supervisors), 134–5
Cecchetti, Stephen, 79
Central Bank of Ireland, 183–4
central banks see individual banks; NCBs
China
  economic rise of, 24–5
  goods to Europe, 60
Chirac, Jacques, 11–12, 64
Clarke, Blánaid, 234–5
Cliffe, Mark, 156
Cline, William, 251–2
cluster firms, 221
Cœuré, Benoît, 257–8
collateral policy, 67–8, 83
collective action clauses, 109
collective bargaining, 216–17, 224
Competitive Advantage of Nations, 221
competitiveness
  divergence in, 73–4
  reforms, 17
Confindustria, 225
convergence criteria, 25, 44–6, 61–2
convergence trades, 60
corporate borrowing costs, 132–3
Corsetti, Giancarlo, 48
Crafts, Nicholas, 267
Crédit Agricole, 124
credit boom, 59, 118–19, 121
credit drought, 117
credit quality threshold, 184
credit risk, debtor countries, 184–6
credit-generated growth, 14
creditor/debtor countries, political
    differences, 9
cross-border bank ownership, 124
cross-border holdings, 76–7
cross-border lending, 119, 123, 128
currency notes / coins introduction, 59
currency notes overstamping, 151,
    167
currency unions
  problems/break-ups, 11–13, 143–9
  and trade, 152

Cyprus
  bail-in policy, 141
  bail-out, 27, 97–8, 116, 139–40
  banks, 116, 128, 244
  as divided country, 38
  ELA (emergency liquidity assistance),
    149–50
  and ESM, 97–8
  financial crisis, 2–5
  growth, 72–3
  junk rating, 203–4
  private debt, x, 8–9
  sovereign bond losses, 129–30
  sovereign debt, 2
Czech–Slovak monetary divorce, 151, 152

D'Antona, Massimo, 225
DBRS, 203–4
De Grauwe, Paul, 15, 189
De Witte, Bruno, 97, 194–5, 254–5
Deauville meeting (2010), 108
debt, joint underwriting, 104–5
debt brake, 106
debt criterion, 48, 60–1
debt financing, 121–2
debt mutualisation, 102
debt restructuring, 109–15, 261–2
debt union, 47
debt unsustainability, 109–15
debtor country credit risk, 184–6
deficit criterion, 61
deficit deadline extensions, 107–8
deflation, 5, 22–3, 250–1
deleveraging, 131
Deleveraging? What deleveraging?, 250–1
Delors, Jacques, 41–2
Delors report, 41–2, 83
Delpla, Jacques, 103
demand deficiency, 253–4
Denmark
  bail-in policy, 141–2
  SCU (Scandinavian Currency Union),
    145–6
DEPA, 236
deutsche mark creation, 32–3
devaluation, 39–40
Dexia, 135
Dijsselbloem, Jeroen, 140
Dini, Lamberto, 164–5
Dombrovskis, Valdis, 259

Draghi, Mario, 3, 15–16, 23–4, 28, 64, 66, 89,
    90, 100–1, 133, 136, 176–7, 185, 187–8,
    189–93, 198, 200, 204–5, 206, 232,
    250–1, 253–4, 256–8, 260–1, 267, 269
Duisenberg, Wim, 64, 65, 66, 68–9

ease of doing business, rankings, 230–1,
    233–4, 238
EBA (European Banking Authority), 135
ECB (European Central Bank)
  ABS purchases, 202–3, 204–5
  after first decade, 58
  authority limitations, 121
  banking supervision, xi, 17–18, 27, 29,
    135–9
  bonds purchase by, 15–16, 22–3, 26–7, 28,
    94, 178–80, 202, 204–5
  capital keys, 63, 97
  collateral policy, 67–8, 83
  covered-bond purchases, 202
  creditor status, 195
  debtor country credit risk, 184–6
  decision-making processes, 259–60
  deposit rate, 67
  Draghi's euro support see Draghi
  establishment of, viii
  and the euro, 30, 187–8, 189–97
  exchange rates, 200
  financial stability, 121–2
  flaws in mandate, 53–4
  full allotment policy, 84
  German view of, 12–13
  identity crisis, 28, 175
  independence of, 64–5
  and inflation, 5, 53–4, 65–7, 199
  and interest rates, 30, 67, 70–1, 200–1
  as lender of last resort, 28
  liquidity provision, 84
  long-term lending to banks, 200–1
  monetary policy setting, 26–7, 52–3, 63, 84
  monetary stability, 64–5
  and NCBs, 62–3, 182–4
  negative interest rates, 200–1
  non-standard measures, 84
  and outright monetary transactions, 3
  price stability policy, x
  quantitative easing, x–xi, 166, 178–9,
    196–7, 199, 203–7
  restrictions on Greek bonds, 205–6
  role as central bank, ix–xi, 9, 28, 121–2, 175

ECB (European Central Bank) (cont.)
  SMP (securities markets programme), 94
  supervisory powers, 256
  three-year funding, 130
ECJ (European Court of Justice), 50, 193,
    194–6
economic diversity, cross-border, 34–5
economic governance, 17–18, 25, 29
ecu (European currency unit), 40–1
education, in Southern Europe, 232–3
EEC (European Economic Community), and
    single currency, 33
EFSF (European Financial Stability Facility),
    96–8, 99–100, 101, 111, 112
EFSM (European Financial Stabilisation
    Mechanism), 96–7
Eichel, Hans, 50
Eichengreen, Barry, 55–7
Einaudi, Luca, 145
ELA (emergency liquidity assistance),
    149–50, 166–7
emigration, 233
Emmott, Bill, 221
Emporiki Bank, 124
EMS (European Monetary System), 40–1
EMU (economic and monetary union), 44–6
Eonia interest rate, 67
EPL (employment protection legislation),
    215–16
  see also labour market flexibility
equity issuance, 138
equity markets, 266–7
ERM (exchange-rate mechanism), 40–1, 44–6
  and interest rates, 40
ESM (European Stability Mechanism), 18,
    97–8, 99–100, 101, 108, 114, 142,
    254–5, 256
Esquirou de Parieu, Félix, 144
Estonia, bank ownership, 123–4
euro
  break-up risks/repercussions, 155–9,
    166–9
  collateral damage to, 264–5
  creation, viii–ix
  criteria for, 44–6, 60–1
  debt and admission, 48, 60–1
  disintegration threat, 184–6
  dollar exchange rate, 85
  Draghi's ECB support, 187–8, 189–97
  and ECB, 30
  and EEC, 33

  and EU membership, 162–3
  and extremist politics, 269
  flaws in, 54–5
  on foreign-exchange markets, 62, 85
  foreign-exchange reserves, 154–5
  German predominance, 267–9
  increasing membership, 259–60
  institutional framework, 262
  irreversibility of, 187–8
  membership irrevocability, 55–7
  and national politics, 12–13, 31, 35–6,
    263
  need for growth 120
  notes/coins introduction, 59
  public support for, 262–3
  as reserve currency, 154–5
  right to leave, 162–3
  strength of, 161–2
  and treaties/constitutions, 262
  UK Treasury five tests, 34–5
euro area
  bank cross-border debt securities,
    153–4
  consumer prices, 197
  GDP (2008–14), 5–7
  government debt, 153
euro crisis, viii–xvi, 2–8, 29
  beginnings of, 58–9, 84–5, 88
  compared to US/UK, 86
  as multidimensional, 7–9
  as national budgetary failings, 106, 108
  and national politics, xii–xiii
euro membership expansion, 59–60
euro tax, 61
The Euro Trap, 245
euro vulnerability, 26–7
eurobonds, 102–5, 206
  and conditionality, 104–5
  and Merkel, 105–6, 206
Eurogroup, 109
European Commission study (2008), 1–2
European Council
  Madrid meeting (1995), 45
  and monetary union, 39–40
European elections (2014), 18–19, 269
European Investment Bank, 204
European Monetary Institute, 64
euro-plus pact, 209–10
Europe's Deadlock, 259–60
Europe's Unfinished Currency, 145
evergreening loans, 120–1

exchange rate, 14, 24–5, 27–8, 35–6, 45–6, 59, 60
exchange-rate, 34–5
  Bretton Woods system, 39–40, 45–6
  ERM (exchange-rate mechanism), 40–1
  gold standard, 39–40, 55–7
  nominal, 73
exit discount rates, 111–12
extremist politics, 269

failing banks resolution, 138–9
family-firm predominance, 219–20, 221
Fazio, Antonio, 37
Federal Deposit Insurance Corporation, 138–9
Feldstein, Martin, 1–2
Financial Services Authority, 121
Financial Stability Board, 141–2
Fine Gael, 163
Finland
  debt test, 60–1
  and Greece, 99
fiscal compact (2012), 105–6
fiscal development and policy, 9, 51
  budget balancing, 49
  budgetary discipline, 89
  budgetary sovereignty, 52
  budgetary surveillance, 18
  common fiscal policy, 106
Fitch, 203–4
Five Star Movement, 18–19, 163
four presidents report, 256–7
France
  corporate debt, 130–1
  current-account deficit, 247
  debt test, 60–1
  deficit deadline extensions, 107–8
  ease of doing business rankings, 230–1
  ECB bank assessment, 137–8
  fiscal discipline, 12
  and France Télécom, 61–2
  Macron law, 238–9
  and monetary union, 36, 38–9
  pensions system, 61–2, 237–8
  price-stability test, 45
  sovereign debt, 79–81
  structural reform, 28–9, 237–9
  taxation, 237–8
Frankel, Jeffrey, 31
Friedman, Milton, 34–5, 39

G20 (2011), 164–5
G20 (2012), 165
Garber, Peter, 54
Geithner, Timothy, 92
German Council of Economic Experts, 8, 104, 106
Germany
  AAA status, 203–4
  bail-in provision, 141–2
  balance of payments, 74–6, 247, 248–50
  bank recapitalisation, 120
  benefits from euro, xiv
  capital key, 63
  constitutional court, 193–4
  corporate debt, 130–1
  in early euro period, 210–11
  ease of doing business rankings, 230–1
  and ECB (European Central Bank), 12–13
  EPL (employment protection legislation), 215
  euro exit, 155–9
    risks/repercussions, 158–60
  financial support, 23–4, 99–100
  fiscal policy, 12, 52–3, 254
  governance, 63
  and Greece, 9, 89, 90, 99–100, 113–14, 171–3, 258, 264–5
  growth, 70
  Hartz reforms, 210–11, 232
  inflation, 198
  pension reforms, 208, 211
  private debt, 77–9
  and quantitative easing, 205–6
  SMEs (small and medium-sized enterprises), 122
  sovereign debt, 79–81
  and structural reforms, 208–13
  trade union cooperation, 211
  and Ukraine crisis, 261
Gieve, Sir John, 125
GLF (Greek Loan Facility), 93–4
Glick, Reuven, 151–2
global banking glut, 118–19
global competition, 73
global financial crisis (2008), 1, 58
global saving glut, 118–19
*Going for Growth*, 209, 231–2
gold standard, 39–40, 55–7, 144, 267
*Good Italy, Bad Italy*, 221
Goodhart, Charles, 118

Gosbank, 148
governance *see* economic governance
government debt *see* sovereign debt
Greece
  and Argentina's currency crisis experience, 167, 168, 169–70
  bail-outs, xii–xiii, 9, 20–2, 47, 89, 91–6, 97, 98–9, 109–15, 116, 173
  banks, 111–12, 120, 122–3, 126–7, 150, 244, 263, 264
  capital controls imposition, 264
  competitiveness concerns, 245
  and credit rating agencies, 82–3
  currency change, 167–9
  currency overstamping, 167
  current-account deficits, 14
  default implications, 91–5
  ease of doing business rankings, 230–1, 233–4
  ECB bond purchase, 180, 205–6
  economy, 112–13, 164
  ELA (emergency liquidity assistance), 149–50, 166–7
  election (2009), 85, 90–1
  elections (2012), 113–14, 165–6, 171
  election (January 2015), xii, 20–3, 113–14
  and ESM, 97–8, 114
  and euro crisis, 114
  and euro exit (Grexit), 10, 14–15, 20–2, 27–8, 143, 152–3, 156–8, 161, 166–9, 171–4
  exchange rates, 245
  external indebtedness, 187
  financial crises, xii–xiii, 2–5, 7–9, 47
  of 2015, xiii
  financial reporting, 81–2, 85, 90–1
  fiscal policy, 26–7, 70, 89, 90–1, 112–13, 243
  GDP and euro exit, 156
  and Germany, 9, 89, 90, 99–100, 113–14, 171–3, 258, 264–5
  goods exports, 220, 246
  growth, 70, 72–3
  growth/competitiveness reforms, 17
  inflation, 168–9
  interest payment deferment, 244
  interest rates, 132–3
  junk rating, 203–4
  labour market reforms, 224
  leadership changes, 165
  in LMU, 145
  loss of confidence, 113–14
  and Merkel *see* Greece, and Germany
  and monetary union, 37
  and OMT, 190
  pension system, 226–7
  and PPC power company, 228–9
  preferred-creditor status, 190
  private debt, 114–15
  privatisation programme, 235–6
  referendum (2015), 150, 172, 264
  retrofit collective-action clause, 111
  scrip payments, 167
  self-employment level, 220–1
  sovereign debt, 2, 14–15, 16, 26–7, 70, 79–81, 88, 89, 90–1, 94, 109–15, 129–30, 242–3, 247–8, 264–5
  stabilisation mechanism for, 94
  structural reform, 221–2, 224, 229, 235–6
  structural weaknesses, 37, 218–19, 228, 233–4, 235–6
  Syriza policies damage, 263–4, *see also* Syriza party
  tax system corruption, 220–1
  US pressure to support, 92
  Worldwide Governance Indicators, 219
Green Line (Cyprus), 38
Grexit *see* Greece
Grillo, Beppe, 163
Gros, Daniel, 158–9
G-SIB (global systemically important bank), 141–2
Guardia, Anton La, 23
Guindos, Luis de, 172
Gulati, Mitu, 109–10

haircut
  on collateral value, 83
  on Greek bonds, 109–10
Hanover summit (1988), 41–2
Hardiman, Niamh, 234–5
Hartz reforms, 210–11, 232
Hellenic Financial Stability Fund, 112
Henkel, Hans-Olaf, 155–9
Hollande, François, 18–22, 237–8
housing-market bubbles, 70–1

Iglesias, Pablo, 20–2
IMF (International Monetary Fund), 5, 22–3, 86, 92, 93, 94, 95, 98–9, 156, 221–2, 264–5

inflation, 44–6, 60, 64–7, 68–9
and monetary growth, 39
inflation fall
ECB remedies, 199
effects of, 197–9
insider–outsider gap, 216
integration proposals, 256–9
interacting crises, 10–11
interbank market, 153–4
interest rates, 67
corporate borrowing, 132–3
and ECB, 130
and inflation fall, 199
long-term, 24–5, 44–6, 70–1
negative, 200–1
zero lower bound, 66
intergovernmentalism, 254–5
internal devaluation, 34, 214
Ireland
bail-out, 97, 116
balance of payments, 74–6, 245–6
banks, 76–7, 116, 117–18, 120, 122–3, 124
budgetary surplus, 81
capital flight, 181–2
Celtic Tiger economy, 213–14
credit-generated growth, 14
ease of doing business rankings, 230–1
ECB bank assessment, 136
ECB bond purchase, 180
economic boom, 71–2
ELA (emergency liquidity assistance), 149–50
election (2011), 163
exports, 246
external indebtedness, 187
financial crisis (2010), 2–5, 7–9
governance failures, 234–5
government debt / GDP ratio, 247–8
and Greek Loan Facility, 93–4
growth, 70, 72–3
house prices, 71, 163
interest payment deferment, 244
labour market flexibility, 211–13
OMT eligibility, 240
price-stability test, 45
private debt, x, 8–9, 77–9
sovereign bonds, 2, 15–16, 79–81, 86, 108, 129–30
sterling link with UK, 152
structural reform, 221–2, 236

Worldwide Governance Indicators, 219
Issing, Otmar, 51–2, 80, 94
Italy
balance of payments surpluses, 245–6
banks, 59, 120, 122–3, 126–7, 234–5
capital outflows, 173
corporate debt, 130–1
and credit rating agencies, 82–3
debt test, 60–1
ease of doing business rankings, 230–1, 233–4
ECB bank assessment, 137–8
ECB bond purchases, 180
education/skills, 232–3
euro exit, 164–5
eurobonds, 104
financial crisis (2010), 2–5
governance failures, 234–5
government debt / GDP ratio, 247–8
growth, 72–3
interest rates, 132–3
judicial system, 234
long-term interest rates, 70–1
LTROs, 185–6
and monetary union, 1–2
pension system, 225–6, 232
private debt, 8–9, 77–9
recessions, 5
self-employment level, 220–1
SMEs (small and medium-sized enterprises), 122
sovereign debt, 2, 79–81, 84–5, 100, 103, 126–7, 129–30, 153, 251–2
structural reforms, 17, 28–9, 100–1, 221–2, 225–6, 227–8, 229, 231–2, 233–4, 236–7
utilities monopolies, 219
Worldwide Governance Indicators, 219

James, Harold, 32, 40–1, 56
Japan
banking crisis, 133
deflation record, 250–1
job protection see EPL; labour market flexibility
Jobs Study, 209
joint deposit-guarantee scheme, 138–9
joint and several liability, 102–3
joint underwriting, 104–5
Juncker, Jean-Claude, 140, 248, 256–7

Kenen, Peter, 35
Kindleberger, Charles, 32
Kohl, Helmut, 11–12, 36, 38, 44, 64
Kraemer, Moritz, 248–50
Krugman, Paul, 81

labour market flexibility/reforms, 34, 35, 36, 37, 46, 54–5, 209, 210–11, 214–17, 222–4, 232, *see also* EPL
Lagarde, Christine, 5, 95, 107, 197
Laiki Bank, 129, 139–40
Landesbanken, 117–18
Lane, Philip, 250–1
Latvia
    bank ownership, 123–4
    euro membership, 259–60
    price-stability test, 45
Le Pen, Marine, 18–19
Leigh, Daniel, 107
lex monetae, 159–61
liability/control balance, 261–2
Liikanen, Erkki, 188
liquidity, provision by ECB, 84, 129
Lisbon agenda, 209
Lisbon Treaty, 63, 95, 162–3
Lithuania
    bank ownership, 123–4
    euro membership, 259–60
LMU (Latin Monetary Union), 144–5
loan-to-deposit ratios, 122–3
London Debt Agreement, 86
lowflation, 5, 202, 250–1
LTROs (longer term refinancing operations), 185–6
Luxembourg
    AAA status, 203–4
    bank recapitalisation, 120
    debt test, 60–1
    and monetary union, 37, 39

Maastricht Treaty, 25, 44–6, 47, 51, 148, 178, 251, 261–2
MacDougall report, 47
macroeconomic imbalances, 10–11
macroeconomic rebalancing, 245–7
Macron, Emmanuel, 238–9
Macron law, 238–9
*Managing the Euro Area Debt Crisis*, 251–2
Marcegaglia, Emma, 225
marked to market assets/securities, 120–1

Marsh, David, 23, 60, 259–60
Mayer, Thomas, 23, 145, 167
Merkel, Angela, xii–xiii, 3, 15–16, 19–22, 23–4, 89, 90, 99, 105–6, 108, 152–3, 164–5, 171–3, 191–2, 193, 206, 209–10, 211, 254, 258, 261, 268
Mersch, Yves, 199
Mitterrand, François, 11–12, 36
mobility of labour, 31
Moedas, Carlos, 222
monetary financing, 178
monetary growth, and inflation, 39
monetary policy pillars, 65
monetary policy setting, 37, 51–3, 58–9
monetary stability, 64–5
monetary union *see* euro
Monti, Mario, 17, 104, 106, 164–5, 186–7, 222, 225–6, 231–2
Moody's, 203–4
mortgage-backed securities, 117–19
mortgages, 34, 35–6, 37
Muellbauer, John, 104–5
Mundell, Robert, 32–4, 37–8

Napolitano, Giorgio, 164–5
national economic output diversity, 34–5
national power/money link, 32–4, 37–9
national sovereignty, 257–8
NCBs (national central banks), 12–13, 17–19, 20, 23–4, 27, 35, 47, 48–52, 60–1, 83, 89, 106, 107, 112–13
    balance sheets, 182–4
    borrowing by, 181
    and capital keys, 63
    collateral policy, 67–8
    community system, 39
    ELA (emergency liquidity assistance), 149–50
    and eurozone sovereign debt, 205–6
    funding by, 129
    as lenders of last resort, 15–16, 28, 31
    and monetary policy, 63
    and monetary union, 40–1
    permitted lending risks, 150–1
    public debt purchase, 178–9
    rogue behaviour by, 149
    Target2 payments system, 166–7, 181
Netherlands
    balance of payments, 74–6, 247
    bank recapitalisation, 120

deficit deadline extensions, 107–8
exchange-rate test, 45–6
household debt, 8–9
and monetary union, 35–6
New Democracy party, 10
NIIP (net international investment position),
183–4
no bail-out rule, 10, 47, 85, 91, 92, 95
nominal exchange rates, 73
nominal interest rates, 66
Norway, SCU (Scandinavian Currency
Union), 145–6
Novo Banco, 127

Obama, Barack, 92
Obstfeld, Maurice, 54
OECD (Organisation for Economic
Cooperation and Development), 55,
61, 75, 209, 221–2, 230–1
OMT (outright monetary transactions)
policy, 3, 17–18, 189–97, 240
One market, one money, 42–3
optimal currency area theory, 25, 32–6, 47, 55
output gap, 253–4
overnight interbank interest rate, 67
overstamping currency notes, 151, 167

pact for competitiveness, 209–10
Padoan, Pier Carlo, 231–2
Papademos, Lucas, 165
Papandreou, George, 85, 90–1, 113–14,
165, 171
Passos Coelho, Pedro, 163, 222, 240
Peet, John, 23
pension reforms, 208, 211
peripheral-countries
balance of payments, 74–7
banks, 122–3, 129, 131–3
boom sustainability, 76–7
corporate borrowing costs, 132–3
credit booms, 26–7, 59
crises, 7–9
debt, 3
growth, 70
structural reforms, 28–9
unit labour costs, 73–4
see also individual countries
permanent rescue fund, 17–18, 29
Pisani-Ferry, Jean, 23

PMR (product-market regulation), 217–18,
229, 238
Podemos party, 18–19, 20–2
Pöhl, Karl Otto, 41–2
Portas, Paulo, 240
Porter, Michael, 221
Portugal
bail-out, 113, 116, 127, 241–2
balance of payments, 17, 74–6, 245–6
banks, 116, 127
constitutional court decisions, 236
corporate debt, 130–1
and credit rating agencies, 82–3
deficit deadline extensions, 107–8
ease of doing business rankings, 230–1
ECB bond purchase, 180
economy, 113, 164, 241–2, 252–3
education/skills, 232–3
election (2011), 163
emigration, 233
EPL (employment protection legislation),
215, 224
exports, 247
external indebtedness, 187
financial crisis (2010), 2–5
fiscal policy, 232, 243
GDP per person change, 265–6
government debt / GDP ratio, 247–8
and Greek Loan Facility, 93–4
interest payment deferment, 244
interest rates, 132–3
junk rating, 203–4, 241
loan-to-deposit ratios, 122–3
long-term interest rates, 70–1
and monetary union, 37
pension system, 61–2, 227
private debt, 8–9, 17, 77–9
public finance reporting, 82
quantitative easing, 266–7
self-employment level, 220–1
sovereign debt, 2, 8–9, 15–16, 17, 79–81,
84–5, 113–14, 129–30, 240
structural reforms, 17, 72–3, 221–2, 224,
229, 236, 245
Worldwide Governance Indicators, 219
PPC power company, 228–9
Praet, Peter, 176–7
pretend and extend strategy, 251
price stability, 68–9

price-stability test, 45, 60
private asset buying, 204–5
private creditors participation, 108
private debt, x, 8–9, 10–11, 14, 17, 29, 70–1,
    77–9, 131, 250–1
  and inflation fall, 198
Prodi, Romano, 49, 62
product market reforms, 227–8, 232
productivity growth, 69–73
professional cartels, 218–19, 228
public debt *see* sovereign debt

QE (quantitative easing), x–xi, 22–3, 25, 28,
    66–7, 84, 130, 166, 178–9, 196–7, 199,
    202–3, 266–7

Rajoy, Mariano, 186–7, 191–2, 223, 227, 236
redemption fund, 103–4
referendums, xi–xii, 18–19, 150, 163, 172,
    262, 264
refinancing interest rate, 67
Regling, Klaus, 100
Rehn, Olli, 107–8
Reichenbach, Horst, 235
Reichlin, Lucrezia, 250–1
Reinhart, Vincent, 250–1
Renzi, Matteo, 18–20, 234, 236–7, 254
rescue fatigue, 9
retrofit collective-action clause, 111
Rose, Andrew, 31, 143–4, 151–2
Ross, Wilbur, 141
Roubini, Nouriel, 48
rouble area, 147–8
Rueff, Jacques, 38–9

S&P (Standard & Poor's), 203–4, 248–50
Sachs, Jeffrey, 35
Sala-i-Martin, Xavier, 35
Samaras, Antonis, 10, 171
Santander, 125
Sapin, Michel, 254
Sarko trade, 130
Sarkozy, Nicolas, 3–5, 18–19, 108, 130, 164–5
Schäuble, Wolfgang, 3, 20–2, 152–3, 162–3,
    171, 172, 173, 254, 262
Schorkopf, Frank, 195–6
Schröder, Gerhard, 30, 210–11
SCU (Scandinavian Currency Union), 145–6
sectoral shocks, 34–5
Shambaugh, Jay, 8
Shin, Hyun Song, 119

Sibert, Anne, 83
single currency *see* euro
Single Resolution Fund, 254–5
Sinn, Hans-Werner, 23, 181–2, 202, 245
six-pack rules, 255
skills, in Southern Europe, 232–3
Slovakia, and Greek Loan Facility, 93–4
Slovenia
  banks, 116, 127–8, 241, 245
  deficit deadline extensions, 107–8
  ease of doing business rankings, 230–1
  ECB bank assessment, 136
  growth, 72–3
  unsustainable lending, 76–7, 127–8
  Worldwide Governance Indicators, 219
small-firm predominance, 219–20, 221
SMEs (small and medium-sized
    enterprises), 122
Smith, Adam, 53–4
SMP (securities markets programme), 94,
    178–80, 190–1
sovereign bond holdings, 129–30
sovereign bonds, ECB purchase, ix, 204–5
sovereign debt, x, 2, 8–9, 12, 14–15, 16, 17,
    26–7, 29, 63, 70, 79–81, 86, 88, 89, 100,
    103, 113–15, 126–7, 204–5, 251–2
  and assets denationalisation, 153
  and banks, 126–7, 135
  and inflation fall, 198
  sustainability, 108
sovereign signature, 100–1, 102
sovereign-bond buying, 12–13, 94
sovereign-bond markets, 14–15
sovereign-bond yields, 3, 15–16, 123
  convergence/divergence, 84–5
Spain
  bail-out, 116
  balance of payments, 14, 74–6, 245–6
  banks, 116, 122–3, 125–6, 244
  budgetary surplus, 81
  capital flow, 173, 181–2
  competitiveness concerns, 245
  corporate debt, 130–1
  covered bond market, 202–3
  credit boom, 59
  deficit deadline extensions, 107–8
  dynamic provision policy, 125
  ease of doing business rankings, 230–1
  ECB bank assessment, 136
  ECB bond purchases, 180
  economy, 71–2, 241–2, 252–3

education/skills, 232–3
emigration, 233
EPL (employment protection
    legislation), 215
and ESM, 97–8
exports, 246
external indebtedness, 187
financial difficulties, 186–7
governance failures, 234–5
growth, 70
interest rates, 132–3
labour market inflexibility, 215, 216–17
labour market reform, 222–4
long-term interest rates, 70–1
LTROs, 185–6
pension system, 227
private debt, x, 8–9, 77–9
property boom, 71, 125
quantitative easing, 266–7
SMEs (small and medium-sized
    enterprises), 122
sovereign debt, 16, 79–81, 86, 100, 129–30
structural reforms, 221–4
tax reform, 236
unsustainable lending, 76–7
Worldwide Governance Indicators, 219
Spanish paradox, 246
SRM (Single Resolution Mechanism),
    138–9
stability-and-growth pact, 48–51
    enforcement of, 50
    escape clauses, 50–1
    flaws in, 49–50, 52
    reforms to, 50–1
Stark, Jürgen, 94, 100–1, 176–8, 179–80, 191
Steffen, Sascha, 137–8
Steinbrück, Peer, 85, 152–3
Strauss-Kahn, Dominique, 92, 95
stress testing, 133–5, 137
structural budget balance, 106
structural reforms, 208–13
    need for, 221–2
sub-prime mortgage crisis, 24–5, 117–18
Sweden
    banking crisis, 133
    price-stability test, 45
    SCU (Scandinavian Currency Union),
        145–6
Syriza party, xii, 10–11, 18–19, 20–3, 113–14,
    165–6, 172, 205, 236, 263

taper tantrum, 240
Target2 system, 166–7, 181–2, 183–5
Thomsen, Poul, 228
Tietmeyer, Hans, 63–4
Toniolo, Gianni, 39
Towards a Genuine Economic and Monetary
    Union, 256–7
trade cartels, 218–19, 228
trade intensity, 46
    cross-border, 35
Trebesch, Christoph, 110
Trichet, Jean-Claude, 1, 28, 58, 63, 64, 66,
    68–9, 100–1, 123, 175–8, 185, 256–7,
    260–1
Tsipras, Alexis, xii, 10–11, 20–1, 88, 150,
    165–6, 172, 173, 264
two-pack rules, 255

UK
    monetary policy, 25, 51
    private debt, 9
    sovereign debt, 9
    status of pound, 58
    sterling link with Ireland, 152
    Treasury tests for euro, 34–5, 46
Ukraine crisis, 261
unemployment rate, 265–6
unit labour costs, 73–4
US
    GDP (2008–14), 5–7
    and Greek default crisis, 92
    private debt, 9
    sovereign debt, 9
    sub-prime mortgage crisis, 24–5, 117–18
    Tarp (troubled asset relief programme), 134
utilities monopolies, 219

Van Rixtel, Adrian, 128–9
Van Rompuy, Herman, 256–7
Varoufakis, Yanis, 20, 172
Venizelos, Evangelos, 165
Villa Schifanoia meeting (2011), 109–10
Villalón, Pedro Cruz, 194–5
vulture funds, 170

wage flexibility, 7
Weber, Axel, 64, 94, 100–1, 176–7, 179–80
Weidmann, Jens, 15–16, 100–1, 175, 188, 191,
    192–3, 260, 261–2
Weizsäcker, Jakob von, 103

Werner, Pierre, 39
Werner report, 39, 47, 75
Whelan, Karl, 72
White, William, 121
Wolfson, Lord, 169
World Bank, ease of doing business rankings, 230–1, 233–4, 238
Worldwide Governance Indicators, 219

Young Plan, 40–1
Yugoslavia, and Austro-Hungarian empire, 146–7

Zapatero, José Luis Rodríguez, 126, 223, 227
Zettelmeyer, Jeromin, 110, 111–12
zombie banks, 137–8